macOS Programming for Absolute Beginners

Developing Apps Using Swift and Xcode

Wallace Wang

Apress®

macOS Programming for Absolute Beginners: Developing Apps Using Swift and Xcode

Wallace Wang
San Diego, California, USA

IISBN-13 (pbk): 978-1-4842-2661-2   ISBN-13 (electronic): 978-1-4842-2662-9
DOI 10.1007/978-1-4842-2662-9

Library of Congress Control Number: 2017935026

Managing Director: Welmoed Spahr
Editorial Director: Todd Green
Acquisitions Editor: Aaron Black
Development Editor: Jim Markham
Technical Reviewer: Bruce Wade
Coordinating Editor: Jessica Vakili
Copy Editor: Mary Behr
Compositor: SPi Global
Indexer: SPi Global
Artist: SPi Global
Cover image designed by Freepik

Distributed to the book trade worldwide by Springer Science+Business Media New York, 233 Spring Street, 6th Floor, New York, NY 10013. Phone 1-800-SPRINGER, fax (201) 348-4505, e-mail orders-ny@springer-sbm.com, or visit www.springeronline.com. Apress Media, LLC is a California LLC and the sole member (owner) is Springer Science + Business Media Finance Inc (SSBM Finance Inc). SSBM Finance Inc is a **Delaware** corporation.

For information on translations, please e-mail rights@apress.com, or visit www.apress.com/rights-permissions.

Apress titles may be purchased in bulk for academic, corporate, or promotional use. eBook versions and licenses are also available for most titles. For more information, reference our Print and eBook Bulk Sales web page at www.apress.com/bulk-sales.

Any source code or other supplementary material referenced by the author in this book is available to readers on GitHub via the book's product page, located at www.apress.com/9781484226612. For more detailed information, please visit www.apress.com/source-code.

Printed on acid-free paper

This book is dedicated to everyone who dreams of writing a computer program. Anyone can learn to program a computer. The problem often boils down to not knowing where to start and feeling intimidated by the whole process. So this book is dedicated to everyone who has longed for a gentle introduction to computer programming for the Macintosh. Welcome to the future where your dreams are only limited by your imagination.

Contents at a Glance

Contents

About the Author

Wallace Wang has written dozens of computer books over the years, beginning with ancient MS-DOS programs like WordPerfect and Turbo Pascal, and graduating up to Windows programs like Visual Basic and Microsoft Office.

When he's not helping people discover the joys of computing programming with a computer that's actually fun to use, he performs stand-up comedy and appears on two radio shows on KNSJ in San Diego (http://knsj.org) called "Notes From the Underground" and "Laugh In Your Face Radio" (www.laughinyourfaceradio.com).

He also writes a screenwriting blog called "The 15 Minute Movie Method" (http://15minutemoviemethod.com), a blog about the latest cat news on the Internet called "Cat Daily News" (http://catdailynews.com), a blog about the latest trends in technology called "Top Bananas" (www.topbananas.com), and a blog about programming called "Games For Geeks" (www.gamesforgeeks.com).

About the Technical Reviewer

Bruce Wade is a software engineer from British Columbia, Canada. He started software development when he was 16 years old by coding his first website. He went on to study Computer Information Systems at DeVry Institute of Technology in Calgary, and to further enhance his skills, he studied Visual and Game Programming at The Art Institute Vancouver. Over the years he has worked for large corporations as well as several start-ups. His software experience includes C/C++, Python, Objective-C, Swift, Postgres, and JavaScript. In 2012, he started the company Warply Designed to focus on mobile 2D/3D and OS X development. Aside from hacking out new ideas, he enjoys spending time hiking with his Boxer, Rasco, working out, and exploring new adventures.

Acknowledgments

Thanks go to all the wonderful people at Apress for giving me a chance to write about the wonderfully bizarre, yet fascinating, world of personal computing.

Additional thanks go to Dane Henderson and Elizabeth Lee (www.echoludo.com), who share the airwaves with me on our radio show called "Notes From the Underground" on KNSJ.org. More thanks go to Chris Clobber, Diane Jean, and Ikaika Patria for letting me share their friendship and lunacy every week on another KNSJ radio show called "Laugh In Your Face Radio" (www.laughinyourfaceradio.com) where we combine comedy with political activism and commentary.

A special mention goes to Michael Montijo and his indomitable spirit, which has had him drive from Phoenix to Los Angeles at least once a month for the past 20 years to meet with Hollywood executives. One day when you hear about his cartoon series "Life of Mikey" and "Pachuko Boy," you'll know how they finally appeared on television because he never gave up on his dream despite all the obstacles in his way.

Thanks also go to my wife, Cassandra, and my son, Jordan, for putting up with a house filled with more gadgets than actual living people. Final thanks go to my cats, Oscar and Mayer, for walking over the keyboard, stepping on the trackpad and mouse, and chewing on power cords at the most inconvenient times of the day.

Introduction

If you're a complete novice looking to get started in programming, or someone familiar with programming but curious about learning more, or a seasoned programmer comfortable with other programming languages but unfamiliar with Macintosh programming, this book is for you. Whatever your skill level, this book will help everyone understand how to use Apple's latest programming language, Swift, to create macOS programs for the Macintosh.

Now you may be wondering, why learn Swift and why program for the Macintosh? The answers are simple.

First, Swift is Apple's newest programming language and it's designed to make creating macOS and iOS programs faster, easier, and more reliable than before. Previously, you had to use Objective-C to create macOS and iOS apps. While powerful, Objective-C is much harder to learn, more complicated to read and write, and because of its complexity, more prone to introducing errors or bugs in a program.

Swift is just as powerful as Objective-C (actually, it's more powerful, as you'll soon see), far easier to learn, much simpler to read and write, and it minimizes common programming errors. Swift gives you all the benefits of Objective-C with none of the drawbacks. Plus, Swift provides features that Objective-C doesn't offer, which makes Swift a far better programming language to learn and use today and tomorrow. Since Swift is Apple's official programming language, you can be certain that learning Swift will lead to greater opportunities now and long into the future.

But why should you want to learn to create Macintosh programs? The hot trend is learning to create iOS apps for the iPhone, iPad, and Apple Watch. If you plan on developing software, you definitely want to use Swift to create iOS apps.

However, learning Swift means understanding the following:

- The principles of programming, and object-oriented programming in particular

- The syntax of the Swift programming language

- Xcode's features

- Apple's software development framework (called Cocoa), which forms the foundation of every macOS and iOS program

- The principles of user interface design

Does this sound like a lot to learn? Don't worry. I'll go through each process step by step so you won't feel lost. The point is that to create macOS programs and iOS apps, you need to learn multiple topics, but creating iOS apps poses an additional challenge.

For example, an iOS app needs to respond to touch gestures with one finger, two fingers, swipes, shakes, and motion, in addition to adapting to changes when the user flips an iPhone or iPad left, right, upside down, or right side up.

In comparison, a Macintosh program only needs to respond to keyboard and mouse input. This means macOS programs are much simpler to create and understand, which also means that learning Swift to create macOS programs is far easier than learning Swift to create iOS apps.

Best of all, the principles are exactly the same. What you learn creating macOS programs are the exact same skills you need to create iOS apps. The difference is that creating macOS programs is far simpler, less confusing, and much less intimidating than creating iOS apps.

Trying to create iOS apps right from the start can be like trying to swim across the English Channel before you even know how to hold your breath underwater.

You don't want to frustrate yourself unnecessarily. That's why it's much easier to learn the principles of iOS app programming by first learning macOS programming. Once you're familiar with macOS programming, you'll find it's trivial to transfer your programming skills to creating iOS apps. By learning to create macOS programs in Swift, you'll learn everything you need to know to eventually create iOS apps in Swift, plus you'll know how to create macOS programs so you can tap into the growing Macintosh market as well.

Following Lucrative Programming Trends

The introduction of a new computer platform has always ushered in a lucrative period for programmers. In the early 80s, the hottest platform was the Apple II computer. If you wanted to make money writing programs, you wrote programs to sell to Apple II computer owners, like Dan Bricklin, an MBA graduate student at the time, did when he wrote the first spreadsheet program, VisiCalc.

The next big computing platform shift occurred in the mid-80s with the IBM PC and MS-DOS. People made fortunes off the IBM PC, including Bill Gates and Microsoft, which went from a small start-up company to the most dominant computer company in the world. The IBM PC made millionaires out of hundreds of people including Scott Cook, a former marketing director at Proctor & Gamble, who developed the popular money manager program, Quicken.

Microsoft helped usher in the next computer platform when it shifted from MS-DOS to Windows and put a friendly graphical user interface on IBM PCs. Once again, programming for Windows became the number one way that programmers and non-programmers alike made fortunes by writing and selling their own Windows programs. Microsoft took advantage of the shift to Windows by releasing several Windows-only programs that have become fixtures of the business world, such as Outlook, Access, and Excel.

Now the world is shifting towards the new computer platform of Apple products running macOS and iOS. Thousands of people just like you are eager to start writing programs to take advantage of the Macintosh's rising market share along with the dominant position of the iPhone and the iPad in the smartphone and tablet categories, the Apple Watch in the wearable computer market, and the Apple TV in the TV market.

Likewise, experienced developers, amateurs, hobbyists, and professionals in other fields are also interested in writing their own games, utilities, and business software specific to their particular niche.

Many programmers have gone from knowing nothing about programming to earning thousands of dollars a day by creating iPhone/iPad apps or Macintosh programs. As the Macintosh, iPhone, iPad, Apple Watch, and Apple TV continue to gain market share all over the world, more people will use one or more of these products, increasing the potential market for you.

All of this means that it's a perfect time for you to start learning how to program your Macintosh right now, because the sooner you understand the basics of Macintosh programming, the sooner you can start creating your own Macintosh programs along with iPhone/iPad/Apple Watch/Apple TV apps.

What to Expect From This Book

Whether you're a complete novice or a seasoned programmer coming from another programming environment, this book will minimize technical jargon and focus on helping you understand what to do and why.

If you just want to get started and learn the basics of programming in Swift, this book is for you. If you're already an experienced Windows programmer and want to get started programming the Macintosh, this book can be especially helpful in teaching you the basics in a hurry.

If you've never programmed before in your life, or if you're already familiar with programming but not with Macintosh programming, then this book is for you. Even if you're experienced with Macintosh programming, you may still find this book handy as a reference to help you achieve certain results without having to wade through several books to find an answer.

You won't learn everything you need to create your own super-sophisticated programs, but you'll learn just enough to get started, feel comfortable using Xcode, and be able to tackle other programming books with more confidence and understanding. Fair enough? If so, then turn the page and let's get started.

Chapter 1

Understanding Programming

Programming is nothing more than writing step-by-step instructions for a computer to follow. If you've ever written down the steps for a recipe or scribbled directions for taking care of your pets while you're on vacation, you've already gone through the basic steps of writing a program. The key is simply knowing what you want to accomplish and then making sure you write the correct instructions that will tell someone how to achieve that goal.

Although programming is theoretically simple, it's the details that can trip you up. First, you need to know exactly what you want. If you want a recipe for chicken chow mein, following a recipe for baked salmon won't do you any good.

Second, you need to write down every instruction necessary to get from your starting point to your desired result. If you skip a step or write steps out of order, you won't get the same result. Try driving to a restaurant when the list of driving instructions omits telling you when to turn on a specific road. It doesn't matter if 99% of the instructions are right; if just one instruction is wrong, you won't get to your desired goal.

The simpler your goal, the easier it is to achieve it. Writing a program that displays a calculator on the screen is far simpler than writing a program to monitor the safety systems of a nuclear power plant. The more complex your program, the more instructions you'll need to write, and the more instructions you need to write, the greater the chance you'll forget an instruction, write an instruction incorrectly, or write instructions in the wrong order.

© Wallace Wang 2017
W. Wang, *macOS Programming for Absolute Beginners*,
DOI 10.1007/978-1-4842-2662-9_1

Programming is nothing more than a way to control a computer to solve a problem, whether that computer is a laptop, smartphone, tablet, or wearable watch. Before you can start writing your own programs, you need to understand the basic principles of programming.

> **Note**   Don't get confused between learning programming and learning a particular programming language. You can actually learn the principles of programming without touching a computer at all. Once you understand the principles of programming, you can easily learn any particular programming language, like Swift.

Programming Principles

To write a program, you have to write instructions that the computer can follow. No matter what a program does or how big it may be, every program in the world consists of nothing more than step-by-step instructions for the computer to follow, one at a time. The simplest program can consist of a single line, such as

```
print ("Hello, world"!)
```

Obviously, a program that consists of a single line won't be able to do much, so most programs consist of multiples lines of instructions (or code), such as

```
print ("Hello, world!")
print ("Now the program is done.")
```

This two-line program starts with the first line, follows the instructions on the second line, and then stops. Of course, you can keep adding more instructions to a program until you have a million instructions that the computer can follow sequentially, one at a time.

Listing instructions sequentially is the basis for programming. Unfortunately, it's also limiting. For example, if you want to print the same message five times, you can use the following code:

```
print ("Hello, world!")
print ("Hello, world!")
print ("Hello, world!")
print ("Hello, world!")
print ("Hello, world!")
```

Writing the same five instructions is tedious and redundant, but it works. What happens if you want to print this same message a thousand times? You'd have to write the same instruction a thousand times.

Writing the same instruction multiple times is clumsy. To make programming easier, the goal is to write the least number of instructions to get the most work done. One way to avoid writing the same instruction multiple times is to organize your instructions using a second basic principle of programming, which is called a loop.

The idea behind a loop is to repeat one or more instructions multiple times, but only by writing those instructions down once. A typical loop might look like this:

```
for i in 1...5 {
  print ("Hello, world!")
}
```

The first line tells the computer to repeat the loop five times. The second line tells the computer to print the message "Hello, world" on the screen. The third line just defines the end of the loop.

Now if you want to make the computer print a message a thousand times, you don't need to write the same instruction a thousand times. Instead, you just need to modify how many times the loop repeats:

```
for I in 1...1000 {
  println ("Hello, world!")
}
```

Although loops are slightly more confusing to read and understand than a sequential series of instructions, loops make it easier to repeat instructions without writing the same instructions multiple times.

Most programs don't exclusively list instructions sequentially or in loops, but use a combination of both, such as

```
print ("Hello, world!")
print ("Now the program is starting.")
for I in 1...1000 {
  print ("Hello, world!")
}
```

In this example, the computer follows the first two lines sequentially and then follows the last three lines repetitively in a loop. Generally, listing instructions sequentially is fine when you only need the computer to follow those instructions once. When you need the computer to run instructions multiple times, that's when you need to use a loop.

What makes computers powerful isn't just the ability to follow instructions sequentially or in a loop, but in making decisions. Decisions mean that the computer needs to evaluate some condition and then, based on that condition, decide what to do next.

For example, you can write a program that locks someone out of a computer until that person types in the correct password. If the person types the correct password, the program gives that person access. However, if the person types an incorrect password, the program blocks access to the computer. The following is an example of this type of decision-making:

```
if password == "secret" {
    print ("Access granted!")
} else {
    print ("Login denied!")
}
```

In this example, the computer asks for a password, and when the user types in a password, the computer checks to see if it matches the word "secret". If so, then the computer grants that person access to the computer. If the user does not type "secret", then the computer denies access.

Making decisions is what makes programming flexible. If you write a sequential series of instructions, the computer will follow these lists of instructions exactly the same way, every time. However, if you include decision-making instructions, also known as branching instructions, then the computer can respond according to what the user does.

Consider a video game. No video game could be written entirely with instructions organized sequentially because then the game would play exactly the same way every time. Instead, a video game needs to adapt to the player's actions at all times. If the player moves an object to the left, the video game needs to respond differently than if the player moves an object to the right or does nothing at all. Using branching instructions gives computers the ability to react differently so the program never runs exactly the same way.

To write a computer program, you need to organize instructions in one of the following three ways, as graphically show in Figure 1-1.

- **Sequentially**: The computer follows instructions one after another.

- **Loop**: The computer repetitively follows one or more instructions.

- **Branching**: The computer chooses to follow one or more groups of instructions based on outside data.

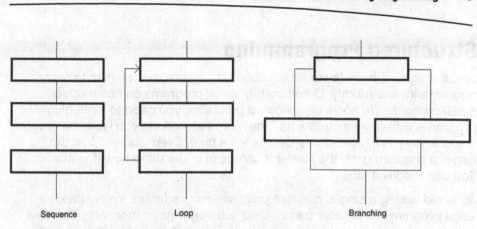

Figure 1-1. The three basic building blocks of programming

While simple programs may only organize instructions sequentially, every large program organizes instructions sequentially, in loops, and in branches. What makes programming more of an art and less of a science is that there is no single best way to write a program. In fact, it's perfectly possible to write two different programs that behave exactly the same.

Because there is no single "right" way to write a program, there are only guidelines to help you write programs easily. Ultimately, what matters is that you write a program that works.

When writing any program, there are two, often mutually exclusive, goals. First, programmers strive to write programs that are easy to read, understand, and modify. This often means writing multiple instructions that clearly define the steps needed to solve a particular problem.

Second, programmers try to write programs that perform tasks efficiently, making the program run as fast as possible. This often means condensing multiple instructions as much as possible by using tricks or exploiting little known features that are difficult to understand and confusing even to experienced programmers.

In the beginning, strive towards making your programs as clear, logical, and understandable as possible, even if you have to write more instructions or type longer instructions to do it. Later, as you gain more experience in programming, you can work on creating the smallest, fastest, most efficient programs possible, but remember that your ultimate goal is to write programs that just work.

Structured Programming

Small programs have fewer instructions so they are much easier to read, understand, and modify. Unfortunately, small programs can only solve small problems. To solve complicated problems, you need to write bigger programs with more instructions. The more instructions you type, the greater the chance you'll make a mistake (called a bug). Even worse is that the larger a program gets, the harder it can be to understand how it works so you can modify it later.

To avoid writing a single, massive program, programmers simply divide a large program into smaller parts called subprograms or functions. The idea is that each function solves a single task. This makes it easy to write and insure that it works correctly.

Once all of your separate functions work, you can connect them to create a single, large program, as shown in Figure 1-2. This is like building a house out of bricks rather than trying to carve an entire house out of one massive rock.

| Instructions for printing |
| Instructions for saving files |
| Instructions for displaying graphics |
| Instructions for opening files |

Figure 1-2. Dividing a large program into multiple subprograms or functions helps make programming more reliable

Dividing a large program into smaller programs provides several benefits. First, writing smaller functions is fast and easy, and small functions make it easy to read, understand, and modify the instructions.

Second, functions act like building blocks that work together, so multiple programmers can work on different functions, and then combine the separate functions together to create a large program.

Third, if you want to modify a large program, you just need to yank out, rewrite, and replace one or more functions. Without functions, modifying a large program means wading through all the instructions stored in a large program and trying to find which instructions you need to change.

A fourth benefit of functions is that if you write a useful function, you can plug that function into other programs. By creating a library of tested, useful functions, you can create other programs quickly and easily by reusing existing code, thereby reducing the need to write everything from scratch.

When you divide a large program into multiple functions, you have a choice. You can store all your programs in a single file or you can store each function in a separate file, as shown in Figure 1-3. By storing functions in separate files, multiple programmers can work on different files without affecting anyone else.

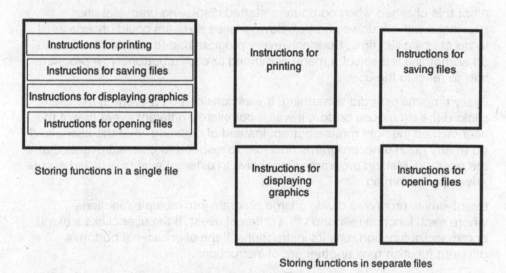

Figure 1-3 content:

Storing functions in a single file:
- Instructions for printing
- Instructions for saving files
- Instructions for displaying graphics
- Instructions for opening files

Storing functions in separate files:
- Instructions for printing
- Instructions for saving files
- Instructions for displaying graphics
- Instructions for opening files

Figure 1-3. You can store functions in a single file or in multiple files

Storing all your functions in a single file makes it easy to find and modify any part of your program. However, the larger your program, the more instructions you'll need to write, which can make searching through a single large file as clumsy as flipping through the pages of a non-alphabetized dictionary looking for a specific word.

In addition, storing all functions in a single file makes it impossible for multiple programmers to work on separate parts of your program since each programmer will need the same file.

Storing all of your functions in separate files means that you need to keep track of which file contains which function. However, the benefit is that modifying a function is much easier because once you open the correct file, you only see the instructions for a single function, not for a dozen or more other functions.

Because today's programs can get so large, it's common to store functions in separate files.

Event-Driven Programming

In the early days of computers, most programs worked by starting with the first instruction and then following each instruction line by line until reaching the end. Such programs tightly controlled how the computer behaved at any given time.

All of this changed when computers started displaying graphical user interfaces with windows and pull-down menus so users could choose what to do at any given time. Suddenly every program had to wait for the user to do something like select a menu command or click a button. Now programs had to react to the user.

Every time the user did something, it was considered an event. If the user clicked the left mouse button, it was a completely different event than if the user clicked the right mouse button. Instead of dictating what the user could do at any given time, programs now had to respond to different events that the user did. Making programs responsive to different events is called event-driven programming.

Event-driven programs divide a large program into multiple functions where each function responds to a different event. If the user clicks a menu command, a function runs its instructions. If the user clicks a button, a different function runs another set of instructions.

Event-driven programming always waits to respond to the user's action.

Object-Oriented Programming

Dividing a large program into multiple functions makes it easy to create and modify a program. However, trying to understand how such a large program works is often confusing since there is no simple way to determine which functions work together or what data they might need from other functions.

Even worse, functions often modify data that other functions use. This means sometimes a function will modify data before another function can use it. Using the wrong data will cause the other function to fail, causing the whole program to fail. Not only does this situation create less reliable software, but it also makes it much harder to determine how and where to fix the problem.

To solve this situation, computer scientists created object-oriented programming. The goal is to divide a large program into smaller functions, but organized related functions together into groups known as objects.

To make object-oriented programs easier to understand, objects also model physical items in the real world.

Suppose you need to write a program to control a robot. Dividing this problem by tasks, you might create one function to move the robot, a second function to tell the robot how to see nearby obstacles, and a third function to calculate the best path to follow. If there is a problem with the robot's movement, you won't know if the problem is in the function controlling the movement, the function controlling how the robot sees obstacles, or the function calculating the best path to follow.

Dividing this same robot program into objects might create a Legs object (for moving the robot), an Eye object (for seeing nearby obstacles), and a Brain object (for calculating the best path to avoid obstacles). Now if there is a problem with the robot's movement, you can isolate the problem to the code stored in the Legs object.

Besides isolating data within an object, a second idea behind object-oriented programming is to make it easy to reuse and modify a large program. Suppose you replace a robot's legs with treads. Now you must modify the function for moving the robot since treads behave differently than legs. Next, you must modify the function for calculating the best path around obstacles since treads force a robot to go around obstacles while legs allow a robot to walk over small obstacles and go around larger obstacles.

If you want to replace a robot's legs with treads, object-oriented programming simply allows you to yank out the Legs object and replace it with a new Treads object, without affecting or needing to modify any additional objects that make up the rest of the program.

Since most programs are constantly modified to fix errors (known as bugs) or add new features, object-oriented programming allows you to create a large program out of separate building blocks (objects), and modify a program by only modifying a single object.

The key to object-oriented programming is to isolate parts of a program and promote reusability through three features known as encapsulation, inheritance, and polymorphism.

Encapsulation

The main purpose of encapsulation is to protect and isolate one part of a program from another part of a program. To do this, encapsulation hides data so it can never be changed by another part of a program. In addition, encapsulation also holds all functions that manipulate data stored in that object. If any problems occur, encapsulation makes it easy to isolate the problem within a particular object.

Every object is meant to be a completely independent of any other part of a program. Objects store data in properties. The only way to manipulate these properties is to use functions called methods, which are also encapsulated in the same object. The combination of properties and methods, isolated within an object, makes it easy to create large programs quickly and reliably by using objects as building blocks, as shown in Figure 1-4.

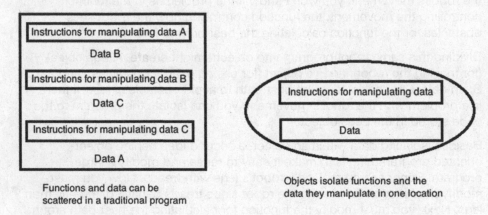

Instructions for manipulating data A

Data B

Instructions for manipulating data B

Data C

Instructions for manipulating data C

Data A

Functions and data can be
scattered in a traditional program

Instructions for manipulating data

Data

Objects isolate functions and the
data they manipulate in one location

Figure 1-4. Objects encapsulate related functions and data together, hidden from the rest of a program

Inheritance

Creating a large, complicated program is hard, but what makes that task even harder is writing the whole program from scratch. That's why most programmers reuse parts of existing programs for two reasons. First, they don't have to rewrite the feature they need from scratch. This means they can create a large program faster. Second, they can use tested code that's already proven to work correctly. This means they can create more reliable software faster by reusing reliable code.

One huge problem with reusing code is that you never want to make duplicate copies. Suppose you copied a function and pasted it into a second location. Now you have two copies of the exact same code stored in two separate places in the same program. This wastes space, but more importantly, it could cause problems in the future.

Suppose you found a problem in a function. To fix this problem, you'd need to fix this code everywhere you copied and pasted it in other parts of your program. If you copied and pasted this code in two other places in your program, you'd have to find and fix that code in both places. If you copied and pasted this code in a thousand places in your program, you'd have to find and fix that code in a thousand different places.

Not only is this inconvenient and time-consuming, but it also increases the risk of overlooking code and leaving a problem in that code. This creates less reliable programs.

To avoid the problem of fixing multiple copies of the same code, object-oriented programming uses something called inheritance. The idea is that one object can use all the code stored in another object but without physically making a copy of that code. Instead, one object inherits code from another object, but only one copy of that code ever exists.

Now you can reuse one copy of code as many times as you want. If you need to fix a problem, you only need to fix that code once and those changes automatically appear in any object that reuses that code through inheritance.

Basically, inheritance lets you reuse code without physically making duplicate copies of that code. This makes it easy to reuse code and easily modify it in the future.

Polymorphism

Every object consists of data (stored in properties) and functions (called methods) for manipulating that data. With inheritance, one object can use the properties and methods defined in another object. However, inheritance can create a problem when you need a function (method) to use different code.

Suppose you create a video game. You define a car as one object and a monster as a second object. If the monster throws rocks at the car, the rocks are a third object. To make the car, monster, and rocks move on the screen, you create a method named Move.

Unfortunately, a car needs to move differently on the screen than a monster or a thrown rock. You could create three functions and name them MoveCar, MoveMonster, and MoveRock. However, a simpler solution is to just give all three functions the same name, such as Move.

In traditional programming, you can never give the same name to two or more functions since the computer won't know which function you want to run. However, in object-oriented programming, you can use duplicate function names because of polymorphism.

Polymorphism lets you use the same method name but replace it with different code. The reason why polymorphism works is because each Move function (method) gets stored in a separate object such as one object that represents the car, a second object that represents the monster, and a third object that represents a thrown rock. To run each Move function, you identify the object that contains the Move function you want to use, such as

```
Car.Move
Monster.Move
Rock.Move
```

By identifying both the object that you want to manipulate and the function that you want to use, object-oriented programming can correctly identify which set of instructions to run even though one function has the identical name as another function.

Essentially, polymorphism lets you create descriptive function names and reuse that descriptive name as often as you like when you also use inheritance.

The combination of encapsulation, inheritance, and polymorphism forms the basis of object-oriented programming. Encapsulation isolates one part of a program from another. Inheritance lets you reuse code. Polymorphism lets you reuse method names but with different code.

Understanding Programming Languages

A programming language is nothing more than a particular way to express ideas much like human languages such as Spanish, Arabic, Chinese, or English. Computer scientists create programming languages to solve specific types of problems. That means one programming language may be perfect for solving one type of problem but horrible at solving a different type of problem.

The most popular programming language is C, which was designed for low-level access to the computer hardware. As a result, the C language is great for creating operating systems, anti-virus programs, and hard disk encryption programs. Anything that needs to completely control hardware is a perfect task for the C programming language.

Unfortunately, C can be cryptic and sparse because it was designed for maximum efficiency for computers without regard for human efficiency for reading, writing, or modifying C programs. To improve C, computer scientists created an object-oriented version of C called C++. A more refined version of C++ soon appeared called Objective-C, which was the language Apple adopted for macOS and iOS programming.

Because C was originally designed for computer efficiency at the expense of human efficiency, all variants of C including C++ and Objective-C can also be difficult to learn, use, and understand. That's why Apple created Swift. The purpose of Swift is to give you the power of Objective-C while being far easier to learn, use, and understand. Swift is basically an improved version of Objective-C, which itself is an improved version of C++, which is an improved version of C.

Each evolution of computer programming builds on the previous programming standards. When you write programs in Swift, you can use Swift's unique features along with object-oriented programming, event-driven programming, structured programming, and the three basic building blocks of programming (sequential, loops, and branching).

Swift, like all computer programming languages, contains a fixed list of commands known as keywords. To tell a computer what to do, you use keywords to create statements that cause the computer to perform a single task.

You've already seen the `print` keyword that prints text such as

```
print ("Hello, world!")
```

This Swift keyword is `print` (which stands for print); then you have to tell the keyword what you want to print, enclosed in parentheses. Just as learning a human language requires first learning the basic symbols used to write letters such as an alphabet or other symbols, so does learning a programming language require first learning the keywords of that particular programming language.

Although Swift contains dozens of keywords, you don't have to learn all of them at once to write programs in Swift. You just have to learn a handful of keywords initially. As you get more experienced, you'll gradually need to learn additional Swift keywords.

To make programming as easy as possible, Swift (like many programming languages) uses keywords that look like ordinary English words such as `print` or `var` (short for variable). However, many programming languages also use symbols that represent different features.

Common symbols are mathematical symbols for addition (+), subtraction (-), multiplication (*), and division (/).

To identify the beginning and end of commands that work together, Swift (like C) uses curly brackets to enclose code such as

```
{
    print ("This is a message");
}
```

Unlike human languages where you can misspell a word or forget to end a sentence with a period and people can still understand what you're saying, programming languages are not so forgiving. With a programming language, every keyword must be spelled correctly and every symbol must be used where needed. Misspell a single keyword, use the wrong symbol, or put the right symbol in the wrong place and your entire program will fail to work.

Programming languages are precise. The key to programming is to write

- As little code as possible
- Code that does as much as possible
- Code that's as easy to understand as possible.

You want to write as little code as possible because the less code you write, the easier it will be to make sure that it works correctly.

You want code that does as much as possible because this makes your program more capable of solving bigger problems.

You want code that's easy to understand because this makes it easy to fix problems and add features.

Unfortunately, these three criteria are often at odds with one another, as shown in Figure 1-5.

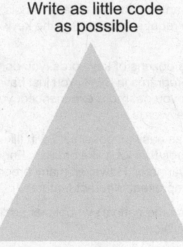

Write as little code
as possible

Code that does as
much as possible

Code that's easy
to understand

Figure 1-5. The three, often contradictory, goals of programming

If you write as little code as possible, this usually means your code can't do much. This is why programmers often resort to shortcuts and programming tricks to condense the size of their code, but this then increases the complexity of their code, making it harder to understand.

If you write code that does as much as possible, this usually means writing large numbers of commands, which makes the code harder to understand.

If you write code that's easy to understand, it usually won't do much. If you write more code to make it do more, this makes it harder to understand.

Ultimately, computer programming is more of an art than a science. In general, it's better to focus on making code as easy to understand as possible because this will make it easier to fix problems and add new features. In addition, code that's easy to understand means other programmers can fix and modify your program if you can't do it.

This is why Apple created Swift: to make code easier to understand than Objective-C without sacrificing the power of Objective-C. Despite being more powerful than Objective-C, Swift code can often be shorter than equivalent Objective-C code. For this reason, the future programming language of Apple will be Swift.

The Cocoa Framework

Keywords (and symbols) let you give instructions to a computer, but no programming language can provide every possible command you might need to create all types of programs. To provide additional commands, programmers use keywords to create functions that perform a specific task.

When they create a useful function, they often save it in a library of other useful functions. When you write a program, you can use the programming language's keywords plus any functions stored in libraries. By reusing functions stored in libraries, you can create more powerful and reliable code.

For example, one library may contain functions for displaying graphics. Another library may contain functions for saving data to a disk and retrieving it again. Still another library may contain functions for calculating mathematical formulas. To make writing macOS and iOS programs easier, Apple has created a library framework of useful functions called the Cocoa framework.

There are two reasons for reusing an existing framework. First, reusing a framework keeps you from having to write your own instructions to accomplish a task that somebody else has already solved. Not only does a framework provide a ready-made solution, but a framework has also been tested by others, so you can just use the framework and be assured that it will work correctly.

A second reason to use an existing framework is for consistency. Apple provides frameworks for defining the appearance of a program on the screen, known as the user interface. This defines how a program should behave from displaying windows on the screen to letting you resize or close a window by clicking the mouse.

It's perfectly possible to write your own instructions for displaying windows on the screen, but chances are good that writing your own instructions will take time to create and test, and the end result will be a user interface that may not look or behave identically to other macOS or iOS programs.

However, by reusing an existing framework, you can create your own program quickly and insure that your program behaves the same way that other programs behave. Although programming might sound complicated, Apple provides hundreds of prewritten and tested functions that help you create programs quickly and easily. All you have to do is write the custom instructions that make your program solve a specific, unique problem.

To understand how Apple's Cocoa framework works, you need to understand object-oriented programming for two reasons. First, Swift is an object-oriented programming language, so to take full advantage of Swift, you need to understand the advantages of object-oriented programming.

Second, Apple's Cocoa framework is based on object-oriented programming. To understand how to use the Cocoa framework, you need to use objects.

> **Note**   The Cocoa framework is designed for creating macOS programs.
> A similar framework called Cocoa Touch is designed for creating iOS apps.
> Because the Cocoa Touch framework (iOS) is based on the Cocoa framework
> (macOS), they work similarly but offer different features.

By relying on the Cocoa framework, your programs can gain new features each time Apple updates and improves the Cocoa framework. For example, spell-checking is a built-in feature of the Cocoa framework. If you write a program using the Cocoa framework, your programs automatically get spell-checking capabilities without you having to write any additional code whatsoever. When Apple improves the spell-checking feature in the Cocoa framework, your program automatically gets those improvements with no extra effort on your part.

The Cocoa framework is a general term that describes all of Apple's pre-written and tested libraries of code. Some different parts of the Cocoa framework can give your programs audio playing capabilities, graphics capabilities, contact information storage abilities such as names and addresses, and Internet capabilities.

The Cocoa framework creates the foundation of a typical macOS program. All you have to do is write Swift code that makes your program unique.

The View-Model-Controller Design

It's possible to write a large program and store all your code in a single file. However, this makes finding anything in your program much harder. A better solution is to divide a large program into parts and store related parts in separate files. This way you can quickly find the part of your program you need to modify and make it easy for multiple programmers to work together since one programmer can work on one file and a second programmer can work on a second file.

When you divide a program into separate files, it's best to stay organized. Just as you might store socks in one drawer and t-shirts in a second drawer so you can easily find the clothes you need, so should you organize your program into multiple files so each file only contains related data. This way you can find the file you need to modify quickly and easily.

The type of data you can store in a file generally falls into one of three categories, shown in Figure 1-6:

- Views (user interface)
- Models
- Controllers

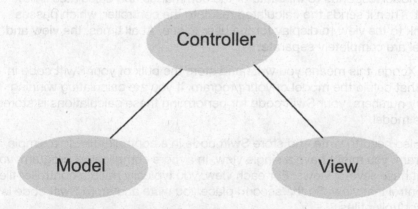

Figure 1-6. Dividing a program into a model-view-controller design

The view or user interface is what the user sees. The purpose of every user interface is to display information, accept data, and accept commands from the user. In the old days, programmers often created user interfaces by writing code. While you can still do this in Swift, it's time-consuming, error-prone, and inconsistent because one programmer's user interface may not look and behave exactly like a second programmer's user interface.

A better option is to design your user interface visually, which is what Xcode lets you do. Just draw objects on your user interface such as buttons, text fields, and menus, and Xcode automatically creates an error-free, consistent-looking user interface that only takes seconds to create. When you create a user interface using Xcode, you're actually using Apple's Cocoa framework to do it.

By itself, the user interface looks good but does nothing. To make a program do something useful, you need to write code that solves a specific problem. For example, a lottery-picking program might analyze the latest numbers picked and determine the numbers most likely to get picked the coming week. The portion of your code that calculates a useful result is called the model.

The model is actually completely separate from the view (user interface). This makes it easy to modify the user interface without affecting the model (and vice versa). By keeping different parts of your program as isolated as possible from other parts of your program, you reduce the chance of errors occurring when you modify a program.

Since the model is always completely separate from the view, you need a controller. When a user chooses a command or types data into the user interface, the controller takes that information from the view and passes it to the model.

The model responds to this data or the commands and calculates a new result. Then it sends the calculated result to the controller, which passes it back to the view to display for the user to see. At all times, the view and model are completely separate.

With Xcode, this means you write and store the bulk of your Swift code in files that define the model of your program. If you are calculating winning lottery numbers, your Swift code for performing these calculations is stored in the model.

You also need to write and store Swift code in a controller file. In a simple program, you might have a single view. In a more complicated program, you might have several views. For each view, you typically need a controller file to control that view. So the second place you write and store Swift code is in the controller files.

In simple programs, it's common to combine a model with a controller in one file. However for larger, more complicated programs, it's better to create one (or more) files for your model and one file for each controller. The number of controller files is usually equal to the number of views that make up your user interface.

Once you've clearly separated your program into models, views, and controllers, you can easily modify your program quickly and easily by replacing one file with a new file. For example, if you want to modify the user interface, you simply design a different view, connect it to your controller, and you're done, without touching your model files.

If you want to modify the model to add new features, you just update your model files and connect it to your controller, without touching your view.

In fact, this is exactly how programmers create programs for both macOS and iOS. Their model remains unchanged. All they do is write one controller and view for macOS and one controller and view for iOS. Then they can create both macOS and iOS apps with the exact same model.

How Programmers Work

In the early days, a single programmer could get an idea and write code to make that program work. Nowadays, programs are far more complicated and user expectations are much higher, so you need to design your program before writing any code. In fact, most programmers actually don't spend much of their time writing or editing code at all. Instead, programmers spend the bulk of their time thinking, planning, organizing, and designing programs.

When a programmer has an idea for a program, the first step is to decide if that idea is even any good. Programs must solve a specific type of problem. For example, word processors make it easy to write, edit, and format text. Spreadsheets make it easy to type in numbers and calculate new results from those numbers. Presentation programs make it easy to type text and insert graphics to create a slideshow. Even video games solve the problem of relieving boredom by offering a challenging puzzle or goal for players to achieve.

> **Note**   The number one biggest failure of software development is not defining a specific problem to solve. The second biggest failure of software development is identifying a specific problem to solve but underestimating the complexity of the steps needed to solve that problem. You have to know what problem to solve and how to solve that problem. If you don't know either one, you can't write a useful program.

Once you have an idea for a problem to solve, the next step is defining how to solve that problem. Some problems are simply too difficult to solve. For example, how would you write a program to write a best-selling novel? You may be able to write a program that can help you write a novel, but unless you know exactly how to create a best-selling novel predictably, you simply can't write such a program.

Knowing a problem to solve is your target. Once you clearly understand your problem, you need to identify all the steps needed to solve that problem. If you don't know how to solve a particular problem, you won't be able to tell a computer how to solve that problem either.

After defining the steps needed to solve a problem, now you can finally write your program. Generally, you write your program in parts and test each part before continuing. In this way, you gradually expand the capabilities of your program while making sure that each part works correctly.

The main steps you go through while using Xcode are

- Write code and design your user interface
- Edit your code and user interface
- Run and test your program

When your program is finally done, guess what? It's never done. There will always be errors you'll need to fix and new features you'll want to add. Programmers actually spend more time editing and modifying existing programs than they ever do creating new programs.

When you write and edit code, you use an editor, which is a program that resembles a word processor that lets you type and edit text. When you design and modify your user interface, you use a feature in Xcode called Interface Builder, which resembles a drawing program that lets you drag, drop, and resize objects on the screen. When you run and test your program, you use a compiler, which converts (or compiles) your Swift code into an actual working macOS program.

To create a macOS program, you just need a copy of Xcode, which is Apple's free programming tool that you can download from the Mac App Store. With Xcode installed on your Macintosh, you can create your own programs for free just by learning Xcode and Swift.

Summary

To learn how to write programs for the Macintosh, you need to learn several separate skills. First, you need to understand the basic principles of programming. This includes organizing instructions in sequences, loops, or branches, and understanding structured programming techniques, event-driven programming, and object-oriented programming.

Second, you need to learn a specific programming language. For the Macintosh, you'll be learning Swift. That means you'll learn the keywords used in Swift along with learning how to write and organize your Swift code in separate files.

Third, you need to know how to use Xcode, which is Apple's programming tool for creating macOS and iOS apps. Xcode lets you write and edit Swift code as well as letting you visually design and modify your user interface.

Fourth, you need to learn how to use Apple's Cocoa framework so you can focus solely on writing instructions that make your program do something unique.

Whether you want to write your own software to sell, or sell your programming skills to create custom software for others, you'll find that programming is a skill that anyone can learn.

Remember, programming is nothing more than problem-solving. By knowing how to solve problems using Swift and Xcode, you can create your own programs for the Macintosh much easier and far faster than you might think.

Chapter **2**

Getting to Know Xcode 8

To write programs in Swift for the Macintosh, you need to use Xcode. Apple developed Xcode as a professional programming tool that they give away free to encourage everyone to write software for macOS and their other operating systems such as iOS, tvOS, and watchOS. Despite being a free program, Xcode is a powerful program used by major companies including Microsoft, Adobe, Google, and even Apple. With Xcode on a Macintosh, you have one of the most powerful programming tools for creating macOS programs and iOS, tvOS, and watchOS apps.

Although Xcode contains dozens of features specifically for professional programmers, anyone can learn to use Xcode. Xcode's sheer number of features may seem confusing and intimidating at first glance, but relax. To use Xcode, you don't need to learn every possible feature. Instead, you can just learn the handful of features you need and ignore all the rest. As you get more experienced, you can gradually learn Xcode's other features. However, you may never use all of Xcode's features.

Xcode lets you create a macOS program or an iOS, tvOS, or watchOS app from start to finish without ever needing another program. Within Xcode you can do the following:

- Create a new project.
- Write and edit Swift code.
- Design and modify user interfaces.
- Manage files that make up a single project.
- Run and test your project.
- Debug your Swift code.

© Wallace Wang 2017
W. Wang, *macOS Programming for Absolute Beginners*,
DOI 10.1007/978-1-4842-2662-9_2

You can download and install Xcode for free through the Mac App Store. On your Macintosh, just click the Apple menu and choose App Store. When the App Store window appears, click in the Search text field in the upper right corner, type **Xcode**, and press Return. Click the button underneath the Xcode icon to download it, as shown in Figure 2-1. Since Xcode is a fairly large file, you'll need a fast Internet connection and plenty of disk space to install it on your Macintosh.

Figure 2-1. *When you search for Xcode, it will likely appear in the upper left corner of the App Store window*

The four most common parts of Xcode you'll use regularly are

- The project manager
- The editor
- Interface Builder
- The compiler

A project represents a single macOS or iOS, tvOS, or watchOS program. In the old days when programs were simple, you could store code in a single file. Now with programs being much larger and more complicated, it's far more common to store code in separate files. A collection of files that work together form a single project, so the Xcode project manager lets you create, rearrange, and delete files within a project.

Every project contains a code file, identified by the .swift file extension. Code files are where you store, edit, and type Swift code. By using Xcode's editor, you can open a code file, copy and paste code, delete code, and write new code to save in that file. An editor basically acts like a simple word processor designed just for helping you write code in the Swift programming language.

Besides a code file containing Swift code, every project also contains a user interface stored in a separate file identified by the .xib or .storyboard file extension. A simple program might only have a single file containing its user interface but a more complicated program might have several files containing different parts of the user interface. The feature in Xcode that lets you design, create, and modify user interfaces is called Interface Builder.

After you've written Swift code and designed your user interface, you'll need to convert all the files in your project into an actual working program. The process of translating Swift code into a language that the computer can understand (called machine code) is called compiling, so the part of Xcode that does this is called a compiler.

You'll often use these four main parts of Xcode in different order. For example, you may create a project and modify its files using the project manager feature. Then you may use the editor to write Swift code and Interface Builder to design your user interface. Finally, you'll test your program using the compiler. If problems occur, you'll likely go back to the editor or Interface Builder as many times as necessary until your program works correctly. You may even create new files and rearrange them in the project manager.

Ultimately, there is no single "best" or "right" way to use Xcode. Xcode offers features for you to use whenever you need them.

Giving Commands to Xcode

Like many programs, Xcode offers multiple ways to do the exact same task. For example, to open a project, you can choose File ➤ Open or press Command+O. In general, Xcode typically offers three ways to perform common types of commands:

- Use the pull-down menus from the menu bar that appears at the top of the screen.

- Press a unique keystroke combination such as Command+O.

- Click an icon that represents a command.

Pull-down menus can be convenient to help you find specific commands, but they can be slower and clumsier to use because you have to click a menu title to pull down a menu, and then you have to click a command that appears on that menu.

Keystroke combinations are faster and easier, but they force you to memorize cryptic keystroke combinations for commonly used commands. To help you learn which commands have keystroke combinations, look on each pull-down menu and you'll see keystroke combinations displayed to the right of different commands, as shown in Figure 2-2. (However, not all commands have keystroke combinations.)

File	Edit	View	Find	Navigate	Editor
New					▶
Add Files to "TestPlayground"...					⌥⌘A
Open...					⌘O
Open Recent					▶
Open Quickly...					⇧⌘O
Close Window					⌘W
Close Tab					
Close "TestPlayground.playground"					^⌘W
Close Playground					⌥⌘W
Save					⌘S
Duplicate...					⇧⌘S
Revert to Saved...					
Unlock...					
Export...					
Show in Finder					
Open with External Editor					
Save As Workspace...					
Playground Settings...					
Page Setup...					⇧⌘P
Print...					⌘P

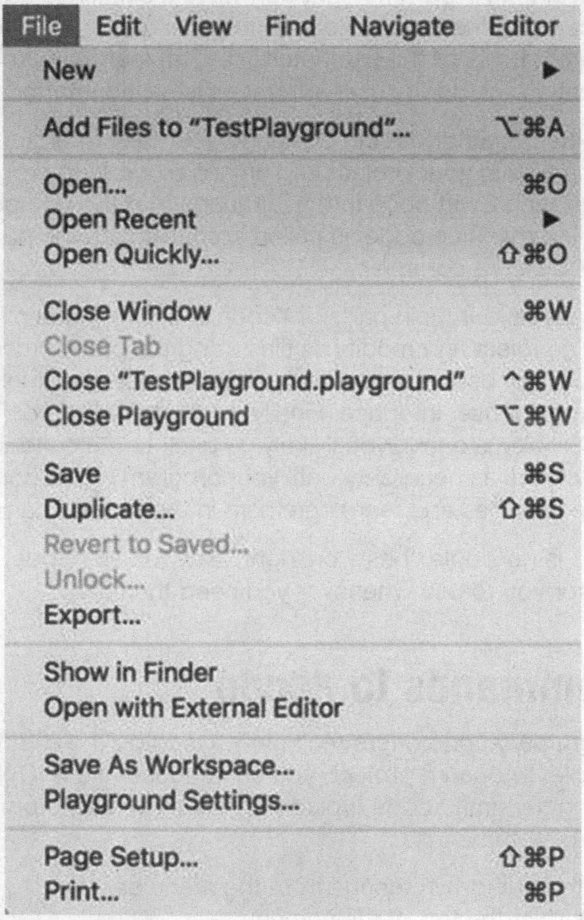

Figure 2-2. Keystroke combinations appear to the right of commands on pull-down menus

Keystroke combinations usually include a modifier key plus a letter or function key. The four modifier keys include Command, Control, Option, and Shift, as shown in Figure 2-3.

⌘	Command key
^	Control key
⌥	Option key
⇧	Shift Key

Figure 2-3. Symbols used to represent common modifier keys

Clicking icons to choose a command may be the fastest method of all, but you have to know the command that each icon represents. To help you understand what an icon does, just move the mouse pointer over an icon and wait a few seconds. A tiny window will appear, briefly describing the purpose of that icon; see Figure 2-4.

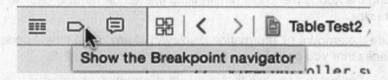

Figure 2-4. Hovering the mouse pointer over an icon displays a brief description of that icon's function

Some people only use pull-down menus, others rely more on icons and keystroke shortcuts, and others use a mix of all three methods. Generally, people begin with pull-down menus but when they start using the same commands often, they gradually switch to icons and keystroke shortcuts.

Choose whatever method you like but be aware that you almost always have alternatives. The main point is to get comfortable using Xcode via your preferred method so you can spend more time being creative and less time trying to find the commands you need.

Modifying the Xcode Window

Because Xcode offers so many features, the Xcode window can look cluttered at times. To simplify the appearance of Xcode, you have several options:

- Resize the Xcode window to make it larger (or smaller).

- Close panes to hide parts of Xcode.

- Open panes to view parts of Xcode.

Like all Macintosh windows, the most straightforward way to resize the Xcode window is to move the mouse pointer over the edge or corner of the Xcode window until the mouse pointer turns into a two-way pointing arrow. Then drag the mouse to resize the window.

A second way to resize the Xcode window is to click the green dot in the upper left corner of the Xcode window. This expands the Xcode window to take up the full screen and hides the Xcode menu bar at the same time. To exit out of full screen mode, just move the mouse pointer to the top of the screen to make the Xcode menu bar appear again. Then click the green dot in the upper left corner of the window once more.

A third way to resize the Xcode window is to choose Window ➤ Zoom. This toggles between expanding the Xcode window to fill the screen while still displaying the Xcode menu bar or shrinking the Xcode window back to its previous size.

To reduce the amount of information displayed at any given time, Xcode has three panes that you can hide (or open), as shown in Figure 2-5:

- The Navigator pane that displays information about your project

- The Debug area that lets you search for errors or bugs in your program

- The Utilities pane that lets you customize different items on your user interface

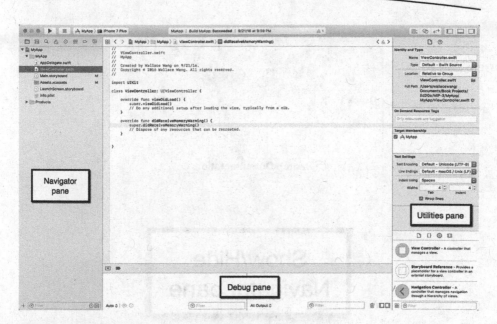

Figure 2-5. Xcode's Navigator pane, Debug pane, and Utilities pane

The Navigator pane displays several icons that let you switch between viewing different types of information. The most common use for the Navigator pane is to let you select a file to open by displaying the Project Navigator. To toggle between hiding and showing the Navigator pane, you have three options:

- Choose View ➤ Navigators ➤ Show/Hide Navigator.

- Press Command+0 (the number zero).

- Click the Show/Hide Navigator Pane icon in the upper right corner of the Xcode window, as shown in Figure 2-6.

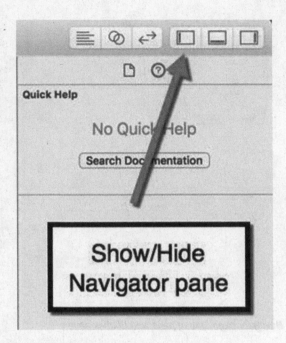

Figure 2-6. The Show/Hide Navigator Pane icon

The Debug area is used when you want to check if your program is working correctly. While you're designing your user interface or writing Swift code, you'll likely want to hide this Debug area. To toggle between hiding and showing the Debug area, you have three options:

- Choose View ➤ Debug Area ➤ Show/Hide Debug Area.

- Press Shift+Command+Y.

- Click the Show/Hide Debug Area icon in the upper right corner of the Xcode window, as shown in Figure 2-7.

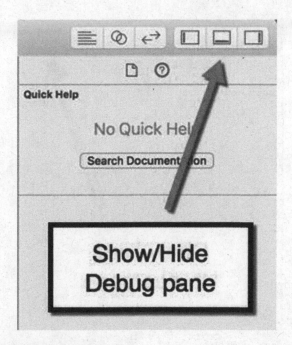

Figure 2-7. The Show/Hide Debug Area icon

The Utilities pane displays several icons that let you switch between showing different types of information. The most common use for the Utilities pane is to help you design and modify a user interface. To toggle between hiding and showing the Utilities pane, you have three options:

- Choose View ➤ Utilities ➤ Show/Hide Utilities.

- Press Option + Command + 0 (the number zero).

- Click the Show/Hide Utilities icon in the upper right corner of the Xcode window, as shown in Figure 2-8.

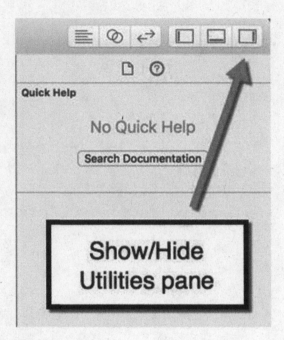

Figure 2-8. *The Show/Hide Utilities icon*

By selectively showing or hiding the Navigator pane, the Debug area, or the Utilities pane, you can make the Xcode window look less cluttered and provide more room for the parts of Xcode that you want to see. To quickly open or hide these three panes, it's usually faster to click the Show/Hide Navigator, Debug area, or Utilities icons in the upper right corner of the Xcode window.

Creating and Managing Files

Any time you need to create a project (that represents a brand new program) or a file (to add to an existing project), you have two choices:

- Choose File ➤ New to display a submenu, as shown in Figure 2-9.

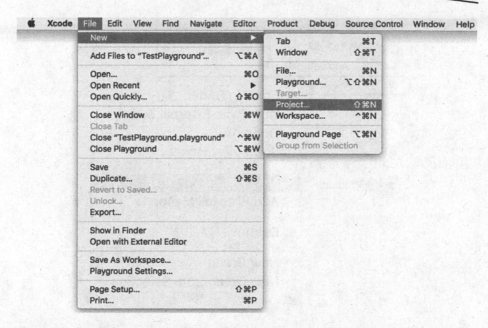

| Xcode | File | Edit | View | Find | Navigate | Editor | Product | Debug | Source Control | Window | Help |

New	▶
Add Files to "TestPlayground"...	⌥⌘A
Open...	⌘O
Open Recent	▶
Open Quickly...	⇧⌘O
Close Window	⌘W
Close Tab	
Close "TestPlayground.playground"	^⌘W
Close Playground	⌥⌘W
Save	⌘S
Duplicate...	⇧⌘S
Revert to Saved...	
Unlock...	
Export...	
Show in Finder	
Open with External Editor	
Save As Workspace...	
Playground Settings...	
Page Setup...	⇧⌘P
Print...	⌘P

Tab	⌘T
Window	⇧⌘T
File...	⌘N
Playground...	⌥⇧⌘N
Target...	
Project...	⇧⌘N
Workspace...	^⌘N
Playground Page	⌥⌘N
Group from Selection	

Figure 2-9. *The File ➤ New command displays a submenu that lets you choose to create a file or a project*

- Right-click any file displayed in the Navigator pane to display a pop-up menu, as shown in Figure 2-10.

Figure 2-10. Right-clicking a file in the Navigator pane displays a pop-up menu that lets you choose to create a file

Note   Right-clicking may be disabled on some Macintosh computers. You can simulate a right-click by holding down the Control key while clicking. To turn on right-clicking, click the Apple menu, choose System Preferences, and click the Mouse or Trackpad icon. Then select the "Secondary click" check box to turn on right-clicking.

When you create a new file, you can choose whether to create a file for a macOS or iOS, tvOS, or watchOS project. In this book, you'll always create files for macOS.

Besides choosing to create a file for macOS, you also need to choose what type of file to create. The two most common types of files you'll create will be either files that can hold Swift code (organized under the Source category, as shown in Figure 2-11) or files that can hold a user interface (organized under the User Interface category, as shown in Figure 2-12).

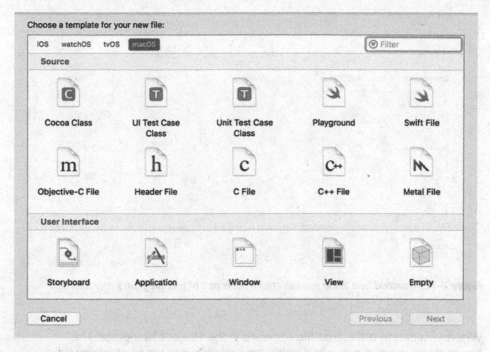

Figure 2-11. One type of file you can create holds Swift code

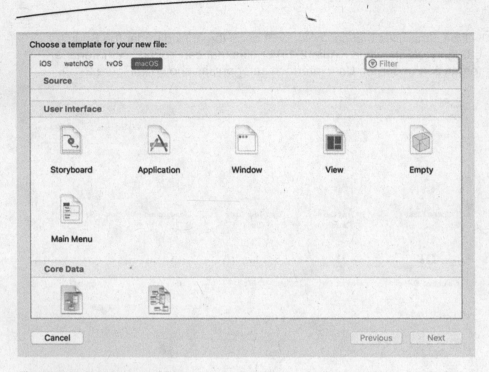

Figure 2-12. A second type of file you can create holds part of your program's user interface

When you create a file, that file appears in the Project Navigator. The Navigator pane can actually display several different types of information, but the most common is the Project Navigator, which lists of all the files that make up your project. To open the Project Navigator within the Navigator pane, you have three choices:

- Choose View ➤ Navigators ➤ Show Project Navigator.

- Press Command+1.

- Click the Show the Project Navigator icon, as shown in Figure 2-13.

Figure 2-13. The Project Navigator pane lists all the files that make up a project

The Project Navigator closely resembles the Finder by displaying files and folders. To rename a file or folder, just select it and press Return to edit its name.

To move a file or folder, just drag it with the mouse and drop it in a new location.

To select one or more items, hold down the Command key and click a file or folder.

Just like the Finder, the Project Navigator lets you organize files into folders. This lets you group related files together and tuck them out of sight so they don't clutter the Project Navigator. To create a folder, click a file or folder in the Project Navigator and then do one of the following actions:

- Choose File ➤ New ➤ Group (or Group from Selection to store one or more selected files in a folder).

- Press Option + Command + N.

- Right-click any file or folder in the Project Navigator and when a pop-up menu appears, choose New Group (or New Group from Selection to store one or more selected files in a folder).

To delete a file or folder, select a file or folder and then do one of the following:

- Choose Edit ➤ Delete.
- Press the Delete key or Command+Backspace.
- Right-click any file or folder in the Project Navigator and when a pop-up menu appears, choose Delete.

> **Note** When you delete a file or folder, you have the option of Remove Reference (which removes a file/folder from a project but does not physically delete it from your Macintosh) or Move to Trash (which removes a file/folder from a project and physically deletes it from your Macintosh).

Perhaps the most important use for the Project Navigator is to let you edit a file in a project. When you click a file in the Project Navigator, the middle pane of the Xcode window displays the contents of your selected file, which will either hold Swift code or your user interface (see Figure 2-14).

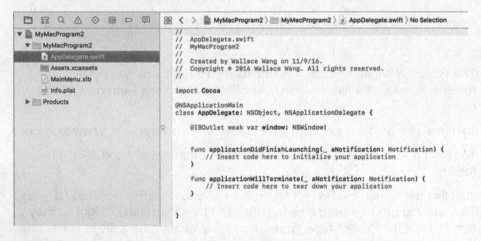

Figure 2-14. Selecting a file in the Navigator pane displays the contents of that file

Creating and Customizing a User Interface

The Utilities pane is most often used for creating and customizing your project's user interface. With macOS programs, user interface files may be one of two types:

- .xib files

- .storyboard files

When you create a project, you can choose which type you want to use. In general, .xib files are used for single window user interfaces while .storyboard files are used for multiple windows that are linked to appear in a certain order. It's possible to mix both .xib and .storyboard files to create a user interface or just use .xib or .storyboard files exclusively.

Whether you use .xib or .storyboard files, you need to use the Utilities pane for two purposes. First, you need to drag and drop items onto your user interface, such as buttons, text fields, and pictures. Second, you need to customize those user interface items by changing their names, color, or size.

To design a user interface, you start with the Object Library, which appears at the bottom of the Utilities pane, as shown in Figure 2-15. To open the Object Library, you can do the following:

- Choose View ➤ Utilities ➤ Show Object Library.

- Press Contrl + Option + Command + 3.

- Click the Show Object Library icon.

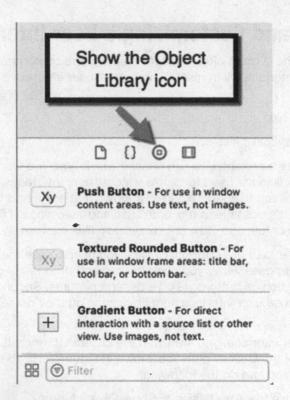

Figure 2-15. The Object Library contains different user interface items

To find a user interface item in the Object Library, you can simply scroll up and down the list. However, if you know the name of the item you want, a faster method is to click in the Search field at the bottom of the Object Library window, type all or part of the name of the item you want, and press Return. The Object Library will then show only those items that match what you typed. So if you typed "Button," the Object Library would only display different buttons you can add to your user interface.

After you have placed one or more items on your user interface, the second step is to customize those items using the Inspector pane. The Inspector pane can display several types of panes but the two most common you'll use to customize user interface items are

- The Attributes Inspector
- The Size Inspector

The Attributes Inspector lets you modify the appearance of an item. The Size Inspector lets you modify the size and position of an item on the user interface.

To open the Attributes Inspector, you can do one of the following:

- Choose View ➤ Utilities ➤ Show Attributes Inspector.

- Press Option + Command + 4.

- Click the Show Attributes Inspector, as shown in Figure 2-16.

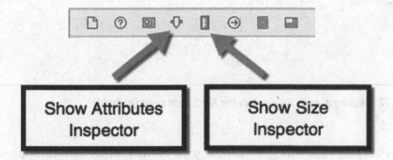

Figure 2-16. *The Show Attributes Inspector and Show Size Inspector icons*

To open the Size Inspector, you can do one of the following:

- Choose View ➤ Utilities ➤ Show Size Inspector.

- Press Option + Command + 5.

- Click the Show Size Inspector, as shown in Figure 2-16.

After opening the Attributes or Size Inspectors, you can then click a user interface item to modify it (such as a button or text field) and then type or choose different options to modify that item's appearance.

The Standard and Assistant Editors

You'll spend most of your time using the editor or Interface Builder. The editor acts like a word processor and lets you type and edit Swift code. Interface Builder acts like a drawing program and lets you drag and drop, resize, and move items on the user interface such as buttons, text fields, and graphics.

To edit Swift code, just click any file in the Project Navigator pane that contains the .swift file extension. When you click a .swift file, the contents of that file appears in the middle Xcode pane, as shown in Figure 2-17.

```
//
//  NyanCatCanvas.swift
//  touchbar_nyancat
//
//  Created by Aslan Vatsaev on 05/11/2016.
//  Copyright © 2016 AVatsaev. All rights reserved.
//

import Cocoa

class NyanCatCanvas: NSImageView {

    override func draw(_ dirtyRect: NSRect) {
        super.draw(dirtyRect)

        // Drawing code here.

        self.frame = CGRect(x: 0, y: 0, width: 685, height: 30)

        self.animates = true
        self.image = NSImage(named: "nyan_long@2x.gif")!
        self.canDrawSubviewsIntoLayer = true
    }

}
```

Figure 2-17. Clicking a .swift file displays the Swift code stored in that file

To edit your user interface, just click any file in the Project Navigator pane that contains the `.xib` or `.storyboard` file extension. This displays the contents of that user interface in the middle Xcode pane, as shown in Figure 2-18.

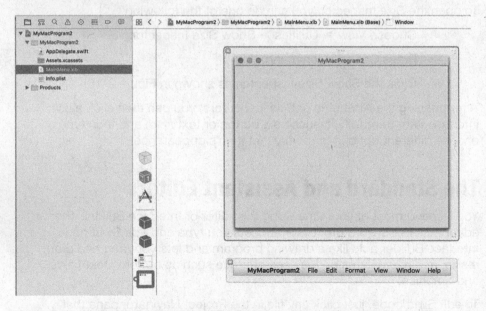

Figure 2-18. Clicking a .xib or .storyboard file displays the user interface stored in that file

Each time you click a different file in the Project Navigator pane, Xcode displays the contents of that new file in the middle pane of the Xcode window.

When Xcode displays the contents of a single file in its middle pane, that's called the Standard Editor. However, it's often useful to view the contents of two files side by side. When Xcode displays two file contents side by side, that second file pane is called the Assistant Editor.

The most common reason to open the Assistant Editor is when you have the user interface displayed in the left pane and a Swift file displayed in the right pane, as shown in Figure 2-19. The purpose for this is to let you link your user interface to your Swift code.

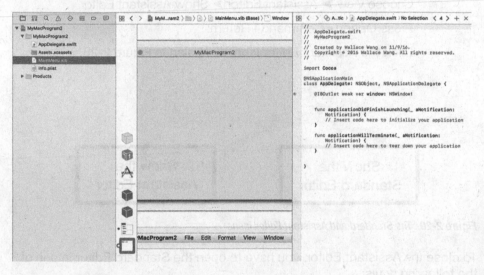

Figure 2-19. The Assistant Editor displays two file contents side by side

When you create a user interface, it's completely independent from your Swift code (and vice versa). This gives you the freedom to replace your user interface with a new user interface without affecting how your Swift code behaves. Likewise, this also lets you modify your Swift code without worrying about affecting your user interface.

In the old days, programmers had to create their user interfaces using code, which meant changing the code often affected the user interface, increasing the chance of errors or bugs in the program. By separating the user interface from the code, Xcode eliminates this problem and helps you create more reliable software.

When you create a user interface initially, it won't do anything. That's why you need to link some of your user interface items to Swift code that makes the user interface actually work. For example, if your user interface displays a button, clicking that button won't do anything. You have to write Swift code to tell that button what to do. Then you have to link your button to your Swift code.

This is the purpose of the Assistant Editor. By displaying your user interface next to your Swift code file, the Assistant Editor makes it easy to drag the mouse from your user interface to your Swift code files, creating a link between your user interface and your Swift code.

To open the Assistant Editor, you can choose one of the following:

- Choose View ➤ Assistant Editor ➤ Show Assistant Editor.
- Press Option + Command + Return.
- Click the Assistant Editor icon, as shown in Figure 2-20.

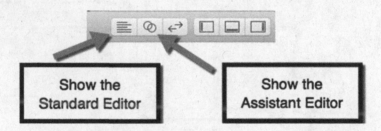

Figure 2-20. The Standard and Assistant Editor icons

To close the Assistant Editor, you have to open the Standard Editor in one of the following ways:

- Choose View ➤ Standard Editor ➤ Show Standard Editor.
- Press Command + Return.
- Click the Standard Editor icon (see Figure 2-20).

One problem with using the Assistant Editor is that Xcode displays both file contents in narrow panes. If you prefer seeing two or more files in a wider view, you can display them in separate tabs. This lets you see the contents of each file in the middle pane of Xcode and simply click a tab to see a different file's contents.

The drawback of tabs is that you can only see the contents of one file at a time. A second drawback is that you can't see your user interface next to your Swift code so you can't connect user interface items to your Swift code.

To create a tab, choose one of the following:

- Choose File ➤ New ➤ Tab.
- Press Command + T.

Now you can click on each tab to view the contents of that file. To close a tab, move the mouse over the tab and choose one of the following:

- Click the close icon (it looks like a big X) in the left of the tab.
- Right-click the tab and when a pop-up menu appears, click Close Tab, as shown in Figure 2-21.

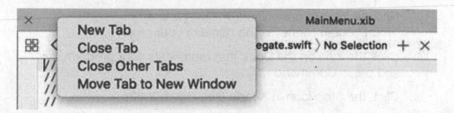

Figure 2-21. Right-clicking a tab displays a pop-up menu

Running a Program

Typically you run your program multiple times to test and make sure it works right. When you run a program, Xcode compiles it into a file that you can distribute to others if you wish. Running a program lets you test your program directly on your Macintosh.

The three ways to run a program are

- Choose Product ➤ Run.
- Press Command + R.
- Click the Run icon, as shown in Figure 2-22.

Figure 2-22. The Run and Stop icons let you test your macOS project

Once your program is running, you can stop it in several ways:

- Choose YourProgramName ➤ Quit (where "YourProgramName" is the name of your project).

- Click the icon on the Dock that represents your program and press Command+Q.

- Click the Stop icon in Xcode (see Figure 2-22).

If your program has major errors that prevent it from responding to any commands, you can also use the Force Quit command to shut down your program. To use Force Quit, click the Apple menu and choose Force Quit.

When the Force Quit window appears, click your program's name and then click the Force Quit button to shut it down.

Summary

This chapter introduced you to the major features of Xcode and showed various ways to choose common commands. Don't worry about memorizing or fully understanding everything in this chapter just yet. Think of this chapter as an introduction to Xcode that you can refer back to whenever you have a question.

In the next chapter, you'll actually go through the typical process of creating a macOS program using Xcode. This way you can see the purpose of the various Xcode features that you learned about in this chapter.

Just remember that with Xcode, there are often two or more ways to choose the exact same command, but you don't have to learn all of these different ways. Choose the method you like best and ignore the other methods.

As you can see, Xcode offers everything you need to turn your ideas into a fully functional macOS program that you can sell and distribute to others. By learning Xcode, you'll be learning to use the programming tool that professional programmers use to create macOS and iOS, tvOS, or watchOS software. The more you use Xcode, the more comfortable you'll get and the less intimidating Xcode's user interface will feel. Pretty soon you'll be using Xcode like a pro.

Remember, the real key to programming isn't having the best programming tools but knowing how to use them. The more you use Xcode, the more you'll understand how to turn your great ideas into actual working programs. Learning Xcode is your path to writing software for the Macintosh and Apple's many other devices such as the iPhone, iPad, Apple Watch, and Apple TV. By learning Xcode today, you can take advantage of the many lucrative programming opportunities that will be available now and far into the future.

Welcome to the world of Xcode!

Chapter 3

The Basics of Creating a Mac Program

Whatever type of macOS program you want to create, such as a video game or a custom program for dentists or real estate agents, you'll always go through the same basic steps. First, you'll need to create a macOS project. This creates a bare-bones macOS program that includes a generic user interface.

Second, you'll need to customize this generic macOS program in two ways: by adding items to the user interface and by writing Swift code to make the program actually do something.

Third, you'll need to run and test your program. After running and testing your program, you'll likely need to constantly go back and modify your user interface or Swift code to fix problems and add new features. Eventually your program will reach a point where it's complete (for now) and you can ship it. Then you'll repeat these basic steps all over again to add new features once more.

Generally, you'll spend more time modifying a program than creating new ones. However, it's useful to create small programs to test out different features. Once you get these smaller, experimental programs working, you can add them to another program. By doing this, you don't risk messing up a working program.

© Wallace Wang 2017
W. Wang, *macOS Programming for Absolute Beginners*,
DOI 10.1007/978-1-4842-2662-9_3

Creating a Project

The first step to creating a program is to create a new project. When you create a project, Xcode gives you the option of choosing different templates, which provide basic functions. All you have to do is customize the template. The three categories of macOS templates are shown in Figure 3-1:

- Application

- Framework & Library

- Other

Figure 3-1. The three categories of macOS templates for creating a project

Most of the time you'll choose a template in the Application category. The most common template is Cocoa Application, which creates a standard macOS program with pull-down menus and a window.

The other two Application templates are Game (for creating video games) and Command Line Tool (for creating programs that don't need a traditional graphical user interface).

The Framework & Library category is meant to create reusable software libraries. The Other category is meant for creating programs that don't fit into the other categories such as creating plug-ins or drivers.

In this book, you'll always use the Cocoa Application under the macOS Application category. The other macOS categories are designed for advanced programmers and won't be covered in this book.

When you create a Cocoa Application project, you need to define several items, as shown in Figure 3-2:

- The name of your product

- The programming language to use (Objective-C or Swift)

- Whether to use storyboards or not for your user interface

- Whether to create a document-based application

- Whether to use Core Data

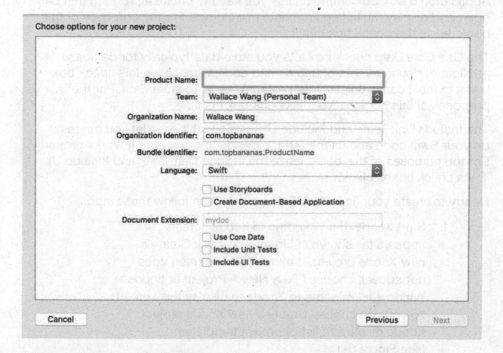

Choose options for your new project:

Product Name:	
Team:	Wallace Wang (Personal Team)
Organization Name:	Wallace Wang
Organization Identifier:	com.topbananas
Bundle Identifier:	com.topbananas.ProductName
Language:	Swift
	☐ Use Storyboards
	☐ Create Document-Based Application
Document Extension:	mydoc
	☐ Use Core Data
	☐ Include Unit Tests
	☐ Include UI Tests

Cancel   Previous   Next

Figure 3-2. Defining a Cocoa Application project

Your product's name is completely arbitrary but should be descriptive since Xcode will store all your files in a folder using your chosen name.

Your organization name and identifier are also arbitrary and are typically assigned from your Apple Developer account. Both of them can also be arbitrary strings if you want, but if you plan on distributing your programs through the Mac App Store, they should be linked to your Apple Developer account.

The Language pop-up menu lets you choose Objective-C or Swift. For the purposes of this book, you'll always choose Swift. Objective-C is a more complicated programming language that Apple still supports, but it's no longer considered Apple's official programming language.

The Use Storyboards check box lets you create a user interface that either consists of a single window (a .xib file if the "Use Storyboards" check box is clear) or a series of windows linked together (a .storyboard file if the "Use Storyboards" check box is selected). I'll go over both methods for creating a user interface later in this book.

The Create Document-Based Application option means that Xcode creates a Cocoa Application that can open and manage multiple windows, such as the multiple windows available in a word processor. Managing multiple windows is more complicated so leave the Create Document-Based Application check box empty unless you need to create a program that can open and display multiple documents in windows. For the purposes of this book, leave this check box blank.

The Use Core Data check box lets you store data typically for database applications such as lists of names and addresses. Leave this check box blank in most cases unless your program needs to store data. For the purposes of this book, leave this check box blank.

The Include Unit Tests and Include UI Tests check boxes let you run tests on your Swift code and user interface design to make sure it works properly. For the purposes of this book, leave the Include Unit Tests and Include UI Tests check boxes blank.

Ready to create your first macOS program? Then follow these steps:

1. Start Xcode. If a Welcome to Xcode screen appears (as shown in Figure 3-3), click Create a new Xcode project. If this welcome screen does not appear, choose File ➤ New ➤ Project or choose Window ➤ Welcome to Xcode to display this screen so you can choose Create a new Xcode project. Xcode displays a list of project templates (see Figure 3-1).

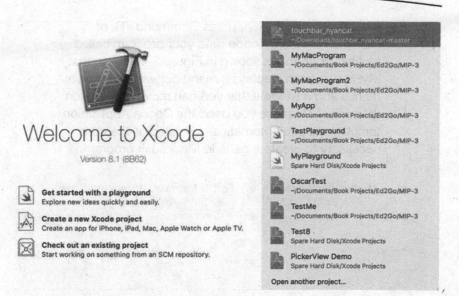

Figure 3-3. *The Welcome to Xcode opening screen*

2. Click Application under the macOS category. A list of different macOS application templates appears.

3. Click Cocoa Application and then click the Next button. Xcode now asks for your project name (see Figure 3-2).

4. Click in the Product Name text field and type **MyFirstProgram**.

5. Click in the Language pop-up menu and make sure Swift appears.

6. Make sure all check boxes are empty and then click the Next button. Xcode now asks where you want to store your project.

7. Click a folder where you want to store your Xcode project and click the Create button. Congratulations! You've just created your first macOS program. At this point, Xcode just created a generic Macintosh program but you haven't had to write a single line of Swift code or even design the user interface to create an actual working program.

8. Choose Product ➤ Run, press Command + R, or
    click the Run icon. Xcode runs your program called
    MyFirstProgram, as shown in Figure 3-4. Notice that
    MyFirstProgram displays a menu bar with pull-down
    menus and a window that you can move or resize on
    the screen. Because you used the Cocoa Application
    template, Xcode automatically created all the code
    necessary to create a generic Macintosh program.

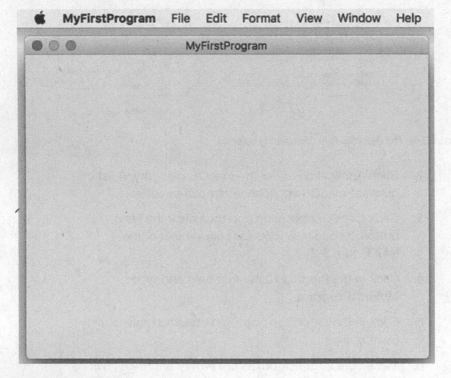

Figure 3-4. The MyFirstProgram running

9. Choose MyFirstProgram ➤ Quit MyFirstProgram.
    Xcode appears. Keep your MyFirstProgram project
    open in Xcode for the next section.

Without doing a thing, you managed to create a program that looks and
behaves like a typical Macintosh program. Of course, this bare-bones
Macintosh program won't do anything interesting until you customize the
user interface and write Swift code to make the program do something
useful.

Designing a User Interface

When designing a user interface, keep in mind the three purposes for any user interface:

- ■ To display information to the user
- ■ To get data from the user
- ■ To let the user give commands to the program

When you design a user interface, every element must satisfy one of these criteria. Colors and lines might just seem decorative, but they can be useful to organize a user interface so users will know where to find information, how to input data, or how to give commands to the program.

To create a user interface in Xcode, you need to follow a two-step process:

- ■ Use the Object Library to drag and drop items on to your user interface.
- ■ Use the Inspector pane to customize each user interface item.

To see how to use the Object Library, let's add a label, a text field, and a button to the MyFirstProgram user interface. The label will display text to the user, the text field will let the user type in data, and the button will make the program take the text from the text field, modify it by capitalizing every character, and place the modified uppercase text into the label.

To do this, follow these steps:

1. Make sure your MyFirstProgram project is loaded into Xcode.

2. Choose View ➤ Navigators ➤ Show Project Navigator or press Command + 1 to view the list of all the files that make up your MyFirstProgram project.

3. Click the MainMenu.xib file. Xcode displays the user interface. Notice that the actual window of your MyFirstProgram is not visible until you click the MyFirstProgram icon.

4. Click the Window icon that appears in the pane between the Project Navigator and the user interface. This displays the window of the MyFirstProgram user interface, as shown in Figure 3-5.

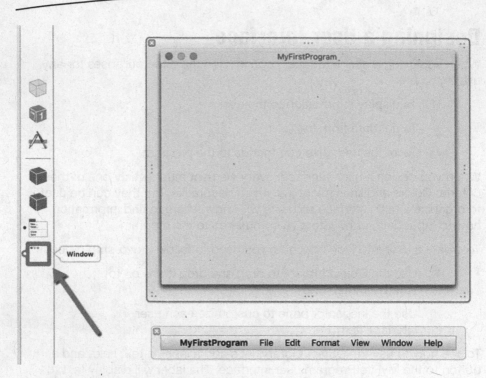

Figure 3-5. The Window icon displays the MyFirstProgram user interface

5. Choose View➤ Utilities ➤ Show Object Library. The Object Library appears in the bottom right corner of the Xcode window.

6. Drag a push button from the Object Library and drop it near the bottom of your MyFirstProgram window. Notice that when you place the button in the middle and near the bottom of the window, blue guidelines appear to help you align user interface items, as shown in Figure 3-6.

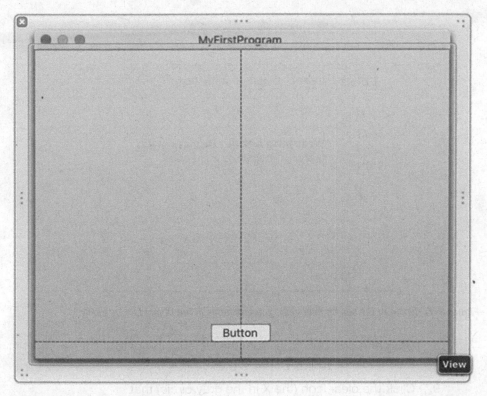

Figure 3-6. Using blue guidelines to place a push button near the bottom of the MyFirstProgram window

7.   Click in the Search field at the Object Library and type **label**. Notice that the Object Library now only displays label user interface items, as shown in Figure 3-7.

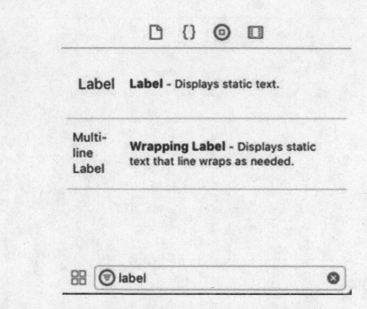

Figure 3-7. *Typing in the search field helps you find items in the Object Library easily*

8. Drag and drop the label from the Object Library to the middle of your MyFirstProgram window.

9. Click the clear icon (the X in the gray circle) that appears to the right of the Search field at the bottom of the Object Library. The Object Library now displays all possible user interface items.

10. Scroll through the Object Library until you find the text field item.

11. Drag and drop the text field above the label so your entire user interface appears as shown in Figure 3-8. (Don't worry about the exact position of each user interface item.)

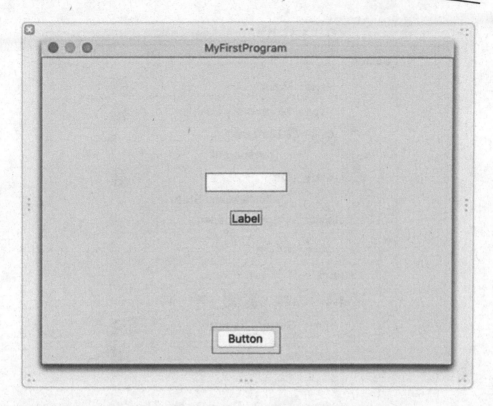

Figure 3-8. A label, text field, and button on the MyFirstProgram user interface

At this point, you've customized the generic user interface. Now you have to customize each user interface item using the Inspector pane. Through the Inspector pane, you can choose different options for a user interface item, such as typing the exact width of a button or choosing a background color for a text field.

When resizing or moving an item on the user interface, you can either type exact values into the Size Inspector pane, or you can just drag the mouse to resize or move an item. Either way is acceptable but the Size Inspector pane gives you precise control over items. Let's see how to use the Inspector pane to customize the generic user interface.

1. Click the push button near the bottom of the MyFirstProgram window to select it.

2. Choose View ➤ Utilities ➤ Show Attributes Inspector. The Attributes Inspector pane appears in the upper right corner of the Xcode window, as shown in Figure 3-9.

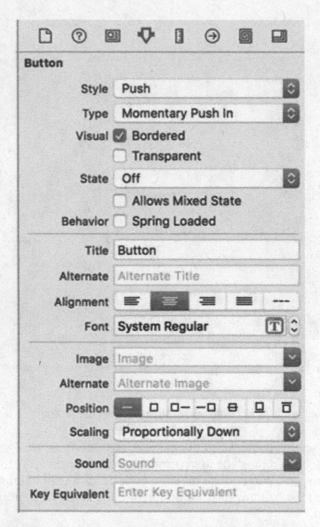

Figure 3-9. The Attributes Inspector pane lets you customize the appearance of items

3. Click in the Title text field that currently displays "Button." Delete any existing text in the Title text field, type **Change Case**, and press Return. The text on the push button now displays "Change Case." However, the button width is too narrow.

4. Choose View ➤ Utilities ➤ Show Size Inspector. The Size Inspector pane appears in the upper right corner of the Xcode window.

5. Click in the Width text field, change the value to 120 (as shown in Figure 3-10), and press Return. Xcode changes the width of the push button.

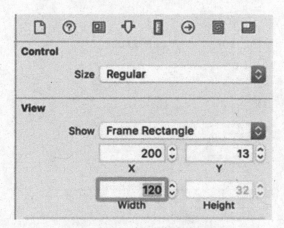

Figure 3-10. The Width text field appears in the Size Inspector pane

6. Click the label to select it. To modify the size of the label, you need to open the Size Inspector pane, which you can do by choosing View➤Utilities➤Show Size Inspector, but there's a faster method using either keystroke shortcuts or icons.

7. Press Option+Command+5 or just click the Size Inspector icon (it looks like a vertical ruler). The Size Inspector pane appears in the upper right corner of the Xcode window.

8. Click in the Width text field, type 250, and press Return. Xcode widens the width of your label.

9. Click the text field to select it.

10. Press Option+Command+5 or just click the Size Inspector icon (it looks like a vertical ruler). The Size Inspector pane appears in the upper right corner of the Xcode window.

11. Click in the Width text field, type 250, and press Return. Xcode widens the width of your text field. At this point, all the user interface items appear off center.

12. Drag each item until you see a blue guideline
     showing that you've centered it in the
     MyFirstProgram window, as shown in Figure 3-11.

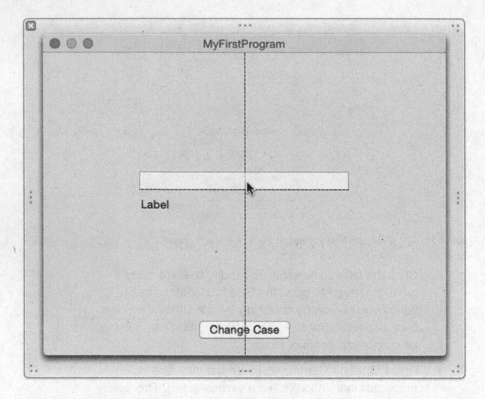

Figure 3-11. Using blue guidelines to center items on the user interface

At this point, you've customized the appearance of your user interface. If you
run this program, the user interface will look good but it won't actually do
anything. To make a user interface work, you need to finish two more steps:

- Write the Swift code.
- Connect your user interface to your Swift code.

You need to write the Swift code to make your program calculate some
useful result. You need to connect your user interface to your Swift code so
you can retrieve data from the user interface and display information back
on the user interface.

In this example, you'll write Swift code that retrieves text from the text field,
changes it to uppercase, then displays the uppercase text back on to the
label when the user clicks the Change Case push button.

So you need to write Swift code that converts text to uppercase. Then you need to connect the text field and the label so the Swift code can retrieve data from the text field and put new data on the label.

To send or retrieve data from a user interface item so the Swift code can access it, you need to use something called an IBOutlet. An IBOutlet essentially represents a user interface item (such as a label or a text field) as a variable that Swift code can use.

To help you create an IBOutlet, use the Assistant Editor. The Assistant Editor lets you display the user interface in the left pane and your Swift code in the right pane. Then you can use the mouse to drag between your user interface items to your Swift code to create an IBOutlet that connects the label or text field to an IBOutlet. Let's see how that works:

1. Make sure the MainMenu.xib file is selected to display the MyFirstProgram user interface window on the screen. (If not, click the MainMenu.xib file in the Project Navigator and then click the MyFirstProgram icon to display the user interface window.)

2. Choose View ➤ Assistant Editor ➤ Show Assistant Editor. The Assistant Editor displays the Swift code in the AppDelegate.swift file next to the user interface in the MainMenu.xib file, as shown in Figure 3-12.

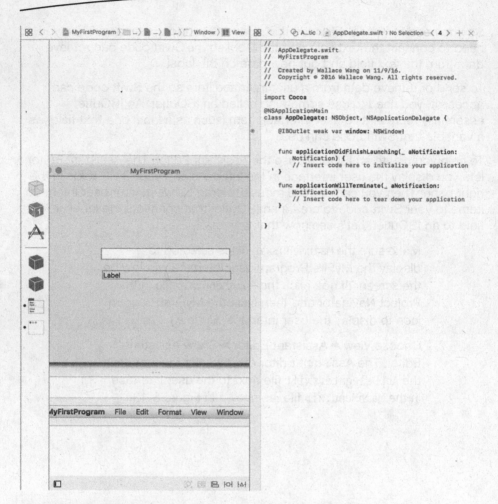

Figure 3-12. The Assistant Editor lets you view the user interface and the Swift code file side by side

3. Click the label on your MyFirstProgram window.

4. Hold down the Control key and drag the mouse from the label underneath the @IBOutlet line in the AppDelegate.swift file until you see a horizontal line appear in the Swift code file, as shown in Figure 3-13.

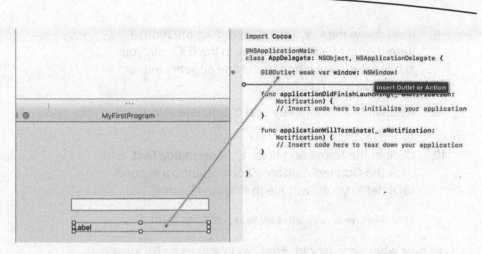

```
import Cocoa

@NSApplicationMain
class AppDelegate: NSObject, NSApplicationDelegate {

    @IBOutlet weak var window: NSWindow!

    func applicationDidFinishLaunching(_ aNotification:
        Notification) {
        // Insert code here to initialize your application
    }

    func applicationWillTerminate(_ aNotification:
        Notification) {
        // Insert code here to tear down your application
    }

}
```

Figure 3-13. Control-dragging creates a connection between a user interface item and your Swift code

5. Release the Control key and the mouse. A pop-up window appears, as shown in Figure 3-14.

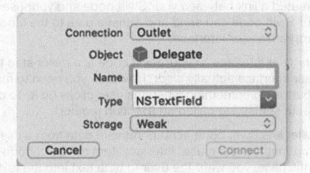

Connection	Outlet
Object	Delegate
Name	
Type	NSTextField
Storage	Weak

Cancel   Connect

Figure 3-14. A pop-up window lets you define a name for your IBOutlet

6. Click in the Name text field, type **labelText**, and click the Connect button. (The name you choose should be descriptive but can be anything you want.) Xcode creates an IBOutlet in your Swift file that looks like this:

```
@IBOutlet weak var labelText: NSTextField!
```

7. Click the text field to select it.

8. Hold down the Control key and drag the mouse from the text field to underneath the IBOutlet you just created until a horizontal line appears in the `AppDelegate.swift` file.

9. Release the Control key and the mouse. A pop-up window appears.

10. Click in the Name text field, type **messageText**, and click the Connect button. Xcode creates a second IBOutlet in your Swift file that looks like this:

```
@IBOutlet weak var messageText: NSTextField!
```

Let's go over what you just did. First, you created an IBOutlet to represent the label and the text field. The label is now represented by the name "labelText" and the text field is now represented by the name "messageText." When your Swift code needs to store or retrieve data from the label or text field on the user interface, it can just refer to them by the names "labelText" or "messageText."

Second, you created a link between your Swift code and your user interface items. Now your Swift code can send and retrieve data to the label and text field on your program's user interface.

Connecting your user interface to your Swift code is a major step towards making your user interface actually work. However, you need to make the Change Case button do something when the user clicks on it. To do that, you need to create something called an IBAction method.

Where an IBOutlet lets Swift code send or retrieve data from a user interface item, an IBAction method lets a user interface item run Swift code that does something. In this case, you want the user to type text into the text field. Then the program will take that text, capitalize it, and display this capitalized text back into the label.

To do this, you need to know how to do the following:

- Create an IBAction method.
- Retrieve text from the text field.
- Capitalize all the text retrieved from the text field.
- Store the capitalized text in the label.

Storing and retrieving text from a text field and label is similar because both are defined by IBOutlet variables. Let's take a look at what these IBOutlets mean:

```
@IBOutlet weak var labelText: NSTextField!
@IBOutlet weak var messageText: NSTextField!
```

All user interface items in the Object Library are based on class files, which make up the Cocoa framework. In this case, you created two IBOutlet variables called labelText and messageText, which are both based on the NSTextField class file.

If you look up the NSTextField class file in Xcode's documentation, you'll see a long list of all the properties that anything based on the NSTextField can hold. However, you won't find anything that describes the property that holds text.

However, if you remember from Chapter 1, object-oriented programming means that class files can inherit from other class files. In this case, the NSTextField class inherits from another class called NSControl. Looking up NSControl in Xcode's documentation (which you'll learn how to do in the next chapter), you can see that NSControl has a property that holds text called stringValue, as shown in Figure 3-15.

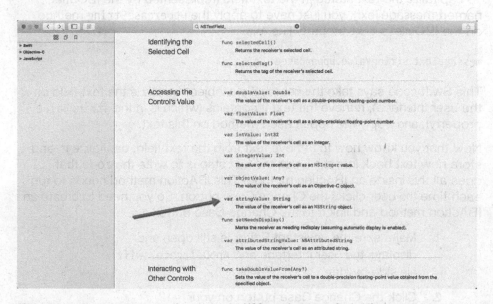

Figure 3-15. Xcode's documentation shows the NSControl property for holding text

To access text stored in the text field, you need to identify the text field by name (messageText) and its property that holds the text (stringValue) such as

```
messageText.stringValue
```

To display text in the label, you need to identify the label by name (labelText) and its property that holds text (stringValue) such as

```
labelText.stringValue
```

The next question is, how can you capitalize text? Swift stores text in a data type called String, which has a method called uppercased, as shown in Figure 3-16.

```
func uppercased(with: Locale?)
    Returns a version of the string with all letters converted to uppercase, taking into account the
    specified locale.
```

Figure 3-16. Xcode's documentation shows that the NSString class has a method for capitalizing text called uppercaseString

To capitalize the text stored in the text field (represented by the IBOutlet named messageText), you just have to apply the uppercaseString method on the IBOutlet's text property like this:

```
messageText.stringValue.uppercased
```

This Swift code says take the messageText object (which is the text field on the user interface), retrieve the text it contains (which is in the stringValue property), and apply the uppercased method on this text.

Now that you know how to retrieve text from the text field, capitalize it, and store new text back into the label, the last step is to write the code that does all this inside an IBAction method. This IBAction method needs to run each time the user clicks the Change Case button. So you need to create an IBAction method and link it to the Change Case button.

1. Make sure the Assistant Editor is still open and displays the user interface and AppDelegate.swift file side by side.

2. Click the Change Case button on your MyFirstProgram user interface to select it.

3. Hold down the Control key and drag the mouse above the last curly bracket until a horizontal line appears, as shown in Figure 3-17.

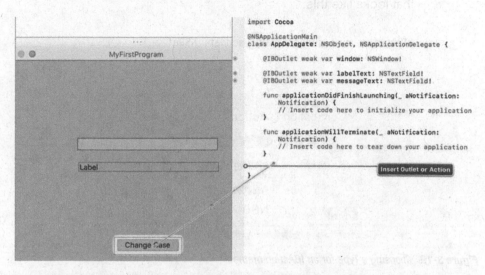

```
import Cocoa

@NSApplicationMain
class AppDelegate: NSObject, NSApplicationDelegate {

    @IBOutlet weak var window: NSWindow!

    @IBOutlet weak var labelText: NSTextField!
    @IBOutlet weak var messageText: NSTextField!

    func applicationDidFinishLaunching(_ aNotification:
        Notification) {
        // Insert code here to initialize your application
    }

    func applicationWillTerminate(_ aNotification:
        Notification) {
        // Insert code here to tear down your application
    }
}
```

Figure 3-17. Control-dragging from the button to the AppDelegate.swift file

4. Release the Control key and the mouse. A pop-up window appears.

5. Click in the Connection pop-up menu and choose Action, as shown in Figure 3-18.

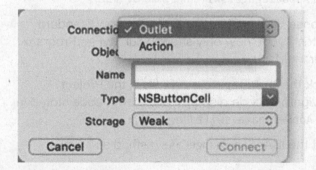

Figure 3-18. Creating an Action connection

6. Click in the Name text field and type **changeCase**. (The name you choose should be descriptive but can be anything you want.)

7. Click in the Type pop-up menu and choose NSButton, as shown in Figure 3-19. Then click the Connect button. Xcode creates an IBAction method that looks like this:

```
@IBAction func changeCase(_ sender: NSButton) {
}
```

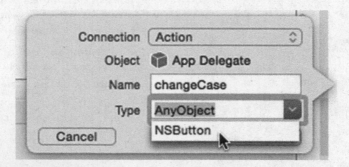

Figure 3-19. *Choosing a Type for an IBAction method*

At this point, you've created an IBAction method that runs every time the user clicks the Change Case button. Of course, there's no Swift code inside that IBAction, so now you need to type Swift code inside those curly brackets that defines the beginning and ending of the IBAction method.

1. Make sure Xcode still displays your user interface and AppDelegate.swift file side by side.

2. Choose View➤Standard Editor➤Show Standard Editor. Xcode now only shows your MyFirstProgram user interface.

3. Click the AppDelegate.swift file in the Project Navigator. Xcode displays all the Swift code stored in the AppDelegate.swift file.

4. Edit the IBAction changeCase method as follows:

```
@IBAction func changeCase(_ sender: NSButton) {
        labelText.stringValue = messageText.stringValue.
uppercased()
}
```

5. Choose Product➤Run. Your MyFirstProgram runs.

6. Click in the text field of your MyFirstProgram user interface and type **hello, world**.

7. Click the Change Case button. The label displays HELLO, WORLD, as shown in Figure 3-20.

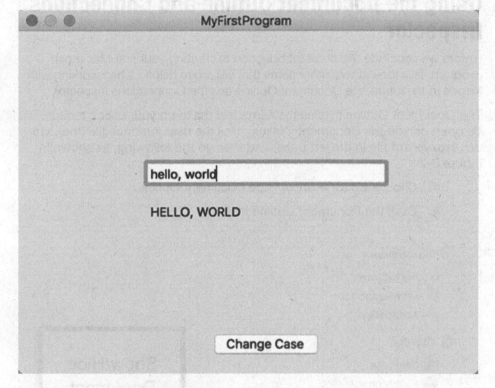

Figure 3-20. Running the MyFirstProgram

8. Choose MyFirstProgram ➤ Quit MyFirstProgram. Xcode appears again.

As you can see, you created a simple Macintosh program without writing much Swift code at all. The Swift code you did write was just a single line that took the text stored in the text field, changed it to uppercase, and then stored this uppercase text in the label.

Much of the power of Swift comes from relying on Apple's Cocoa framework as much as possible, which displays a window that the user can move or resize. In addition, the Cocoa framework also creates pull-down menus that you can modify. To understand the Cocoa framework, you have to understand object-oriented programming and how classes define properties (to store data) and methods (to manipulate data), and use inheritance, which you'll learn more about in the next chapter.

The main point is to see how Xcode creates generic macOS programs so you just need to design and customize the user interface and then write Swift code to make it all work.

Using the Document Outline and Connections Inspector

Before we conclude this short introduction to creating your first Macintosh program, let's look at two other items that will prove helpful when working with Xcode in the future: the Document Outline and the Connections Inspector.

The Document Outline lists all the items that make up your user interface. To open or hide the Document Outline, click the user interface file (the .xib or .storyboard file in the left pane) and then do the following, as shown in Figure 3-21:

- Choose Editor➤Show/Hide Document Outline.
- Click the Document Outline icon.

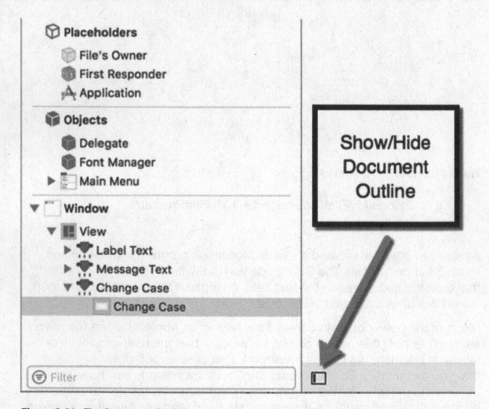

Figure 3-21. The Document Outline

The Document Outline makes it easy to select different items on your user interface. In your MyFirstProgram, there are only three items (a label, text field, and button) but in more complicated user interfaces, you could have many more items that could be hidden behind other items or too small to see easily.

If you click an item in the Document Outline, Xcode selects that item in the user interface (and vice versa), as shown in Figure 3-22.

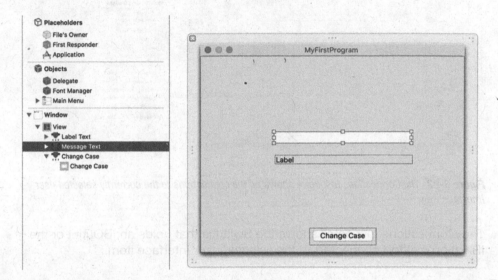

Figure 3-22. Clicking an item in the Document Outline window selects that item on the user interface

Think of the Document Outline as a fast way to see all the parts of a user interface and select just the items you want.

Once you start connecting user interface items to your Swift code through IBOutlets and IBAction methods, you may wonder what items are connected to which IBOutlets and IBAction methods. To see the connections between IBOutlets/IBAction methods and user interface items, you have two options.

First, you can use the Connections Inspector. Second, you can use the Assistant Editor.

To open the Connections Inspector, first click any item in the user interface that you want to examine and then do one of the following to display the Connections Inspector that appears in the upper right corner of the Xcode window, as shown in Figure 3-23:

- ▣ Choose View ➤ Utilities ➤ Show Connections Inspector.

- ▣ Press Option + Command + 6.

- ▣ Click the Show Connections Inspector icon.

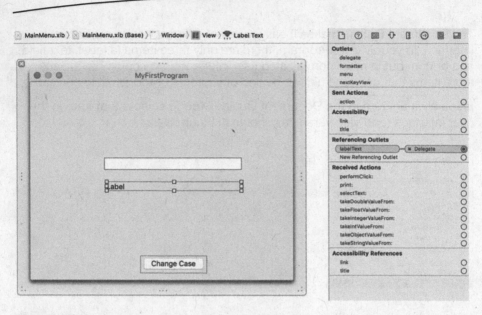

Figure 3-23. *The Connections Inspector shows all the connections to the currently selected user interface item*

The Connections Inspector shows the Swift file that holds an IBOutlet or the IBAction method connected to the selected user interface item.

> **Note**   If you look carefully, the Connections Inspector displays an X to the left of the Swift file that links to the currently selected user interface item. If you click this X, you can break the link between a user interface item and its IBOutlet or IBAction method.

Another way to see which IBOutlets and IBAction methods are connected to user interface items is to open the user interface (such as clicking the MainMenu.xib file) and then open the Assistant Editor.

To the left of each IBOutlet and IBAction method in your Swift file, you'll see a gray circle. When you move the mouse pointer over a gray circle, Xcode highlights the user interface item that's connected to that IBOutlet or IBAction method, as shown in Figure 3-24.

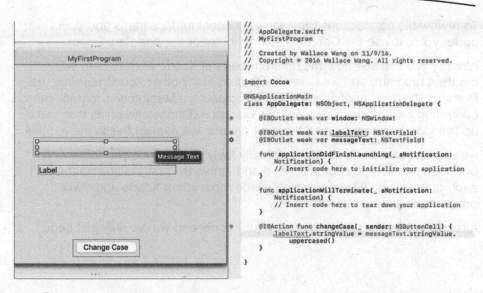

```
//
//  AppDelegate.swift
//  MyFirstProgram
//
//  Created by Wallace Wang on 11/9/16.
//  Copyright © 2016 Wallace Wang. All rights reserved.
//

import Cocoa

@NSApplicationMain
class AppDelegate: NSObject, NSApplicationDelegate {

    @IBOutlet weak var window: NSWindow!

    @IBOutlet weak var labelText: NSTextField!
    @IBOutlet weak var messageText: NSTextField!

    func applicationDidFinishLaunching(_ aNotification:
        Notification) {
        // Insert code here to initialize your application
    }

    func applicationWillTerminate(_ aNotification:
        Notification) {
        // Insert code here to tear down your application
    }

    @IBAction func changeCase(_ sender: NSButtonCell) {
        labelText.stringValue = messageText.stringValue.
            uppercased()
    }
}
```

Figure 3-24. The Assistant Editor lets you see which IBOutlet and IBAction methods are connected to user interface items

Summary

Xcode is the only program you need to design, write, and modify your own macOS programs. When you want to create a macOS program, you just follow the same basic steps:

- Pick a project template to use (typically Cocoa Application).

- Design and customize the user interface.

- Connect the user interface items to IBOutlets and IBAction methods.

- Write Swift code to make IBAction methods do something.

- Run and test your program.

To design your user interface, you need to drag and drop items from the Object Library. Then you need to use the Attributes and Size Inspectors to customize each user interface item. To help you select user interface items, you can use the Document Outline.

After designing your user interface, you need to connect your user interface to your Swift code through IBOutlets (for retrieving or displaying data) and IBAction methods (to make your user interface do something) using the Assistant Editor.

To review the connections between your user interface items and your Swift code, you can use the Connections Inspector or the Assistant Editor.

Already you can see how the different parts of Xcode work to help you create a program, and we haven't explored many other Xcode features yet. Perhaps the most confusing part about creating a Macintosh program can be writing Swift code and using methods stored in the class files that make up the Cocoa framework, so the next chapter will explain this in more detail.

As you can see, using Xcode is actually fairly simple once you focus only on those features you actually need and ignore the rest. As you go through each chapter, you'll keep learning a little more about Xcode and Swift programming.

Already you've learned so much about Xcode, and you've only just begun.

Chapter **4**

Getting Help

The best way to learn any new skill is to have someone show you what you need to learn. Since that's not always possible, you'll be happy to know that Xcode comes with plenty of built-in help features to make using Xcode less stressful and more enjoyable.

To use Xcode's help, you first need to understand how Swift programs work and how they work with the Cocoa framework. Once you understand how a typical macOS program works and how it relies on the Cocoa framework, you'll be better able to understand how to get the help you need and how you can understand the help you do find through Xcode.

Understanding the Cocoa Framework

When using Xcode, you have to understand that every program you create is based on the Cocoa framework, which contains classes that contain various properties and methods. By using these existing classes, you can save time by not writing and testing your own code. Instead, you can just use the existing code in the Cocoa framework that already works. This frees you to spend more time focusing on writing the code that's unique to your particular program.

To use the Cocoa framework, you must understand the principles of object-oriented programming and how objects work. To create an object, you must first define a class. A class contains the actual code that defines properties (to hold data) and methods (to manipulate data stored in its properties). Once you've defined a class, you can define one or more objects based on that class.

Just as a cookie cutter defines the shape of a cookie but isn't the actual cookie, so do classes define an object but aren't the actual object.

© Wallace Wang 2017
W. Wang, *macOS Programming for Absolute Beginners*,
DOI 10.1007/978-1-4842-2662-9_4

The Cocoa framework consists of multiple class files where many class files inherit properties and methods from other class files. When you create a macOS program, you'll typically create objects based on Cocoa framework class files. In fact, every user interface item that you create from the Object Library is based on a Cocoa framework class.

To see what class file each user interface item is based on, let's examine the three user interface items you created: a label, a text field, and a button.

1.   Open the MyFirstProgram project in Xcode.

2.   Click the `MainMenu.xib` file. Xcode displays your user interface.

3.   Choose View ➤ Utilities ➤ Show Object Library. The Object Library appears in the lower right corner of the Xcode window.

4.   Click the push button item. A pop-up window appears, as shown in Figure 4-1. Notice that this pop-up window tells you the class file (NSButton) and describes what the NSButton class file does.

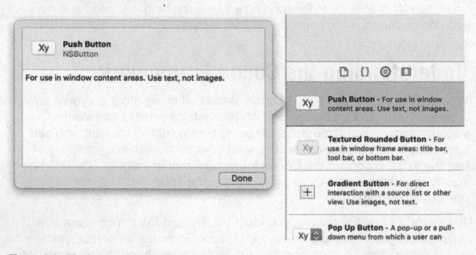

Figure 4-1. Finding the class file of a push button

5.   Click the Done button to make the pop-up window go away.

6. Scroll through the Object Library and click the label item. A pop-up window appears, as shown in Figure 4-2. This pop-up window tells you the class file (NSTextField), describes what an NSTextField class file does, and also tells you that the NSTextField class inherits (is a subclass) from the NSControl class.

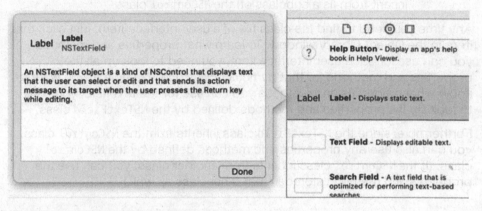

Figure 4-2. Finding the class file of a label

7. Scroll through the Object Library and click the text field item. A pop-up window appears, as shown in Figure 4-3. In case you haven't noticed by now, user interface items that can store data often inherit properties and methods from the NSControl class file.

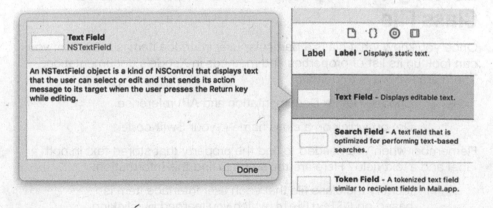

Figure 4-3. Finding the class file of a text field

By using Xcode's simple help pop-up windows for each item in the Object Library, you've learned the following about your user interface:

- The push button is based on the NSButton class file.

- The label is based on the NSTextField class file.

- The text field is also based on the NSTextField class file.

- Both the NSButton class and the NSTextField class inherit from (is a subclass of) the NSControl class.

Any time you need to find the class file of a user interface item, just click that item in the Object Library window. To learn what properties and methods you can use for each user interface item, you need to look up all the properties and methods for that particular class. For example, if you want to know what properties and methods you can use for the text field, you have to look up the properties and methods defined by the NSTextField class.

Furthermore, since the NSTextField class inherits from the NSControl class, you can also use any properties and methods defined by the NSControl class. (If the NSControl class inherits from another class, you can use the properties and methods stored in that other class as well.)

> **Note**   The NS prefix in front of each class name stands for NextStep, which was the company that originally created macOS and the Cocoa framework. When Apple acquired NextStep, they simply kept the NS prefix.

Looking Up Properties and Methods in a Class File

Once you know what class a particular user interface item is based on, you can look up its list of properties and methods in Xcode's documentation. There are two ways to do this:

- Choose Help➤Documentation and API reference.

- Option+click on a class name in your Swift code.

Remember when you needed to find the property that stored text in both a label and a text field? Here are the steps to find this information:

- Identify the class file that each user interface item is based on (NSTextField, which you learned by clicking that item in the Object Library).

- Look up Xcode's documentation about the NSTextField class file.

- If you can't find the information you need in the NSTextField class file, look up the NSControl class file since the NSTextField class inherits all properties and methods from the NSControl class.

Looking Up Class Files with the Help Menu

Xcode's menu bar and pull-down menus are usually the most straightforward way to find any command. So the first step is to open Xcode's documentation window, as shown in Figure 4-4, in one of two ways:

- Choose Help ➤ Documentation and API Reference.

- Press Shift + Command + 0 (the number zero).

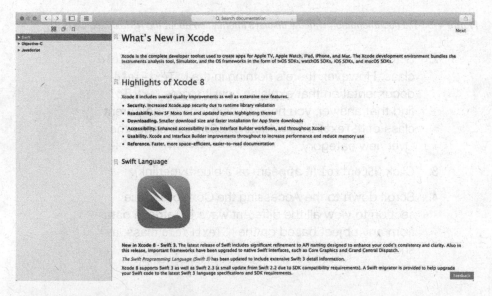

Figure 4-4. The Xcode Documentation window

1. Click in the Search documentation text field at the top of the Documentation window, type **NSTextField**, and press Return. The Documentation window displays information about the NSTextField class, as shown in Figure 4-5.

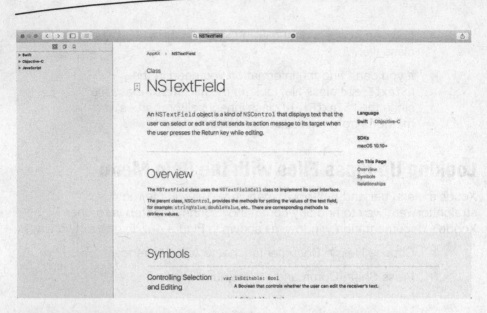

Figure 4-5. The documentation window displays information about the NSTextField class

2. Scroll through the information about the NSTextField class. However, there's nothing in the NSTextField documentation that explains how it stores text. To find that answer, you need to next look in the parent class of NSTextField, which is NSControl under the Overview category.

3. Click NSControl (it appears as a blue hyperlink).

4. Scroll down to the Accessing the Control's Value section to view all the different ways to retrieve data from any object based on the NSTextField class, as shown in Figure 4-6.

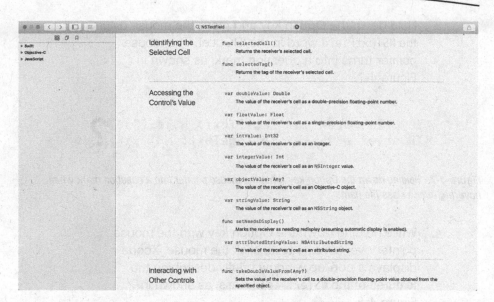

Figure 4-6. The Documentation window lists all the properties in NSTextField that store data

Once you know that you can use the `stringValue` property to hold text data from any object based on the `NSTextField` class, you know you can access the text data of both the label and text field using the `stringValue` property.

Looking Up Class Files with Quick Help

Using the Documentation window to look up class files can be handy, but Xcode offers another method called Quick Help. To use Quick Help, you move the cursor or mouse pointer over a class file name in a file containing Swift code, and then choose one of the following methods:

- Choose Help ➤ Quick Help for Selected Item.

- Press Control + Command + Shift + ?.

- Hold down the Option key and click a class file name.

Quick Help then displays a pop-up window containing a brief description of the selected class file, giving you the option to view the full description in the Documentation window if you choose. To see how Quick Help works using the Option key and the mouse, follow these steps:

1. Make sure the MyFirstProgram is loaded into Xcode.

2. Click the `AppDelegate.swift` file in the Project Navigator. Xcode displays the contents of the `AppDelegate.swift` file in the middle pane.

3. Hold down the Option key and move the mouse over
    the NSTextField word in the IBOutlet. The mouse
    pointer turns into a question mark, as shown in
    Figure 4-7.

```
@IBOutlet weak var labelText: NSTextFiel
@IBOutlet weak var messageText: NSTextField!
```

Figure 4-7. *Holding down the Option key turns the mouse pointer into a question mark when*
hovering over a class file name

4. While holding down the Option key with the mouse
    pointer over NSTextField, click the mouse. Xcode
    displays a pop-up window briefly describing the
    features of the NSTextField class, as shown in
    Figure 4-8.

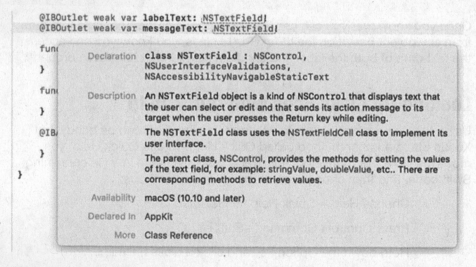

Figure 4-8. *Option + clicking on a class file name displays a pop-up window describing that*
class file

5. Click Class Reference at the bottom of the pop-up
    window next to the Reference label. Xcode displays
    the Documentation window listing the NSTextField
    class file (see Figure 4-5).

Option+clicking is just a way to open the Documentation window without going through the Help➤Documentation and Reference API command and typing a class file name.

Browsing the Documentation

Quick Help can display information about specific class files, but what if you know you need information but don't know where to find it? That's when you can spend time browsing through the Documentation window and skimming through the different help topics until you find what you want.

Even if you don't find what you want, chances are good you'll stumble across some interesting information about Xcode or macOS that could come in handy in the future.

If you find something interesting, you can bookmark it so that you can find it quickly again later. You can also send information by e-mail or text messaging, so feel free to share useful information with others.

To browse through the Documentation, follow these steps:

1. Choose Help➤Documentation and API Reference. The Documentation window appears.

2. Click the Browse the API reference documentation icon. The left pane displays a list of different frameworks available to use when creating a macOS program, as shown in Figure 4-9.

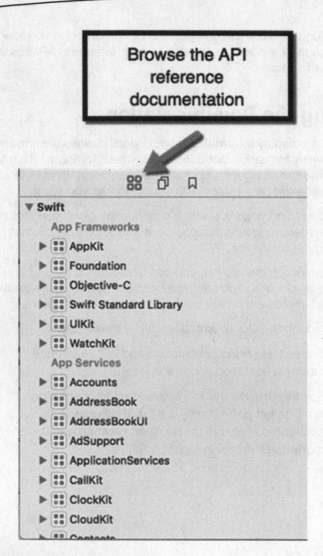

Figure 4-9. Viewing the frameworks available

3. Click the gray disclosure triangle that appears to the left of a category such as the HealthKit or Core Data. A list of additional topics (with their own gray disclosure triangles) appears. By continuing to click the disclosure triangle of topics, you will eventually find lists of topics that you can click to view that information, as shown in Figure 4-10.

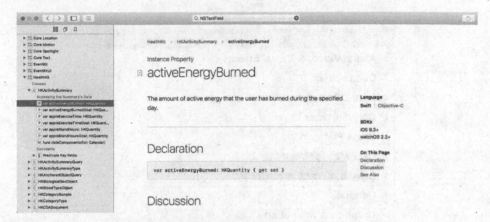

Figure 4-10. Each category lists several other categories of various topics

4. Click in the Browse guides and sample code icon. A list of different topics appears, as shown in Figure 4-11.

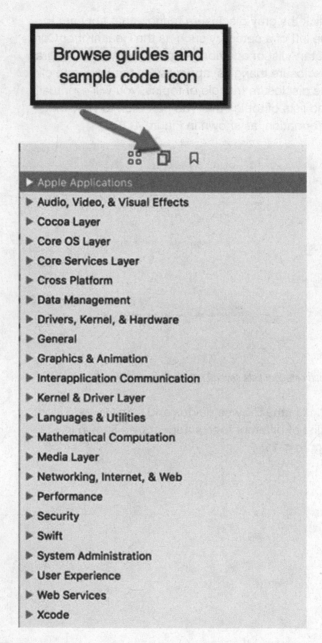

Figure 4-11. The Browse guides and sample code icon display various topics for macOS programming

5. Click the gray disclosure triangle that appears to the left of a category, such as the Security or Graphics & Animation. A list of additional topics (with their own gray disclosure triangles) appears. By continuing to click the disclosure triangle of topics, you will eventually find lists of topics that you can click on to view that information, as shown in Figure 4-12.

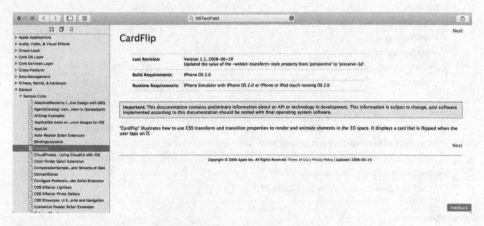

Figure 4-12. Viewing information about specific programming techniques or sample code

Searching the Documentation

Quick Help can display information about specific class files, and browsing the documentation can help you explore the vast information about the Cocoa framework and macOS programming. The problems are that Quick Help is only useful for finding information about class files and browsing the documentation can be time-consuming. If you know what you want to find, you can just search for it instead.

When searching for information, type as much as possible to narrow your search results. If you just type a single letter or word, Xcode's documentation will bombard you with irrelevant results.

To see how searching the documentation window works, try the following:

1. Choose Help ➤ Documentation and API Reference. The Documentation window appears.

2. Click in the Search documentation text field and type **text**. A menu of different text results appears that you can click to get more information, as shown in Figure 4-13.

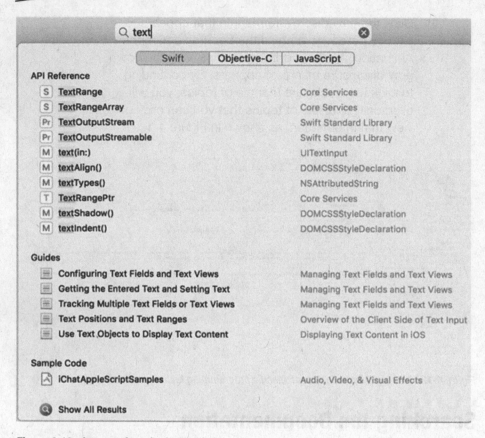

Figure 4-13. A menu of results for "text"

3.   Click a topic to view that information.

By searching through Xcode's documentation, you can find what you need quickly and easily.

Using Code Completion

In Chapter 3, when you started typing Swift code, you may have noticed something odd. Each time you typed part of a Swift command, the Xcode editor may have displayed grayed text and a menu of possible commands that match what you partially typed; see Figure 4-14.

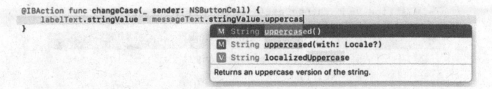

```
@IBAction func changeCase(_ sender: NSButtonCell) {
    labelText.stringValue = messageText.stringValue.uppercas|
}
```

M String uppercased()
M String uppercased(with: Locale?)
V String localizedUppercase

Returns an uppercase version of the string.

Figure 4-14. Code completion suggests a likely command you may be trying to type

This feature is called code completion and it is Xcode's way of helping you insert long commands without actually typing every character yourself. When you see grayed out text and a menu, you have three choices:

- Press the Tab key to let Xcode automatically type part of the grayed out text. (You may need to press the Tab key several times to completely select all the grayed out text.)

- Double-click a command in the pop-up menu to type that command automatically.

- Keep typing.

If you keep typing, Xcode keeps displaying new grayed out text that it thinks you may be trying to type along with a menu of different commands that match what you've typed so far. Let's see how code completion works.

To see how searching the documentation window works, try the following:

1. Make sure your MyFirstProgram is loaded in Xcode.

2. Click AppDelegate.swift in the Project Navigator pane. The contents of the AppDelegate.swift file appear in the middle Xcode pane.

3. Modify the @IBAction changeCase (sender: NSButton) code by deleting the one line between the curly brackets so it now appears as follows:

   ```
   @IBAction func changeCase(_ sender: NSButton) {

   }
   ```

4. Move the cursor between the curly brackets of this @IBAction method and type **labelText.s** and notice that grayed out text appears and a menu of possible commands also appears, as shown in Figure 4-15.

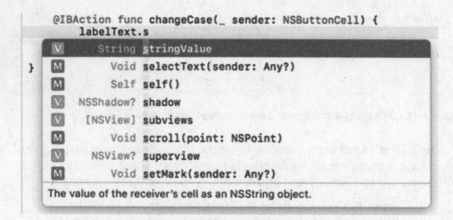

```
@IBAction func changeCase(_ sender: NSButtonCell) {
    labelText.s
    V      String stringValue
}   M       Void selectText(sender: Any?)
    M       Self self()
    V  NSShadow? shadow
    V   [NSView] subviews
    M       Void scroll(point: NSPoint)
    V   NSView? superview
    M       Void setMark(sender: Any?)
```

The value of the receiver's cell as an NSString object.

Figure 4-15. Code completion suggests stringValue as a possible command

5. Tap the Tab key. The first time you tap the Tab key, Xcode types "string".

6. Tap the Tab key a second time and now Xcode types the complete "stringValue".

7. Type = **messageText.stringValue.uppercased()**. Notice that as you type, code C\completion keeps showing different grayed out text and commands in the pop-up menu.

By using code completion, you can type commands faster and more accurately. If you start typing a command and you don't see code completion's grayed out text or menu appear, this could be a signal that you mistyped the command. Code completion is just one more way Xcode tries to make typing code easier for you.

Understanding How macOS Programs Work

To help you better understand what all of Xcode's help documentation means, you need to understand how macOS programs work. In the old days when programs were small, programmers stored all program commands in a single file. Then the computer started at the first command at the top of the file, worked its way down line by line, and stopped when it reached the end of the file.

Today programs are much larger so they're often divided into multiple files. No matter how many files you divide your program into, Xcode treats everything as if it were stored in a single file. Dividing a program into files is for your convenience.

Let's examine your MyFirstProgram line by line so you can understand what's happening. When you view Swift code in Xcode, you'll notice that the Xcode editor color codes different text. These colors help you identify the purpose of different text as follows:

- **Green**: Comments, which Xcode completely ignores. Comments are meant to explain something about the nearby code.

- **Purple**: Keywords of the Swift language

- **Red**: Text strings

- **Blue**: Class file names

- **Black**: Commands

The very first line tells Xcode to import or include all the code in the Cocoa framework as part of your program. This line looks like this:

```
import Cocoa
```

The next line runs a Swift function that loads your user interface (MainMenu.xib) and creates an object from your AppDelegate class. This basically gets your whole program running as a generic Macintosh program. This line looks like this:

```
@NSApplicationMain
```

The next line defines a class called AppDelegate that is based on the NSObject class and uses the NSApplicationDelegate protocol (which you'll learn about shortly). This line looks like this:

```
class AppDelegate: NSObject, NSApplicationDelegate {
```

The next three lines define IBOutlets that connect this Swift code to the user interface items: the window of the user interface along with the label and text field. The window is based on the NSWindow class (defined in the Cocoa framework) while the label and text field are based on the NSTextField class. These lines look like this:

```
@IBOutlet weak var window: NSWindow!
@IBOutlet weak var labelText: NSTextField!
@IBOutlet weak var messageText: NSTextField!
```

Every time Xcode creates a new macOS Cocoa Application project, you'll see two empty functions that don't do anything. If you typed code inside of these functions, the code would run right after your program started up (applicationDidFinishLaunching) or it would run as soon as your program ended (applicationWillTerminate). For now, leave these functions alone and ignore them.

The next three lines define an IBAction method that's connected to the push button on the user interface. The code takes the text stored in messageText (the text field) and converts it to uppercase. Then it stores the uppercase text into labelText (the label). Both the label and text field are based on the NSTextField class (defined in the Cocoa framework). These lines look like this:

```
@IBAction func changeCase(_ sender: NSButton) {
    labelText.stringValue = messageText.stringValue.uppercased()
}
```

When MyFirstProgram runs, it imports the Cocoa framework and runs to display a generic Macintosh program on the screen that includes your user interface. The applicationDidFinishLaunching function runs, but since it doesn't contain any code, nothing happens. Now the program stops and waits for something to happen.

If the user quits out of the program, the applicationWillTerminate function will run, but since it doesn't contain any code, nothing happens.

When the user clicks the Change Case button, it runs the IBAction changeCase method. The only Swift command in this IBAction method takes the text from the text field (stored in the stringValue property of messageText), capitalizes it, and stores the capitalized text in the label (displayed by the stringValue property of labelText).

Now that you've seen how the MyFirstProgram works, let's look at macOS programming from a more theoretical standpoint. First, creating a program involves using class files defined by the Cocoa framework. When you place items on a user interface, you're using Cocoa framework class files (such as NSTextField and NSButton).

When you define a class in your AppDelegate.swift file, you're also using a class from the Cocoa framework file (NSObject).

A typical macOS program creates objects from the class files in the Cocoa framework and any class files you may define in your Swift files. Objects now communicate with one another in one of two ways:

- Storing or retrieving data from properties stored in other objects
- Calling methods stored in other objects

To store data in an object's property, you have to specify the object name and its property on the left side of an equal sign and a value on the right, like this:

```
labelText.stringValue = "Hello, world!"
```

To retrieve data from an object's property, you have to specify a variable to hold data on the left side of an equal sign and the object name and its property on the right, like this:

```
let warning = labelText.stringValue
```

To call a method stored in another object, you have to specify the object's name and the method to use, like this:

```
messageText.stringValue.uppercased()
```

This command tells Xcode to run the uppercased() method on the stringValue property stored in the messageText object.

Setting property values, retrieving property values, and calling methods to run are the three ways objects communicate with each other.

When you create a class, you must define the class file to use, such as

```
class AppDelegate: NSObject
```

This line tells Xcode to define a class called AppDelegate and base it on the class file called NSObject (which is defined in the Cocoa framework).

When you create a class based on an existing class, that class automatically includes all the properties and methods defined by that class. So in the above line of code that defines the AppDelegate class, any object created from the AppDelegate class automatically has all the properties and methods defined by the NSObject class.

Sometimes a class file doesn't have all the methods you may need. To fix this, you can inherit from an existing class and then define a new method in your class. However, if you create a method name that you want other classes to use, a second alternative is to define something called a protocol.

A protocol is nothing more than a list of related method names together but doesn't include any Swift code to make those methods actually do anything. In the code below, the AppDelegate class is not only based on the NSObject class file, but also uses methods defined by the NSApplicationDelegate protocol.

If you open the Documentation window and search for NSApplicationDelegate protocol, you'll see a list of method names defined by the NSApplicationDelegate protocol, such as applicationDidFinishLaunching or applicationWillTerminate, as shown in Figure 4-16.

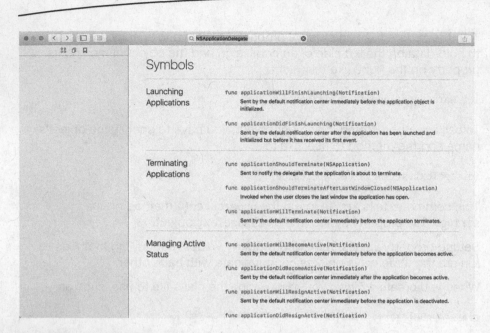

Figure 4-16. The NSApplicationDelegate protocol in the Documentation window

The AppDelegate class inherits properties and methods from the NSObject class and also uses the method names defined by the NSApplicationDelegate protocol. Any class based on a protocol must write Swift code to make those protocol methods actually do something. In technical terms, this is known as "implementing or conforming to a protocol."

So the Cocoa framework actually consists of classes and protocols. Classes define objects and protocols define commonly used method names that different classes may need.

When you write macOS programs, you'll often use both Cocoa framework classes and protocols. When you use a Cocoa framework class, you can use methods that already work, such as the uppercased() method that knows how to capitalize text.

When you use a Cocoa framework protocol, you'll need to write Swift code to make that method actually work. When browsing through Xcode's documentation, keep your eye out for this difference between classes and protocols.

Let's see an example of both classes and protocols in the Xcode documentation window:

1. Make sure your MyFirstProgram is loaded in Xcode.

2. Click the AppDelegate.swift file in the Project Navigator. Xcode's middle pane displays the contents of that .swift file.

3. Move the cursor in NSApplicationDelegate.

4. Choose Help ➤ Quick Help for Selected Item, or hold down the Option key and click NSApplicationDelegate. A Quick Help pop-up window appears, as shown in Figure 4-17, explaining how NSApplicationDelegate is a protocol.

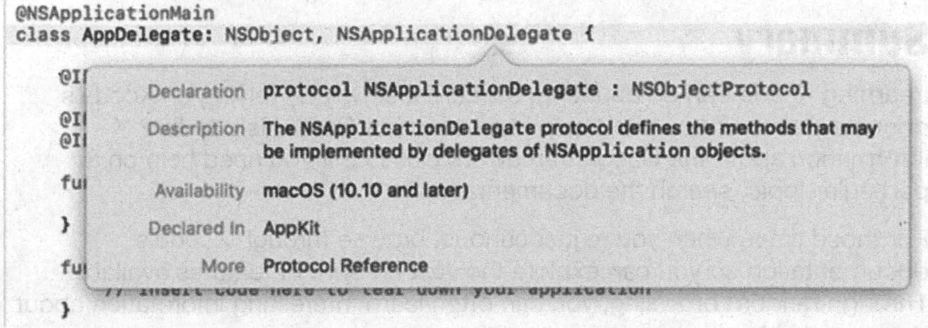

```
@NSApplicationMain
class AppDelegate: NSObject, NSApplicationDelegate {
```

Declaration	protocol NSApplicationDelegate : NSObjectProtocol	
Description	The NSApplicationDelegate protocol defines the methods that may be implemented by delegates of NSApplication objects.	
Availability	macOS (10.10 and later)	
Declared In	AppKit	
More	Protocol Reference	

Figure 4-17. The NSApplicationDelegate Quick Help pop-up window

5. Click Protocol Reference at the bottom of this window. The NSApplicationDelegate protocol reference appears in the Documentation window (see Figure 4-16).

Protocols add methods to a class without the need to create a new class, but you never need to use protocols. When you write programs in Xcode, you'll use Cocoa framework classes and protocols. For the unique purposes of your program, you'll likely create your own classes and protocols as well.

When browsing through Xcode's documentation, look for properties and methods in classes before writing your own code. If you don't find the properties and methods you need in one class, look in the parent class.

For example, in the MyFirstProgram project, you could have written Swift code to capitalize text typed into the text field. However, it was much easier to just use the existing uppercased() method instead. This saved you the time it would take to write code and debug it, when you could just use proven code in the Cocoa framework instead.

The more you know about the Cocoa framework, the less work you'll have to do when writing your own programs. Use Xcode's documentation to help you better understand all the classes and protocols that make up the entire Cocoa framework.

Since the Cocoa framework is so large, don't bother trying to learn everything at once. Just learn what you need and ignore the rest. The more you use Xcode and write programs, the more likely you'll need and learn the other parts of the Cocoa framework.

The general idea is to rely on the Cocoa framework as much as possible and only write Swift code when you have to. This makes it easy to write reliable software quickly with less effort.

Summary

Learning Xcode can be daunting, so learn it slowly by relying on Xcode's documentation. If you need help in a hurry, use Quick Help to find information about the Cocoa framework classes. If you need help on a particular topic, search the documentation.

For those times when you're just curious, browse through Xcode's documentation so you can explore the vast amount of features available. Through random browsing, you can often learn interesting information about Xcode or writing programs for macOS.

As you can see, learning to write programs involves learning about Xcode, learning about the Cocoa framework, and learning the Swift programming language. Just take it easy, learn only what you need to know, and gradually keep expanding your knowledge. Through steady progress, you'll learn more and more until one day you'll realize how much you actually know.

Learning to write macOS programs with Xcode won't happen overnight, but you'll be surprised how much you can learn through steady progress over time. Just practice writing programs and rely on Xcode's documentation available from the Help menu. Before you know it, you'll be capable of writing small programs with confidence and then larger and more complicated programs.

Chapter 5

Learning Swift with Playgrounds

To write any program, you need to choose a programming language. A programming language lets you define commands for the computer to follow. There's no one "best" programming language because every programming language is meant to solve a specific problem. This means that a certain programming language may be great at solving certain types of problems, but horrible at solving other types of programs.

With most programming languages, there's a tradeoff between ease of use and efficiency. For example, the BASIC programming language is meant to be easy to learn and use, while the C programming language is meant to give you complete control over the computer. By maximizing computer efficiency, the C language is great for creating complicated programs like operating systems or hard disk utility programs.

Since BASIC was never designed for maximum control over a computer, BASIC would never be used to create an operating system or a hard disk utility program. Since C was designed for maximum computer efficiency, it's difficult for novices to learn and even difficult for experienced programmers to use. The majority of errors or bugs in many programs are due solely to the complexity of the C programming language, which confounds even professional programmers with decades of experience.

Apple's official programming language used to be Objective-C, which was a superset of the C programming language and an alternative to the object-oriented C++ language. Unfortunately, Objective-C can be difficult to learn and even harder to master. By making programming harder than it needs

© Wallace Wang 2017
W. Wang, *macOS Programming for Absolute Beginners*,
DOI 10.1007/978-1-4842-2662-9_5

to be, Objective-C makes creating macOS and iOS software difficult for novices and experienced programmers alike.

That's why in 2014, Apple introduced a new programming language called Swift. Swift is meant to be just as powerful as Objective-C while also being much easier to learn. Because Apple will use Swift for macOS, iOS, tvOS, and watchOS programming, Swift is now the future programming language for the Macintosh, iPhone, iPad, Apple Watch, Apple TV, CarPlay, and any other future products from Apple.

Since so many people have written programs using Objective-C, there will always be a need for programmers to modify existing Objective-C programs. However, you can always mix Objective-C and Swift in a program. This means over time, there will be less of a need for Objective-C programmers and more of a need for Swift programmers. If you want to learn the most powerful programming language for writing macOS and iOS programs, you want to learn Swift.

> **Note** If you're already familiar with Objective-C, you'll notice several ways that Swift makes coding far easier. First, Swift doesn't require a semicolon to end each line. Second, Swift doesn't need asterisks to represent pointers or square brackets to represent method calls to objects. Third, Swift stores everything in a single `.swift` file in comparison to Objective-C, which needs to create an `.h` header file and an `.m` implementation file. If you know nothing about Objective-C, just look at any program written in Objective-C and see how confusing the code can be. One look at Objective-C code will make you realize how much easier learning and using Swift can be.

Using Playgrounds

In the old days, programmers had two types of tools to help them learn programming. The first is called an interpreter. An interpreter lets you type in a command and then immediately shows you the results. This way you can see exactly what you are doing right or wrong.

The drawback with interpreters is that they are slow and you can't use them to create programs you can sell. To run a program in an interpreter, you need both the interpreter and the file (called the source code) that contains all your commands written in a particular programming language. Because you have to give away your source code to run programs in an interpreter, others can easily copy your program and steal it. As a result, interpreters aren't practical for selling software but are great for learning a programming language.

The second tool programmers use to learn programming is called a compiler. A compiler takes a list of commands, stored in a file, and converts them to machine language so the computer can understand them. The advantage of a compiler is that it keeps others from seeing the source code of your program.

The problem with using a compiler is that you have to write a complete program and compile it just to see if your commands work or not. If your commands don't work, now you have to go back and fix the problem. Unlike the interactive nature of an interpreter, a compiler makes learning a programming language much slower and clumsier.

With an interpreter you can write a command and immediately see if it works or not. With a compiler, you have to write a command, compile your program, and run your program to see if it works or not.

Interpreters are better for learning, and compilers are better for creating software you can distribute to others without giving away your source code. Fortunately, Xcode gives you the best of both worlds..

When you run your program, you're using Xcode's compiler. However, if you only want to experiment with some commands, you can use Xcode's interpreter, called a playground.

Playgrounds let you experiment with Swift code to see if it works or not. When you get it to work, then you can copy and paste the code into your project files and compile them to create a working program. By giving you the ability to use both an interpreter and a compiler, Xcode makes it easy to learn Swift and practical for creating programs you can sell or give away to others.

To create a playground, follow these steps:

1. Start Xcode.

2. Choose File ➤ New ➤ Playground. (If you see the Xcode welcome screen, you can also click on Get started with a playground.) Xcode asks for a playground name and platform, as shown in Figure 5-1.

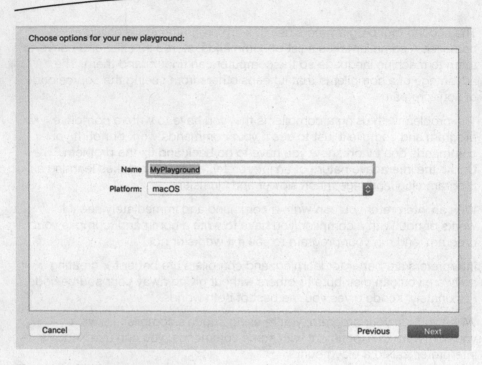

Figure 5-1. Creating a playground file

3. Click in the Name text field and type
    IntroductoryPlayground.

4. Click in the Platform pop-up menu and choose
    macOS. Xcode asks where you want to save your
    playground file.

5. Click a folder where you want to save your
    playground file and click the Create button. Xcode
    displays the playground file, as shown in Figure 5-2.

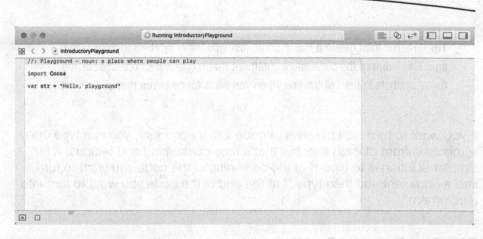

Figure 5-2. The playground window

6. Edit the second line as follows:

```
var str = "This is the Swift interpreter"
```

Notice that the playground window immediately displays the results of your code change in the right margin, as shown in Figure 5-3.

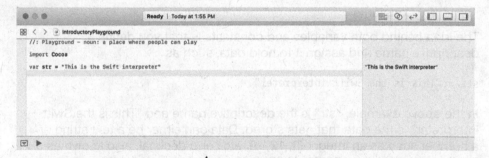

Figure 5-3. The playground window displays code changes immediately

Playgrounds let you freely experiment with Swift and access every class in the Cocoa framework without worrying about getting your Swift code to work with a user interface.

When you type Swift code, Xcode may display certain text in different colors. Notice that the top line in your playground displays text in green. In Swift, this is known as a comment, which means any text that begins with the // symbols are ignored by Xcode and exist solely for people to read. Any time you type // in front of any line of code, Xcode will turn the text green and ignore it.

> **Tip**   Rather than delete a line of code, just type the // symbols in front of that
> line. This will turn the code into a comment that Xcode will ignore. Just delete
> the // symbols in front of the line when you want Xcode to run that code again.

If you want to turn multiple lines of code into a comment, you can type the //
symbols in front of each line, but that's time-consuming and tedious. A far
simpler solution is to type /* at the beginning of the code you want to turn
into a comment and then type */ at the end of the code you want to turn into
a comment.

Storing Data in Swift

Every program needs to accept data, manipulate that data somehow, and
display that result to the user. To accept data, programs need to store
data temporarily in memory. Technically, computers store data in memory
addresses, which can be confusing to remember. To make it easier to know
where data gets stored, programming languages let you give those memory
addresses descriptive names. In Swift, those two choices are called

- Variables
- Constants

The idea behind both variables and constants is that you define a
descriptive name and assign it to hold data, such as

```
str = "This is the Swift interpreter"
```

In the above example, "str" is the descriptive name and "This is the Swift
interpreter" is the data that gets stored. Data can either be a text string or
a number such as an integer (3, 12, -9, etc.) or a decimal, also known as a
floating-point number (12.84, -0.83, 8.02, etc.). At any given time, you can
store one chunk of data in a descriptive name, which can be defined as a
variable or a constant.

The main difference between a variable and a constant is that you can reuse
a variable by storing new data as many times as you want (hence the name
"variable"). A constant only lets you store data in it once.

To define a variable, you have to use the var keyword, like this:

```
var str = "This is the Swift interpreter"
```

To define a constant, you have to use the let keyword like this:

```
let str = "This is the Swift interpreter"
```

The first time you store data in a variable or a constant, Swift infers the data type, which can be either

- Text strings (defined as String)
- Integers (defined as Int)
- Decimal numbers (defined as Double)

Knowing the data type a variable or constant can hold is crucial because it can only hold one type of data and nothing else. So if you create a variable and store a string in it, that variable can only store strings from now on.

> **Note** Swift is known as a type-safe programming language because it forces you to explicitly define the type of data each variable or constant can store. This prevents your program from trying to work with incorrect data, such as trying to add a number to a text string like "John".

To make it clear what type of data a variable or constant can hold, you can explicitly define one of four common data types, such as

```
var cat: String
var dog: Int
var fish: Float
var snake: Double
```

String data types can only contain characters enclosed within double quotation marks such as "This is a string" and "15". Anything within double quotation marks is treated as a string.

Int (Integer) data types can only hold whole numbers such as -25, 4, and 3,928. If you need to store any whole number between -2,147,483,648 and 2,147,483,647, use the Int data type.

Float and Double data types can hold decimal numbers such as 2.01, -0.577, and 51.634. The main difference between the two is that a Float data type can hold seven digits after the decimal point while Double data types can hold twice the number of digits after the decimal point.

For example, suppose you want to store the number 0.123456789123456789 in a variable. If you store it in a variable that can only hold Float values, Swift will actually store the value 0.1234568 (rounding up the last digit).

```
var floatVar: Float = 0.123456789123456789
// 0.1234568
```

However, if you store that exact same number in a variable that can only hold Double values, Swift will store all the digits up to fourteen decimal places, such as

```
var doubleVar: Double = 0.123456789123456789
// 0.12345671234568
```

Because Swift is a type-safe language, you cannot manipulate Float and Double data types together. As a general rule, use Double data types for storing decimal numbers unless you have a specific reason to use Float data types.

If you try to store the wrong type of data in a variable or constant, Swift won't let you. This is to prevent problems when a program tries to use the wrong type of data. For example, if a program asks the user for how many items to order and the user types in "five" instead of the number 5, the program will have no idea how to do a mathematical calculation on "five," which will cause the program to either crash or work erratically.

Swift gives you three ways to define a variable or a constant:

- `let cat = "Oscar" // Infers String data type`
- `let cat: String = "Oscar"`
- `let cat: String`

  `cat = "Oscar"`

The first method lets you store data directly into a variable or constant. Based on the type of data you first store, Swift infers the data type as String, Int, or Double (not a Float, because a Float stores less precise decimal numbers than Double, and Swift assumes you want exact precision).

The second method lets you explicitly declare the data type and store data into that variable or constant. While this can be wordier, it's clear exactly what type of data you want to store.

The third method takes two lines. The first line defines the data type. The second line actually stores the data. This can be handy for variables that may get assigned different data in various parts of your program. You can declare the variable near the top of your file to make it easy to find, and then assign data to it later when you need it.

When creating multiple variables of the same data type, you can place each variable declaration on a different line, like this:

```
var cat : Int
var dog : Int
```

As a shortcut, you can declare variables of the same data type on a single line, like this:

```
var cat, dog : Int
```

The above line declares cat and dog as variables that can hold Int data types, which is identical to the two lines that declare cat as an Int data type and then dog as another Int data type. By putting all data type variable declarations on a single line, you can easily see which variables use identical data types.

To see how to declare variables and constants in Swift, follow these steps:

1. Make sure your IntroductoryPlayground file is loaded into Xcode.

2. Modify the Swift code in the playground file as follows:

```
import Cocoa

let cat: String
cat = "Oscar"

cat = "Bo"
```

Notice that when you try to assign new data to a constant that already holds data, you get a warning. Clicking that warning icon in the left margin displays an error message, as shown in Figure 5-4.

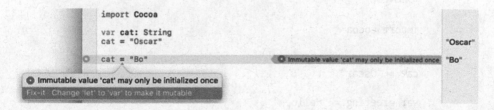

Figure 5-4. An error message warns that you cannot store data in a constant more than once

> **Note**   Constants are also called "immutable" because they cannot be changed after you've stored data in them. Variables are called "mutable" because you can constantly change the data that they store. Just remember that variables can only hold one chunk of data at a time. The moment you store new data in a variable, any existing data in that variable gets wiped out.

3. Modify the Swift code in the playground file by changing the constant to a variable (replacing `let` with var) as follows:

```
import Cocoa

var cat: String
cat = "Oscar"

cat = 42.7
```

Notice that when you try to assign a number to a variable that can only hold strings, you get a warning. Clicking on that warning icon in the left margin displays an error message, as shown in Figure 5-5.

Figure 5-5. An error message warns that you cannot store the wrong type of data

4. Modify the Swift code in the playground file as follows:

```
import Cocoa

var cat: String
cat = "Oscar"

var greeting = "Hello, "
var period : String = "."

print (greeting + cat + period)
```

In Figure 5-6, you can see that the playground displays the results of your Swift code in the right margin.

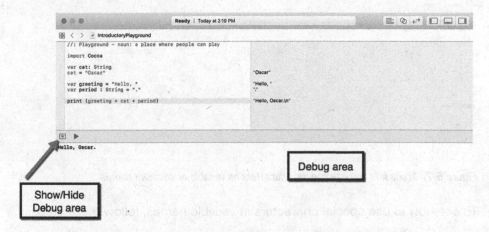

Figure 5-6. *The right margin of the playground window constantly shows the result of your code*

When you use the `print` command, Swift's playground displays the result in both the right margin and the bottom of the playground window in the Debug area. To toggle between showing or hiding the Debug area, click the Show/Hide Debug area icon (see Figure 5-6).

By hiding the Debug area, you can view more of your playground Swift code. By showing the Debug area, you can view the results of the `print` command in your Swift code.

Using Unicode Characters as Names

In most programming languages, variables and constants are limited to a specific range of characters, often excluding foreign language characters. To help make Swift more accessible to programmers comfortable with other languages, Swift lets you use Unicode characters for your variable and constant names.

Unicode is a new universal standard that represents different characters. If you choose Edit ➤ Emojis & Symbols, you can choose from a limited number of characters that you can use instead of or in addition to ordinary letters and numbers, as shown in Figure 5-7.

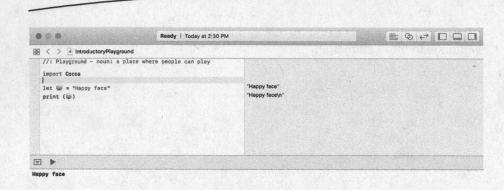

Figure 5-7. Xcode lets you use special characters as variable or constant names

To see how to use special characters in variable names, follow these steps:

1. Make sure your IntroductoryPlayground file is loaded in Xcode.

2. Delete all the code in your playground except for the "import Cocoa" line.

3. Underneath the "import Cocoa" line, type **let** and press the spacebar.

4. Choose Edit➤Emojis & Symbols. A pop-up window appears, as shown in Figure 5-8.

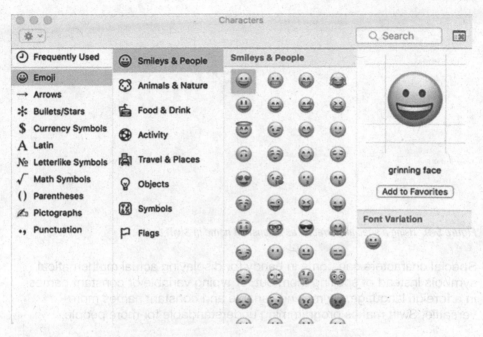

Figure 5-8. A pop-up window with different categories of special characters

5. Double-click any character that looks interesting. Xcode types that character as your constant name.

6. Type = **"Funny symbol here"** and press Return.

7. Copy the character and paste it in between the parentheses of the print command. Notice that the right margin of the playground window displays the contents of your constant variable, as shown in Figure 5-9.

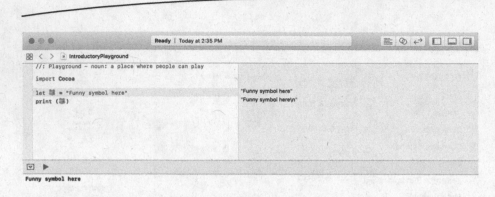

Figure 5-9. Using a special character as a constant name in Swift code

Special characters can come in handy for displaying actual mathematical symbols instead of spelling them out, or typing variable or constant names in a foreign language. By making variable and constant names more versatile, Swift makes programming understandable for more people.

Converting Data Types

If you have a number stored as an integer and need to convert it to a decimal, or if you have a decimal and need to convert it to an integer, what can you do? The answer is that you can convert one number data type to another just by specifying the data type you want, such as

```
Int(decimal)
```

The Int data type in front tells Swift to convert the number inside the parentheses to an integer. If the number is a decimal, converting it to an integer basically means dropping all numbers after the decimal point, so a number like 4.9 is turned into the integer 4.

When Swift converts an integer to a decimal number, it simply tacks on a decimal point with zeroes. So if you convert the integer 75 to a floating-point number, Swift now stores it as 75.0. To see how converting integers to decimals (and vice versa) works, follow these steps:

1. Make sure your IntroductoryPlayground file is loaded in Xcode.

2. Modify the code in the playground file as follows:

```
import Cocoa
var whole : Int = 4
var decimal : Double = 4.902

print (Int(decimal))
print (Double(whole))
```

Notice how Swift turns an integer into a decimal (changing 4 to 4.0) and how it turns a decimal into an integer by dropping every value to the right of the decimal point (changing 4.902 to 4), as shown in Figure 5-10.

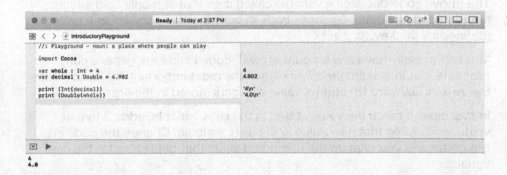

Figure 5-10. Changing integers to decimals and vice versa

Computed Properties

Up until this point, declaring variables and constants, and then assigning data to those variable or constants, is little different than in other programming languages. If you have one variable related to another one, you could do something like this:

```
var cats = 4
var dogs: Int

dogs = cats + 2
print (dogs)
```

Unfortunately, this separates the variable declaration for "dogs" from the actual setting of the value of the dogs variable. To keep a variable declaration linked with the code that defines it, Swift offers something called computed properties.

With a computed property, you don't store data directly into a variable. Instead, you define the data type a variable can hold and then use other variables or constants to calculate a new value to store in that variable. This calculation is known as a getter, with code that looks like this:

```
var dogs : Int {
    get {
        return cats + 2 // Code to calculate a value
    }
}
```

The above code declares a variable called dogs that can only hold integer (Int) data types. Then it encloses code in curly brackets known as a getter (defined by the keyword get).

You can actually have any amount of Swift code inside the getter's curly brackets, but this example only includes the most important line, which uses the return keyword to return a value that gets stored in the dogs variable.

In this case, it takes the value stored in the cats variable, adds 2 to that value, and stores that new value in the dogs variable. Change the code in the getter and you change the computed value that gets stored in the dogs variable.

Let's see how this works by following these steps:

1. Make sure your IntroductoryPlayground file is loaded in Xcode.

2. Modify the code in the playground file as follows:

```
import Cocoa

var cats = 4

var dogs : Int {
    get {
        return cats + 2 // Code to calculate a value
    }
}

print (dogs)
```

Notice that the right margin of the playground window shows the value of dogs, as shown in Figure 5-11.

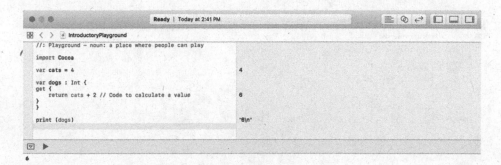

Figure 5-11. The right margin of the playground window shows how the getter portion works

Getters use code to calculate the value of a variable. A second type of computed property is known as a setter, which runs code that calculates the value of a different variable.

A setter runs every time its variable gets assigned a value. To see how getters and setters work, follow these steps:

1. Make sure your IntroductoryPlayground file is loaded in Xcode.

2. Modify the code in the playground file as follows:

```
import Cocoa

var cats = 4
var dogs : Int {
    get {
        return cats + 2 // Code to calculate a value
    }
    set(newValue) {
        cats = 3 * newValue
    }
}

print (dogs)
print (cats)
dogs = 5
print (dogs)
print (cats)
```

Notice how the value of the cats and dogs variables change when you assign a different value to the dogs variable, as shown in Figure 5-12.

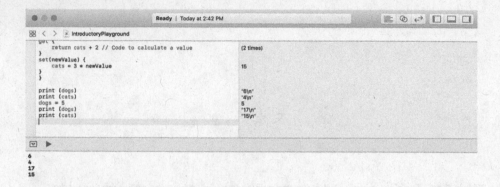

Figure 5-12. The right margin of the playground window shows how the getter and setter code works

Let's go through this code line by line. First, the number 4 gets stored in the cats variable. Using the cats variable (4) in the getter returns cats + 2 or 4 + 2 (6). So the first print (dogs) command prints 6.

The second print (cats) prints the value of the cats variable, which is still 4.

When the dogs variable gets assigned the number 5, it runs the setter. The temporary variable newValue gets assigned the number 5, which calculates a new value for cats as 3 * newValue, which is 3 * 5 or 15. The value of the cats variable is now set to 15.

Now the next print (dogs) command runs, using the value of dogs, which is calculated by the getter. Since the value of cats is 15, the getter calculates cats + 2 or 15 + 2, which is 17. So the next print (dogs) command prints 17 and the last print (cats) command prints 15.

> **Note**   Computed properties can run code when assigning a value to a variable. However, use computed properties sparingly since they can make your code harder to understand. Computed properties are most often used for class properties in object-oriented programming. For example, if an object represents a square drawn on the screen, changing the width of the square must also change the height of that square at the same time (and vice versa).

Using Optional Variables

The biggest flaw when you declare a variable is that you can't use that variable until you store data in it. If you try using a variable before it stores any data, your program will fail and crash. To avoid this problem, many programmers initially store "dummy" data in a variable. Unfortunately, such "dummy" data can still be used by a program and cause errors.

To avoid this problem, Swift offers something called optional variables. An optional variable can store data or nothing at all. If an optional variable contains nothing, it's considered to hold a value called nil. By using optional variables, you avoid crashing a program if a variable doesn't contain any data.

To create an optional variable, you just declare a variable and its data type with a question mark, like this:

```
var fish : String?
```

The question mark identifies a variable as an optional. You can use optional variables exactly like ordinary variables to store data in them, such as

```
fish = "goldfish"
```

Although storing data in an optional variable is no different than storing data in an ordinary variable, retrieving data from an optional variable requires extra steps. First, you must check if the optional variable even has data in it or not. Once you know that an optional variable contains data, you have to unwrap that optional to get to the actual data by using an exclamation mark, such as

```
print (fish!)
```

To see how optional variables work, try the following:

1. Make sure your IntroductoryPlayground file is loaded in Xcode.

2. Modify the code as follows:

```
import Cocoa

var fish : String?
fish = "goldfish"
print (fish)
print (fish!)
```

Notice that fish by itself is actually an optional variable but when you use the exclamation mark to unwrap it, you access the actual data inside the optional, as shown in Figure 5-13.

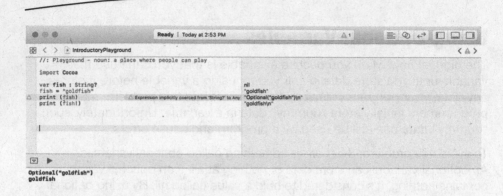

Figure 5-13. Seeing the difference between an optional and the unwrapped data inside an optional

3. Type two additional lines of code underneath:

```
var str : String
str = fish
```

Notice that you can't assign the optional variable fish to str because str can only hold String data types. Instead, you must unwrap the optional variable fish and retrieve its actual string content by using the exclamation mark, like this:

```
var str : String
str = fish!
```

Before unwrapping optional variables to get to their data, always check to see if the optional variable contains a nil value or a variable. If you try to use an optional variable when it contains a nil value, your program could crash.

To check if an optional variable holds a nil value or not, you have two options. First, you can explicitly check for a nil value, like this:

```
if fish != nil {
    print ("The optional variable is not nil")
}
```

This code checks if the fish optional variable is not equal to (!=) nil. If an optional variable is not nil, then it must hold a value, so it's safe to retrieve it.

A second way to check if an optional variable has a value or not is to assign it to a constant, like this:

```
if let food = fish {
    print ("The optional variable has a value")
    print (food)
}
```

If the optional variable has a value, it stores that value in the constant. Now you can access that value through the constant. To see how this works, follow these steps:

1. Make sure your IntroductoryPlayground file is loaded in Xcode.

2. Modify the code as follows:

    ```
    import Cocoa
    var fish : String?
    fish = "goldfish"

    if fish != nil {
        print ("The optional variable is not nil")
        var str : String
        str = fish!
        print (str)
    }

    if let food = fish {
        print ("The optional variable has a value")
        print (food)
    }
    ```

Notice that you can retrieve the value in an optional variable by unwrapping it with an exclamation mark or storing it in a constant and then using that constant, as shown in Figure 5-14.

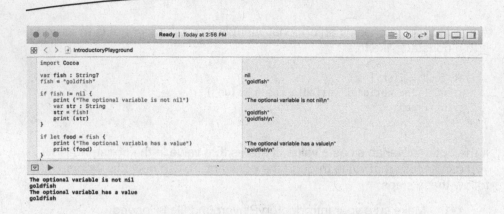

```
import Cocoa

var fish : String?                                      nil
fish = "goldfish"                                       "goldfish"

if fish != nil {
    print ("The optional variable is not nil")          "The optional variable is not nil\n"
    var str : String
    str = fish!                                         "goldfish"
    print (str)                                         "goldfish\n"
}

if let food = fish {
    print ("The optional variable has a value")         "The optional variable has a value\n"
    print (food)                                        "goldfish\n"
}
```

```
The optional variable is not nil
goldfish
The optional variable has a value
goldfish
```

Figure 5-14. Two ways to access a value stored in an optional variable

Linking Swift Code to a User Interface

Every program needs to store data, and one of the most common ways to store data in a variable is to retrieve data from a user interface. To link a user interface item to Swift code, you need to create an IBOutlet variable.

If you have a text field connected to an IBOutlet variable, anything the user types in the text field automatically gets stored in the IBOutlet variable. Likewise, anything you store in the IBOutlet variable suddenly appears in the text field. IBOutlet variables act like a link between your Swift code and your user interface, as shown in Figure 5-15.

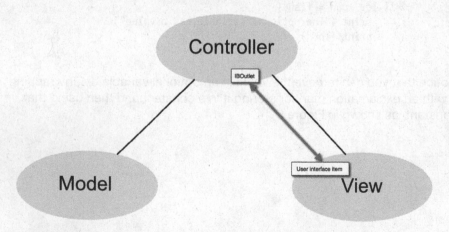

Figure 5-15. IBOutlet variables link your user interface items with Swift code

Since user interface items like text fields may initially be empty, IBOutlet variables are defined as implicitly unwrapped optional variables defined by an exclamation mark, like this:

```
@IBOutlet weak var labelText: NSTextField!
```

If an IBOutlet is a regular variable and is connected to an empty text field, your program will risk crashing without any data in the IBOutlet variable.

If an IBOutlet is an optional variable, you can define it with a question mark, like this:

```
@IBOutlet weak var labelText: NSTextField?
```

Unfortunately, every time you want to access the data stored in this optional variable, you must type an exclamation mark. If you access this IBOutlet variable multiple times, each time you must type an exclamation mark, which can get annoying and will make your code harder to read.

To let you access an IBOutlet variable without typing exclamation marks all the time, it's easier to create an IBOutlet variable as an implicitly unwrapped optional variable, which means that if it holds a value, you can access it without typing the unwrapping exclamation mark.

To see how Xcode creates IBOutlets as implicitly unwrapped optional variables, open the MyFirstProgram project that you created earlier.

1. Make sure your MyFirstProgram is loaded in Xcode.

2. Click the AppDelegate.swift file in the Project Navigator. Xcode's middle pane displays the contents of that .swift file. Notice that all the IBOutlet variables are declared with an exclamation mark, meaning they're implicitly unwrapped optional variables:

    ```
    @IBOutlet weak var labelText: NSTextField!
    @IBOutlet weak var messageText: NSTextField!
    ```

Also notice that the IBAction changeCase method lets you access the contents of these implicitly unwrapped optional variables without using an exclamation mark.

```
@IBOutlet weak var labelText: NSTextField!
@IBOutlet weak var messageText: NSTextField!
```

```
@IBAction func changeCase(_ sender: NSButton) {
      labelText.stringValue = messageText.stringValue.uppercased()
      let warning = labelText.stringValue
  }
```

3. Replace the exclamation marks at the end of each
    IBOutlet variable with a question mark, like this:

```
@IBOutlet weak var labelText: NSTextField?
@IBOutlet weak var messageText: NSTextField?
```

Notice that Xcode now displays error messages each time you use an
IBOutlet variable. That's because you need to unwrap each optional variable
with an exclamation mark, like this:

```
@IBAction func changeCase(_ sender: NSButton) {
    labelText!.stringValue=messageText!.stringValue.uppercased()
    let warning=labelText!.stringValue
}
```

If you define your IBOutlets as regular optional variables (defined by a
question mark), then you must unwrap each optional variable with an
exclamation mark to access its value.

If you simply define your IBOutlets as implicitly unwrapped optional
variables (which Xcode does for you), then you don't need to type an
exclamation mark to unwrap the optional variables.

Basically, let Xcode create your IBOutlets as implicitly unwrapped variables
(with an exclamation mark) to make typing Swift code easier.

So when should you use an optional variable (defined by ?) and when should
you use an implicitly unwrapped optional variable (defined by !)?

In general, use implicitly unwrapped optional variables for IBOutlets to make
it easy to write Swift code without typing exclamation marks all over. If you
use implicitly unwrapped optional variables any other time, your variable
could contain a nil value and Xcode won't catch any potential errors if you
try to use it.

To see the danger of using implicitly unwrapped optional variables, follow
these steps:

1. Make sure your IntroductoryPlayground file is loaded
    in Xcode.

2. Modify the code as follows:

```
import Cocoa

var safe : Int?  // optional variable
var danger : Int!// implicitly unwrapped optional variable

print (danger * 2)
print (safe * 2)
```

Notice that neither integer variable has a value in it, but Xcode cheerfully lets you perform a calculation with a nil value in an implicitly unwrapped optional but flags a possible error with a regular optional variable, as shown in Figure 5-16.

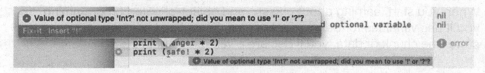

Figure 5-16. *Xcode can identify possible problems with undefined optional variables but not undefined implicitly unwrapped optional variables*

By making you unwrap optional variables with an exclamation mark (!), Xcode forces you to acknowledge you're using an optional variable so you can remember to check if it has a nil value or not.

Since implicitly unwrapped optional variables let you type the variable name without typing additional symbols, it's much easier to forget you're working with optional variables and check for a possible nil value before trying to use it. Optional variables can't prevent problems, but they can force you to remember you're working with potentially nil values.

Summary

If you're coming from another programming environment, you've already seen numerous ways that Swift differs from other languages. Swift's playground interpreter lets you test your code in a safe environment before copying and pasting it into an actual program. Playgrounds give you the freedom to experiment freely with Swift commands.

The three most common data types are integers (Int), decimal numbers (Float or Double), and text strings (String). To avoid mixing data types when storing decimal numbers, use Double data types unless you have a specific reason to use a Float data type instead.

To make variable names more flexible, you can use Unicode characters that can represent symbols or foreign language characters.

Storing data in a variable can be as simple as assigning it to a value. Swift also offers computed properties that let you modify a variable or another variable when assigned a new value. Computed properties are far more useful when working with classes and object-oriented programming.

Even more important are optional variables that let you handle nil values without crashing your program. Optional variables are especially important when using IBOutlets to connect Swift code to user interface items such as labels and text fields.

When you create an optional variable (with a question mark), you need to unwrap it to access its actual data (using an exclamation mark).

Variables are crucial for storing data temporarily so you'll use them often. When you start learning about classes and object-oriented programming, you'll use variables for defining properties. Essentially, any time you need to store one chunk of data, you'll declare a variable to hold it.

Chapter 6

Manipulating Numbers and Strings

Every program needs to store data temporarily in variables. However, for a program to be useful, it must also manipulate that data somehow to calculate a useful result. A spreadsheet lets you add, subtract, multiply, and divide numbers. A word processor manipulates text to correct your spelling and format text. Even a video game responds to joystick movements to calculate a new position for the player's object such as a cartoon person, airplane, or car. Using data to calculate a new result is the whole purpose of every program.

To manipulate numbers, Swift includes four basic mathematic operators for addition (+), subtraction (-), multiplication (*), division (/), and a remainder operator (%). You can even manipulate strings using the addition operator (+) when you want to combine two strings into one.

Although Swift includes multiple operators for manipulating numbers and text, the Cocoa framework includes plenty of more powerful functions for manipulating numbers and strings. If none of these functions prove suitable, you can always create your own functions to manipulate text and numeric data. By creating miniature programs called functions, you can manipulate data in any way you like and reuse your function as often as necessary.

Using Mathematical Operators

The simplest way to manipulate numbers is to perform addition, subtraction, division, or multiplication. When manipulating numbers, first make sure all your numbers are the same data type, such as all integers or all Float or

Double decimal numbers. Since mixing integers with decimal numbers can lead to calculation errors, Swift will force you to use the same data types in a calculation. If all your data isn't the same data type, you need to convert one or more data types such as

```
var cats = 4
var dogs = 5.4

dogs = Double(cats) * dogs
```

In this case, Swift infers that cats is an Int data type and dogs is a Double data type. To multiply cats and dogs, they must be the same data type (Double), so you must first convert the cats value to a Double data type and then the calculation can proceed safely..

When using multiple mathematical operators, use parentheses to define which calculations should occur first. Swift normally calculates mathematical operators from left to right, but multiplication and division occur before addition and division. If you typed the following Swift code, you'd get two different results based solely on the order of the mathematical calculations:

```
var cats, dogs : Double

dogs = 5 *  9 - 3 /  2 + 4      // 47.5
cats = 5 * (9 - 3) / (2 + 4)    // 5.0
```

For clarity, always group mathematical operators in parentheses. The most common mathematical operators are known as binary operators because they require two numbers to calculate a result, as shown in Table 6-1.

Table 6-1. Common Mathematical Operators in Swift

Mathematical Operator	Purpose	Example
+	Addition	5+9=14
-	Subtraction	5-4=1
*	Multiplication	5*9=45
/	Division	45/9=5
%	Remainder	5%9=5

Out of all these mathematical operators, the remainder operator may need some additional explanation. Essentially the remainder operator divides one number into another and returns just the remainder of that division. So 5 divided by 9 is 0 with a remainder of 5, and 26 divided by 5 gives a remainder of 1.

Compound Assignment Operators

If you want to add or subtract a number to a variable, you can use Swift code like this:

```
temp = temp + 5
```

This command tells Swift to add 5 to the current value stored in the temp variable. While this type of code will work, it can be clumsy to type the same variable name twice.

As a shortcut, Swift offers a compound assignment operator that looks like (+=) or (-=). To use a compound assignment operator, you need to specify a variable, the compound assignment operator you want to use, and then the value you want to add or subtract, such as

```
temp += 5
```

This is equivalent to

```
temp = temp + 5
```

To see how compound assignment operators work, follow these steps:

1. Open the IntroductoryPlayground file in Xcode.

2. Edit the code as follows:

```
import Cocoa

var temp = 2
temp += 57                    // Equivalent to temp = temp + 57
print (temp)
temp -= 7                     // Equivalent to temp = temp - 7
print (temp)
```

As Figure 6-1 shows, the += compound assignment operator adds 57 to the current value of temp. Then the -= compound assignment operator subtracts 7 from the current value of temp.

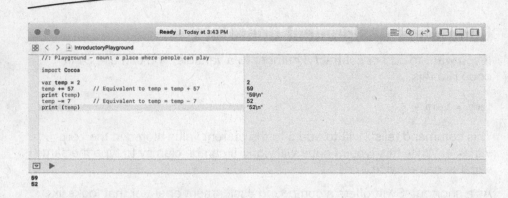

```
●  ●  ●                    Ready | Today at 3:43 PM                            ≣  ⊘  ↩    ☐ ☐ ☐
⌗  <  >   ⌷ IntroductoryPlayground
   //: Playground - noun: a place where people can play

   import Cocoa

   var temp = 2                                                   2
   temp += 57      // Equivalent to temp = temp + 57              59
   print (temp)                                                   "59\n"
   temp -= 7       // Equivalent to temp = temp - 7               52
   print (temp)                                                   "52\n"



   ▽  ▶
   59
   52
```

Figure 6-1. Seeing how compound assignment operators work

By combining mathematical operators, you can create any type of calculation. However, if you need to perform common mathematical operations such as finding the square root or logarithm of a number, it's much simpler and more reliable to use built-in math functions that are part of the Cocoa framework.

Using Math Functions

The Cocoa framework provides dozens of math functions that you can use. Some of the more common math functions include the following:

- Rounding functions

- Calculation functions (sqrt, cbrt, min/max, etc.)

- Trigonometry functions (sin, cosine, tangent, etc.)

- Exponential functions

- Logarithmic functions

Rounding Functions

When you're working with decimal numbers, you may want to round them to the nearest place value. However, there are many ways to round numbers in Swift, such as

- **round**: Rounds up from 0.5 and higher and rounds down from 0.49 and lower

- **floor**: Rounds to the lowest integer

- **ceil**: Rounds to the highest integer

- **trunc**: Drops the decimal value

To see how these different rounding functions work, create a new playground by following these steps:

1. Make sure the IntroductoryPlayground file is loaded in Xcode.

2. Edit the code as follows:

```
import Cocoa

var testNumber : Double

testNumber = round(36.98)
testNumber = round(-36.98)
testNumber = round(36.08)

testNumber = floor(36.98)
testNumber = floor(-36.98)
testNumber = floor(36.08)

testNumber = ceil(36.98)
testNumber = ceil(-36.98)
testNumber = ceil(36.08)

testNumber = trunc(36.98)
testNumber = trunc(-36.98)
testNumber = trunc(36.08)
```

Figure 6-2 shows how each type of rounding function works differently with both negative and positive numbers as well as how each function rounds up or down.

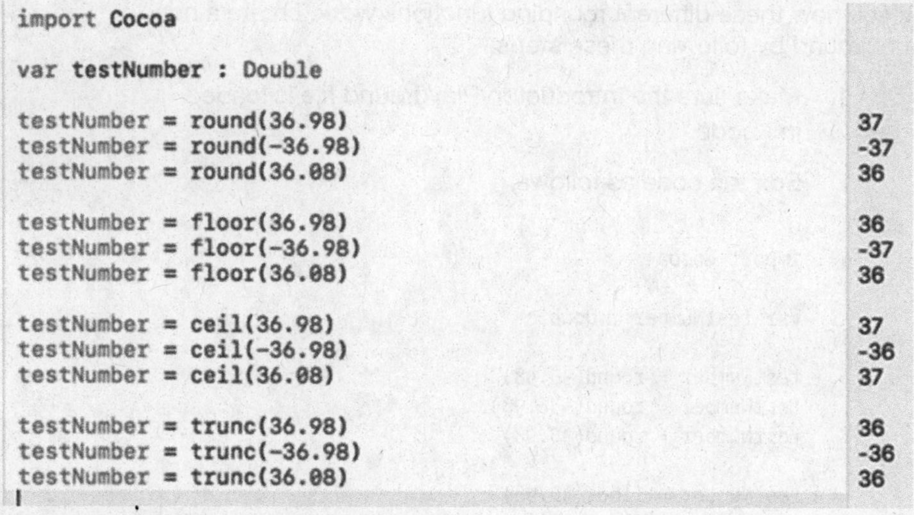

```
import Cocoa

var testNumber : Double

testNumber = round(36.98)                    37
testNumber = round(-36.98)                   -37
testNumber = round(36.08)                    36

testNumber = floor(36.98)                    36
testNumber = floor(-36.98)                   -37
testNumber = floor(36.08)                    36

testNumber = ceil(36.98)                     37
testNumber = ceil(-36.98)                    -36
testNumber = ceil(36.08)                     37

testNumber = trunc(36.98)                    36
testNumber = trunc(-36.98)                   -36
testNumber = trunc(36.08)                    36
```

Figure 6-2. Seeing how different rounding functions work

Calculation Functions

You can combine Swift's four basic mathematical (addition, subtraction, division, and multiplication) to create sophisticated calculations of any kind. However, the Cocoa framework includes common types of mathematical functions that you can use so you don't have to create them yourself. Some common calculation functions include

- **fabs**: Calculates the absolute value of a number

- **sqrt**: Calculates the square root of a positive number

- **cbrt**: Calculates the cube root of a positive number

- **hypot**: Calculates the square root of (x*x + y*y)

- **fmax**: Identifies the maximum or largest value of two numbers

- **fmin**: Identifies the minimum or smallest value of two numbers

To see how these different calculation functions work, follow these steps:

1. Make sure your IntroductoryPlayground is loaded in Xcode.

2. Edit the code as follows:

```
import Cocoa

var testNumber : Double
testNumber = fabs(52.64)
testNumber = fabs(-52.64)

testNumber = sqrt(5)
testNumber = cbrt(5)
testNumber = hypot(4, 9)
testNumber = fmax(34.2, 89.2)
testNumber = fmin(34.2, 89.2)
```

Figure 6-3 shows how each type of calculation function works differently.

```
import Cocoa

var testNumber : Double
testNumber = fabs(52.64)            52.64
testNumber = fabs(-52.64)           52.64

testNumber = sqrt(5)                2.23606797749979
testNumber = cbrt(5)                1.709975946676697
testNumber = hypot(4, 9)            9.848857801796104
testNumber = fmax(34.2, 89.2)       89.2
testNumber = fmin(34.2, 89.2)       34.2
```

Figure 6-3. Seeing how different calculation functions work

Trigonometry Functions

If you remember from school (or even if you don't), trigonometry is a mathematical field involving angles between intersecting lines. Since trigonometry can actually be handy in the real world, the Cocoa framework provides plenty of functions for calculating cosines, hyperbolic sines, inverse tangents, and inverse hyperbolic cosines. Some common trigonometry functions include

- **sin**: Calculates the sine of a degree measured in radians

- **cos**: Calculates the cosine of a degree measured in radians

- **tan**: Calculates the tangent of a degree measured in radians

- **sinh**: Calculates the hyperbolic sine of a degree measured in radians

- **cosh**: Calculates the hyperbolic cosine of a degree measured in radians

- **tanh**: Calculates the hyperbolic tangent of a degree measured in radians

- **asin**: Calculates the inverse sine of a degree measured in radians

- **acos**: Calculates the inverse cosine of a degree measured in radians

- **atan**: Calculates the inverse tangent of a degree measured in radians

- **asinh**: Calculates the inverse hyperbolic sine of a degree measured in radians

- **acosh**: Calculates the inverse hyperbolic cosine of a degree measured in radians

- **atanh**: Calculates the inverse hyperbolic tangent of a degree measured in radians

To see how these different trigonometry functions work, follow these steps:

1. Make sure your IntroductoryPlayground is loaded in Xcode.

2. Edit the code as follows:

```
import Cocoa

var testNumber : Double
testNumber = sin(1)
testNumber = cos(1)
testNumber = tan(1)

testNumber = sinh(1)
testNumber = cosh(1)
testNumber = tanh(1)

testNumber = asin(1)
testNumber = acos(1)
testNumber = atan(1)

testNumber = asinh(1)
testNumber = acosh(1)
testNumber = atanh(1)
```

Figure 6-4 shows how each type of trigonometry function works differently.

```
import Cocoa

var testNumber : Double
testNumber = sin(1)                    0.8414709848078965
testNumber = cos(1)                    0.5403023058681398
testNumber = tan(1)                    1.557407724654902

testNumber = sinh(1)                   1.175201193643801
testNumber = cosh(1)                   1.543080634815244
testNumber = tanh(1)                   0.7615941559557649

testNumber = asin(1)                   1.570796326794897
testNumber = acos(1)                   0
testNumber = atan(1)                   0.7853981633974483

testNumber = asinh(1)                  0.881373587019543
testNumber = acosh(1)                  0
testNumber = atanh(1)                  inf
```

Figure 6-4. Seeing how different trigonometry functions work

Exponential Functions

Exponential functions involve multiplication such as multiplying the number 2 by itself a fixed number of times. Some common exponential functions include

- **exp**: Calculates e**x where x is an integer

- **exp2**: Calculates 2**x where x is an integer

- **__exp10**: Calculates 10**x where x is an integer

- **expm1**: Calculates e**x-1 where x is an integer

- **pow**: Calculates x raised to the power of y

To see how these different trigonometry functions work, follow these steps:

1. Make sure your IntroductoryPlayground file is loaded in Xcode.

2. Edit the code as follows:

```
import Cocoa

var testNumber : Double
testNumber = exp(3)
testNumber = exp2(3)
testNumber = __exp10(3)
testNumber = expm1(3)
testNumber = pow(2,4)
```

Figure 6-5 shows how each type of trigonometry function works differently.

```
import Cocoa

var testNumber : Double
testNumber = exp(3)                        20.08553692318767
testNumber = exp2(3)                       8
testNumber = __exp10(3)                    1000
testNumber = expm1(3)                      19.08553692318767
testNumber = pow(2,4)                      16
```

Figure 6-5. Seeing how different exponential functions work

Logarithmic Functions

Logarithm functions allow multiplication, division, and addition of large numbers in calculations similar to exponential functions. Some common logarithmic functions include

- **log**: Calculates the natural logarithm of number

- **log2**: Calculates the base-2 logarithm of a number

- **log10**: Calculates the base-10 logarithm of a number

- **log1p**: Calculates the natural log of $1+x$

To see how these different logarithmic functions work, follow these steps:

1. Make sure your IntroductoryPlayground file is loaded in Xcode.

2. Edit the code as follows:

    ```
    import Cocoa

    var testNumber : Double
    testNumber = log(3)
    testNumber = log2(3)
    testNumber = log10(3)
    testNumber = log1p(3)
    ```

Figure 6-6 shows how each type of logarithmic function works differently.

```
import Cocoa

var testNumber : Double
testNumber = log(3)
testNumber = log2(3)
testNumber = log10(3)
testNumber = log1p(3)
```

```
1.09861228866811
1.584962500721156
0.4771212547196624
1.386294361119891
```

Figure 6-6. Seeing how different logarithmic functions work

Using String Functions

Just as the Cocoa framework provides dozens of math functions, so does it also contain a handful of string manipulation functions. Some common string functions include

- **+**: Concatenates or combines two strings together such as "Hello " + "world", which creates the string "Hello world"

- **characters.count**: Returns the length of a string

- **capitalized**: Capitalizes the first letter of each word

- **lowercased()**: Converts an entire string to lowercase letters

- **uppercased()**: Converts an entire string to uppercase letters

- **isEmpty**: Checks if a string is empty or has at least one character

- **hasPrefix**: Checks if certain text appears at the beginning of a string

- **hasSuffix**: Checks if certain text appears at the end of a string

When using the + operator to append or combine strings, be careful of spaces. If you omit spaces, you might get unwanted results. For example, "Hello" + "world" creates the string "Helloworld" without any spaces. That's why you need to make sure you put a space in between words such as "Hello " + "world" to create "Hello world".

To see how these different string functions work, follow these steps:

1. Make sure IntroductoryPlayground is loaded in Xcode.

2. Edit the code as follows:

```
import Cocoa

var text : String = "Hello everyone!"

print (text.characters.count)
print (text.capitalized)
print (text.lowercased())
print (text.uppercased())
print (text.isEmpty)
print (text.hasPrefix ("Hello"))
print (text.hasSuffix ("world"))
```

Figure 6-7 shows how each type of logarithmic function works differently.

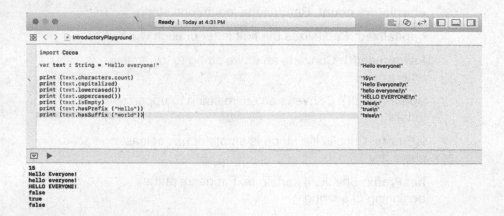

Figure 6-7. Seeing how different string functions work

Summary

The heart of any program is its ability to accept data, manipulate that data, and then return a useful result. The simplest way to manipulate numeric data is through common mathematical operators such as + (addition), - (subtraction), / (division), * (multiplication), and % (remainder). The common way to manipulate strings is through concatenation using the + operator, which combines two strings together.

As a shortcut, you can use the increment and decrement operators to add or subtract 1 from a variable. If you need to add or subtract values other than 1, you can use compound assignment operators instead.

Beyond these basic operators, you can also manipulate data through functions defined by the Cocoa framework. You don't have to know how these functions work; you just have to know they exist so you can use them in your own program by calling these function names.

Chapter 7

Making Decisions with Branches

After a program receives data, it needs to manipulate that data somehow to return a useful result. Simple programs manipulate data the same way, but more complicated programs need to make decisions on how to manipulate that data.

For example, a program might ask the user for a password. If the user types in a valid password, then the program gives the user access. If the user does not type in a valid password, then the program must display an error message and block access.

When a program analyzes data and makes a decision based on that data, it uses things called Boolean values and branching statements.

Boolean values represent either a true or false value. Branching statements give your program the option of choosing between two or more different sets of commands to follow. Boolean values combined with branching statements give programs the ability to respond to different data.

Understanding Comparison Operators

Earlier you learned about the common data types such as Int, Double, and String. Swift also includes a Boolean data type that can hold either a true or false value. You can create a Boolean variable by declaring a Bool data type, such as

```
var flag : Bool
```

© Wallace Wang 2017
W. Wang, *macOS Programming for Absolute Beginners*,
DOI 10.1007/978-1-4842-2662-9_7

139

Bool represents a Boolean data type. Any variable defined as a Bool data type can only hold one of two values, such as

```
flag = true
flag = false
```

While you can directly assign true and false to variables that represent Boolean data types, it's far more common to calculate Boolean values using comparison operators. Some common comparison operators are shown in Table 7-1.

Table 7-1. Common Comparison Operators in Swift

Comparison Operator	Purpose	Example	Boolean Value
==	Equal	5==14	False
<	Less than	5<14	True
>	Greater than	5>14	False
<=	Less than or equal to	5<=14	True
>=	Greater than or equal to	5>=14	False
!=	Not equal	5!=14	True

> **Note** The equal (==) comparison operator is the only comparison operator that can also compare strings such as "Joe" == "Fred" (which evaluates to false) or "Joe" == "Joe" (which evaluates to true).

Comparison operators compare two values, such as 38 == 8 or 29.04 > 12. The result of any comparison is always true or false. Since using actual values with comparison operators always returns the same true or false value, it's far more common to use comparison operators to compare a fixed value with a variable or to compare two variables, such as

```
let myValue = 45
myValue > 38          // Evaluates to true

let yourValue = 39
myValue < yourValue   // Evaluates to false
```

When you compare one or more variables, the results can change depending on the current value of those variables. However, when using the equal (==) comparison operator, be careful when working with decimal values. That's because 45.0 is not the same number as 45.0000001. When working with decimal values, it's best to use greater than or less than comparison operators.

To see how comparison operators create either a true or false value, follow these steps:

1.   Open the IntroductoryPlayground file in Xcode.

2.   Edit the code as follows:

```
import Cocoa
4 > 9
23 >= 12
3.4 < 8.5
73 <= 29
3.0 == 3.01
3.0 != 3.01
```

Notice that the right margin displays the Boolean value of each comparison operator, as shown in Figure 7-1.

```
import Cocoa

4 > 9                                                              false
23 >= 12                                                           true
3.4 < 8.5                                                          true
73 <= 29                                                           false
3.0 == 3.01                                                        false
3.0 != 3.01                                                        true
```

Figure 7-1. Comparison operators always evaluate to a true or false Boolean value

Understanding Logical Operators

Any comparison operator, such as 78 > 9, evaluates to a true or false value. However, Swift provides special logical operators just for working with two or more Boolean values, as shown in Table 7-2.

Table 7-2. Common Logical Operators in Swift

Comparison Operator	Purpose
&&	Add
||	Or
!	Not

Both the And (&&) and Or (||) logical operators take two Boolean values and convert them into a single Boolean value. The Not (!) logical operator takes one Boolean value and converts it to its opposite. Table 7-3 shows how the Not (!) logical operator works.

Table 7-3. The Not (!) Logical Operator

Example	Value
!true	False
!false	True

The And (&&) operator takes two Boolean values and calculates a single Boolean value based on Table 7-4.

Table 7-4. The And (&&) Logical Operator in Swift

First Boolean Value	Second Boolean Value	Result	
True	&&	True	True
True	&&	False	False
False	&&	True	False
False	&&	False	False

The Or (||) operator takes two Boolean values and calculates a single Boolean value based on Table 7-5.

Table 7-5. The Or (ll) Logical Operator in Swift

First Boolean Value	Second Boolean Value	Result	
True	||	True	True
True	||	False	True
False	||	True	True
False	||	False	False

To see how Boolean values work with comparison and logical operators, create a new playground by following these steps:

1. Open the IntroductoryPlayground file in Xcode.

2. Edit the code as follows:

```
import Cocoa

var x, y, z : Int

x = 35
y = 120
z = -48

x == y
x < y
x > z
y != z
z > -48

// And && operator

(y != z) && (x > z)
(y != z) && (x == y)
(x == y) && (x < y)
(z > -48) && (x == y)

// Or || operator

(y != z) || (x > z)
(y != z) || (x == y)
(x == y) || (x < y)
(z > -48) || (x == y)
```

Figure 7-2 shows how the comparison operators evaluate to true or false and how the logical operators (And and Or) take two Boolean values and return a single true or false value.

```
import Cocoa

var x, y, z : Int

x = 35                                                    35
y = 120                                                   120
z = -48                                                   -48

x == y                                                    false
x < y                                                     true
x > z                                                     true
y != z                                                    true
z > -48                                                   false


// And && operator

(y != z) && (x > z)                                       true
(y != z) && (x == y)                                      false
(x == y) && (x < y)                                       false
(z > -48) && (x == y)                                     false


// Or || operator

(y != z) || (x > z)                                       true
(y != z) || (x == y)                                      true
(x == y) || (x < y)                                       true
(z > -48) || (x == y)                                     false
```

Figure 7-2. Evaluating Boolean values with comparison and logical operators

Ultimately every Boolean value must be

■ A true or false value

■ A comparison of two values that is true or false

■ A combination of Boolean values using logical operators
   that evaluate to true or false

The if Statement

Boolean values are crucial for letting programs make choices. If someone
types in a password, a program checks to see if the password is valid.
If true (the password is valid), then the program grants access. If false
(the password is not valid), then the program blocks access.

To decide what to do next, every program needs to evaluate a Boolean value. Only then can it decide what to do next based on the value of that Boolean value.

The simplest type of branching statement in Swift is an if statement, which looks like this:

```
if BooleanValue == true {

}
```

To simplify this if statement, you can eliminate the "== true" portion so the if statement looks like this:

```
if BooleanValue {

}
```

This shortened version says, "If the BooleanValue is true, then run the code inside the curly brackets. If the BooleanValue is false, then skip all the code inside the curly brackets without running it."

To see how Boolean values work with an if statement, follow these steps:

1. Open the IntroductoryPlayground file in Xcode.

2. Edit the code as follows:

```
import Cocoa

var BooleanValue = true

if BooleanValue {
    print ("The BooleanValue is true")
}
```

Figure 7-3 shows the results of the if statement running. Change the value of BooleanValue to false and you'll see that the if statement no longer prints the string "The BooleanValue is true".

```
import Cocoa
var BooleanValue : Bool = true                                   true

if BooleanValue {
    print ("The BooleanValue is true")          "The BooleanValue is true\n"
}
```

Figure 7-3. Running an if statement

The if-else Statement

The major limitation of the if statement is that it either runs code or it runs nothing. If you want one set of code to run if a Boolean value is true and a second set of code to run if a Boolean value is false, you could write two separate if statements, as follows:

```
if BooleanValue {

}

if !BooleanValue {

}
```

The first if statement runs if the BooleanValue is true. If not, then it does nothing.

The second if statement runs if the BooleanValue is false. If not, then it does nothing.

The problem with writing two separate if statements is that the logic of your program isn't as clear. To fix this problem, Swift offers an if-else statement that looks like this:

```
if BooleanValue {
    // First set of code to run if true
} else {
    // Second set of code to run if false
}
```

An if-else statement offers exactly two different branches to follow. If a Boolean value is true, then the first set of code runs. If a Boolean value is false, then the second set of code runs. At no time is it possible for both sets of code to run in an if-else statement.

To see how Boolean values work with an if-else statement, follow these steps:

1. Open the IntroductoryPlayground file in Xcode.

2. Edit the code as follows:

    ```
    import Cocoa

    var BooleanValue = true
    ```

```
    if BooleanValue {
        print ("The BooleanValue is true")
    } else {
        print ("The BooleanValue is false")
    }
```

Figure 7-4 shows how the if-else statement works when BooleanValue is true. Change BooleanValue to false and see how the if-else statement now runs the second set of code.

```
import Cocoa

var BooleanValue : Bool = true                          true

if BooleanValue {
    print ("The BooleanValue is true")                  "The BooleanValue is true\n"
} else {
    print ("The BooleanValue is false")
}
```

Figure 7-4. Running an if-else statement

The if-else-if Statement

An if statement either runs one set of code or it runs nothing. An if-else statement always runs one set of code or a second set of code. However, what if you want a choice of running two or more possible sets of code? In this case, you need to use an if-else-if statement.

Like an if statement, an if-else-if statement may not run any code at all. The simplest if-else-if statement looks like this:

```
if BooleanValue {
    // First set of code to run if true
} else if BooleanValue2 {
    // Second set of code to run if true
}
```

With an if-else-if statement, a Boolean value must be true to run code. If no Boolean value is true, then it's possible that no code will run at all. An if-else-if statement is equivalent to multiple if statements like this:

```
if BooleanValue {
    // First set of code to run if true
}

if BooleanValue2 {
    // Second set of code to run if true
}
```

With an if-else-if statement, you can check for as many Boolean values as you want, such as

```
if BooleanValue {
    // First set of code to run if true
} else if BooleanValue2 {
    // Second set of code to run if true
} else if BooleanValue3 {
    // Third set of code to run if true
} else if BooleanValue4 {
    // Fourth set of code to run if true
} else if BooleanValue5 {
    // Fifth set of code to run if true
}
```

As soon as the if-else-if statement finds one Boolean value is true, then it runs the accompanying code trapped within curly brackets. However, it's possible that no Boolean value will be true, in which case no code inside the if-else-if statement will run.

If you want to insure that at least one set of code will run, then you need to add a final else clause to the end of an if-else-if statement, such as

```
if BooleanValue {
    // First set of code to run if true
} else if BooleanValue2 {
    // Second set of code to run if true
} else if BooleanValue3 {
    // Third set of code to run if true
} else if BooleanValue4 {
    // Fourth set of code to run if true
} else if BooleanValue5 {
    // Fifth set of code to run if true
} else {
    // This code runs if every other Boolean value is false
}
```

To see how Boolean values work with an if-else statement, follow these steps:

1. Open the IntroductoryPlayground file in Xcode.

2. Edit the code as follows:

    ```
    import Cocoa

    var BooleanValue = false
    var BooleanValue2 = false
    var BooleanValue3 = false
    ```

```
if BooleanValue {
    print ("BooleanValue is true")
} else if BooleanValue2 {
    print ("BooleanValue2 is true")
} else if BooleanValue3 {
    print ("BooleanValue3 is true")
} else {
    print ("This prints if everything else is false")
}
```

Notice that because every Boolean value is false, the only code that runs occurs in the final else portion of the if-else if statement, as shown in Figure 7-5.

```
import Cocoa

var BooleanValue : Bool = false          false
var BooleanValue2 : Bool = false         false
var BooleanValue3 : Bool = false         false

if BooleanValue {
    print ("BooleanValue is true")
} else if BooleanValue2 {
    print ("BooleanValue2 is true")
} else if BooleanValue3 {
    print ("BooleanValue3 is true")
} else {
    print ("This prints if everything else is false")    "This prints if everything else is false\n"
}
```

Figure 7-5. Running an if-else if statement with multiple Boolean values

If you change different Boolean values to true, you can see how the if-else-if statement behaves differently by running a different set of code.

With an if-else-if statement,

■ It's possible that no code will run unless the last part is just a regular else statement.

■ The program can choose between two or more sets of code.

■ The number of possible options is not limited to just two options like an if-else statement.

Since an if-else-if statement checks multiple Boolean values, what happens if two or more Boolean values are true? In this case, the if-else-if statement only runs the set of code associated with the first true Boolean value and ignores all the rest of the code, as shown in Figure 7-6.

```
import Cocoa

var BooleanValue : Bool = true                    true
var BooleanValue2 : Bool = true                   true
var BooleanValue3 : Bool = true                   true

if BooleanValue {
    print ("BooleanValue is true")                "BooleanValue is true\n"
} else if BooleanValue2 {
    print ("BooleanValue2 is true")
} else if BooleanValue3 {
    print ("BooleanValue3 is true")
} else {
    print ("This prints if everything else is false")
}
```

Figure 7-6. Running an if-else-if statement with multiple true Boolean values

The switch Statement

An if-else-if statement lets you create two or more sets of code that can possibly run. Unfortunately, an if-else-if statement can be hard to understand when there's too many Boolean values to check. To fix this problem, Swift offers a switch statement.

A switch statement works much like an if-else-if statement except that it's easier to read and write. The main difference is that instead of checking multiple Boolean values, a switch statement checks the value of a single variable. Based on the value of this single variable, the switch statement can choose to run different sets of code.

The simplest switch statement checks if a variable is exactly equal to different values, such as

```
switch value/variable/expression {
    case value1: // First set of code to run if variable = value1
    case value2: // Second set of code to run if variable = value2
    case value3: // Third set of code to run if variable = value3
        default: // Fourth set of code to run if nothing else runs
}
```

A switch statement starts by examining a fixed value (such as 38 or "Bob"), a variable (which represents data), or an expression (such as 3 * age where age is a variable). Ultimately, the switch statement needs to identify a single value and match that value to the first "case" statement it finds. The moment it finds an exact match, it runs one or more lines of code associates with that "case" statement.

To see how Boolean values work with a case statement, follow these steps:

1. Open the IntroductoryPlayground file in Xcode.

2. Edit the code as follows:

```
import Cocoa

var whatNumber = 3

switch whatNumber {
    case 1: print ("The number is 1")
    case 2: print ("The number is 2")
    case 3: print ("The number is 3")
        print ("Isn't this amazing?")
    case 4: print ("The number is 4")
    case 5: print ("The number is 5")
    default: print ("The number is undefined")
}
```

Because the value of the whatNumber variable is 3, the switch statement matches it with case 3: and then runs the Swift code that appears after the colon, as shown in Figure 7-7. Note that you can store multiple lines of code after the colon and you do not need to enclose the code within curly brackets. Change the value of the whatNumber variable to see how it affects the behavior of the switch statement.

```
import Cocoa

var whatNumber : Int = 3                                    3

switch whatNumber {
case 1: print ("The number is 1")
case 2: print ("The number is 2")
case 3: print ("The number is 3")          "The number is 3\n"
print ("Isn't this amazing?")              "Isn't this amazing?\n"
case 4: print ("The number is 4")
case 5: print ("The number is 5")
default: print ("The number is undefined")
}
```

Figure 7-7. Running a switch statement to match an exact value

> **Note** Unlike other programming languages like Objective-C, you do not need to use a break command to separate code stored in different "case" statements of the switch statement.

The above switch statement is equivalent to

```
if whatNumber == 1 {
    print ("The number is 1")
} else if whatNumber == 2 {
    print ("The number is 2")
} else if whatNumber == 3 {
    print ("The number is 3")
    print ("Isn't this amazing?")
} else if whatNumber == 4 {
    print ("The number is 4")
} else if whatNumber == 5 {
    print ("The number is 5")
} else {
    print ("The number is undefined")
}
```

As you can see, the switch statement is cleaner and simpler to read and understand.

What creating a switch statement, you must handle all possibilities. In the above switch statement, the whatNumber variable can be any integer, so the switch statement can explicitly handle any value from 1 to 5. If the value does not fall within this 1 to 5 range, then the default portion of the switch statement handles any other value. If you fail to include a default, then Xcode will flag your switch statement as a possible error. This is to protect your code from possibly crashing if the switch statement receives data it doesn't know how to handle.

This example of a switch statement tries to match a value/variable/ expression with exactly one value. However, a switch statement can try matching more than one value. There are three ways a switch statement can check a range of values:

- Explicitly list all possible values, separated by a comma

- Define the starting and ending range of numbers separated by three dots (...)

- Define the starting number and the ending range with two dots and a less-than sign (..<)

When a case statement lists all values separated by commas, its code will run only if the switch value/variable/expression exactly matches one of those values. For example, consider the following case statement:

```
switch whatNumber {
    case 1, 2, 3: print ("The number is 1, 2, or 3")
        default: print ("The number is undefined")
}
```

Only if the value of whatNumber is 1, 2, or 3 will its code print "The number is 1, 2, or 3".

Explicitly listing all possible values may be fine for a handful of numbers, but for multiple numbers, it can get tedious to write every possible number. As a shortcut, Swift lets you specify a range. If you want to match a number between 4 and 20, the case portion of the switch statement might look like this:

```
switch whatNumber {
        case 4...20: print ("The number is between 4 and 20")
        default: print ("The number is undefined")
}
```

In this case, whatNumber could be 4, 20, or any number in between. The three dots signify a range that includes the starting and ending number of the range (4 and 20).

Swift can also check a half range that consists of two dots and a less-than symbol, such as

```
switch whatNumber {
        case 20..<49: print ("The number is between 20 and 48")
        default: print ("The number is undefined")
}
```

This 20..<49 half range matches only if whatNumber is 20, 48, or any number in between. Notice that if whatNumber is 49, it will not match the half range but if whatNumber is 20, then it will match.

To see how all three variations of multiple values works, follow these steps:

1. Open the IntroductoryPlayground file in Xcode.

2. Edit the code as follows:

   ```
   import Cocoa

   var whatNumber = 49

   switch whatNumber {
       case 1, 2, 3: print ("The number is 1")
           println ("Isn't this amazing?")
       case 4...20: print ("The number is between 4 and 20")
           case 20..<49: print ("The number is between 20 and 48")
           default: print ("The number is undefined")
   }
   ```

When the value is 49, the switch statement matches nothing so it uses the default portion of the switch statement, as shown in Figure 7-8.

```
import Cocoa

var whatNumber : Int = 49                            49

switch whatNumber {
case 1, 2, 3: print ("The number is 1")
    print ("Isn't this amazing?")
case 4...20: print ("The number is between 4 and 20")
case 20..<49: print ("The number is between 20 and 48")
default: print ("The number is undefined")           "The number is undefined\n"
}
```

Figure 7-8. Running a switch statement that checks for multiple values

Change the value of the whatNumber variable to 2, 12, and 48 to see how the switch statement matches different values.

In the previous example, the switch statement could check for multiple values (1, 2, 3) or a range of values (4...20) and (20..<49). However, sometimes you may want to check if a value is less than, less than or equal, greater than, or greater than or equal. To check for <, <=, >, or >= in a switch statement, you have to use the following:

```
case _ where variableName < value:
```

The _ where code tells Swift to match this case if a specific variable is <, <=, >, or >= to a certain value. To see how to check for <. <=. >, or >= in a switch statement, follow these steps:

1. Open the IntroductoryPlayground file in Xcode.

2. Edit the code as follows:

```
import Cocoa

var whatNumber = 49

switch whatNumber {
        case _ where whatNumber < 1: print ("The number is less
        than 1")
        case _ where whatNumber <= 10: print ("The number is less
        than or equal to 10")
        case _ where whatNumber >= 11 : print ("The number is
        greater than or equal to 11")
        default: print ("The number is undefined")
}
```

When the value is 49, the switch statement matches the >= 11 case statement so it prints "The number is greater than or equal to 11"; see Figure 7-9.

```
import Cocoa

var whatNumber : Int = 49                                    49

switch whatNumber {
case _ where whatNumber < 1: print ("The number is less
    than 1")
case _ where whatNumber <= 10: print ("The number is
    less than or equal to 10")
case _ where whatNumber >= 11 : print ("The number is     "The number is greater than or equal to 11\n"
    greater than or equal to 11")
default: print ("The number is undefined")
}
```

Figure 7-9. Running a switch statement that checks for multiple values

Making Decisions in an macOS Program

Using playground files to test out Swift code can be fun and simple because you can focus solely on learning how Swift works without the interference of other parts of writing a program. However, eventually you'll need to see how Swift code works outside of your playground file.

In this sample program, the user needs to type an employee ID number and password. The employee ID number must fall within a range of 100 to 150 to be valid. The password must exactly match the string "password" (which isn't a very secure password).

This means you'll be using two comparison operators to check if the name and password are valid. Then you'll use a logical operator to make sure that both are valid.

Create a new macOS project by following these steps:

1. From within Xcode choose File ➤ New ➤ Project.

2. Click Application under the macOS category.

3. Click Cocoa Application and click the Next button. Xcode now asks for a product name.

4. Click in the Product Name text field and type **BranchingProgram**.

5. Make sure the Language pop-up menu displays Swift and that no check boxes are selected.

6. Click the Next button. Xcode asks where you want to store the project.

7. Choose a folder to store your project and click the Create button.

8. Click the `MainMenu.xib` file in the Project Navigator.

9. Click the Window icon to make the window of the user interface appear, as shown in Figure 7-10.

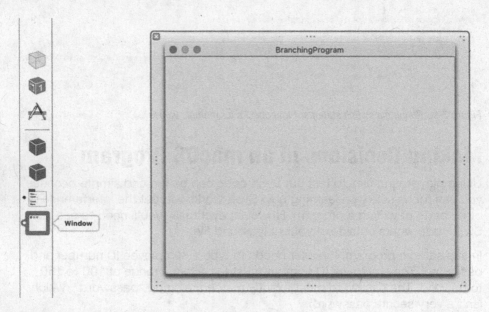

Figure 7-10. Making the window of the user interface visible

10. Choose View ➤ Utilities ➤ Show Object Library to make the Object Library appear in the bottom right corner of the Xcode window.

11. Drag two labels, two text fields, and a push button on the user interface so it looks similar to Figure 7-11.

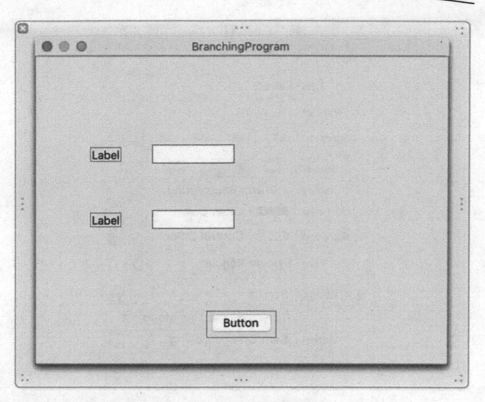

Figure 7-11. Creating a basic user interface with labels, text fields, and a push button

12. Click the top label to select it. Then choose
    View ➤ Utilities ➤ Show Attributes Inspector. The
    Attributes Inspector pane appears in the upper right
    corner of the Xcode window, as shown in Figure 7-12.

Figure 7-12. The Attributes Inspector pane for a label

13. Click in the Title text field and replace Label with **ID**. Press Return. Notice that the top label now displays reads ID. When you change a label's Title property, you change the text that appears on that label. Let's see a second and faster way to change the text on a label.

14. Double-click the second label. Xcode highlights your chosen label, as shown in Figure 7-13.

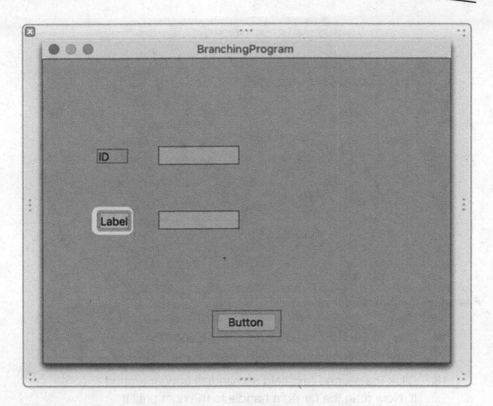

Figure 7-13. *Double-clicking on a label lets you change the text without using the Attributes Inspector pane*

15. Type **Password** and press Return. Notice that the second label now displays Password. By double-clicking a label, you can change text on that label without opening the Attributes Inspector pane.

16. Click the top text field and choose View ➤ Utilities ➤ Show Size Inspector. The Size Inspector pane appears in the upper right corner of the Xcode window, as shown in Figure 7-14.

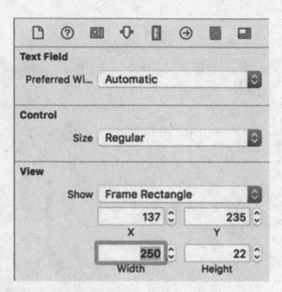

Figure 7-14. The Size Inspector pane

17. Click in the Width text field and type **250**. Then press Return. Xcode expands with width of the text field.

18. Click the second text field so handles appear around it. Now drag the far right handle to the right until it aligns with the top text field, as shown in Figure 7-15.

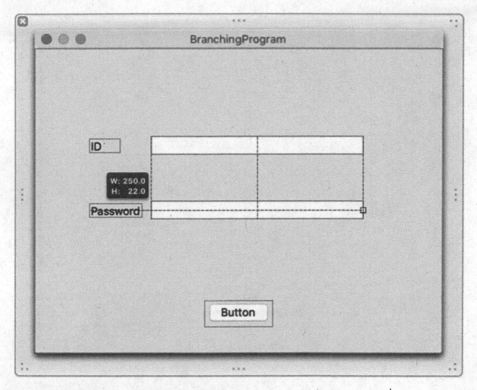

Figure 7-15. Aligning a text field using the mouse

19. Release the mouse button. Just as you can modify
     text on a label by using either the Attributes
     Inspector pane or double-clicking directly on that
     label, so can you modify the size of an item through
     the Size Inspector pane or by resizing that item with
     the mouse.

20. Double-click the push button to select it and type
     Check Password. Then press Return. Your completed
     interface should look similar to Figure 7-16.

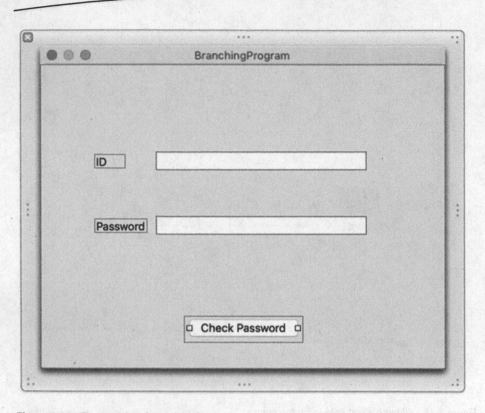

Figure 7-16. The completed user interface

With this user interface, the user will type an ID (an integer) into the ID text field, a password (string) in the Password text field, and then click the Check Password button to see if the ID and password are valid. Once you have a user interface, the next step is to connect the user interface to Swift code using IBOutlets and IBAction methods.

Remember, IBOutlets let you retrieve or display information to a user interface. IBAction methods let the user interface make your program do something.

In this example, you'll need two IBOutlet variables to connect to each text field so you can retrieve the data the user types in. Then you'll need one IBAction method to connect to the Check Password button. This way, when the user clicks the Change Password button, the IBAction method can verify the ID and password.

To connect Swift code to your user interface, follow these steps:

1. With your user interface still visible in the Xcode window, choose View ➤ Assistant Editor ➤ Show Assistant Editor. The AppDelegate.swift file appears next to the user interface, as shown in Figure 7-17.

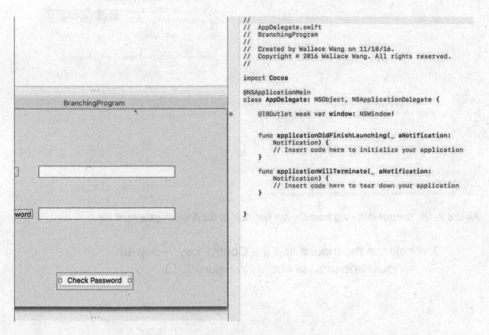

```swift
//
//  AppDelegate.swift
//  BranchingProgram
//
//  Created by Wallace Wang on 11/10/16.
//  Copyright © 2016 Wallace Wang. All rights reserved.
//

import Cocoa

@NSApplicationMain
class AppDelegate: NSObject, NSApplicationDelegate {

    @IBOutlet weak var window: NSWindow!

    func applicationDidFinishLaunching(_ aNotification:
        Notification) {
        // Insert code here to initialize your application
    }

    func applicationWillTerminate(_ aNotification:
        Notification) {
        // Insert code here to tear down your application
    }

}
```

Figure 7-17. The Assistant Editor displays the user interface next to the AppDelegate.swift file

2. Move the mouse over the top text field, hold down the Control key, and drag from the top text field to underneath the existing @IBOutlet line in the AppDelegate.swift file, as shown in Figure 7-18.

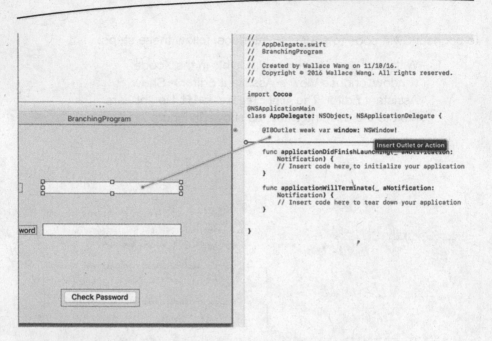

```
//
//  AppDelegate.swift
//  BranchingProgram
//
//  Created by Wallace Wang on 11/10/16.
//  Copyright © 2016 Wallace Wang. All rights reserved.
//

import Cocoa

@NSApplicationMain
class AppDelegate: NSObject, NSApplicationDelegate {

    @IBOutlet weak var window: NSWindow!

    func applicationDidFinishLaunching(_ aNotification:
        Notification) {
        // Insert code here, to initialize your application
    }

    func applicationWillTerminate(_ aNotification:
        Notification) {
        // Insert code here to tear down your application
    }

}
```

BranchingProgram

word

Check Password

Figure 7-18. Control-dragging from the top text field to the AppDelegate.swift file

3. Release the mouse and the Control key. A pop-up
    window appears, as shown in Figure 7-19.

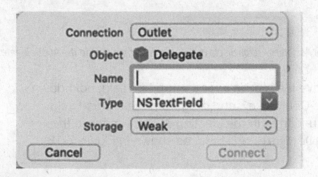

Figure 7-19. The pop-up window for defining an IBOutlet

4. Click in the Name text field and type **IDField** and
    click the Connect button. Xcode creates an IBOutlet.

5. Move the mouse over the bottom text field,
    hold down the Control key, and drag the mouse
    underneath the @IBOutlet line in the AppDelegate.
    swift file.

6. Release the mouse and the Control key. A pop-up window appears.

7. Click in the Name text field and type **PasswordField** and click the Connect button. Xcode creates another IBOutlet. You should now have two IBOutlets that represent the two text fields on your user interface:

```
@IBOutlet weak var IDField: NSTextField!
@IBOutlet weak var PasswordField: NSTextField!
```

8. Move the mouse over the Check Password push button, hold down the Control key, and drag the mouse above the last curly bracket in the AppDelegate.swift file, as shown in Figure 7-20.

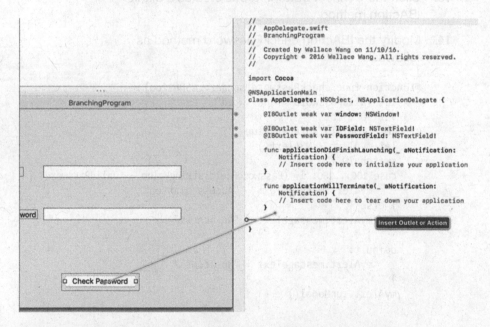

Figure 7-20. Control dragging from the push button to the AppDelegate.swift file

9. Release the mouse and the Control key. A pop-up window appears.

10. Click in the Connection pop-up menu and choose Action to create an IBAction method.

11. Click in the Name text field and type **checkPassword**.

12. Click in the Type pop-up menu and choose NSButton, as shown in Figure 7-21.

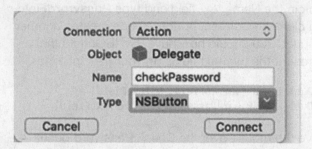

Figure 7-21. Defining an IBAction method

13. Click the Connect button. Xcode creates a blank IBAction method.

14. Modify the IBAction checkPassword method as follows:

```
@IBAction func checkPassword(sender: NSButton) {
    let validPassword = "password"
    var ID : Int
    ID = IDField.integerValue
    let myAlert = NSAlert()
    switch ID {
    case 100...150: if (PasswordField.stringValue == validPassword) {
        myAlert.messageText = "Access granted"
    } else {
        myAlert.messageText = "No access"
        }
    default:
        myAlert.messageText = "No access"
    }
    myAlert.runModal()

}
```

This IBAction method uses a switch statement to check if the user typed an ID that falls within the 100...150 range. If so, then it checks if the user typed "password" in the Password text field. If this is also true, then the switch statement displays "Access granted" in an Alert dialog. If the ID does not fall within the 100...150 range or the Password text field does not contain "password", then the Alert dialog displays "No access."

In the above IBAction code, you could also replace these two lines:

```
var ID : Int
ID = IDField.integerValue
```

with a single line that uses type inference like this:

```
var ID = IDField.integerValue
```

> **Note** You may be wondering where `stringValue` and `integerValue` came from in the above code. If you look at your IBOutlets, you'll see that each text field IBOutlet is based on the `NSTextField` class. Look up `NSTextField` in Xcode's documentation and you'll see that `NSTextField` is based on the `NSControl` class. The `NSControl` class contains properties like `stringValue` and `integerValue` so that means anything based on `NSTextField` (such as the IBOutlets that represent the text fields on your user interface) can also use these `stringValue` and `integerValue` properties.

15. Choose Product ➤ Run. Xcode runs your BranchingProgram project.

16. Click in the ID text field of your BranchingProgram user interface and type **120**.

17. Click in the Password text field of your BranchingProgram user interface and type **password**.

18. Click the Check Password push button. An Alert dialog appears, as shown in Figure 7-22.

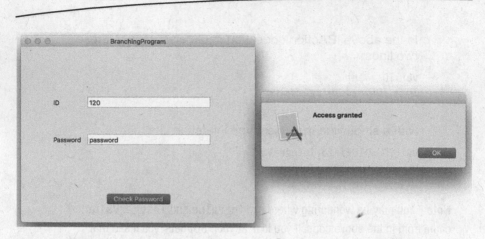

Figure 7-22. Displaying an Alert dialog

19. Click the OK button in the Alert dialog to make it go away.

20. Click in the ID text field of your BranchingProgram user interface and type **1**.

21. Click the Check Password push button. Notice that now the Alert dialog displays "No access."

22. Click the OK button in the Alert dialog to make it go away.

23. Choose BranchingProgram ➤ Quit BranchingProgram.

Summary

To respond intelligently to the user, every program needs a way to make decisions. The first step to making a decision is to define a Boolean value, which is either true or false. Boolean values can be calculated through comparison operators or logical operators.

Once you can determine a Boolean value, then you can use that Boolean value to decide which code to follow in a branching statement. The simplest branch is an if statement that either runs a set of code or does nothing at all.

Another branch is the if-else statement, which offers exactly two sets of code to run. If a Boolean value is true, then the first set of code runs. Otherwise, the second set of code runs.

If you want to choose between three or more sets of code to run, you can use an if-else-if statement. However, it's often simpler to use a switch statement instead. When using a switch statement, you must anticipate all possible values.

A switch statement lets you match an exact value, a list of values, a range of values (which includes the beginning and ending numbers), a half range of values (which only includes the beginning number but not the end), or <, <=, >, and >= comparisons.

Branching statements combined with Boolean values gives your program the ability to make decisions and run different code based on the data it receives. Branching statements essentially let your program respond intelligently to outside data.

Chapter 8

Repeating Code with Loops

The basic goal of programming is to write as little code as possible that does as much as possible. The less code you write, the easier the program will be to understand and to modify later. The more your code does, the more powerful your program will be.

One way to write less code is to reuse code stored in functions. A second way to reuse code is through loops. A loop runs one or more lines of code multiple times, thereby eliminating the need to write multiple, redundant lines of code.

For example, if you want to print a message five times, you can write the following:

```
print ("Hello")
print ("Hello")
print ("Hello")
print ("Hello")
print ("Hello")
```

This is tedious but it will work. However, if you suddenly decide you need to print a message a thousand times, now you must write that command a thousand times. Not only is typing the same command tedious, but it increases the chance of making a mistake in one of those commands.

A far simpler method is to use a loop. A loop lets you write one or more commands once and then run those commands as many times as you want, such as

© Wallace Wang 2017
W. Wang, *macOS Programming for Absolute Beginners*,
DOI 10.1007/978-1-4842-2662-9_8

```
var counter = 1
while counter <= 5 {
    print ("Hello")
    counter = counter + 1
}
```

The above loop runs five times and prints "Hello" five times. If you want to print "Hello" a thousand times, you can just replace the number 5 with the number 1000. Loops make code easier to write and modify while doing more work at the same time.

The while Loop

The simplest loop in Swift is called the while loop, which looks like this:

```
while BooleanValue {

}
```

Before the while loop does anything, it first checks if a Boolean value is true or false. If it's true, then it runs the code inside its curly brackets once. Then it checks its Boolean value again to see if it's changed to false or if it's still true. The moment this Boolean value becomes false, the while loop stops.

Because the while loop checks a Boolean value before doing anything, it's possible that the while loop may never run any of its code. More importantly, the while loop only runs if its Boolean value is true. This means somewhere inside the while loop's curly brackets, there must be code that eventually changes this Boolean value to false.

If a while loop fails to change its Boolean value from true to false, then the loop will run forever, which is known as an endless loop. An endless loop may crash or freeze your program so it no longer responds to the user.

At the simplest level, a while loop's Boolean value can just be true or false, such as

```
while true {

}
```

More commonly, while loops use comparison operators to determine a Boolean value, such as

```
while counter <= 5 {

}
```

As long as counter <=5 remains true, the while loop will run. The moment counter <= 5 is no longer true, the while loop will stop.

When using while loops, you need to define the Boolean value before the loop begins (to make sure it's either true or false) and then you must change the Boolean value somewhere inside the while loop (to make sure the while loop eventually stops).

To see how Boolean values work with a while loop, create a new playground by following these steps:

1. Open the Introductory Playground file in Xcode.

2. Edit the code as follows:

```
import Cocoa

var counter = 1

while counter <= 10 {
    print ("Hello")
    counter = counter + 1
}
```

Note that the var counter = 1 line defines the variable that the while loop uses to determine a Boolean value (true or false). Also note the counter = counter + 1 line inside the while loop. This constantly changes the variable used by the while loop to determine when to stop. By changing the Boolean comparison (counter <=10), you can change how many times the while loop runs.

To make sure you can see what the print command does, click the Show Debug area icon in the bottom left corner to make the Debug area appear, as shown in Figure 8-1.

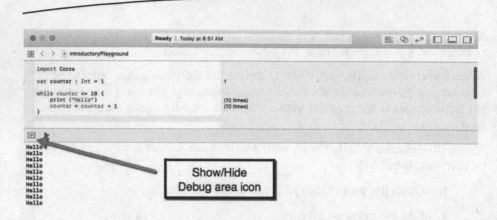

Figure 8-1. Running a while loop in a playground

When using a while loop, keep in mind the following:

- Before the while loop, make sure to define any variables used by the while loop's Boolean value (such as the var counter = 1 line).

- A while loop may run zero or more times.

- Inside the while loop, make sure the Boolean value used by the while loop can change to false eventually to avoid creating an endless loop (such as the counter = counter + 1 line).

The repeat-while Loop

As an alternative to the while loop, Swift also offers a repeat-while loop that works exactly the same way. The only difference is that instead of checking a Boolean value before running, the repeat-while loop checks its Boolean value after it runs.

This means the repeat-while loop will always run at least once. The structure of a repeat-while loop looks like this:

```
repeat {

} while BooleanValue
```

Like the while loop, the repeat-while loop also needs code inside its loop that can change its Boolean value from true to false, and it also needs code before the repeat-while loop to initialize any variables that are used to calculate the repeat-while loop's Boolean value.

To see how Boolean values work with a repeat-while loop, follow these steps:

1. Make sure the IntroductoryPlayground file is loaded in Xcode.

2. Edit the code as follows:

```
import Cocoa

var counter = 1
repeat {
    print ("Goodbye")
    counter = counter + 1
} while counter <= 10
```

Notice that the Boolean value (counter <= 10) determines how many times the repeat-while loop runs, as shown in Figure 8-2.

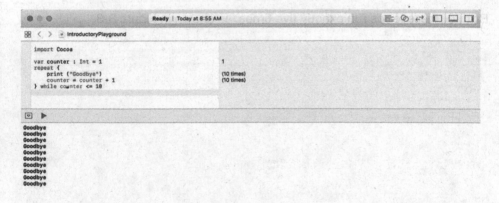

Figure 8-2. Running a repeat-while loop in a playground

Remember, the main difference between the while loop and the repeat-while loop is that the repeat-while loop always runs at least once while the while loop may never run at all if its Boolean value is initially false.

The for-in Loop

How many times will a while or repeat-while loop repeat? It all depends on its Boolean value. If you want to run a loop a fixed number of times, you can simply count using either a while or repeat-while loop, such as

```
var counter = 1

while counter <= 5 {
    print ("while loop \(counter)")
    counter = counter + 1
}

counter = 1

repeat {
    print ("repeat loop \(counter)")
counter = counter + 1
} while counter <= 5
```

Both of these loops run exactly five times, as shown in Figure 8-3.

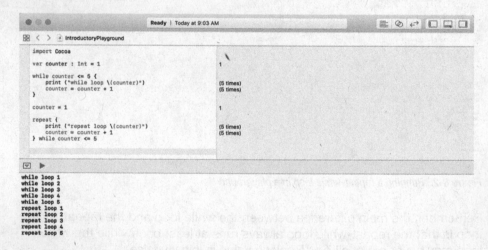

Figure 8-3. *A while and repeat-while loop can run a fixed number of times*

Note that the print command can only print strings. Any time you want to use a non-string value in the print command, you can enclose it within parentheses with a \ symbol in front of it such as \(counter).

Using a while or repeat-while loop to count can be clumsy because you must make sure you create a counting variable and that you constantly update that counting variable within the while or repeat-while loop to avoid an endless loop.

When you want a loop to run a fixed number of times, it's far better to use a for-in loop. The main advantage is that the for-in loop automatically knows how to count so you don't have to specify when to stop.

To use the for-in loop, you need to specify the following:

- A starting value

- An ending value

- The range between the starting and ending values, such as ... or ..<

The structure of a for-in loop looks like this:

```
for countingVariable in startingValue...endingValue {

}
```

This tells Swift to start counting by 1 at the startingValue and stop when it reaches the endingValue, such as

```
for i in 1...5 {
    print ("Loop \(i)")
}
```

The above for-in loop counts from 1, 2, 3, 4, and stops after 5. The following similar for-in loop uses a different range that tells Swift to stop counting before the endingValue:

```
for i in 1..<5 {
    print ("Second loop \(i)")
}
```

Unlike the previous for-in loop, this for-in loop counts from 1, 2, 3, and stops after 4, as shown in Figure 8-4.

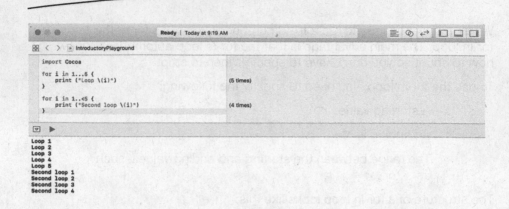

Figure 8-4. Comparing different ranges in a for-in loop

Notice that the for-in loop is far simpler than the while or repeat-while loop that requires initializing a counting variable and then updating that counting variable within the loop to prevent an endless loop.

By default, the for-in loop always counts by 1. If you want to count by values other than 1, you can specify an increment value as follows:

```
for i in startValue...endValue where i%incrementValue == 0 {

}
```

This for-in loop uses the remainder operator (%) to determine which values to count. So if you want to count by 3, you can use the following for-in loop:

```
for i in 1...20 where i%3 == 0 {

}
```

This for-in loop starts counting at 1 but before it runs any code inside the curly brackets, it divides the counting variable (i) by 3 to determine if it's evenly divisible by 3 (equals to 0 as shown in the Swift code == 0). If the counting variable (i) is evenly divisible by 3, then it runs the code inside the loop.

To see if the for-in loop works by counting in increments, create a new playground by following these steps:

1. Open the Introductory Playground file in Xcode.

2. Edit the code as follows:

   ```
   for i in 1...20 where i%3 == 0 {
       print ("Loop \(i)")
   }
   ```

This for-in loop starts at 1, but 1%3 is not equal to 0 so it skips to 2. However, 2%3 is also not equal to it skips to 3. Since 3%3 is equal to 0, it runs the code inside the curly brackets and prints "Loop 3". This continues until the counting variable (i) reaches 20, as shown in Figure 8-5.

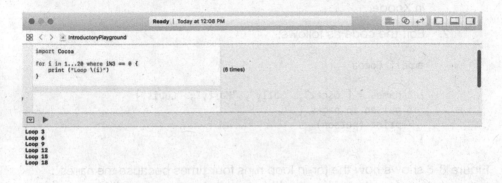

Figure 8-5. *The for-in loop can count in increments*

If you replace i%3 with i%4, the for-in loop will count by 4. Just by changing this value, you can define how the for-in loop counts in increments other than 1.

Counting Through Arrays with the for-in Loop

The most straightforward way to use a for-in statement is to specify a starting and ending value to count from 1 to 10 or 0 to 34. However, the for-in loop can also be especially handy for counting through lists of data stored in an array (which is a type of data structure). The for-in loop automatically knows where to begin and end so you never have to worry about counting how many items yourself.

The structure of a for-in loop for counting through a list of data looks like this:

```
for countingVariable in listOfItems {

}
```

The countingVariable counts each item in a list of some kind, and listOfItems represents a list of some kind such as an array (which consists of a list of data). To see how for-in loops can work, follow these steps:

1. Make sure the IntroductoryPlayground file is loaded in Xcode.

2. Edit the code as follows:

```
import Cocoa

let names = ["Oscar", "Sally", "Marty", "Louis"]
for person in names {
    print (person)
}
```

Figure 8-6 shows how the for-in loop runs four times because the names array contains four items. If you add or subtract a name from this array, the for-in loop automatically counts the new number of items in the array.

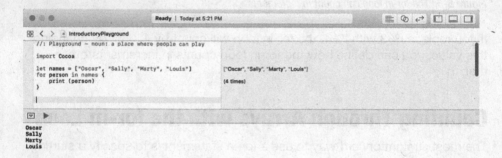

Figure 8-6. Counting through an array with a for-in loop

Exiting Loops Prematurely

Normally loops run until a Boolean value changes. However, you can prematurely exit out of a loop by using the break command. Normally this loop will run four times:

```
let names = ["Oscar", "Sally", "Marty", "Louis"]
for person in names {
    print (person)
}
```

If you insert a break command, you can make this loop exit after running only once, like this:

```
let names = ["Oscar", "Sally", "Marty", "Louis"]
for person in names {
    print (person)
    break
}
```

This for-in loop will run once, print the name "Oscar", hit the break command, and exit out of the for-in loop. Of course, it's rather pointless to put a break command inside a for-in loop to stop it prematurely all the time, so it's more common to use the break command with a branching statement. That way if a certain Boolean value is true, the loop exits prematurely. Otherwise, the loop keeps running.

To see how to exit out of the loop prematurely, follow these steps:

1. Make sure the IntroductoryPlayground file is loaded in Xcode.

2. Edit the code as follows:

    ```
    import Cocoa

    let employees = ["Fred", "Jane", "Sam", "Kelly"]
    for person in employees {
        if person == "Sam" {
            print ("Break command")
            break
        }
        print (person)
    }
    ```

This for-in loop will normally run four times because the employees array contains four names. However, as soon as the for-in loop finds the name "Sam", it prints that name, hits the break command, and prematurely exits out of the for-in loop, so it only runs three times, as shown in Figure 8-7.

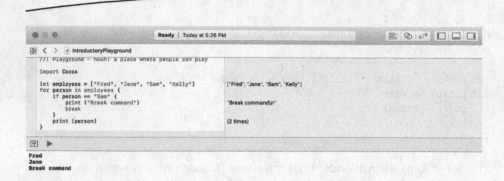

Figure 8-7. Using the break command to exit out of a loop prematurely

Using Loops in an macOS Program

In the following sample program, the computer picks a random number between 1 and 10. The user must guess that number. To keep the user from guessing a number outside the range of 1 and 10, the user interface will let the user choose a value from a slider.

Each time the user guesses incorrectly, a label will display a message that the guess is too high or too low. When the user correctly guesses the number, a loop will print a list of each guess and display it in an alert dialog.

Create a new macOS project by following these steps:

1. From within Xcode choose File ➤ New ➤ Project.

2. Click Application under the macOS category.

3. Click Cocoa Application and click the Next button. Xcode now asks for a product name.

4. Click in the Product Name text field and type **LoopingProgram**.

5. Make sure the Language pop-up menu displays Swift and that no check boxes are selected.

6. Click the Next button. Xcode asks where you want to store the project.

7. Choose a folder to store your project and click the Create button.

8. Click the `MainMenu.xib` file in the Project Navigator.

9.   Click the Window icon to make the window of the
     user interface appear, as shown in Figure 8-8.

Figure 8-8. Making the window of the user interface visible

10.   Choose View ➤ Utilities ➤ Show Object Library to
      make the Object Library appear in the bottom right
      corner of the Xcode window.

11.   Drag a horizontal slider, two labels, and a push
      button on the user interface and resize them so the
      user interface looks similar to Figure 8-9.

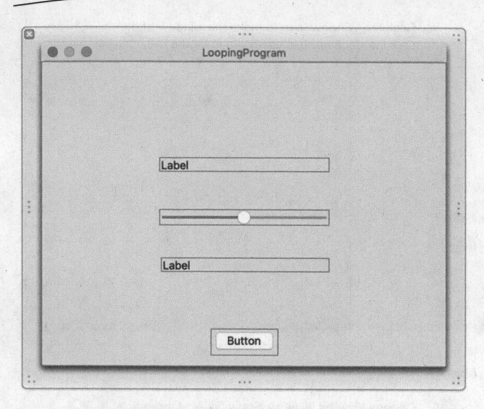

Figure 8-9. *Creating a basic user interface with two labels, a horizontal slider, and a push button*

12. Double-click the top label to select it. Then choose View ➤ Utilities ➤ Show Attributes Inspector. The Attributes Inspector pane appears in the upper right corner of the Xcode window.

13. Click in the Title text field and type **Guess a number**.

14. Click the Center alignment icon, as shown in Figure 8-10.

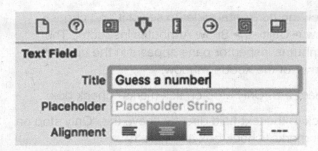

Figure 8-10. The Attributes Inspector pane for a label

15. Double-click the bottom label and type **Your guesses =** and then press Return.

16. Double-click the push button, type **Guess**, and then press Return. Your user interface should look like Figure 8-11.

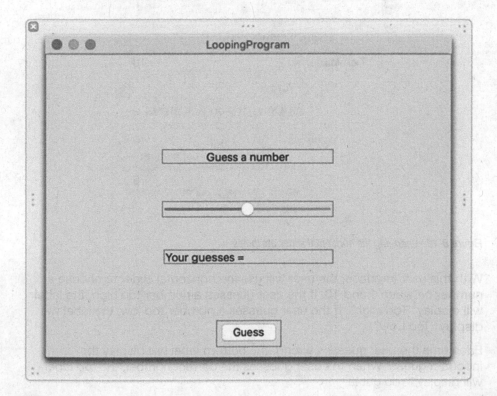

Figure 8-11. The completed user interface

17. Click the horizontal slider to select it and choose View ➤ Utilities ➤ Show Attributes Inspector. The Attributes Inspector pane appears in the upper right corner of the Xcode window.

18. Select the "Only stop on tick marks" check box.

19. Click in the text field directly above the "Only stop on tick marks" check box and type **10**.

20. Click in the Minimum text field and type **1**.

21. Click in the Maximum text field and type **10**.

22. Click in the Current text field and type **5**, as shown in Figure 8-12.

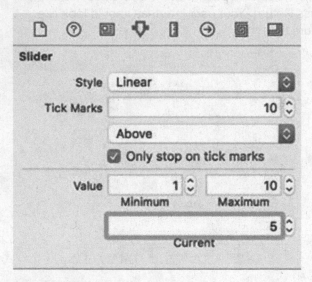

Figure 8-12. Changing the horizontal slider attributes

With this user interface, the user will use the horizontal slider to choose a number between 1 and 10. If the user guesses a number too high, the label will display "Too High". If the user guesses a number too low, the label will display "Too Low".

Each time the user guesses wrong, the bottom label will display the incorrect guess. When the user guesses the correct number, the top label will display "You got it!"

In this example, you need two IBOutlet variables to connect to each label so you can display information on each label. Then you need one IBAction method to connect to the Guess button. This way, when the user clicks the Guess button, the IBAction method can check if the user picked the correct number using the horizontal slider.

You need to write Swift code that chooses a random number between 1 and 10. Then you use a loop to list all the guesses the user made and display those results in an alert dialog.

Don't worry if you don't completely understand all the Swift code in the example. Just make sure you understand what the code is doing but don't worry about the specific details of how the code actually works. At this point, it's just important to see a more complex program actually work.

To connect Swift code to your user interface, follow these steps:

1. With your user interface still visible in the Xcode window, choose View ➤ Assistant Editor ➤ Show Assistant Editor. The AppDelegate.swift file appears next to the user interface.

2. Move the mouse over the top label, hold down the Control key, and drag from the top text field to underneath the existing @IBOutlet line in the AppDelegate.swift file, as shown in Figure 8-13.

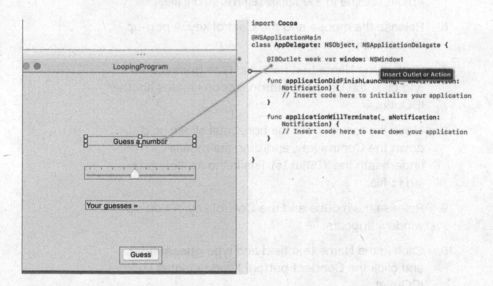

Figure 8-13. Control-dragging from the top label to the AppDelegate.swift file

3. Release the mouse and the Control key. A pop-up window appears, as shown in Figure 8-14.

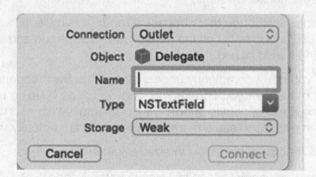

Figure 8-14. The pop-up window for defining an IBOutlet

4. Click in the Name text field and type **messageLabel** and click the Connect button. Xcode creates an IBOutlet.

5. Move the mouse over the bottom label, hold down the Control key, and drag the mouse underneath the @IBOutlet line in the AppDelegate.swift file.

6. Release the mouse and the Control key. A pop-up window appears.

7. Click in the Name text field and type **guessLabel** and click the Connect button. Xcode creates another IBOutlet.

8. Move the mouse over the horizontal slider, hold down the Control key, and drag the mouse underneath the @IBOutlet line in the AppDelegate. swift file.

9. Release the mouse and the Control key. A pop-up window appears.

10. Click in the Name text field and type **guessSlider** and click the Connect button. Xcode creates another IBOutlet.

11. You should now have three IBOutlets that represent
     the two text fields in your user interface:

```
@IBOutlet weak var messageLabel: NSTextField!
@IBOutlet weak var guessLabel: NSTextField!
@IBOutlet weak var guessSlider: NSSlider!
```

12. Move the mouse over the Guess push button, hold
     down the Control key, and drag the mouse above the
     last curly bracket in the AppDelegate.swift file.

13. Release the mouse and the Control key. A pop-up
     window appears.

14. Click in the Connection pop-up menu and choose
     Action to create an IBAction method.

15. Click in the Name text field and type **checkGuess**.

16. Click in the Type pop-up menu and choose
     NSButton, as shown in Figure 8-15.

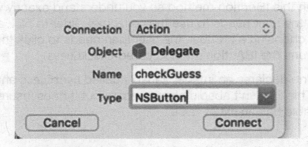

Figure 8-15. Defining an IBAction method

17. Click the Connect button. Xcode creates a blank
     IBAction method.

18. Modify the IBAction checkGuess method as follows:

```
@IBAction func checkGuess(_ sender: NSButton) {
    var userGuess = 0

    // Get guess from horizontal slider
    userGuess = guessSlider.integerValue

    // Store guess in guessArray
    guessArray.append(userGuess)
```

```
                    if userGuess < randomNumber {
                        messageLabel.stringValue = "Too Low"
                    } else if userGuess > randomNumber {
                        messageLabel.stringValue = "Too High"
                    } else {
                        messageLabel.stringValue = "You got it!"

                        arrayTotal = guessArray.count

                        for i in 0..<arrayTotal {
                            guessHistory += "Guess \(i+1) = \(guessArray[i])" + "\r\n"
                        }
                        let myAlert = NSAlert()
                        myAlert.messageText = guessHistory
                        myAlert.runModal()
                    }
                    guessLabel.stringValue = guessLabel.stringValue + " \(userGuess)"
                    }
                    guessLabel.stringValue = guessLabel.stringValue + " \(userGuess)"

        }
```

Let's go through this IBAction method so you understand exactly what happens. First, the user needs to use the horizontal slider to pick a number to guess. After choosing a number, the user then needs to click the Guess button, which runs the IBAction method called checkGuess.

The following line declares an integer variable called userGuess and sets its value to 0. This line isn't absolutely necessary but it does insure that the userGuess variable has an initial value.

```
var userGuess = 0
```

The next line retrieves the value from the horizontal slider, which is represented by the IBOutlet variable called guessSlider. To retrieve the integer that the horizontal slider represents, you have to use the integerValue property. This stores the value from the horizontal slider into the userGuess variable that you just declared as an integer variable.

```
userGuess = guessSlider.integerValue
```

The next line adds the value stored in the userGuess variable into the array called guessArray. This array must be defined earlier in your program.

```
guessArray.append(userGuess)
```

The if-else if statement creates three branches. The first branch runs if the userGuess variable is less than the randomNumber variable, which must be defined earlier in the program. This displays the text "Too Low" into the label represented by the messageLabel IBOutlet.

```
if userGuess < randomNumber {
    messageLabel.stringValue = "Too Low"
```

The second branch runs if the userGuess variable is greater than the randomNumber variable. This displays the text "Too High" into the label represented by the messageLabel IBOutlet.

```
} else if userGuess > randomNumber {
    messageLabel.stringValue = "Too High"
```

The third branch runs if the userGuess variable is neither less than or greater than the randomNumber variable, which means that it must be exactly equal to the randomNumber variable. This displays the text "You got it!" into the label represented by the messageLabel IBOutlet.

```
} else {
    messageLabel.stringValue = "You got it!"
```

Then it counts the total number of items stored in the guessArray and puts this value in the arrayTotal variable, which must be defined earlier in the program.

```
arrayTotal = guessArray.count
```

Now it uses a for loop to count from 0 to arrayTotal - 1 (i < arrayTotal) and increments by 1 (i++). It creates a string that stores the guess number, such as Guess 1, and the guess that the user chose in the string variable called guessHistory, which must be defined earlier in the program. Notice that you can print numbers in a string by using the \() characters where a non-string value appears inside the parentheses. This lets you store non-string values in a string without converting them to a string data type first.

Also notice that if you simply type Guess \(i) then the first string will hold the value Guess 0 as the first guess. To avoid this, you need to add 1 to the current value of i.

Notice that the string also contains the characters "\r\n" at the end. These symbols represent a carriage return and a newline character, respectively. These are invisible characters that tell Xcode that if you add more text, it will appear on the next line down.

```
for var i in 0..<arrayTotal {
guessHistory += "Guess \(i+1) = \(guessArray[i])" + "\r\n"
}
```

The code inside the for loop uses a compound assignment operator (+=) to add this string to any existing string stored in the guessHistory variable. Because of the "\r\n" characters that create a carriage return and a newline, any new string that gets added will appear on the next line down.

The next three lines create an alert dialog (NSAlert), store the string from the guessHistory variable into the messageText property of the alert dialog, and then display the dialog to display how many guesses you took and the numbers you chose in each guess, as shown in Figure 8-16.

```
var myAlert = NSAlert()
myAlert.messageText = guessHistory
myAlert.runModal()
```

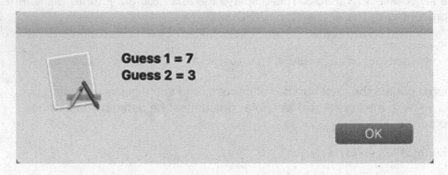

Figure 8-16. The typical results that appear in an alert dialog

The last line of the IBAction method simply stores the user's guesses in the guessLabel IBOutlet, which makes the text appear in the bottom label.

```
guessLabel.stringValue = guessLabel.stringValue + " \(userGuess)"
```

19. Edit the code above the IBAction method so it looks like this:

```
import Cocoa

@NSApplicationMain

class AppDelegate: NSObject, NSApplicationDelegate {

    @IBOutlet weak var window: NSWindow!
    @IBOutlet weak var messageLabel: NSTextField!
```

```
@IBOutlet weak var guessLabel: NSTextField!
@IBOutlet weak var guessSlider: NSSlider!

var randomNumber : Int
var guessHistory : String
var guessNumber : Int
var guessArray = [Int]()
var arrayTotal : Int

override init () {
    self.guessHistory = ""
    self.guessNumber = 0
    self.guessArray = []
    self.arrayTotal = 0
    self.randomNumber = 1 + Int(arc4random_uniform(10))
    // Int(arc4random_uniform(10)) chooses a random number
    between 0 and 9, so you need to add 1 so it chooses a
    random number from 1 to 10
}

func applicationDidFinishLaunching(aNotification:
NSNotification) {
    // Insert code here to initialize your application
}

func applicationWillTerminate(aNotification: NSNotification) {
    // Insert code here to tear down your application
}
```

The IBOutlet variables connect to the items on your user interface:

```
@IBOutlet weak var window: NSWindow!
@IBOutlet weak var messageLabel: NSTextField!
@IBOutlet weak var guessLabel: NSTextField!
@IBOutlet weak var guessSlider: NSSlider!
```

The next five lines declare variables the entire class AppDelegate can use:

```
var guessHistory : String
var guessNumber : Int
var guessArray = [Int]()
var arrayTotal : Int
var randomNumber : Int
```

When you define variables (called properties) inside a class, you need to give them an initial value. That's the purpose of the override init method:

```
override init () {
    self.guessHistory = ""
    self.guessNumber = 0
    self.guessArray = []
    self.arrayTotal = 0
    self.randomNumber = 1 + Int(arc4random_uniform(10))
    // Int(arc4random_uniform(10)) chooses a random number between 0 and 9,
    so you need to add 1 so it chooses a random number from 1 to 10
}
```

The self keyword tells Xcode that all of these variables are defined inside the same class (class AppDelegate). The last line creates a random number between 1 and 10.

The way this entire program works is that it first creates all its variables. Then it runs the override init method to store initial values in these variables.

At this point, the program now waits for the user to choose a value in the horizontal slider and click the Guess button.

20. Choose Product ➤ Run. Xcode runs your LoopingProgram project.

21. Click a value in the horizontal slider to guess a number.

22. Click the Guess push button. If you guess too low or too high, the "Too Low" or "Too High" message appears. Eventually when you guess the correct number, an alert dialog appears, as shown in Figure 8-17.

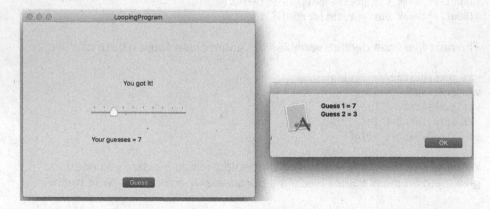

Figure 8-17. Displaying an alert dialog

23.   Click the OK button in the alert dialog to make it go away.

24.   Choose LoopingProgram ➤ Quit LoopingProgram.

Summary

Loops let you repeat one or more lines of code by running code until a Boolean value becomes false. A while loop checks a Boolean value first, which means it can run zero or more times. A repeat-while loop checks a Boolean value last, which means it can run one or more times.

When creating a while or repeat-while loop, always make sure the loop has a way to end. If a loop never ends, it becomes an endless loop, which will make your program appear to freeze and be unresponsive.

A for-in loop lets you specify how many times the loop can run based on a starting value and an ending value. To make a for-in loop count in increments other than 1, you can use the remainder operator (%) along with the where command. Besides counting through a range of values, the for-in loop can also count items in a list automatically.

Each type of loop has its advantages and disadvantages, but you can always make each loop duplicate the features of the other loops. If you need to exit out of a loop prematurely, you can use the break command along with an if statement.

Loops give your program the power to do repetitive tasks without requiring you to write duplicate commands. Just make sure that your loops always end eventually and that they run the proper number of times before stopping.

Chapter 9

Arrays and Dictionaries

Almost every program needs to accept data so it can manipulate that data and calculate a useful result. The simplest way to store data temporarily is through variables that can store numbers or text strings. However, what if you need to store multiple chunks of data such as a list of names or a list of product numbers? You could create multiple variables like this:

```
var employee001, employee002, employee003 : String
```

Unfortunately, creating separate variables to store related data can be clumsy. What if you don't know how many items you need to store? Then you may create too many or not enough variables. Even worse, storing related data in separate variables means it's easy to overlook the relationship between data.

For example, if you stored the names of three employees in three different variables, how do you know if there isn't a fourth, fifth, or sixth variable containing additional employee names? Unless you keep variables together in your code, it's easy to lose track of related data stored in separate variables.

That's why Swift offers two additional ways to store data called arrays and dictionaries. The main idea behind both data structures is that you create a single variable that can hold multiple items. Now you can store related data in one location and easily find and retrieve it again.

Both arrays and dictionaries are designed to store multiple copies of similar data such as a list of names or a list of numbers. In most cases, you'll store a list of identical data types in an array or dictionary. However, you can also use arrays and dictionaries to hold different data types by declaring that the

© Wallace Wang 2017

W. Wang, *macOS Programming for Absolute Beginners*,
DOI 10.1007/978-1-4842-2662-9_9

array or dictionary can store any type of data (using the "Any" data type) such as an integer and a string. Consider the following:

```
var mixedArray: [Any] = [1, "Temp", 2.6]
```

As a general rule, it's usually best to store the same type of data in an array or dictionary so you always know what type of data to expect.

Using Arrays

You can think of an array as an endless series of buckets that can hold exactly one chunk of data. To help you find data stored in an array, each array element (bucket) is identified by a number called an index. The first item in an array is defined at index 0, the second item is defined at index 1, the third item is defined at index 2, and so on, as shown in Figure 9-1.

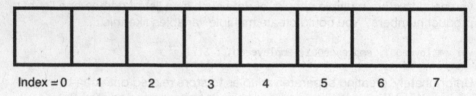

Index = 0   1   2   3   4   5   6   7

Figure 9-1. The structure of an array

To create an array, you can define the name of the array and the type of data the array can hold. One way to create an array is like this:

```
var arrayName : [DataType] = []
```

Once you've created an array and defined the type of data it can hold, you can store data to that array like this:

```
var arrayName : [Int] = []
arrayName = [34, 89, 70, 1, -24]
```

Rather than define an empty array and its data type, and then assign data to the array, it's much simpler to define an array name and set it equal to a list of items of the same data type on a single line, like this:

```
var myArrray = [34, 89, -2, 84]
```

Swift then infers the data type of the array based on the data. Just make sure all data in the array are the same data type such as Int, Float, Double, or String.

> **Note** When you declare an array with the var keyword, you can add and delete items in that array. If you don't want an array to change, declare it with the let keyword like this: let arrayName = [34, 89, 70, 1, -24]. An array declared with the let keyword can never be modified.

When you store data in an array, each item in that array appears in a fixed location. In the previous examples of arrays that hold integers, the first number (34) is located at index 0, the second number (89) is located at index 1, the third number (70) is located at index 2, the fourth number (1) is located at index 3, and the fifth number (-24) is located at index 4. Because Swift arrays count the index numbers starting with 0, they are known as zero-based arrays. (Some programming languages count the index of arrays starting with 1 so they're called one-based arrays.)

If you want to retrieve the second item in an array (located at index 1), you can retrieve that item and store it in a variable like this:

```
var arrayName = [4, 5, 9, -3]

var number : Int

number = arrayName[1]
```

The above Swift code creates an array that holds four integers (4, 5, 9, -3) and then creates a variable called number that can hold integer data types. The third line then retrieves the item stored in the 1 index position in arrayName. In this case, the number variable now holds the value 5.

Adding Items to an Array

Whether an array is empty or already filled with data, you can always add more items to an array by using the append command, like this:

```
arrayName.append(data)
```

You must specify the array name to add data to and put the actual data in parentheses. Make sure the data you add is of the proper data type. So if you want to add data to an array that can only hold integers, you can only add another integer to that array.

Instead of using the append command, you can use the addition compound assignment operator to add items to the end of an array, like this:

```
arrayName3 += [data1, data2, data3, ... dataN]
```

The += compound assignment operator can add multiple items to the end of an array while the append command only adds one item at a time to the end of an array..

The append command always adds new items to the end of an array. If you want to add a new item to a specific location in an array, you can use the insert and at commands, like this:

```
arrayName.insert(data, at: index)
```

With the insert command, you must add data that's the proper data type for that array. Then you must also specify the index number. If you choose an index number larger than the array size, the insert command won't work.

To see how to create an array and add data to it, follow these steps:

1. Open the IntroductoryPlayground file in Xcode.

2. Edit the code as follows:

```
import Cocoa

var arrayName = Array<Int>(arrayLiteral: 34, 89, 70, 1, -24)

var arrayName2 = [Int](arrayLiteral: 34, 89, 70, 1, -24)

arrayName.append(2)
arrayName2.append(2)

arrayName.insert(-37, at: 2)
arrayName2.insert(-37, at: 2)
```

Notice how the append command adds data to the end of the array but the insert command can add data in a specific location in the array, as shown in Figure 9-2.

```
import Cocoa

var arrayName = Array<Int>(arrayLiteral: 34, 89, 70, 1,     [34, 89, 70, 1, -24]
    -24)

var arrayName2 = [Int](arrayLiteral: 34, 89, 70, 1, -24)   [34, 89, 70, 1, -24]

arrayName.append(2)                                         [34, 89, 70, 1, -24, 2]
arrayName2.append(2)                                        [34, 89, 70, 1, -24, 2]

arrayName.insert(-37, at: 2)                                [34, 89, -37, 70, 1, -24, 2]
arrayName2.insert(-37, at: 2)                               [34, 89, -37, 70, 1, -24, 2]
```

Figure 9-2. Two ways to add data to an array

Deleting Items from an Array

Just as you can add items to an array, so can you also delete items from an array. To remove the last item in an array, you can use the removeLast command like this:

```
arrayName.removeLast()
```

Not only will this delete the last item in an array, but it will also return that value. If you want to save the last item of an array in a variable, you can do something like this:

```
var item = arrayName.removeLast()
```

If you want to remove a specific item from an array, you can identify the index number of that item with the removeAtIndex command, like this:

```
arrayName.remove(at: number)
```

So if you want to remove the second item in an array, you specify an index of 1. Like the removeLast command, the remove(at: index) command also returns a value that you can store in a variable, like this:

```
var item = arrayName.remove(at: 1)
```

If you want to remove all items from an array, you can use the removeAll command, like this:

```
arrayName.removeAll()
```

To see how to delete items from an array, follow these steps:

1. Make sure the IntroductoryPlayground file is loaded in Xcode.

2. Edit the code as follows:

```
import Cocoa

var arrayName = [Int](arrayLiteral: 3, 8, 9, 21)
var item = arrayName.removeLast()
print (arrayName)
print (item)

item = arrayName.remove(at: 1)
print (arrayName)
print (item)

arrayName.removeAll()
```

Notice how the different commands work when deleting items from an array as shown in Figure 9-3. When specifying index values, you must make sure your index number exists. This means if an array consists of three items, the first item is at index 0, the second is at index 1, and the third is at index 2. So you can remove an item from this array at index values 0, 1, or 2 but any other index number will not work.

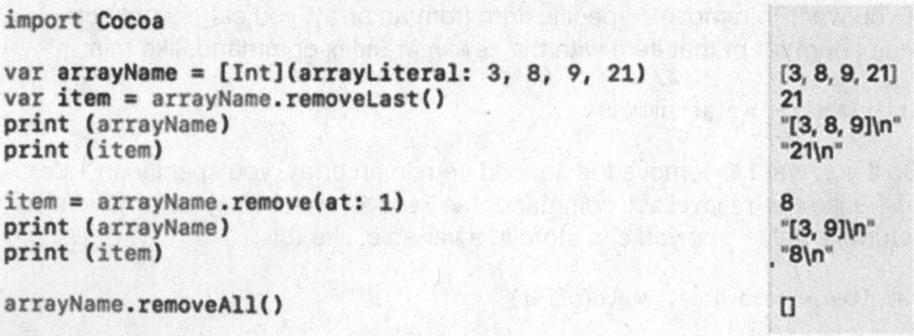

```
import Cocoa

var arrayName = [Int](arrayLiteral: 3, 8, 9, 21)      [3, 8, 9, 21]
var item = arrayName.removeLast()                     21
print (arrayName)                                     "[3, 8, 9]\n"
print (item)                                          "21\n"

item = arrayName.remove(at: 1)                        8
print (arrayName)                                     "[3, 9]\n"
print (item)                                          "8\n"

arrayName.removeAll()                                 []
```

Figure 9-3. Deleting items from an array

Deleting items from an array physically removes that item from that array. Rather than delete an item from an array, you can also replace an existing item with a new value. All you have to do is specify the index value of the array item you want to replace and assign new data to it, like this:

```
arrayName[index] = newData
```

So if you want to replace the second item in an array (at index value 1) with new data, you can do the following:

```
arrayName[1] = 91
```

Whatever existing value was stored in the array at index value 1 gets replaced with the number 91. When replacing data, the new data must be of the same data type as the rest of the items in the array, such as integers or strings.

Querying Arrays

When you have an array, you might want to know if the array is empty (has zero items stored in it), or if the array does have items, how many items it contains. To determine if an array is empty or not, you can use the isEmpty command that returns a Boolean value, like this:

```
arrayName.isEmpty
```

If you want to store this Boolean value in a variable, you can do this:

```
var flag = arrayName.isEmpty
```

If you want to know how many items are stored in an array, you can use the count command, like this:

```
arrayName.count
```

If you want to store this integer value in a variable, you can do this:

```
var total = arrayName.count
```

Manipulating Arrays

Two common ways to manipulate an array is to reverse the order of all the items or rearrange the items in ascending or descending order. This simply reverses the order of all items in an array without regard to their actual values, such as

```
arrayName.reversed()
```

When you sort an array in ascending order, the lowest value gets stored in the first item of the array and the highest value gets stored in the last item of the array. When you sort strings, Swift sorts them in alphabetical order. To sort an array in ascending order, use this:

```
myArray.sort { $0 < $1 }
```

When you sort an array in descending order, the highest value gets stored in the first item of the array and the lowest value gets stored in the last item of the array. When you sort strings, Swift sorts them in reverse alphabetical order. To sort an array in descending order, use this:

```
myArray.sort { $1 < $0 }
```

To see how reversing and sorting an array works, follow these steps:

1. Make sure the IntroductoryPlayground file is loaded in Xcode.

2. Edit the code as follows:

```
import Cocoa

var myArray = ["Bob", "Fred", "Alice", "Mary"]
let backwardsArray : [String]

backwardsArray = myArray.reversed()

myArray.sort { $0 < $1 }
print (myArray)
myArray.sort { $1 < $0 }
print (myArray)
```

Notice that reversing an array simply rearranges the items but sorting an array actually changes the position of items based on their content, as shown in Figure 9-4.

```
import Cocoa

var myArray = ["Bob", "Fred", "Alice", "Mary"]          ["Bob", "Fred", "Alice", "Mary"]
let backwardsArray : [String]

backwardsArray = myArray.reversed()                     ["Mary", "Alice", "Fred", "Bob"]

myArray.sort { $0 < $1 }                                (5 times)
print (myArray)                                         "["Alice", "Bob", "Fred", "Mary"]\n"
myArray.sort { $1 < $0 }                                (7 times)
print (myArray)                                         "["Mary", "Fred", "Bob", "Alice"]\n"
```

Figure 9-4. Sorting and reversing an array

Using Dictionaries

Arrays can be useful for storing lists of related data. The biggest drawback with array comes when you want to retrieve specific data. Unless you know the exact index number of an item in an array, retrieving data can be cumbersome.

That's the purpose of a dictionary. Unlike an array that just stores data, a dictionary stores two chunks of data known as a key-value pair. The value represents the data you want to save and the key represents a quick way to retrieve your data.

For example, consider a list of phone numbers. If you stored phone numbers in an array, you would have to retrieve a specific phone number by knowing its exact index value. However, if you stored phone numbers in a dictionary, you could store each phone number (value) with a name (key). Now if you wanted to retrieve a particular phone number, you just search for the key (the person's name).

Regardless of where that data might be stored in the dictionary, you can quickly retrieve a value using a key. This makes retrieving data from a dictionary far easier than retrieving similar data from an array.

Think of a dictionary like an array, but instead of storing one chunk of data, you're storing a pair of data (a key and a value). Both the key and the value can be of different data types but all the keys and all the values in a dictionary must be of the same data type.

To create a dictionary, you must define the dictionary and the data types for both the key and its associated value. One way to define a dictionary is to do this:

```
var DictionaryName = [keyDataType: valueDatatype]()
```

This defines an empty dictionary but specifies the data type of both the key and the value.

A second way to define a dictionary is to create a list of key:value pairs like this:

```
var DictionaryName = [102: "Fred", 87: "Valerie"]
```

When you directly assign key:value pairs, Swift infers the data type of the key and the value. In this case, the key data type is an integer (Int) and the value data type is a string (String).

Adding Items to a Dictionary

Whether a dictionary is empty or already filled with data, you can always add more items to a dictionary by specifying the dictionary name and its key value, and then assigning a value such as

```
DictionaryName [key] = value
```

To see how to create a dictionary and add data to it, create a new playground by following these steps:

1. Open the IntroductoryPlayground file in Xcode.

2. Edit the code as follows:

```
import Cocoa

var DictionaryName = [102: "Fred", 87: "Valerie"]

DictionaryName [120] = "John"
DictionaryName [96] = "Jane"

print (DictionaryName)
```

This Swift code defines a dictionary where the key:value data types are Int:String, which Swift infers from the type of data initially stored in the dictionary.

The next two lines define a key (120) and a value ("John"), which gets stored in the dictionary. Then the other line defines a key (96) and a value ("Jane"), which also gets stored in the dictionary. The last print command lets you see how the dictionary has changed, as shown in Figure 9-5.

```
import Cocoa                                         
var DictionaryName = [102: "Fred", 87: "Valerie"]    [102: "Fred", 87: "Valerie"]

DictionaryName [120] = "John"                        "John"
DictionaryName [96] = "Jane"                         "Jane"

print (DictionaryName)                               "[120: "John", 102: "Fred", 87: "Valerie", 96: "Jane"]\n"
```

Figure 9-5. Creating a dictionary and adding new key:value data to it

Retrieving and Updating Data in a Dictionary

Once a dictionary contains key:value pairs, you can retrieve the value by using the key. To do so, you specify the dictionary name and a key. Then you assign this value to a variable such as

```
variable = DictionaryName [key]!
```

The variable must be the same data type as the value stored in the dictionary. Also notice the exclamation mark, which defines an implicitly unwrapped variable. This exclamation mark insures that if the key doesn't exist in the dictionary, the non-existent value does not crash your program.

The following example defines two key:value pairs of data in a dictionary. Then it uses the 87 key to retrieve the value from the dictionary, which is the string "Valeria", as shown in Figure 9-6.

```
var DictionaryName = [102: "Fred", 87: "Valerie"]
var name : String
name = DictionaryName [87]!
print (name)
```

```
import Cocoa

var DictionaryName = [102: "Fred", 87: "Valerie"]          [102: "Fred", 87: "Valerie"]

DictionaryName [120] = "John"                              "John"
DictionaryName [96] = "Jane"                               "Jane"
print (DictionaryName)                                     "[120: "John", 102: "Fred", 87: "Valerie", 96: "Jane"]\n"

var name : String
name = DictionaryName [87]!                                "Valerie"
print (name)                                               "Valerie\n"

DictionaryName.updateValue("Sam", forKey: 87)              "Valerie"
name = DictionaryName [87]!                                "Sam"
print (name)                                               "Sam\n"
```

Figure 9-6. Retrieving a value with a key and updating an existing key with new data

Once you've stored a key:value pair in a dictionary, you can always assign a new value to an existing key using the updateValue command, like this:

```
DictionaryName.updateValue(value, forKey: key)
```

So if you wanted to update the value stored with the 87 key, you could do the following:

```
DictionaryName.updateValue("Sam", forKey: 87)
```

To see how to retrieve a value from a dictionary using a key and then update a value for an existing key, follow these steps:

1. Make sure the IntroductoryPlayground file is loaded in Xcode.

2. Edit the code as follows:

```
import Cocoa
var DictionaryName = [102: "Fred", 87: "Valerie"]

DictionaryName [120] = "John"
DictionaryName [96] = "Jane"
print (DictionaryName)

var name : String
name = DictionaryName [87]!
print (name)

DictionaryName.updateValue("Sam", forKey: 87)
name = DictionaryName [87]!
print (name)
```

Notice that the first time the dictionary retrieves the value associated with the 87 key; it returns the string "Valerie". Then the updateValue command replaces "Valerie" with "Sam" so the next time the dictionary retrieves the value associated with the 87 key, it returns the string "Sam", as shown in Figure 9-6.

Deleting Data in a Dictionary

Once a dictionary contains key:value pairs, you can delete the value associated with a specific key by using the removeValue(forKey:key) command like this:

```
DictionaryName.removeValue(forKey: key)
```

The removeValue(forKey:key) command removes both the key and the value associated with that key. Note that if you specify a key that doesn't exist in the dictionary, the removeValue(forKey:key) command does nothing.

If you want to delete all of the key:value pairs in a dictionary, you can just use the removeAll command, like this:

```
DictionaryName.removeAll()
```

Querying a Dictionary

Once you store key:value pairs in a dictionary, you can use the following commands to get information about a dictionary:

- **count**: Counts the number of key:value pairs stored in a dictionary
- **keys**: Retrieves a list of all the keys stored in a dictionary
- **values**: Retrieves a list of all the values stored in a dictionary

The count command only needs the dictionary name and returns an integer value that you can assign to a variable, such as

```
var total = DictionaryName.count
```

The keys and values commands need a dictionary name and returns a list of items that you can store in an array, such as

```
let myKeys = Array(DictionaryName.keys)
```

To see how to count and retrieve keys and values from a dictionary, follow these steps:

1. Make sure the IntroductoryPlayground file is loaded in Xcode.

2. Edit the code as follows:

```
import Cocoa

var myDictionary = [12: "Joe", 7: "Walter"]

myDictionary.removeValue(forKey: 7)
print (myDictionary)

myDictionary.removeAll()
print (myDictionary)

myDictionary = [25: "Stephanie", 98: "Nancy"]

print (myDictionary.count)
let myKeys = Array(myDictionary.keys)
let myValues = Array(myDictionary.values)
```

Notice how the removeValueForKey command removes an existing key:value pair while the removeAll command empties the entire dictionary. Also notice how the count command counts all key:value pairs while the keys and values commands return a list of the keys and values, respectively, as shown in Figure 9-7.

```
import Cocoa

var myDictionary = [12: "Joe", 7: "Walter"]          [12: "Joe", 7: "Walter"]

myDictionary.removeValue(forKey: 7)                  "Walter"
print (myDictionary)                                 "[12: "Joe"]\n"

myDictionary.removeAll()                             [:]
print (myDictionary)                                 "[:]\n"

myDictionary = [25: "Stephanie", 98: "Nancy"]        [98: "Nancy", 25: "Stephanie"]

print (myDictionary.count)                           "2\n"
let myKeys = Array(myDictionary.keys)                [98, 25]
let myValues = Array(myDictionary.values)            ["Nancy", "Stephanie"]
```

Figure 9-7. Deleting dictionary data, counting, and retrieving keys and values

Using Dictionaries in a macOS Program

In the following sample program, the computer creates a list of data stored in a dictionary. Then through the user interface, the user can add new data to the dictionary, delete existing data, or get information about the dictionary.

Create a new macOS project by following these steps:

1. From within Xcode choose File ➤ New ➤ Project.

2. Click Application under the macOS category.

3. Click Cocoa Application and click the Next button. Xcode now asks for a product name.

4. Click in the Product Name text field and type **DictionaryProgram**.

5. Make sure the Language pop-up menu displays Swift and that no check boxes are selected.

6. Click the Next button. Xcode asks where you want to store the project.

7. Choose a folder to store your project and click the Create button.

8. Click the MainMenu.xib file in the Project Navigator.

9. Click the DictionaryProgram icon to make the window of the user interface appear.

10. Choose View ➤ Utilities ➤ Show Object Library to make the Object Library appear in the bottom right corner of the Xcode window.

11. Drag three push buttons, six labels, and six text fields onto the user interface, and double-click the push buttons and labels to change the text that appears on them so they look similar to Figure 9-8.

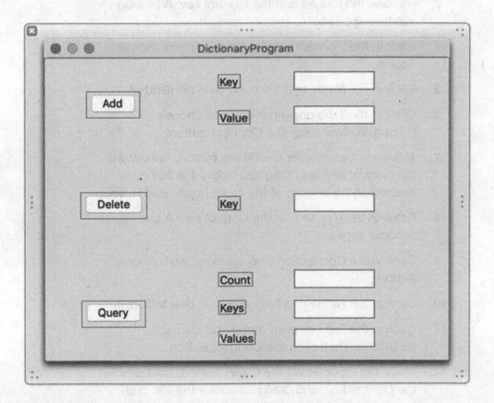

Figure 9-8. The user interface of the DictionaryProgram

The Add button will let you type in a key and value in the text fields on the right. The Delete button will let you specify a key to delete its associated value from a dictionary. The Query button will display the total number of items along with the list of keys and values currently stored in the dictionary.

Each text field will need a separate IBOutlet and each push button will need a separate IBAction method, which you create by Control-dragging each item from the user interface to your AppDelegate.swift file.

1. With your user interface still visible in the Xcode window, choose View ➤ Assistant Editor ➤ Show Assistant Editor. The AppDelegate.swift file appears next to the user interface.

2. Move the mouse over the Add button, hold down the Control key, and drag just above the last curly bracket at the bottom of the AppDelegate.swift file.

3. Release the mouse and the Control key. A pop-up window appears.

4. Click in the Connection pop-up menu and choose Action.

5. Click in the Name text field and type **addButton**.

6. Click in the Type pop-up menu and choose NSButton. Then click the Connect button.

7. Move the mouse over the Delete button, hold down the Control key, and drag just above the last curly bracket at the bottom of the AppDelegate.swift file.

8. Release the mouse and the Control key. A pop-up window appears.

9. Click in the Connection pop-up menu and choose Action.

10. Click in the Name text field and type **deleteButton**.

11. Click in the Type pop-up menu and choose NSButton. Then click the Connect button.

12. Move the mouse over the Query button, hold down the Control key, and drag just above the last curly bracket at the bottom of the AppDelegate.swift file.

13. Release the mouse and the Control key. A pop-up window appears.

14. Click in the Connection pop-up menu and choose Action.

15. Click in the Name text field and type **queryButton**.

16. Click in the Type pop-up menu and choose NSButton. Then click the Connect button. The bottom of the AppDelegate.swift file should look like this:

```
@IBAction func addButton(_ sender: NSButton) {
}

@IBAction func deleteButton(_ sender: NSButton) {
}

@IBAction func queryButton(_ sender: NSButton) {
}
```

17. Move the mouse over the Key text field that appears to the right of the Add button, hold down the Control key, and drag below the @IBOutlet line in the AppDelegate.swift file.

18. Release the mouse and the Control key. A pop-up window appears.

19. Click in the Name text field and type **addKeyField** and click the Connect button.

20. Move the mouse over the Value text field that appears to the right of the Add button, hold down the Control key, and drag below the @IBOutlet line in the AppDelegate.swift file.

21. Release the mouse and the Control key. A pop-up window appears.

22. Click in the Name text field and type **addValueField** and click the Connect button.

23. Move the mouse over the Key text field that appears to the right of the Delete button, hold down the Control key, and drag below the @IBOutlet line in the AppDelegate.swift file.

24. Release the mouse and the Control key. A pop-up window appears.

25. Click in the Name text field and type **deleteKeyField** and click the Connect button.

26. Move the mouse over the Count text field that appears to the right of the Query button, hold down the Control key, and drag below the @IBOutlet line in the AppDelegate.swift file.

27. Release the mouse and the Control key. A pop-up window appears.

28. Click in the Name text field and type **queryCountField** and click the Connect button.

29. Move the mouse over the Keys text field that appears to the right of the Query button, hold down the Control key, and drag below the @IBOutlet line in the AppDelegate.swift file.

30. Release the mouse and the Control key. A pop-up window appears.

31. Click in the Name text field and type **queryKeysField** and click the Connect button.

32. Move the mouse over the Values text field that appears to the right of the Query button, hold down the Control key, and drag below the @IBOutlet line in the AppDelegate.swift file.

33. Release the mouse and the Control key. A pop-up window appears.

34. Click in the Name text field and type **queryValuesField** and click the Connect button.

35. You should now have the following IBOutlets that represent all the text fields on your user interface:

```
@IBOutlet weak var window: NSWindow!
@IBOutlet weak var addKeyField: NSTextField!
@IBOutlet weak var addValueField: NSTextField!
@IBOutlet weak var deleteKeyField: NSTextField!
@IBOutlet weak var queryCountField: NSTextField!
@IBOutlet weak var queryKeysField: NSTextField!
@IBOutlet weak var queryValuesField: NSTextField!
```

At this point you've connected the user interface to your Swift code so you can use the IBOutlets to retrieve and display data on the user interface. You've also created the IBAction methods so the push buttons on the user interface will make the program actually work. Now you just need to write

Swift code to create an initial dictionary and then write more Swift code in each IBAction method to add, delete, or query the dictionary.

1. Underneath the IBOutlet list in the AppDelegate.swift file, type the following to create a dictionary where the keys are integers and the values are strings:

```
var myDictionary = [1:"Joe", 2:"Cindy", 3:"Frank"]
```

2. Modify the addButton IBAction method so it takes a value from the Key and Value text fields and adds them to the dictionary as follows:

```
@IBAction func addButton(_ sender: NSButton) {
    myDictionary.updateValue(addValueField.stringValue, forKey:
    addKeyField.integerValue)
}
```

3. Modify the deleteButton IBAction method so it takes a value from the Key text field and deletes the associates value from the dictionary as follows:

```
@IBAction func deleteButton(_ sender: NSButton) {
    myDictionary.removeValue(forKey: deleteKeyField.integerValue)
}
```

4. Modify the queryButton IBAction method as follows:

```
@IBAction func queryButton(_ sender: NSButton) {
    queryCountField.integerValue = myDictionary.count

    var keyList : String = ""

    for key in myDictionary.keys {
        keyList = keyList + "\(key)" + " "
    }
    queryKeysField.stringValue = keyList

    var valueList : String = ""
    for value in myDictionary.values {
        valueList = valueList + "\(value)" + " "
    }
    queryValuesField.stringValue = valueList

}
```

The myDictionary.count command simply counts the number of key:value pairs in the dictionary and displays that number in the queryCountField IBOutlet. The first for-in loop goes through each key in the dictionary and stores it in a string called keyList. Then it displays this text string in the queryKeysField IBOutlet.

The last for loop goes through each value in the dictionary and stores it in a string called valueList. Then it displays this text string in the queryValuesField IBOutlet.

The complete contents of the AppDelegate.swift file should look like this:

```swift
import Cocoa


@NSApplicationMain
class AppDelegate: NSObject, NSApplicationDelegate {

    @IBOutlet weak var window: NSWindow!

    @IBOutlet weak var addKeyField: NSTextField!
    @IBOutlet weak var addValueField: NSTextField!
    @IBOutlet weak var deleteKeyField: NSTextField!
    @IBOutlet weak var queryCountField: NSTextField!
    @IBOutlet weak var queryKeysField: NSTextField!
    @IBOutlet weak var queryValuesField: NSTextField!

    var myDictionary = [1:"Joe", 2:"Cindy", 3:"Frank"]

    func applicationDidFinishLaunching(_ aNotification: Notification) {
        // Insert code here to initialize your application
    }

    func applicationWillTerminate(_ aNotification: Notification) {
        // Insert code here to tear down your application
    }

    @IBAction func addButton(_ sender: NSButton) {
        myDictionary.updateValue(addValueField.stringValue, forKey:
        addKeyField.integerValue)
    }

    @IBAction func deleteButton(_ sender: NSButton) {
        myDictionary.removeValue(forKey: deleteKeyField.integerValue)
    }

    @IBAction func queryButton(_ sender: NSButton) {
        queryCountField.integerValue = myDictionary.count
```

```
    var keyList : String = ""

    for key in myDictionary.keys {
        keyList = keyList + "\(key)" + " "
    }
    queryKeysField.stringValue = keyList

    var valueList : String = ""
    for value in myDictionary.values {
        valueList = valueList + "\(value)" + " "
    }
    queryValuesField.stringValue = valueList

  }
}
```

The Query button works by just clicking on it to display information about the current dictionary contents.

The Add button works by the user typing in a key (integer) and a name (string) into the Key and Value text fields, and then clicking the Add button.

The Delete button works by the user typing in a key (integer) and then clicking the Delete button.

After clicking either the Add or Delete button, click the Query button again to see your changes. To see how this program works, follow these steps:

1. Choose Product➤Run. Xcode runs your DictionaryProgram project.

2. Click the Query button. The program shows the number of items in the dictionary (3), the list of keys (the numbers 1, 2, and 3), and the list of values ("Joe", "Cindy", and "Frank"). Don't worry about the order of the keys and values. The important point is to see that the order of each key matches up with the correct value such as 1 for "Joe", 2 for "Cindy", and 3 for "Frank".

3. Type 3 in the Key field to the right of the Delete push button and then click the Delete button.

4. Click the Query button. Notice that now the dictionary only contains two items, the keys 1 and 2, and the values "Joe" and "Cindy", as shown in Figure 9-9.

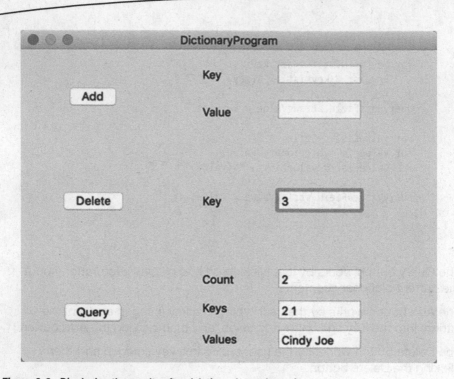

Figure 9-9. Displaying the results after deleting a key:value pair

5.   Click in the Key text field to the right of the Add
      button and type **5**.

6.   Click in the Value text field to the right of the Add
      button and type **Felicia**.

7.   Click the Add button.

8.   Click the Query button. Notice that the count is
      now 3 again, the keys are 1, 2, and 5, and the values
      are "Joe", "Cindy", and "Felicia".

9.   Choose DictionaryProgram➤Quit DictionaryProgram.

Summary

Arrays and dictionaries are two ways to store lists of related data in a
single variable. Arrays make it easy to store data but retrieving data can be
cumbersome since you have to know the exact index value of the data you
want to retrieve.

Dictionaries force you to store data with a key, but that key makes it easy to retrieve that data later without knowing the exact location it may be stored in the dictionary.

In the sample macOS program that you created, you also learned how for-in loops can count automatically through a dictionary. By now you should also be getting more comfortable creating user interfaces and seeing which items need IBOutlets and which items need IBAction methods.

Designing programs can occur in three distinct steps. First, you create the user interface and customize it. Second, you connect your user interface to your Swift file. Third, you write Swift code to make your IBAction methods work.

Think of arrays and dictionaries as super variables that can store multiple data in a single variable name. If you only need to save a single value, then use a variable. If you need to store lists of related data, then use an array or a dictionary.

Chapter **10**

Tuples and Sets

Variables are good for storing individual chunks of data, and arrays and dictionaries are good for storing lists of related data. For greater flexibility, Swift also offers additional data structures called tuples and sets.

A tuple lets you store related data in one place that may consist of different data types such as a string and an integer, which could represent a person's name and an employee ID number. A set is similar to an array or a dictionary in letting you store two or more chunks of related data such as strings or integers.

Perhaps the biggest advantage of both tuples and structures is when you combine them with other data structures. Instead of creating an array of integers, you can create an array of tuples or an array of structures. This gives you the flexibility to store different data types together and store multiple copies of similar data.

Using Tuples

Suppose you want to store somebody's name and age. You can create two separate variables, like this:

```
var name : String
var age : Int
name = "Janice Parker"
age = 47
```

Creating two or more separate variables to store related data can be troublesome because there's no connection between the two variables to show any relationship. To solve this problem, Swift offers a unique data structure called a tuple.

© Wallace Wang 2017
W. Wang, *macOS Programming for Absolute Beginners*,
DOI 10.1007/978-1-4842-2662-9_10

A tuple can store two or more chunks of data in a single variable where the separate chunks of data can even be completely different data types such as a string and an integer. Declaring a tuple is just like declaring a variable. The main difference is that instead of defining a single data type, you can define multiple data types enclosed in parentheses, like this:

```
var tupleName : (DataType1, DataType2)
```

Just like declaring variables, you have to declare a unique name for your tuple. Then you have to define how many different chunks of data to hold and their data types. Tuples can hold two or more chunks of data but the more data a tuple holds, the clumsier it can be to understand and retrieve data.

One way to create a tuple is to declare a tuple name and the data types it can hold. The number of data types listed also defines the number of data chunks the tuple can store. So if you want to store a string and an integer in a tuple, you can use the following Swift code:

```
var person : (String, Int)
```

Then you can store data in that tuple, like this:

```
person = ("Janice Parker", 47)
```

When assigning data to a tuple, make sure you have both the proper data types and the correct number of data chunks. So the following will fail because the person tuple expects a string first and then an integer, not an integer first and then a string:

```
person = (47, "Janice Parker")
```

A second way to define a tuple is to simply give it data and let Swift infer the data type, such as

```
var person = ("Janice Parker", 47)
```

If you define a tuple by listing its data types, or if you let Swift infer the data types by the type of data you store, it's not always clear what each chunk of data represents. To make it easier to identify the different chunks of data, Swift also lets you name your data types, such as

```
var person : (name: String, age: Int)
```

If you want Swift to infer the data types by assigning data directly into the tuple, you can do this:

```
var person = (name: "Janice Parker", age: 47)
```

Named tuples help clarify what each data chunk represents. In this case, the string represents a name and the integer represents an age.

Accessing Data in a Tuple

Once you've created a tuple and stored data in it, you need to retrieve that data eventually. Since a tuple contains two or more chunks of data, Swift offers three ways to retrieve the data you want.

First, you can create multiple variables to access the tuple data, as follows:

```
var petInfo = ("Rover", 38, true)

var (dog, number, yesValue) = petInfo
print (dog)
print (number)
print (yesValue)
```

In the first line of code, petInfo is a tuple that contains three chunks of data: a string ("Rover"), an integer (38), and a Boolean value (true).

The second line of code creates three variables (dog, number, yesValue) and assigns their values to the corresponding data stored in the petInfo tuple. That means dog stores "Rover", number stores 38, and yesValue stores true. The print commands simply print this data out to verify that it retrieved information from the tuple.

To access data from a tuple, you must know the order in which the tuple stores data. So if you want to retrieve a string from the petInfo tuple, you must know that the petInfo tuple stores names (Strings) as its first chunk of data, a number as its second chunk of data, and a Boolean value as its third chunk of data.

If you don't want retrieve all the values stored in a tuple, you can just create a variable to store the data you want and use the underscore character (_) as an empty placeholder to represent each additional value in the tuple that you want to ignore.

This means you still need to know the number of data chunks the tuple holds so you can identify the one chunk of data that you want to retrieve. For example, if a tuple contains three items, you can retrieve the first item like this:

```
var petInfo = ("Rover", 38, true)
var (pet,_,_) = petInfo
print (pet)
```

This will store "Rover" in the pet variable so the println command will print "Rover".

If you just want to retrieve the middle value, you can type the following:

```
var petInfo = ("Rover", 38, true)
var (_,aValue,_) = petInfo
print (aValue)
```

This will store the number 38 into the aValue variable and then the println command will print 38.

The underscore character acts as a placeholder to identify data in a tuple that you want to ignore. If you omit the underscore characters, Swift won't know which particular data you want out of a tuple. To retrieve data from a tuple, you must know the number and order of the items that the tuple stores.

A second way to retrieve values from a tuple is to use index numbers where the first element is assigned index number 0, the second element is assigned index number 1, and so on. For example, you might store data in a tuple like this:

```
var petInfo = ("Rover", 38, true)
print (petInfo.0)
print (petInfo.1)
print (petInfo.2)
```

The first item in the tuple is assigned index number 0 so the combination of the tuple name (such as petInfo) followed by the index number lets you directly retrieve a specific tuple value. So petInfo.0 retrieves "Rover", petInfo.1 retrieves 38, and petInfo.2 retrieves true.

Make sure that when you access tuple data by index number, you use a valid index number. In the above example, the petInfo tuple contains data at index 0, 1, and 2, but if you try to access data in a different index such as index number 3, there is no data so your program won't work.

A third method for accessing data in a tuple involves using names. To use this method, you must first assign names to each tuple data. For example, the following Swift code defines two names called "name" and "age":

```
var tupleName = (name: "Bridget", age: 31)
```

Now you can access the tuple data by referencing the tuple name followed by the identifying name for each data like this:

```
print (tupleName.name)    // Prints "Bridget"
print (tupleName.age)     // Prints 31
```

All three methods give you different ways to access data stored in tuples so just use the method you like best. For clarity, naming the specific elements of a tuple makes your code easier to understand but at the sacrifice of forcing you to name your tuple data. The index number method and the multiple variable method may be simpler, but can be less clear and requires you to know the exact order of the data you want to retrieve.

To see how to work with tuples, create a new playground by following these steps:

1. Open the IntroductoryPlayground file in Xcode.

2. Edit the code as follows:

```
import Cocoa

var tupleName = (greeting: "Happy Birthday", age: 58, happy: true)

// Method #1
var (message, howOld, mood) = tupleName
print (message)
print (howOld)
print (mood)

var (_,stuff,_) = tupleName
print (stuff)

// Method #2

print (tupleName.0)
print (tupleName.1)
print (tupleName.2)

// Method #3

print (tupleName.greeting)
print (tupleName.age)
print (tupleName.happy)
```

When you try all three methods for accessing values from a tuple, you can see how they all work alike. Tuples make it easy to group related data together in a single variable so you can easily keep related information organized. Then you can choose to retrieve data from a tuple using one of three different methods, as shown in Figure 10-1.

```
import Cocoa

var tupleName = (greeting: "Happy Birthday", age: 58,          (.0 "Happy Birthday", .1 58, .2 true)
    happy: true)

// Method #1
var (message, howOld, mood) = tupleName
print (message)                                                "Happy Birthday\n"
print (howOld)                                                 "58\n"
print (mood)                                                   "true\n"

var (_,stuff,_) = tupleName
print (stuff)                                                  "58\n"



// Method #2

print (tupleName.0)                                            "Happy Birthday\n"
print (tupleName.1)                                            "58\n"
print (tupleName.2)                                            "true\n"



// Method #3

print (tupleName.greeting)                                     "Happy Birthday\n"
print (tupleName.age)                                          "58\n"
print (tupleName.happy)                                        "true\n"
```

Figure 10-1. Three different ways to retrieve data from a tuple

Using Sets

Arrays and dictionaries can store lists of the same data types, such as a list
of strings or a list of integers. The difference between arrays and dictionaries
is how you retrieve data. Arrays force you to retrieve data by location using
index values. Dictionaries let you retrieve data using a key, but you must
define a unique key for each chunk of data you store.

Sets represent another way to store lists of identical data types such as
strings or decimal numbers. One speed advantage of a set is determining
if something is stored or not. If you store data in an array, you must
exhaustively search throughout the entire array to determine if an array
stores a particular item. If you store data in a dictionary, you have to know
the key stored with that value, or you have to exhaustively search through
the dictionary's list of values.

Sets let you quickly determine the following far faster than arrays or
dictionaries:

- If an item is stored in a set or not

- If a set contains exactly the same items as another set

- If a set is a subset of another set (contains the same
  items as a larger set)

- If a set is a superset of another set (contains the same items and more than a smaller set)
- If two sets contain the same items or not

Sets make it easy to compare two different groups of data in ways that arrays and dictionaries can't do as easily.

Creating a Set

To create a set, you can define an empty set and the type of data it can hold like this:

```
var setName = Set<DataType>()
```

If you want to create a set and fill a set with data at the same time, list the set contents within square brackets and let Swift infer the data type where all data must be of the same data type, such as

```
var setName = Set ([Data1, Data2, Data2 ... DataN])
```

A third way to create a set is to define a set name, use the Set keyword, and then list the data in the set, like this:

```
var setName :. Set = [Data1, Data2, Data2 ... DataN]
```

Adding and Removing Items from a Set

With a set, you can add new items at any time, just as long as the new item is the same data type as the existing data. To add an item to a set, just specify the set name, the insert command, and the data you want to add inside parentheses, like this:

```
setName.insert(data)
```

You must specify the array name to add data to and put the actual data in parentheses. Make sure the data you add is of the proper data type. So if you want to add data to a set that currently holds only integers, you can only add another integer to that set.

If you try to add data that already exists in the set, nothing will happen. This means if a set contains the number 53, you can't add another copy of 53 into that set.

To remove data from a set, you just specify the set name, the remove command, and the data you want to remove enclosed in parentheses like this:

```
setName.remove(data)
```

If you try to remove data that doesn't exist in the set, the remove command returns a nil value. However, if the remove command succeeds in removing data from a set, it returns an optional variable. This means if you store removed data in a variable, as in

```
var variableName = setName.remove(data)
```

the value stored in the variable can be accessed by using an exclamation mark, as in

```
print (variableName!)
```

If you want to remove all items in a set, specify the set name and the removeAll command, like this:

```
setName.removeAll()
```

To see how to create a set and add and remove data from it, create a new playground by following these steps:

1. Open the IntroductoryPlayground file in Xcode.

2. Enter the code as follows:

```
import Cocoa

var setOne = Set([2, 45, -9, 8, -34])
var setTwo : Set = [34, 90, -83]

setOne
setTwo

setOne.insert(65)
setTwo.insert(-381)

var temp = setOne.remove(45)
print (temp)
print (temp!)

setOne
setTwo

setOne.removeAll()
```

This Swift code creates a set called setOne by storing data directly and letting Swift infer the data types, which are integers. Then it creates a second set called setTwo, which also holds only integers.

After creating setTwo, the two insert commands store different integers into both setOne and setTwo. When the code removes the number 45 from setOne, it stores 45 as an optional variable in the temp variable. To access the actual value, you have to unwrap the optional variable using the exclamation mark (!).

Finally, the removeAll command empties setOne so it contains nothing, as shown in Figure 10-2.

```
import Cocoa

var setOne = Set([2, 45, -9, 8, -34])          {-9, 45, 2, -34, 8}
var setTwo : Set = [34, 90, -83]               {-83, 90, 34}

setOne                                          {-9, 45, 2, -34, 8}
setTwo                                          {-83, 90, 34}

setOne.insert(65)                               (.0 true, .1 65)
setTwo.insert(-381)                             (.0 true, .1 -381)

var temp = setOne.remove(45)                    45
print (temp)                                    "Optional(45)\n"
print (temp!)                                   "45\n"

setOne                                          {-9, 65, 2, -34, 8}
setTwo                                          {-83, -381, 90, 34}

setOne.removeAll()                              Set([])
```

Figure 10-2. Creating sets, inserting data in a set, and removing data from a set

Note that Xcode will display a warning to the left of the print (temp) line. That's because temp represents an optional variable that you need to unwrap (using the ! symbol) to retrieve the actual value.

Querying a Set

Once you have a set, you can use the following commands to get information about that set:

- count: Counts the number of items in a set
- isEmpty: Checks if a set is empty (contains 0 items)
- isSubset (of:): Checks if one set is wholly contained within another set

- isSuperset (of:): Checks if one set contains all the items of another set

- isDisjoint (with:): Checks if two sets have no items in common

Whatever the result of these commands, they never affect the data stored in a set.

The count command returns an integer value and just requires the set name and the count command, like this:

```
setName.count
```

You can also assign this value to a variable, such as

```
var total = setName.count
```

The isEmpty command returns a Boolean value of true if a set has zero items in it. Otherwise, it returns false. Just specify the set name followed by the isEmpty command, like this:

```
setOne.isEmpty
```

The isSubsetOf command checks if one set contains items that are also contained in a second set. Only if this second set contains every item from the first set is it considered a subset.

The isSupersetOf command checks if one set is larger and contains all the same items as a smaller set. Only if this first set is larger and has all its items stored in the second set is it considered a superset.

The isDisjointWith command compares two sets. If they have no items in common, then this command returns true. Otherwise, it returns false.

To see how to query a set, follow these steps:

1. Make sure the IntroductoryPlayground file is loaded in Xcode.

2. Edit the code as follows:

```
import Cocoa

var mySet = Set(["Fred", "Cindy", "Jody", "Grant"])
print (mySet.isEmpty)
mySet.count
mySet.removeAll()
print (mySet.isEmpty)
```

```
var myNewSet = Set(["John", "Oscar"])
var myOtherSet = Set(["John", "Oscar", "Sally"])
var myThirdSet = Set(["Rick", "Vinny"])

myNewSet.isSubset(of: myOtherSet)
myOtherSet.isSuperset(of: myNewSet)
myNewSet.isDisjoint(with: myThirdSet)
```

This code creates a set that holds four strings. It uses the isEmpty command to check if the set is empty (false). Then it counts the set (it has four items). Finally, it removes all the items from the set and uses the isEmpty command again to check if the set is empty (true).

The next batch of code creates three different sets called myNewSet, myOtherSet, and myThirdSet, which are filled with different names. Then the isSubset (of:) command checks if all the items in myNewSet ["John", "Oscar"] are also in the myOtherSet ["John", "Oscar", "Sally"], which is true.

The isSuperset (of:) command checks if myOtherSet ["John", "Oscar", "Sally"] contains more items and also contains all the items stored in myNewSet ["John", "Oscar"], which is also true.

Finally, the isDisjoint (with:) command checks if myNewSet ["John", "Oscar"] has nothing in common with myThirdSet ["Rick", "Vinny"], which is also true, as shown in Figure 10-3.

```
var mySet = Set(["Fred", "Cindy", "Jody", "Grant"])          {"Jody", "Cindy", "Grant", "Fred"}
println (mySet.isEmpty)                                       "false"
mySet.count                                                   4
mySet.removeAll()                                             0 members
println (mySet.isEmpty)                                       "true"

var myNewSet = Set(["John", "Oscar"])                         {"John", "Oscar"}
var myOtherSet = Set(["John", "Oscar", "Sally"])             {"John", "Oscar", "Sally"}
var myThirdSet = Set(["Rick", "Vinny"])                       {"Rick", "Vinny"}

myNewSet.isSubsetOf(myOtherSet)                               true
myOtherSet.isSupersetOf(myNewSet)                             true
myNewSet.isDisjointWith(myThirdSet)                           true
```

Figure 10-3. Querying a set

Manipulating Sets

When you have two or more sets, you can perform operations on both of the sets to create a third set. Some common set operations include

- union: Combines all items from two sets into a new set

- subtracting: Removes the items of a second set from a first set to form a new set

- intersection: Finds the common items in both sets and stores them in a new set

- symmetricDifference: Finds items contained in one set or another, but not items in both sets

Think of the union command as adding two sets together and the subtract command as subtracting one set from another. The union command specifies two set names, like this:

```
firstSet.union(secondSet)
```

Think of this as equivalent to firstSet + secondSet where all items from both sets get combined into a third set.

The subtracting command specifies two set names, but the order makes a difference, such as

```
thirdSet.subtracting(firstSet)
firstSet.subtracting(thirdSet)
```

These two commands can give different results depending on the contents of each set. Suppose thirdSet contains [1, 2, 3, 4, 5] and firstSet contains [1, 3, 5, 7]. The thirdSet.subtracting(firstSet) command works like this:

```
[1, 2, 3, 4, 5] thirdSet
[1, 3, 5, 7] firstSet
```

Both sets contain 1, 3, and 5 so those numbers get eliminated. Take 1, 3, and 5 out of thirdSet and you're left with [2, 4].

The firstSet.subtracting(thirdSet) command works like this:

```
[1, 3, 5, 7] firstSet
[1, 2, 3, 4, 5] thirdSet
```

Both sets contain 1, 3, and 5 so those numbers get eliminated. Take 1, 3, and 5 out of firstSet and you're left with {7}.

The `intersecting` command finds items in common between two sets. The `symmetricDifference` command finds items that are not in both sets. Think of the `symmetricDifference` command as the opposite of the `intersect` command.

To see how these four different ways to manipulate sets work, follow these steps:

1. Make sure the IntroductoryPlayground file is loaded in Xcode.

2. Enter the code as follows:

```
import Cocoa

var firstSet = Set([1, 3, 5, 7])
var secondSet = Set([2, 4, 6, 8])
var thirdSet = Set ([1, 2, 3, 4, 5])

firstSet.union(secondSet)
secondSet.subtracting(firstSet)
firstSet.subtracting(secondSet)
firstSet.subtracting(thirdSet)
thirdSet.subtracting(firstSet)

firstSet.intersection(thirdSet)
firstSet.symmetricDifference(thirdSet)
```

Notice how the subtracting command works differently depending on the order you list the two sets, as shown in Figure 10-4.

```
import Cocoa

var firstSet = Set([1, 3, 5, 7])                {5, 7, 3, 1}
var secondSet = Set([2, 4, 6, 8])               {6, 2, 4, 8}
var thirdSet = Set ([1, 2, 3, 4, 5])            {5, 2, 3, 1, 4}

firstSet.union(secondSet)                       {2, 4, 5, 7, 6, 3, 1, 8}
secondSet.subtracting(firstSet)                 {6, 2, 4, 8}
firstSet.subtracting(secondSet)                 {5, 7, 3, 1}
firstSet.subtracting(thirdSet)                  {7}
thirdSet.subtracting(firstSet)                  {2, 4}

firstSet.intersection(thirdSet)                 {5, 3, 1}
firstSet.symmetricDifference(thirdSet)          {7, 2, 4}
```

Figure 10-4. Manipulating sets

Summary

Tuples are a way to store different data types in a single variable. Like arrays and dictionaries, sets can store lists of the same data type. While arrays are best for storing ordered information and dictionaries are best for fast retrieval of data, sets are best for checking if items belong in a set or not as well as making it easy to manipulate two or more sets.

If you need to store large groups of related data, you can use a tuple, but a tuple gets clumsy with large numbers of data. With tuples, sets, arrays and dictionaries, you can store data in the most flexible way for your particular needs.

Chapter 11

Storing Code in Functions

Every program stores data (in variables or in data structures such as arrays, sets, or dictionaries) and then manipulates that data somehow. Code that manipulates data is called an algorithm.

If you want to use an algorithm in more than one place in your program, you can copy that code and paste it in a separate location. However, this can cause problems if you later want to modify the code. If you made 20 copies of the same algorithm, you'd now have to modify all 20 copies throughout your program. Not only would this be time-consuming, but it would be error-prone as well.

A better solution is to store algorithms in isolated parts of a program called functions. Chapter 6 introduced you to mathematical functions but you can create your own functions as well. Rather than copy algorithms and store them in multiple locations, you just store an algorithm in one place inside a function. Functions serve several purposes:

- To reuse code in different parts of a program
- To group related algorithms in one place
- To make it easy to isolate problems in a program

Think of functions as building blocks. Just as it's easier to build a house out of bricks rather than carving it out of a solid piece of rock, so you would never try to write a complicated program as a list of commands when you can divide a large program into multiple functions instead.

The Cocoa framework contains numerous functions you can use in your own programs. The basic idea behind a function is that you can use it without knowing how it works. To make the code inside a function run, you just need to "call" that function by name.

© Wallace Wang 2017
W. Wang, *macOS Programming for Absolute Beginners*,
DOI 10.1007/978-1-4842-2662-9_11

You should always strive to use the built-in functions of the Cocoa framework as much as possible because this lets you create programs by using pre-tested, reliable code. Of course, the Cocoa framework can't provide every possible function that you may need so you'll eventually need to create your own functions.

The purpose of functions is to simplify code. Functions basically replace multiple lines of code with a single line of code known as a function call.

The three types of functions you can create are

- Functions that do the same thing without accepting any data
- Functions that accept data
- Functions that return values

Remember, functions that accept data can also return values.

Simple Functions Without Parameters or Return Values

The simplest function just consists of a name, like this:

```
func functionName () {

}
```

By inserting one or more lines of code in between the curly brackets, you can make the function do something, such as

```
func simpleFunction () {
    print ("Hello")
    print ("there")
}
```

To run the code inside a function, you just need to call that function by name, such as

```
simpleFunction()
```

To see how this function works, follow these steps:

1. Open the IntroductoryPlayground file in Xcode.

2. Edit the code as follows:

```
import Cocoa

func simpleFunction () {
    print ("Hello")
}

var i = 1
while i <= 5 {
    simpleFunction()
    i = i + 1
}
```

This code defines a simple function that does nothing but print "Hello" and "there". Then it uses a while loop that runs five times and runs or calls the simpleFunction five times, as shown in Figure 11-1.

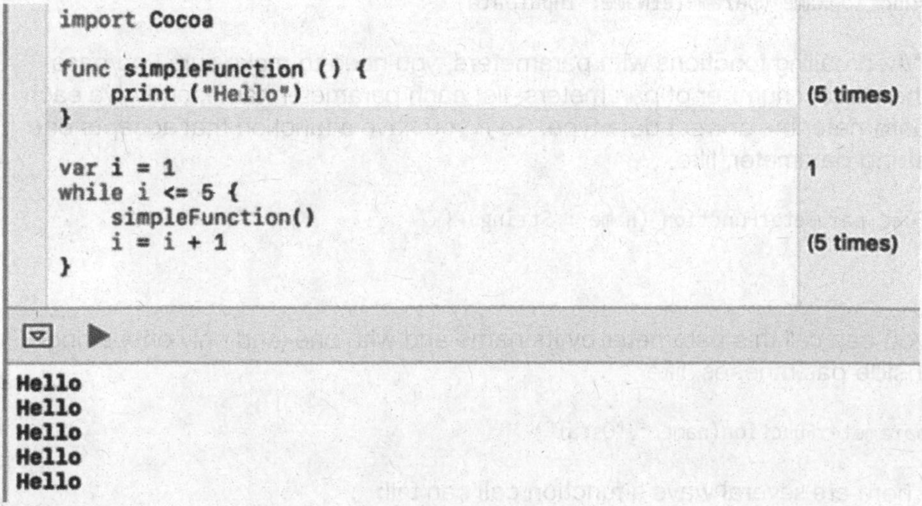

```
import Cocoa

func simpleFunction () {
    print ("Hello")                          (5 times)
}

var i = 1                                    1
while i <= 5 {
    simpleFunction()
    i = i + 1                                (5 times)
}
```

```
Hello
Hello
Hello
Hello
Hello
```

Figure 11-1. Defining and calling a simple function

Simple Functions with Parameters

Simple functions can only do the same thing over and over again regardless of changing circumstances. To make a function more flexible, it's more common to allow functions to accept data as input. Such data are called parameters.

Parameters let functions accept data and use that data to calculate a different result. To define a parameter, you must

- List a descriptive parameter name.

- Specify a data type such as Int or Double.

A function that accepts one parameter looks like this:

```
func functionName (parameterName: dataType) {

}
```

To call a function that defines a parameter, you must specify the parameter name followed by the data you want to give or pass to the function, such as

```
functionName (parameterName: inputData)
```

When calling functions with parameters, you need to make sure you pass the correct number of parameters, list each parameter name, and give each parameter the correct data type. So if you have a function that accepts one string parameter, like

```
func parameterFunction (name : String) {

}
```

you can call this parameter by its name and with one (and only one) string inside parentheses, like

```
parameterFunction(name : "Oscar")
```

There are several ways a function call can fail:

- If you type the function name incorrectly.

- If you don't include the parameter name.

- If you don't pass the correct number of parameters.

- If you don't list or pass parameters of the correct data type.

In this example, the parameterFunction expects one parameter that must be a String data type. Here are all the ways calling this function can fail:

- If you misspell the function name (parameterFunction).

- If you fail to include or misspell the parameter name (name:).

- If you don't pass the correct number of parameters (a single String data type).

- If you don't list or pass parameters of the correct data type (one String data type).

To see how a function with parameters works, follow these steps:

1. Make sure your IntroductoryPlayground file is loaded in Xcode.

2. Edit the code as follows:

```
import Cocoa

func parameterFunction (name : String) {
    print ("Hello, " + name)
}

parameterFunction(name: "Oscar")
```

This Swift program calls parameterFunction and passes it one string parameter ("Oscar"). When the parameterFunction receives this parameter ("Oscar"), it stores it in its name variable. Then it prints "Hello, Oscar", as shown in Figure 11-2.

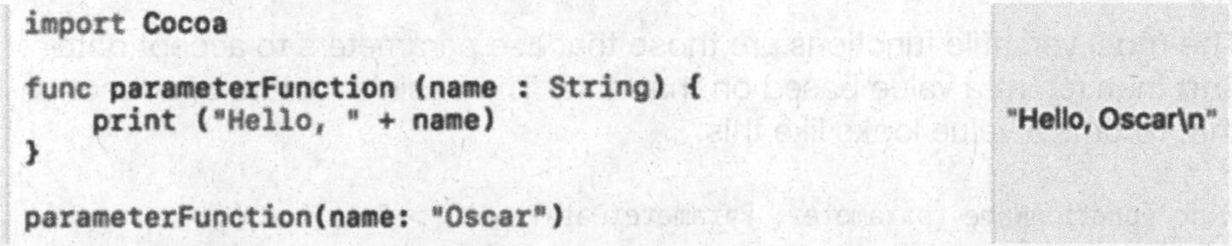

```
import Cocoa

func parameterFunction (name : String) {
    print ("Hello, " + name)
}                                          "Hello, Oscar\n"

parameterFunction(name: "Oscar")
```

Figure 11-2. Passing a string parameter to a function

Although this example uses one parameter, there's no limit to the number of parameters a function can accept. To accept more parameters, you just need to define additional variable names and data types, like this:

```
func functionName (parameter: dataType, parameter2 : dataType) {

}
```

Each parameter can accept different data types so you can pass a function a string and an integer, such as

```
func functionName (parameter: String, parameter2 : Int) {

}
```

To call this function, you specify the function name and its two parameters of the proper data type:

```
functionName (parameter: "Hello", parameter2: 48)
```

If you pass the parameters in the wrong order, the function call won't work:

```
functionName (parameter: 48, parameter2: "Hello")
```

When passing parameters, always make sure you pass the correct number of parameters, the name of each parameter, and the proper data types in the right order as well.

Functions with Parameters That Return Values

The most versatile functions are those that use parameters to accept data and then return a value based on that data. The basic structure of a function that returns a value looks like this:

```
func functionName (parameter: ParameterDataType) -> DataType {
return someValue
}
```

The function name is any arbitrary name you want to use. Ideally, make the function name descriptive of its purpose.

The parameter is much like declaring a variable by specifying the parameter name and its data type that it can accept. Parameters are optional but functions without parameters aren't generally useful since they perform the same tasks over and over.

The -> symbol defines the data type that the function name represents.

The return keyword must be followed by a value or commands that calculate a value. This value must be of the same data type that follows the -> symbols. Any function that returns a value can be stored in a variable of the same data type.

Suppose you had a function defined as follows:

```
func salesTax (amount: Double) -> Double {
    let currentTax = 0.075 // 7.5% sales tax
    return amount * currentTax
}
```

This function name is salesTax, it accepts one parameter called amount, which can store a Double data type. When it calculates a result, that result is also a Double data type as identified by Double after the -> symbol. The return keyword identifies how the function calculates a value to return.

Since this function returns a Double data type, you can store the results in a variable that is also a Double data type.

To see how this function works, follow these steps:

1. Make sure your IntroductoryPlayground file is loaded in Xcode.

2. Edit the code as follows:

```
import Cocoa

func salesTax (amount: Double) -> Double {
    let currentTax = 0.075
    return amount * currentTax
}

let purchasePrice = 59.95
var total : Double
total = purchasePrice + salesTax(amount:purchasePrice)
print ("Including sales tax, your total is =  \(total)")
```

Notice that this code calls the salesTax function by passing it the value stored in purchasePrice. When you type this code in the playground, you'll see the results displayed in the right margin, as shown in Figure 11-3. Change the values stored in purchasePrice and currentTax to see how it affects the results that this Swift code calculates.

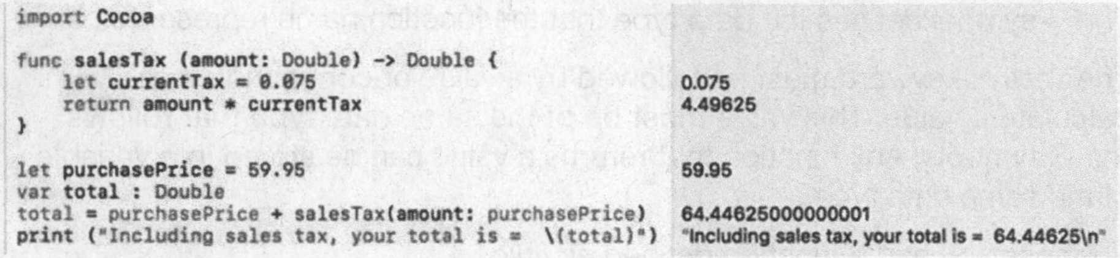

```
import Cocoa

func salesTax (amount: Double) -> Double {          0.075
    let currentTax = 0.075                          4.49625
    return amount * currentTax
}

let purchasePrice = 59.95                           59.95
var total : Double
total = purchasePrice + salesTax(amount: purchasePrice)   64.44625000000001
print ("Including sales tax, your total is = \(total)")   "Including sales tax, your total is = 64.44625\n"
```

Figure 11-3. Defining and calling a function

When a function returns a value, make sure you specify

- The data type the function represents (->dataType)

- The value the function name represents (return)

- That you store the returned function value in a variable that can hold the returned data type

When calling a function that returns a value, make sure the data types match. In the above example, the salesTax function returns a Double data type so in the Swift code, this salesTax function value gets stored in the total variable, which is also a Double data type.

Using Variable Parameters

When a function accepts parameters, it treats that parameter like a constant. This means within the function, Swift code cannot modify that parameter. If you want to modify a parameter within a function, then you need to create a variable parameter by identify the parameter with the var keyword, as follows:

```
func functionName (parameter: dataType {
var parameter = parameter
}
```

To see how variable parameters work, follow these steps:

1.   Make sure your IntroductoryPlayground file is loaded in Xcode.

2.   Edit the code as follows:

```
import Cocoa

func internalChange (name : String) {
    var name = name
    name = name.uppercased()
```

```
        print ("Hello " + name)
    }

    internalChange (name : "Tasha")
```

Within the `internalChange` function, the `name` parameter changes because the parameter is declared as a variable (`var   name = name`). The second line in the `internalChange` function changes the `name` parameter into uppercase. However, any changes the `internalChange` function makes to the `name` parameter has no effect in any other part of your program. All changes stay isolated within the `internalChange` function.

If you want to change a parameter and have those changes take affect outside a function, then you need to use inout parameters instead.

Using Inout Parameters

There are two ways to pass data to a function. One is to pass a fixed value, such as

```
sqrt(5)
```

A second way is to pass a variable that represents a value, such as

```
var z : Double = 45.0
var answer : Double
answer = sqrt(z)
```

In this Swift code, the value of z is 45.0 and is passed to the `sqrt` function. No matter what the `sqrt` function does, the value of z still remains 45.0.

If you want a function to change the value of its parameters, you can create what's called inout parameters. This means when you pass a variable to a function, that function changes that variable.

To define a parameter that a function can change, you just have to identify that parameter using the `inout` keyword, such as

```
func functionName (parameter: inout dataType) {

}
```

If a function has two or more parameters, you can designate one or more parameters as inout parameters. When you identify a parameter as an inout parameter, then the function must change that inout parameter. When you call a function and pass it an inout parameter, you must use the & symbol to identify an inout parameter, such as

```
functionName (parameter: &variable)
```

To see how inout parameters work, follow these steps:

1. Make sure your IntroductoryPlayground file is loaded in Xcode.

2. Edit the code as follows:

```
import Cocoa

func changeMe (name: inout String, age: Int) {
    print (name + " is \(age) years old")
    name = name.uppercased()
}

var animal : String = "Oscar the cat"
changeMe (name: &animal, age: 2)

print (animal)
```

The changeMe function defines two parameters:

- A string parameter called name and identified as an inout parameter

- An integer parameter called age

The changeMe function must modify the inout parameter somehow, which it does by changing the name parameter to uppercase, as shown in Figure 11-4.

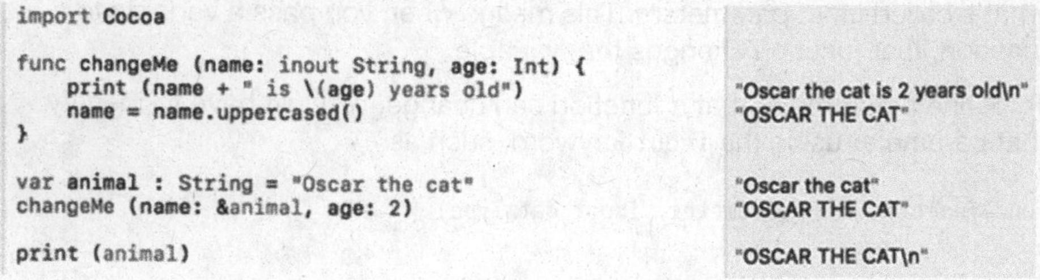

```
import Cocoa

func changeMe (name: inout String, age: Int) {        "Oscar the cat is 2 years old\n"
    print (name + " is \(age) years old")             "OSCAR THE CAT"
    name = name.uppercased()
}

var animal : String = "Oscar the cat"                 "Oscar the cat"
changeMe (name: &animal, age: 2)                      "OSCAR THE CAT"

print (animal)                                        "OSCAR THE CAT\n"
```

Figure 11-4. Using inout parameters

Calling the changeMe function sends it a String variable called "animal", which holds the string "Oscar the cat". The changeMe function expects two parameters where the first one is an inout parameter. This means calling the changeMe function must meet the following criteria:

- The changeMe function expects two parameters: a string and an integer, in that order.

- Since the string parameter is an inout parameter, the first parameter must be a variable identified with the & symbol.

Before calling the changeMe function, the animal variable contains the string "Oscar the cat". After calling the changeMe function, the animal variable now contains the string "OSCAR THE CAT". That's because the inout parameter in the changeMe function modified it.

Returning Multiple Values

To make a function return a value, you must specify two items:

- The data type the function returns, identified by the -> symbols such as -> Double

- The return keyword at the end of the function that identifies a single value

The following function identifies returns an Int value:

```
func add2Numbers (first : Int, second : Int) -> Int {
    return first + second
}

add2Numbers (first: 5, second: 17)
```

In most cases, you want a function to return just a single value, but functions can also return two or more values. If you want a function to return two or more values, you need to do the following:

- Specify all data types (in parentheses) that you want the function to return after the -> symbol.

- Use the return keyword and list all data in the correct order and data type (in parentheses).

- Store the returned multiple values in a tuple.

Remember, a tuple (Chapter 10) is a variable that can hold two or more values where each value can be a different data type, such as

```
var myTuple : (Double, Double, Double)
```

To create a function that returns more than one value, you simply enclose one or more data types in parentheses. So if you want a function to return three Double values, you define a function to return three Double values, like this:

```
func currencyConversion (USD : Double) -> (Double, Double, Double) {

}
```

Inside this function, you need to return three values that are Double data types, such as

```
return (USD * 0.8975, USD * 0.7988, USD * 6.76)
```

To see how to use functions that return multiple values, follow these steps:

1. Make sure your IntroductoryPlayground file is loaded in Xcode.

2. Edit the code as follows:

    ```
    import Cocoa

    var myTuple : (Double, Double, Double)

    func currencyConversion (USD : Double) -> (Double, Double,
    Double) {
        return (USD * 0.8975, USD * 0.7988, USD * 6.76)
    }

    myTuple = currencyConversion (USD: 20)

    print (myTuple.0)
    print (myTuple.1)
    print (myTuple.2)
    ```

To retrieve individual items stored in a tuple, you can use index numbers where the first item in a tuple is located at index 0, the second at index 1, and so on. Figure 11-5 shows how to create a function that returns multiple values, stores the multiple values in a tuple, and accesses each item in the tuple.

```
import Cocoa

var myTuple : (Double, Double, Double)

func currencyConversion (USD : Double) -> (Double,
    Double, Double) {
    return (USD * 0.8975, USD * 0.7988, USD * 6.76)      (.0 17.95, .1 15.976, .2 135.2)
}

myTuple = currencyConversion (USD: 20)                     (.0 17.95, .1 15.976, .2 135.2)

print (myTuple.0)                                         "17.95\n"
print (myTuple.1)                                         "15.976\n"
print (myTuple.2)                                         "135.2\n"
```

Figure 11-5. Returning multiple values from a function and accessing them in a tuple

Understanding IBAction Methods

If you remember in Chapter 3, you linked a button from the user interface to your Swift code to create an IBAction method, which is nothing more than a function that looks like this:

```
@IBAction func changeCase(_ sender: NSButton) {
        labelText.stringValue = messageText.stringValue.uppercased()
}
```

Now that you understand how functions work, let's dissect this line by line. First, @IBAction identifies a function that only runs when the user does something to a user interface item. If you look at the parameter list, you'll see (sender: NSButton), which tells you that when the user clicks on a button, the changeCase function will run the Swift code enclosed within the curly brackets.

The Swift code stored in any IBAction method typically manipulates data somehow. In this case, it converts text from a text field (represented by the IBOutlet variable messageText), converts it to uppercase, and then displays that uppercase text in a label (represented by the IBOutlet variable labelText).

Since it's possible for two or more user interface items to connect to the same IBAction method, the sender parameter identifies which button the user clicked. Since this IBAction method only connects to one button, the sender parameter is ignored.

IBAction methods are nothing more than special functions linked to items on your user interface. Within any program, you'll likely have multiple IBAction methods (functions) along with any additional functions you may have defined.

In addition, you'll likely use functions defined in the Cocoa framework even if you never see the actual code that makes those functions work. When creating any program, you'll use functions in one form or another.

Summary

Functions are mini-programs that perform a single task. Instead of trying to write a large program, you can write multiple smaller programs (functions) and paste them together to create a larger program. Functions act like building blocks.

The simplest function does the same thing over and over again, but more flexible functions accept input so they can use that input to calculate results. When a function accepts one or more chunks of data, it stores them in a parameter, which is like a variable.

Some functions can not only accept data, but can also return a value. To create a function that returns a value, you must specify the data type to return (using the -> symbols) and then use the return keyword inside the function to specify the exact data to send back.

If a function returns a single value, you can store that single value in a variable. Functions can also return multiple values, which you can store in a tuple.

When you connect user interface items (such as a button) to Swift code, you create special functions called IBAction methods. These IBAction methods are functions that run whenever the user clicks or does something on a user interface item.

Every time you write a program in Swift, you need to use functions. You can use functions stored in the Cocoa framework but chances are good you'll need to create your own functions as well.

Chapter 12

Defining Custom Data Types

To store data, Swift provides common data types such as integers (Int), decimal numbers (Float or Double), and text (String). In addition, Swift also offers Boolean data types (Bool) for holding true or false values.

While nearly every program will need to use one or more of these Swift data types, you may find them too limiting. That's why Swift provides several ways to create your own data types based on the basic Swift data types. In addition, Swift offers several ways to organize basic data types (Int, String, Double, etc.) in unique ways. Defining different ways to organize data types is called a data structure.

Essentially, programs consist of algorithms and data structures. Algorithms define how a program manipulates data, and data structures define how a program stores and organizes data.

How a program stores data can greatly determine both the speed and efficiency of a program. If a program organizes data poorly, it may take a long time to find the data it needs. There is no right or wrong way to organize data since every program has different needs.

Creating custom data types makes programs easier to understand. Swift provides several ways to create custom data types:

- Typealiases
- Enumerations

© Wallace Wang 2017
W. Wang, *macOS Programming for Absolute Beginners*,
DOI 10.1007/978-1-4842-2662-9_12

- Structures
- Combinations of different data types

Typealiases

Declaring variables as data types like Int, Double, or String only tells you what type of data it can hold, but doesn't tell you the meaning of that data. For example, if you declare two variables as Int data types, each can hold integers but one variable may represent ages and the other variable may represent employee ID numbers.

To make the purpose of data types clearer, Swift lets you use something called typealiases. A typealias lets you give a descriptive name to a generic data type name, such as

```
typealias EmployeeID = Int
```

Now instead of declaring a variable as an integer (Int) data type, you can declare it as an EmployeeID data type, such as

```
typealias EmployeeID = Int
var employee : EmployeeID

employee = 192
```

This is equivalent to

```
var employee : Int

employee = 192
```

Using Enumerations

One huge problem with the basic data types in Swift is that they tell you what the data contains (integers, strings, etc.) but they don't tell you what that data means. Typealiases can help give meaningful names to data types, but they're only one solution. A second solution is enumerations.

The idea behind enumerations is that they let you create your own data types and list the choices available for that data type. When you declare a variable as an Int data type, you're essentially allowing that variable to hold one of many possible integer values, which will likely be far more than you really need.

Enumerations let you define your own data type with a descriptive name and define the list of possible choices to store. To create an enumeration, you have to define an enumeration name, such as

```
enum EnumerationName {
    // enumeration definition goes here
}
```

The enumerations name is typically capitalized. Once you've created an enumeration name, you need to list the possible choices that enumeration can hold. The list of choices you create does not have to be any data type at all but can be any descriptive name you want.

Suppose you want to create a data type representing acceptable pets. You can create an enumeration like this:

```
enum Pets {
    case dog
    case cat
    case fish
    case bird
}
```

This defines the enumeration to hold only the values dog, cat, fish, or bird. Because you can name an enumeration's data types anything you want, you can make the choices descriptive and meaningful.

Once you've created an enumeration, you need to declare a variable to represent that enumeration, such as

```
var allowed : Pets
```

If you want to assign a value to this variable (declared as a Pets data type), you need to specify one of the choices defined by the enumeration, such as

```
allowed = Pets.cat
```

or as a shortcut,

```
allowed = .cat
```

Since the allowed variable is already declared as a Pets data type, you don't need to type "Pets" again when assigning an allowed choice (.cat instead of Pets.cat).

To see how a function with parameters works, follow these steps:

1. Make sure your IntroductoryPlayground file is loaded in Xcode.

2. Edit the code as follows:

```
enum Pets {
    case dog
    case cat
    case fish
    case bird
}

var allowed : Pets

allowed = .dog

print ("A \(allowed) is an acceptable pet")

allowed = Pets.cat

print ("A \(allowed) is an acceptable pet")
```

The Pets enumeration defines Pets to hold a value of dog, cat, fish, or bird.

The allowed variable is declared as a Pets data type so it can only hold one of those four values (dog, cat, fish, or bird).

Assigning a value to the allowed variable can either list the Pets enumeration name or omit it. Then the print command prints the Pets data in a string, as shown in Figure 12-1.

```
import Cocoa

enum Pets {
    case dog
    case cat
    case fish
    case bird
}

var allowed : Pets

allowed = .dog                                          dog

print ("A \(allowed) is an acceptable pet")            "A dog is an acceptable pet\n"

allowed = Pets.cat                                      cat

print ("A \(allowed) is an acceptable pet")            "A cat is an acceptable pet\n"
```

Figure 12-1. Using enumerations to define descriptive data

What happens if you assign data to a variable that isn't defined by the enumeration? Then Swift will catch the error and keep your program from running. So if you try

```
allowed = .hamster
```

it will fail to run because a hamster is not defined as a possible choice inside the Pets enumeration. Just as Swift won't let you store an integer inside a String variable, so it won't let you store any data in an enumeration that isn't specifically defined.

Using Structures

Suppose you want to store a list of names, street addresses, employee ID numbers, and annual salary amounts for several hundred people. How would you store all this data?

To store one person's information, you could create several variables, such as

```
var name : String
var street : String
var ID : Int
var salary : Double
```

Unfortunately, creating separate variables doesn't clearly identify that each person's name must also include a street address, employee ID, and salary. To get around this problem, you can group related variables in one location known as a structure.

Structures store different types of data in a single place. With a traditional variable, you can only store one chunk of data at a time. With a structure, you can define two or more chunks of data to store in a single variable. Variables declared inside a structure are called properties.

A structure that stores two chunks of data can look like this:

```
struct StructureName {
    var variableName1 : dataType
    var variableName2 : dataType
}
```

Remember, the data type of each variable can be simple data types like Int, String, or Double, or they can be more complicated data types like arrays, tuples, sets, enumerations, or dictionaries.

You can define two or more variables inside a structure where each variable can contain different data types, such as a string or an integer. No matter how many properties a structure holds, you must initialize the properties before you can store data in them.

Swift provides three ways to initialize properties. First, you can define an initial value for each property, like this:

```
struct StructureName {
    var variableName1 : dataType = initialValue
    var variableName2 : dataType = initialValue
}
```

To simplify the property declaration, a second way is to omit the data type and let Swift infer the data type, like this:

```
struct StructureName {
    var variableName1 = initialValue
    var variableName2 = initialValue
}
```

When you assign an initial value to properties, you can create a variable to represent that structure, like this:

```
var variableName = structureName()
```

A third way to initialize structure properties is to create an init function. This means you must create a list of property names and their data types. Then you assign values to those properties when you create a variable to represent that structure.

For example, suppose you want to store information about a person such as their name, e-mail address, and phone number. Instead of creating three separate variables, you can create a single structure, like this:

```
struct Person {
    var name : String
    var email : String
    var phone : String
}
```

If you just define the data types of each property, you need to create an initializer called init, as follows:

```
struct Person {
    var name : String
    var email : String
    var phone : String
    init (name: String, email: String, phone: String) {
        self.name = name
        self.email = email
        self.phone = phone
    }
}
```

When you create a variable based on this structure, you need include initial values, such as

```
var workers = person(name: "Sue", email: "sdk@aol.com", phone: "555-1234")
```

Creating a structure involves three parts:

- Create a structure with two or more variables (properties).

- Initialize all of the structure properties either by assigning values to each property or creating an init function.

- Create a variable to represent that structure.

Storing and Retrieving Items from a Structure

A structure lets you define the type of related data to store. Then you need to create a variable name to represent that structure. To store data using a structure, you need to specify the structure name and the variable name separated by a period, like this:

```
structureVariable.variableName = value
```

To retrieve data from a structure, you can assign a variable to a structure's variable, like this:

```
var variableName = structureVariable.variableName
```

To see how to create a structure, initialize its properties, and add and retrieve data, create a new playground by following these steps:

1. Make sure your IntroductoryPlayground file is loaded in Xcode.

2. Edit the code as follows:

```
import Cocoa

struct Pet {
    var name : String = ""
    var age : Int = 0
}

var dog = Pet()
dog.name = "Fido"
dog.age = 4

print (dog.name)
print (dog.age)

struct Person {
    var name : String
    var email : String
    var phone : String
    init (name: String, email: String, phone: String) {
        self.name = name
        self.email = email
        self.phone = phone
    }
}

var workers = Person(name: "Sue", email: "sdk@aol.com", phone:
"555-1234")

let boss = workers.name
print (boss)

workers.name = "Bo"
print (workers.email)
print (workers.phone)
```

The first structure defines initial values for its properties so there's no need for an init function. This is why you can create a variable with empty parentheses like this:

```
var dog = pet()
```

The second structure does not define initial values for its properties, so when you create a variable to represent that structure, you must define initial values:

```
var workers = person(name: "Sue", email: "sdk@aol.com", phone: "555-1234")
```

To store data in a structure, you need to specify the variable name representing the structure followed by the property name, as shown in Figure 12-2.

```
import Cocoa

struct Pet {                                          
    var name : String = ""                            
    var age : Int = 0                                 
}                                                     

var dog = Pet()                                        Pet
dog.name = "Fido"                                      Pet
dog.age = 4                                            Pet

print (dog.name)                                       "Fido\n"
print (dog.age)                                        "4\n"

struct Person {
    var name : String
    var email : String
    var phone : String
    init (name: String, email: String, phone: String) {
        self.name = name
        self.email = email
        self.phone = phone
    }
}

var workers = Person(name: "Sue", email: "sdk@aol.com",   Person
    phone: "555-1234")

let boss = workers.name                                "Sue"
print (boss)                                           "Sue\n"

workers.name = "Bo"                                    Person
print (workers.email)                                  "sdk@aol.com\n"
print (workers.phone)                                  "555-1234\n"
```

Figure 12-2. Creating a structure and retrieving data

Combining Data Structures

At the simplest level, you can use the basic data types available (Int, Float, Double, String). For more flexibility, you can combine data structures. For example, arrays normally contain a list of single values such as integers or strings. One common combination is to create an array of structures that can contain a list of related information such as names and addresses, as shown in Figure 12-3.

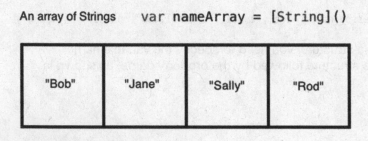

An array of Strings   `var nameArray = [String]()`

| "Bob" | "Jane" | "Sally" | "Rod" |

| "Bob" 12 Oak Street Buffalo | "Jane" 956 Holly Miami | "Sally" 780 Fairlane Dallas | "Rod" 43 Dire Street |

An array of Structures
```
struct Person {
    var name : String
    var address : String
    var state : String
}

var arrayOfStructures = [Person]()
```

Figure 12-3. An array of structures can hold related data

By combining different data structures, you can create unique ways to organize data such as an array of sets, a dictionary that contains arrays, or a structure of tuples. Anywhere you can use a data type like Int or String, you can also use a data structure like an array, set, or dictionary.

One common combination are arrays that hold structures. By themselves, structures can only hold a limited number of data. An array of structures acts like a simple database. The structure defines the type of information to store about a person such as name, address, and age, and the array holds multiple copies of this data.

To show you how to create an array of structures, you'll create a program that will let you type in multiple names, addresses, and phone numbers, and then delete data as well.

1. From within Xcode choose File ➤ New ➤ Project.

2. Click Application under the macOS category.

3. Click Cocoa Application and click the Next button. Xcode now asks for a product name.

4. Click in the Product Name text field and type **StructureProgram**.

5. Make sure the Language pop-up menu displays Swift and that no check boxes are selected.

6. Click the Next button. Xcode asks where you want to store the project.

7. Choose a folder to store your project and click the Create button.

8. Click the MainMenu.xib file in the Project Navigator.

9. Click the StructureProgram icon to make the window of the user interface appear.

10. Choose View ➤ Utilities ➤ Show Object Library to make the Object Library appear in the bottom right corner of the Xcode window.

11. Drag two push buttons, four labels, and four text fields onto the user interface and double-click the push buttons and labels to change the text that appears on them so that it looks similar to Figure 12-4.

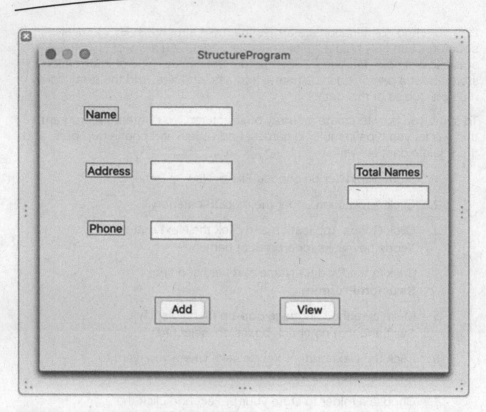

Figure 12-4. The user interface of the StructureProgram

After you type a name, address, and phone number in the appropriate text fields, the Add button will store this information in a structure, and then store this structure in an array. Each time you add another name, address, and phone number, you'll be adding another structure to the array while the Total Names text field constantly lists the total number of structures stored in the array.

The View button removes the last item from the array and displays its contents in an alert dialog so you can verify its contents. Then it displays the new total number of structures in the array.

Each text field will need a separate IBOutlet and each push button will need a separate IBAction method, which you create by Control-dragging each item from the user interface to your AppDelegate.swift file:

1. With your user interface still visible in the Xcode window, choose View ➤ Assistant Editor ➤ Show Assistant Editor. The AppDelegate.swift file appears next to the user interface.

2. Move the mouse over the Add button, hold down the Control key, and drag just above the last curly bracket at the bottom of the AppDelegate.swift file.

3. Release the mouse and the Control key. A pop-up window appears.

4. Click in the Connection pop-up menu and choose Action.

5. Click in the Name text field and type **addData**.

6. Click in the Type pop-up menu and choose NSButton. Then click the Connect button.

7. Move the mouse over the View button, hold down the Control key, and drag just above the last curly bracket at the bottom of the AppDelegate.swift file.

8. Release the mouse and the Control key. A pop-up window appears.

9. Click in the Connection pop-up menu and choose Action.

10. Click in the Name text field and type **viewButton**.

11. Click in the Type pop-up menu and choose NSButton. Then click the Connect button. The bottom of the AppDelegate.swift file should look like this:

```
@IBAction func addData(_ sender: NSButton) {
}

@IBAction func viewData(_ sender: NSButton) {
}
```

12. Move the mouse over the Name text field that appears to the right of the Add button, hold down the Control key, and drag below the @IBOutlet line in the AppDelegate.swift file.

13. Release the mouse and the Control key. A pop-up window appears.

14. Click in the Name text field and type **nameField** and click the Connect button.

15.   Move the mouse over the Address text field that
      appears to the right of the Add button, hold down
      the Control key, and drag below the @IBOutlet line in
      the AppDelegate.swift file.

16.   Release the mouse and the Control key. A pop-up
      window appears.

17.   Click in the Name text field and type **addressField**
      and click the Connect button.

18.   Move the mouse over the Phone text field that
      appears to the right of the Delete button, hold down
      the Control key, and drag below the @IBOutlet line in
      the AppDelegate.swift file.

19.   Release the mouse and the Control key. A pop-up
      window appears.

20.   Click in the Name text field and type **phoneField** and
      click the Connect button.

21.   Move the mouse over the Total Names text field that
      appears to the right of the Query button, hold down
      the Control key, and drag below the @IBOutlet line in
      the AppDelegate.swift file.

22.   Release the mouse and the Control key. A pop-up
      window appears.

23.   Click in the Name text field and type **totalField** and
      click the Connect button. You should now have the
      following IBOutlets that represent all the text fields
      on your user interface:

      ```
      @IBOutlet weak var window: NSWindow!
      @IBOutlet weak var nameField: NSTextField!
      @IBOutlet weak var addressField: NSTextField!
      @IBOutlet weak var phoneField: NSTextField!
      @IBOutlet weak var totalField: NSTextField!
      ```

At this point, you've connected the user interface to your Swift code so you
can use the IBOutlets to retrieve and display data on the user interface.
You've also created the IBAction methods so the push buttons on the user
interface will make the program actually work. Now you just need to write
Swift code to create an initial structure and then write more Swift code to
create an array that holds that structure.

24.   Underneath the IBOutlet list in the `AppDelegate.`
      `swift` file, type the following to create a structure that
      can hold three strings, a name, address, and phone
      number; a variable that represents the structure; and
      an array of structures:

```swift
struct Person {
var name : String = ""
var address : String = ""
var phone : String = ""
}

var employee = Person()

var arrayOfStructures = [Person] ()
```

25.   Modify the `addData` IBAction method so it takes a
      value from the Name, Address, and Phone text fields
      and stores them in the employee structure. Then it
      stores that structure in an array, displays the total
      number of array items in the Total Names text field,
      and clears the Name, Address, and Phone text fields:

```swift
@IBAction func addData(_ sender: NSButton) {
    employee.name = nameField.stringValue
    employee.address = addressField.stringValue
    employee.phone = phoneField.stringValue
    arrayOfStructures.append(employee)
    totalField.integerValue = arrayOfStructures.count

    nameField.stringValue = ""
    addressField.stringValue = ""
    phoneField.stringValue = ""
}
```

26.   Modify the `viewData` IBAction method so it takes
      a value from the Key text field and deletes the
      associates value from the dictionary as follows:

```swift
@IBAction func viewData(_ sender: NSButton) {
    let myAlert = NSAlert()
if arrayOfStructures.isEmpty {
    myAlert.messageText = "Array is empty"
    myAlert.runModal()
```

```
                    } else {
                        var personData = Person()
                        personData = (arrayOfStructures.removeLast())
                        totalField.integerValue = arrayOfStructures.count
                        myAlert.messageText = personData.name + "\r\n" +
                        personData.address + "\r\n" + personData.phone
                        myAlert.runModal()
                    }
                }
```

The code inside the viewData IBAction method creates an alert dialog. Then it checks if the array is empty. If so, it displays "Array is empty" in the alert dialog.

If the array is not empty, then it removes the last structure stored in the array, displays the new total number of array items in the Total Names text field, and displays the removed structure data in the alert dialog.

The complete contents of the AppDelegate.swift file should look like this:

```
import Cocoa

@NSApplicationMain
class AppDelegate: NSObject, NSApplicationDelegate {

    @IBOutlet weak var window: NSWindow!
    @IBOutlet weak var nameField: NSTextField!
    @IBOutlet weak var addressField: NSTextField!
    @IBOutlet weak var phoneField: NSTextField!
    @IBOutlet weak var totalField: NSTextField!

    struct Person {
        var name : String = ""
        var address : String = ""
        var phone : String = ""
    }

    var employee = Person()

    var arrayOfStructures = [Person] ()

    func applicationDidFinishLaunching(_ aNotification: Notification) {
        // Insert code here to initialize your application
    }

    func applicationWillTerminate(_ aNotification: Notification) {
        // Insert code here to tear down your application
    }
```

```
@IBAction func addData(_ sender: NSButton) {
    employee.name = nameField.stringValue
    employee.address = addressField.stringValue
    employee.phone = phoneField.stringValue
    arrayOfStructures.append(employee)
    totalField.integerValue = arrayOfStructures.count

    nameField.stringValue = ""
    addressField.stringValue = ""
    phoneField.stringValue = ""

}

@IBAction func viewData(_ sender: NSButton) {
    let myAlert = NSAlert()
    if arrayOfStructures.isEmpty {
        myAlert.messageText = "Array is empty"
        myAlert.runModal()
    } else {
        var personData = Person()
        personData = (arrayOfStructures.removeLast())
        totalField.integerValue = arrayOfStructures.count
        myAlert.messageText = personData.name + "\r\n" + personData.
        address + "\r\n" + personData.phone
        myAlert.runModal()
    }

}
}
```

To see how this program works, follow these steps:

1. Choose Product ➤ Run. Xcode runs your
   StructureProgram project.

2. Click in the Name text field and type **Bob**.

3. Click in the Address text field and type **123 Main**.

4. Click in the Phone text field and type **555-1234**.

5. Click the Add button. The program shows the
   number of items in the array (1) in the Total Names
   text field.

6. Repeat steps 2–5 except type the name **Jane**,
   the address **90 Oak Lane**, and the phone number
   555-9874. The number 2 appears in the Total Names
   text field.

7. Click the View button. An alert dialog appears, displaying Jane, 90 Oak Lane, and 555-9874, as shown in Figure 12-5.

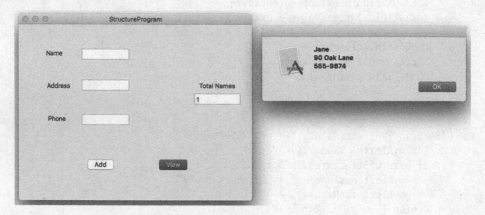

Figure 12-5. An alert dialog showing the last structure added to the array

8. Click OK to make the alert dialog go away.
9. Choose StructureProgram ➤ Quit StructureProgram.

Summary

Every program needs to store and manipulate data. At the simplest level, you can store data in one of Swift's basic data types (Int, Double, Float, String). To make these basic data types more descriptive, you can use typealiases, which lets you choose a more meaningful name to represent a basic data type such as a String or Double.

To create your own data type and restrict the values it can hold, you can use enumerations. Enumerations let you list all possible choices the enumeration can hold so you can create more descriptive names.

If you want to group related data together, regardless of the data type, you can use a structure. By combining structures with another data structure such as arrays, you can create a list of related data. Combining data structures lets you organize data the most efficient way possible for your program.

Chapter 13

Creating Classes and Objects

The heart of programming in Swift using Xcode is object-oriented programming. The main idea is to divide a large program into separate objects where each object ideally represents a physical entity. For example, if you are creating a program to control a car, one object may represent the car's engine, a second object may represent the car's entertainment system, and a third object may represent the car's heating and cooling system.

Now if you want to update the part of a program that controls the car's engine, you just have to modify or replace the object that controls that car engine. Objects not only help you better understand how different parts of a program work together, but also isolate code so you can create building blocks to put together larger, more sophisticated programs.

Objects help you visualize your program as separate building blocks that are independent from each other. Before object-oriented programming, programmers divided programs into functions, which also acted like miniature building blocks. The main difference between functions and objects is that functions can access data used by other functions. This means that if you modify one function, you often inadvertently affect other parts of the program. This makes fixing errors or bugs difficult and also makes modifying programs difficult as well.

With objects, the main idea is to create separate, independent building blocks that work together without affecting each other's data. To keep data isolated, objects use encapsulation. This means an object has its own variables (called properties) and functions (called methods).

© Wallace Wang 2017
W. Wang, *macOS Programming for Absolute Beginners*,
DOI 10.1007/978-1-4842-2662-9_13

The only way you can modify data in an object is to use that object's methods. This way, if something goes wrong, you can isolate the problem to that object's methods. Without objects, any part of a program can interfere with data used by another part of a program, which makes finding and fixing problems nearly impossible.

Objects can communicate with each other in two ways:

- By storing new values in another object's properties
- By calling another object's methods

Ideally, a program should consist of independent objects that perform tasks completely independent from each other. This makes it easy to modify a program by replacing one object with an improved version of that object.

Creating Classes

There are two steps to creating an object. First, you have to create a class. Second, you create an object based on that class.

A class looks and works much like a structure (see Chapter 12). The main difference is that a structure only contains data, while a class can contain data and functions to manipulate that data.

Once you've defined a class, you can create one or more objects based on that class. Think of a class as a cookie cutter that defines the shape of cookies, and objects as different types of dough you can define based on the class.

The simplest type of class you can define looks like this:

```
class ClassName {

}
```

To create an object from this class, you just declare a variable, but instead of defining a data type like Int or String, you define the class name, such as

```
var myObject = ClassName()
```

Of course, a class that contains no code is useless, so the two types of code you can include in a class are variables (known as properties) and functions for manipulate data (known as methods). Creating properties in a class involves creating one or more variables and defining a data type and an initial value, such as

```
class ClassName {
    var name : String = ""
    var ID : Int = 0
    var salary : Double = 0
}
```

Initial values are important because when you create an object based on a class, you don't want uninitialized values that could cause problems if you try to use them.

To define a property, you declare a variable name, a data type, and an initial value. Since Swift can infer data types, you could omit the data type declaration and just assign initial values, like this:

```
class ClassName {
    var name = ""
    var ID  = 0
    var salary = 0
}
```

If you aren't sure what type of initial values you want to store, you can just use optional variables, such as

```
class ClassName {
    var name : String?
    var ID : Int?
    var salary : Double?
}
```

Optional variables have an initial value of nil, so you'll likely want to store actual values eventually.

Whether you define class properties with an initial value or as a nil value with optional variables, you can create an object from a class by just creating a variable name, setting it equal to the class name, and following it with an empty set of parentheses, like this:

```
var myObject = ClassName()
```

Both of the previous methods create the same initial values for the class properties. For more flexibility, you can create an initializer method called init. It lets you define initial values each time you create an object from a class. An initializer in a class might look like this:

```
class SecondClass {
    var name : String
    var ID : Int
    var salary : Double
    init (name: String, ID: Int, salary: Double) {
```

```
        self.name = name
        self.ID = ID
        self.salary = salary
    }
}
```

This initializer method (init) defines a parameter list that accepts three items: a string, an integer, and a double value. Then it stores this information in the name, ID, and salary properties, respectively. When a class has an initializer, you must create an object from that class by including the proper number and data type to match the initializer parameter list.

This means creating an object that includes a string, an integer, and a double value in parentheses, like this:

```
var secondObject = SecondClass (name: "Joe", ID: 102, salary: 120000)
```

Notice that when you include data in the parameter list, you must label each data chunk with the variable name defined in the initializer parameter list. In this case, the three parameter names are name, ID, and salary, so creating an object means identifying the data with those same parameter names.

Accessing Properties in an Object

To access an object's properties, you must specify the object name followed by a period and the property name, such as

```
objectName.propertyName = data
```

You can also assign an object's property values to a variable, like this:

```
var person = myObject.name
```

To access properties, you need to specify the object name, a period, and the property name that you want to access, such as

```
print (person.name)
```

> **Note**   When accessing values stored in properties, make sure you specify the object name, not the class name. If you create a person object from the ClassName class, you access properties by specifying the object name (person) and the property name (name, ID, salary) such as person.name or person. ID. You don't access the property value by using the class name such as ClassName.name or className.ID. If you try this, your code will not work.

Just like ordinary variables, an object's properties can only hold one chunk of data at a time. The moment you store new data in a property, it wipes out the previous data.

To see how to create a class and work with an object's properties, follow these steps:

1. Make sure the IntroductoryPlayground file is loaded in Xcode.

2. Edit the code as follows:

```
import Cocoa

class ClassName {
    var name = ""
    var ID  = 0
    var salary = 0
}

var worker = ClassName()
worker.name = "Bob"
worker.ID = 102
worker.salary = 10

class SecondClass {
    var name : String
    var ID : Int
    var salary : Double
    init (name: String, ID: Int, salary: Double) {
        self.name = name
        self.ID = ID
        self.salary = salary
    }
}

var executive = SecondClass (name: "Joe", ID: 17, salary: 50000)

print (worker.name)
print (worker.ID)
print (worker.salary)

print (executive.name)
print (executive.ID)
print (executive.salary)
```

The first class initializes its properties when they're declared. Then it creates an object (worker) based on the class (ClassName). To store data in the worker object, the code specifies the object name (worker) and property name and assigns it a value.

The second class example uses an initializer to define the property values. The init method accepts three chunks of data, a string, an integer, and a decimal (Double) value, in that order.

To create an object (executive) from this second class (SecondClass), the parentheses need to include the right number of data in the right order, along with the proper data types, in addition to displaying a label to identify what the data means, as shown in Figure 13-1.

```
import Cocoa

class ClassName {
    var name = ""
    var ID  = 0
    var salary = 0
}

var worker = ClassName()                          ClassName
worker.name = "Bob"                               ClassName
worker.ID = 102                                   ClassName
worker.salary = 10                                ClassName


class SecondClass {
    var name : String
    var ID : Int
    var salary : Double
    init (name: String, ID: Int, salary: Double) {
        self.name = name
        self.ID = ID
        self.salary = salary
    }
}

var executive = SecondClass (name: "Joe", ID: 17,    SecondClass
    salary: 50000)

print (worker.name)                                "Bob\n"
print (worker.ID)                                  "102\n"
print (worker.salary)                              "10\n"

print (executive.name)                             "Joe\n"
print (executive.ID)                               "17\n"
print (executive.salary)                           "50000.0\n"
```

Figure 13-1. Creating a class file and accessing properties

Computed Properties in an Object

As an alternative to defining fixed values for properties, you can also use computed properties where one property's initial value depends on the value of another property. The simplest way to create a computed property is to define a property name, a data type, and then in curly brackets write code that calculates a value. Finally, use the return keyword to define the value to store in the property.

This computed property simply takes the value stored in the height property, multiples it by 2, and stores that result in the width property. When you create an object based on the shape class, the initial value of 5 gets stored in the height property and the computed property multiples the height value (5) by 2 to get 10, which it stores in the width property, as shown in Figure 13-2.

```
import Cocoa

class Shape {
    var height : Int = 5
    var width : Int {
        return height * 2                          10
    }
}
var rectangle = Shape()                            Shape
print (rectangle.height)                           "5\n"
print (rectangle.width)                            "10\n"
```

Figure 13-2. *Using computed properties to determine a property's initial value*

In this example of a computed property, the value of one property (width) gets the value of another property (height) to determine its own value. In technical terms, this is known as a getter.

Setting Other Properties

Another option for storing values in a property is to use what's called a setter. With a setter, defining one property sets the value of another property. Since getters and setters are so similar, they're often used within the same property. This way one property uses a getter to calculate its value from another property, so if you set that property with a value, it can change another property. Defining getters and setters looks like this:

```
class Blob {
        var property1 : dataType = value
    var property2 : dataType {
        get {
            return valueHere
        }
        set {
            property1 = valueHere
        }
    }
}
```

In the getter, you always need a return keyword to return a value to the property that has the getter. In the setter, you must assign a property to a value. This value can be a fixed value or a calculation that returns a value.

> **Note**   You don't need both a getter and a setter. You can just have a getter,
> which you can shorten by eliminating the get keyword and just enclose code
> in curly brackets, as in the class shape example in the beginning of this section.
> You can also have just a setter, but you need to use the set keyword.

In the above example, every time property2 gets assigned a new value, it
uses its setter to define a new value for property1.

A setter can also accept a value and use that value to calculate a new result
for a different property. To accept a value for a setter, you just need to create
a variable enclosed in parentheses and use that value to calculate a result
for another property, such as

```
class Blob {
      var property1 : dataType = value
    var property2 : dataType {
        get {
            return valueHere
        }
        set (newValue) {
            property1 = valueHere based on newValue
        }
    }
}
```

To see how getters and setters work, follow these steps:

1. Make sure your IntroductoryPlayground file is loaded
    into Xcode.

2. Edit the code as follows:

```
import Cocoa

class Shape {
    var height : Int = 5
    var width : Int {
      return height * 2
    }
}

var rectangle = Shape()
print (rectangle.height)
print (rectangle.width)
```

```
rectangle.height = 20
print (rectangle.width)

class Blob {
    var height : Int = 5
    var width : Int = 10
    var area : Int {
        get {
            return height * width
        }
        set (newValue) {
            height = newValue + 10
            width = newValue - 5
        }
    }
}

var CEO = Blob()
print (CEO.area)
CEO.area = 247
print (CEO.height)
print (CEO.width)
```

You can think of a getter and setter as a functions that change other properties. Be careful when using getters and setters, though, since they can cause unexpected behavior if you aren't aware of their existence or how they work. Figure 13-3 shows the result of the above code so you can see how the getters and setters affect properties.

```
import Cocoa

class Shape {
    var height : Int = 5
    var width : Int {
        return height * 2                                    (2 times)
    }
}

var rectangle = Shape()                                      Shape
print (rectangle.height)                                     "5\n"
print (rectangle.width)                                      "10\n"

rectangle.height = 20                                        Shape
print (rectangle.width)                                      "40\n"

class Blob {
    var height : Int = 5
    var width : Int = 10
    var area : Int {
        get {
            return height * width                            50
        }
        set (newValue) {
            height = newValue + 10                           Blob
            width = newValue - 5                             Blob
        }
    }
}

var CEO = Blob()                                             Blob
print (CEO.area)                                             "50\n"
CEO.area = 247                                               Blob
print (CEO.height)                                           "257\n"
print (CEO.width)                                            "242\n"
```

Figure 13-3. Using getters and setters to modify properties

Using Property Observers

Swift provides two property observers called willSet and didSet. The willSet property observer runs code before a property receives a value. The didSet property observer runs code after a property receives a value.

Like getters and setters, property observers essentially are functions that run when a property gets a new value. The basic structure for a willSet and didSet property observer is identical to the structure for a getter and setter:

```
var property : dataType = initialValue {
    willSet {

    }
    didSet {

    }
}
```

The willSet property observer runs code before the property gets a new value. The didSet property observer runs code after the property gets a new value. To see how property observers work, follow these steps:

1. Make sure your IntroductoryPlayground file is loaded into Xcode.

2. Edit the code as follows:

```
import Cocoa

class Animal {
    var IQ : Int = 0
    var legs : Int = 0 {
        willSet {
            IQ += 10
        }
        didSet {
            IQ -= 3
        }
    }
}

var pet = Animal()
print (pet.IQ)
pet.legs = 4
print (pet.IQ)
```

In this example, the IQ property has an initial value of 0. Notice that when you set the legs property to 4, it immediately runs the willSet property observer code, which increases the IQ property by 10. Then it immediately runs the code in the didSet property observer, which subtracts 3, as shown in Figure 13-4.

```
import Cocoa

class Animal {
    var IQ : Int = 0
    var legs : Int = 0 {
        willSet {
            IQ += 10
        }
        didSet {
            IQ -= 3
        }
    }
}

var pet = Animal()                    Animal
print (pet.IQ)                        "0\n"
pet.legs = 4                          Animal
print (pet.IQ)                        "7\n"
```

Figure 13-4. Using property observers

Creating Methods

A class that simply stores one or more properties can be convenient for grouping related data together. However, what makes object-oriented programming more useful is when objects can also manipulate their own data. To create mini-programs for objects to run, you need to define functions (called methods) inside a class.

You saw methods when you linked push buttons from the user interface to create an IBAction method in the Swift code file. The simplest method inside a class performs the exact same function:

```
class CountDown {
    var counter = 10
    func decrement() {
        counter = counter - 1
    }
}
```

This decrement method simply subtracts 1 from the counter property, which has an initial value of 10. To make this method run, you have to specify the object name, a period, and the method name, like this:

```
var myObject = CountDown ()
myObject.decrement()
```

This decrement method does the exact same thing every time, which is it subtracts 1 from the counter property. A more interesting and flexible method would accept data (one or more parameters) to modify the code in the method works, such as:

```
class CountDown {
    var counter = 10
    func decrement() {
        counter = counter - 1
    }
    func decrementByValue (step : Int) {
        counter -= step
    }
}
```

The second method, decrementByValue, accepts a single integer that gets stored in a variable called step. Then it subtracts the value of step from the counter property, as shown in Figure 13-5.

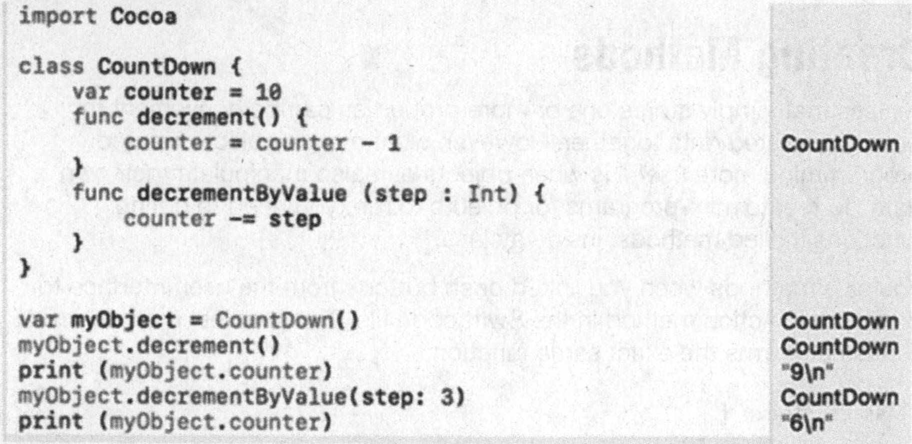

```
import Cocoa

class CountDown {
    var counter = 10
    func decrement() {
        counter = counter - 1                          CountDown
    }
    func decrementByValue (step : Int) {
        counter -= step
    }
}

var myObject = CountDown()                             CountDown
myObject.decrement()                                   CountDown
print (myObject.counter)                               "9\n"
myObject.decrementByValue(step: 3)                     CountDown
print (myObject.counter)                               "6\n"
```

Figure 13-5. Running a method that accepts a value

When a method accepts data, it can also return a specific value. To create such a method, you need to identify the data type the method returns (using the ➤ symbols) along with the return keyword that defines the specific value to return.

So if you want to create a method that returns a Float data type, you can define a method such as

```
class MathBrain {
    var tempValue: Float = 0
    func average (first : Float, second : Float) -> Float {
        return (first + second) / 2
    }
}
```

This method accepts two Float numbers (stored in variables called first and second) and returns a Float value. To call this method, you specify an object name, a period, the method name, and two numbers that are Float data types.

Notice that this method has two parameters called first and second. When passing parameters, you must specify the parameter name (first and second), such as

```
var math = MathBrain()
var temp : Float = math.average(first: 4.0, second: 9.0)
print (temp)
```

To see how to create a set, and add and remove data from it, create a new playground by following these steps:

1. Make sure your IntroductoryPlayground file is loaded into Xcode.

2. Edit the code as follows:

```
import Cocoa

class MathBrain {
    var tempValue: Float = 0
    func average (first : Float, second : Float) -> Float {
        return (first + second) / 2
    }
}

var math = MathBrain()
var temp : Float = math.average(first: 4.0, second: 9.0)
print (temp)
```

The average method accepts two parameters, adds them together, and divides by 2. Then it uses the return keyword to return this value.

When the average method gets passed the numbers 4.0 and 9.0, it returns a value of 6.5, which gets stored in a variable called temp, as shown in Figure 13-6.

```
import Cocoa

class MathBrain {
    var tempValue: Float = 0
    func average (first : Float, second : Float) ->
        Float {
        return (first + second) / 2                    6.5
    }
}

var math = MathBrain()                                 MathBrain
var temp : Float = math.average(first: 4.0, second: 9.0)   6.5
print (temp)                                           "6.5\n"
```

Figure 13-6. Passing parameters to a method in an object

Using Objects in an macOS Program

Objects can contain any number of properties, and those properties can hold simple data types like integers or strings, or more complicated data types like tuples, sets, or arrays. An object can also contain one or more methods that typically manipulate the object's properties.

In this sample program, you'll define one class and create two objects based on that class. You'll also see how to store a class in a separate file. Rather than cram everything into a single file, it's easier to store code in separate files.

The two objects will run methods stored in the other object. The user interface will also retrieve values from both object's properties to display in the text field of the user interface.

To learn more about user interfaces, you'll also see how to connect two buttons to a single IBAction method and determine which button the user clicked. As usual, you'll see how to display data in a user interface item through an IBOutlet. To create the sample program, follow these steps:

1. From within Xcode choose File ➤ New ➤ Project.

2. Click Application under the macOS category.

3. Click Cocoa Application and click the Next button. Xcode now asks for a product name.

4. Click in the Product Name text field and type **ObjectProgram**.

5. Make sure the Language pop-up menu displays Swift and that no check boxes are selected.

6. Click the Next button. Xcode asks where you want to store the project.

7. Choose a folder to store your project and click the Create button.

8. Click the `MainMenu.xib` file in the Project Navigator.

9. Click the ObjectProgram icon to make the window of the user interface appear.

10. Choose View ➤ Utilities ➤ Show Object Library to make the Object Library appear in the bottom right corner of the Xcode window.

11. Drag two push buttons, two labels, and two text fields onto the user interface and double-click the push buttons and labels to change the text that appears on them so that it looks similar to Figure 13-7.

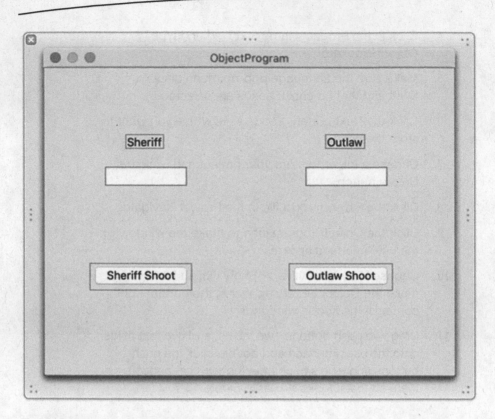

Figure 13-7. The user interface of the ObjectProgram

This user interface will display the number of hit points for two characters: a sheriff and an outlaw. Each time you click either the Sheriff Shoot or the Outlaw Shoot button, an IBAction method will randomly determine if the other character was hit or not. If so, it will also determine how much damage the shot caused, ranging from 1 to 3. Any changes will appear in the text field under the Sheriff or Outlaw label.

The Sheriff Shoot and Outlaw Shoot buttons runs an IBAction method that first determines which button the user clicked, the Sheriff Shoot or the Outlaw Shoot button. To identify which button the user clicked, you need to modify a Tag property on each button so the Sheriff Shoot button has a Tag value of 0 and the Outlaw Shoot button has a Tag value of 1.

After determining whether the sheriff or the outlaw is shooting, the IBAction method runs the shoot method that randomly determines if the shot hit and the damage it caused, which gets subtracted from the hitPoints property of each object.

The total number of hit points appears in the text field under the Sheriff and Outlaw label. The moment the total number of hit points for either the sheriff or outlaw drops to 0 or less, an alert dialog appears to let you know whether the sheriff or the outlaw died. To connect your user interface to your Swift code, follow these steps:

1. With your user interface still visible in the Xcode window, choose View ➤ Assistant Editor ➤ Show Assistant Editor. The AppDelegate.swift file appears next to the user interface.

2. Move the mouse over the Sheriff Shoot button, hold down the Control key, and drag just above the last curly bracket at the bottom of the AppDelegate.swift file.

3. Release the mouse and the Control key. A pop-up window appears.

4. Click in the Connection pop-up menu and choose Action.

5. Click in the Name text field and type **shootButton**.

6. Click in the Type pop-up menu and choose NSButton. Then click the Connect button.

7. Move the mouse over the Outlaw Shoot button, hold down the Control key, and drag over the existing IBAction shootButton method you just created until the entire method appears highlighted, as shown in Figure 13-8.

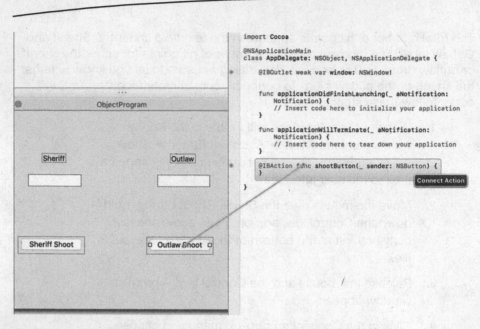

Figure 13-8. Connecting the Outlaw Shoot button to an existing IBAction method

8. Release the mouse and the Control key to connect the Outlaw Shoot button to the existing IBAction `shootButton` method.

9. Move the mouse over the Sheriff text field, hold down the Control key, and drag below the `@IBOutlet` line in the `AppDelegate.swift` file.

10. Release the mouse and the Control key. A pop-up window appears.

11. Click in the Name text field and type **sheriffHitPoints** and click the Connect button.

12. Move the mouse over the Outlaw text field that appears to the right of the Add button, hold down the Control key, and drag below the `@IBOutlet` line in the `AppDelegate.swift` file.

13. Release the mouse and the Control key. A pop-up window appears.

14. Click in the Name text field and type
outlawHitPoints and click the Connect button.
You should now have the following IBOutlets that
represent all the text fields on your user interface:

```
@IBOutlet weak var window: NSWindow!
@IBOutlet weak var sheriffHitPoints: NSTextField!
@IBOutlet weak var outlawHitPoints: NSTextField!
```

At this point, you've connected the user interface to your Swift code so
you can use the IBOutlets to display data on the user interface. You've also
created a single IBAction method to run when the user clicks either of the
two push buttons. Now you need to change the Tag property of the Outlaw
Shoot button.

1. Click on the Outlaw Shoot button to select it.

2. Choose View ➤ Utilities ➤ Show Attributes
Inspector. The Attributes Inspector pane appears in
the upper right corner of the Xcode window.

3. Scroll down to the View category and change the Tag
property to 1, as shown in Figure 13-9.

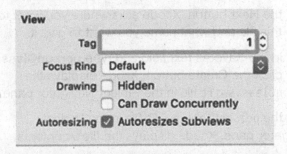

Figure 13-9. The Tag property at the bottom of the Attributes Inspector pane

Now that you've defined the user interface, the next step is to create a
separate Swift file to hold your class, which you can do by following these
steps:

1. Choose File ➤ New ➤ File. A dialog appears asking
for a template to use.

2. Click Source under the macOS category and then
click the Swift File, as shown in Figure 13-10.

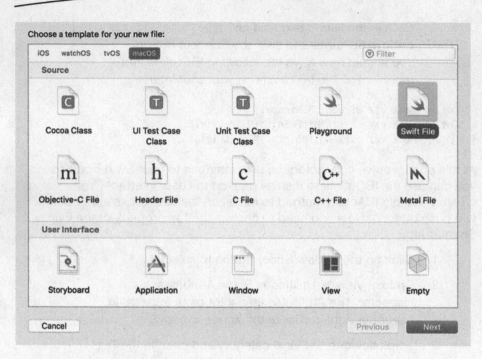

Figure 13-10. Selecting a file to hold the class definition code

3. Click the Next button. Xcode asks where you want to store this file and what name you want to give it.

4. Click in the Save As text field and type **personClass**. Then click the Create button. Xcode displays the personClass.swift file in the Project Navigator pane.

5. Click the personClass.swift file in the Project Navigator pane. Xcode displays the file's contents.

6. Edit the personClass.swift file as follows:

```
import Foundation

class Person {
    var hitPoints = 10
    func shoot () -> Int {
        let odds = 1 + Int(arc4random_uniform(3))
        if odds == 3 {
            // Hit, randomly determine damage from 1..3
            return 1 + Int(arc4random_uniform(3))
```

```
        } else {
            return 0 // Missed
        }
    }
}
```

This class defines one property called `hitPoints`, which it initializes with a value of 10. It also defines one method called shoot, which does not accept any parameters but does return an integer value. Inside the shoot method, it calculates a random number from 1 to 3 and stores this value in the odds variable.

Next, it checks if the value in odds is exactly equal to 3. If so, then it calculates a second random number from 1 to 3 and returns this value. If the value in odds is not 3, then the method returns 0.

Now that you've defined a class in a separate Swift file, it's time to actually use that class to create objects, which you can do by following these steps:

1. Click the `AppDelegate.swift` file in the Project Navigator pane. Xcode displays the contents of the AppDelegate.swift file.

2. Underneath the IBOutlet list in the AppDelegate. swift file, type the following to create two objects based on the person class defined in the personClass.swift file:

```
@IBOutlet weak var window: NSWindow!
@IBOutlet weak var sheriffHitPoints: NSTextField!
@IBOutlet weak var outlawHitPoints: NSTextField!

var sheriff = Person ()
var outlaw = Person ()
```

3. Modify the `applicationDidFinishLaunching` method so it displays the initial values of the hitPoints properties of the sheriff and outlaw objects in the text fields on the user interface. These are the two IBOutlets called sheriffHitPoints and outlawHitPoints:

```
func applicationDidFinishLaunching(aNotification: NSNotification) {
    // Insert code here to initialize your application
    sheriffHitPoints.integerValue = sheriff.hitPoints
    outlawHitPoints.integerValue = outlaw.hitPoints
}
```

4. Modify the `shootButton` IBAction method follows:

```
@IBAction func shootButton(_ sender: NSButton) {
    if sender.tag == 0 {     // Sheriff shooting
        outlaw.hitPoints -= sheriff.shoot()
    } else {     // Outlaw shooting
        sheriff.hitPoints -= outlaw.shoot()
    }

    sheriffHitPoints.integerValue = sheriff.hitPoints
    outlawHitPoints.integerValue = outlaw.hitPoints

    if sheriffHitPoints.integerValue <= 0 {
        let myAlert = NSAlert()
        myAlert.messageText = "The sheriff died."
        myAlert.runModal()
    } else if outlawHitPoints.integerValue <= 0 {
        let myAlert = NSAlert()
        myAlert.messageText = "The outlaw died."
        myAlert.runModal()
    }
}
```

This code checks the Tag property of the `sender` variable, which identifies which button the user clicked. If the Tag property is 0, then the user clicked on the Sheriff Shoot button so it runs the `shoot` method in the sheriff object and subtracts the result (a value from 0 to 3) from the `outlaw.hitPoints` property.

If the user clicked the Outlaw Shoot button, then the `shoot` method runs the `shoot` method in the `outlaw` object and subtracts the result (a value from 0 to 3) from the `sheriff.hitPoints` property.

Whatever the result, it then displays the latest values of the `hitPoints` property from both the sheriff and the outlaw back in the two text fields on the user interface, identified by the `sheriffHitPoints` and `outlawHitPoints` IBOutlets.

Finally, if the `hitPoints` property of either the sheriff or the outlaw falls to 0 or less, then an alert dialog appears to display a message that either the sheriff or the outlaw died. The complete contents of the `AppDelegate.swift` file should look like this:

```
import Cocoa

@NSApplicationMain
class AppDelegate: NSObject, NSApplicationDelegate {

    @IBOutlet weak var window: NSWindow!
    @IBOutlet weak var sheriffHitPoints: NSTextField!
    @IBOutlet weak var outlawHitPoints: NSTextField!
```

```swift
var sheriff = Person ()
var outlaw = Person ()

func applicationDidFinishLaunching(_ aNotification: Notification) {
    // Insert code here to initialize your application
    sheriffHitPoints.integerValue = sheriff.hitPoints
    outlawHitPoints.integerValue = outlaw.hitPoints


}

func applicationWillTerminate(_ aNotification: Notification) {
    // Insert code here to tear down your application
}

@IBAction func shootButton(_ sender: NSButton) {
    if sender.tag == 0 {    // Sheriff shooting
        outlaw.hitPoints -= sheriff.shoot()
    } else {    // Outlaw shooting
        sheriff.hitPoints -= outlaw.shoot()
    }

    sheriffHitPoints.integerValue = sheriff.hitPoints
    outlawHitPoints.integerValue = outlaw.hitPoints

    if sheriffHitPoints.integerValue <= 0 {
        let myAlert = NSAlert()
        myAlert.messageText = "The sheriff died."
        myAlert.runModal()
    } else if outlawHitPoints.integerValue <= 0 {
        let myAlert = NSAlert()
        myAlert.messageText = "The outlaw died."
        myAlert.runModal()
    }
}

}
```

To see how this program works, follow these steps:

1. Choose Product ➤ Run. Xcode runs your ObjectProgram project. Notice that the text fields under both the Sheriff and Outlaw display 10, which represents their total hit points. Each time they're hit, their hit point total will drop. The loser will be the character whose hit points drops to 0 or less.

2. Click the Sheriff Shoot button. If the sheriff hit the outlaw, then you'll see the value under the outlaw label drop from 10 to a lower value such as 8. If the sheriff missed, then the number under the outlaw won't change at all.

3. Click the Outlaw Shoot button.

4. Repeat steps 2 and 3 to alternate clicking the Sheriff Shoot and Outlaw Shoot buttons until one character's hit points drops to 0 or less. Then an alert dialog appears, as shown in Figure 13-11.

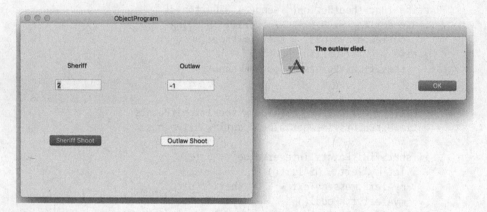

Figure 13-11. When one character's hit point total drops to 0 or less, an alert dialog appears

5. Click OK to make the alert dialog go away.

6. Choose ObjectProgram ➤ Quit ObjectProgram.

Summary

Swift programming depends entirely on objects and the principles of object-oriented programming. To create an object, you must first define a class. A class typically consists of one or more variables (called properties) and one or more functions (called methods). Once you've defined a class, you can create an object that represents that class.

Properties in a class always need to be initialized. You can define initial values for every property at the same time you define those properties, or you can create a special initializer method that lets you accept data to define initial values for an object.

Properties can be initialized with a fixed value, or they can be computed based on values of another property. The value of one property can change the value of a different property.

You can create as many objects from a single class as you want. Typically it's best to store class definitions in separate files to keep your code organized. An object-oriented program works by objects sending data to the properties of other objects, or calling methods stored in other objects. By working together, yet being independent, objects make it easy to create reliable and sophisticated programs much faster than before.

Chapter **14**

Inheritance, Polymorphism, and Extending Classes

In Chapter 13, you learned how objects were created from classes and how classes define properties and methods. To protect its data and methods from other parts of a program, an object isolates or encapsulates its code. Encapsulation is one prime advantage of object-oriented programming because it creates self-contained code that you can easily modify or replace without affecting any other part of a program.

By keeping code as independent as possible from other parts of a program, objects increase reliability. Think of a house built out of playing cards. Remove one card and the whole thing collapses, which is the way most software worked before object-oriented programming.

Objects are like playing cards that you can remove and replace without affecting any other card. Besides encapsulation, object-oriented programming also includes two additional features called inheritance and polymorphism.

The idea behind inheritance is to reuse existing code without physically making another copy of that code. The idea behind polymorphism is that you can replace inherited code without modifying the original code. Through both inheritance and polymorphism, you can reuse existing code, even without understanding how the original code works.

© Wallace Wang 2017
W. Wang, *macOS Programming for Absolute Beginners*,
DOI 10.1007/978-1-4842-2662-9_14

In fact, each time you create a project in Xcode, look at the top of your Swift files and you should see a line that looks like this:

```
import Cocoa
```

This line tells Xcode to use all of the classes that Apple created for you that are stored in the Cocoa framework. In the previous example programs, you used the Cocoa framework to manipulate arrays, sets, and dictionaries. Without the Cocoa framework, you would have to write Swift code to perform these common functions yourself. Not only would this be time-consuming, but it would be error-prone as well since you would have to write code and then test to make sure it worked.

By simply relying on classes in the Cocoa framework, you can add functionality to your program without writing much code at all. As you get more experienced writing your own classes, you can create useful libraries of your own that you can easily plug into other projects to reuse all your hard work.

Understanding Inheritance

The main purpose of inheritance is to make reusing code easy. In the old days, people reused code by simply making another copy of that code. But what happens if you find an error (bug) in the code? You need to fix that bug in every copy of your code. Miss one copy of the faulty code and your program won't work.

Creating multiple copies of the same code causes two problems. First, it wastes space. Second, it makes modifying the code harder, with multiple copies of code scattered all over a program. Inheritance fixes both problems.

First, inheritance never makes a copy of code so it never wastes space. Second, since inheritance only keeps one copy of the code, you just need to modify one copy of code to have your changes automatically affect every part of your program that relies on that code.

Instead of physically copying code, inheritance basically creates pointers or references to one copy of code. When you create a class, you can simply state its name, like this:

```
class ClassName {

}
```

To inherit code from another class, name the other class, like this:

```
class ClassName : SuperClass {

}
```

This code defines a class called ClassName, which inherits code from another class called SuperClass. That means any properties and methods defined in Superclass automatically work in ClassName as well, even though the ClassName class is completely empty.

If you peek at any of the macOS sample programs you created in earlier chapters, you may see code that looks like this:

```
class AppDelegate: NSObject, NSApplicationDelegate {
```

This defines a class called AppDelegate, which inherits code from another class called NSObject. (This code also adds additional code to the AppDelegate class through another file called NSApplicationDelegate, which is a file that you'll learn more about later in this chapter.)

To see how to use inheritance with classes, create a new playground by following these steps:

1. Open the IntroductoryPlayground file in Xcode.

2. Edit the code as follows:

```
import Cocoa

class FirstClass {
    var speed : Int = 0
    var locationX : Int = 3
    var locationY : Int = 5
    func move (X: Int, Y: Int) {
        locationX += X
        locationY += Y
    }
}

class CopyCat : FirstClass {

}

var kitten = CopyCat ()
print (kitten.locationX)
print (kitten.locationY)
```

```
kitten.speed = 4
kitten.move(X: 4, Y: 8)

print (kitten.locationX)
print (kitten.locationY)
```

This Swift code defines two classes. First, it defines a class (called FirstClass) that has three properties (speed, locationX, and locationY) and one method (move). Then it defines a second class (called CopyCat) that's completely empty, but it inherits all of the code from FirstClass.

To show that the CopyCat class inherits code from FirstClass, the Swift code next creates an object called kitten, which is based on the CopyCat class. The kitten object can store data in a speed property and use the move method to change its locationX and locationY properties, yet the CopyCat class is completely empty. Figure 14-1 shows the results of running this Swift code in a playground.

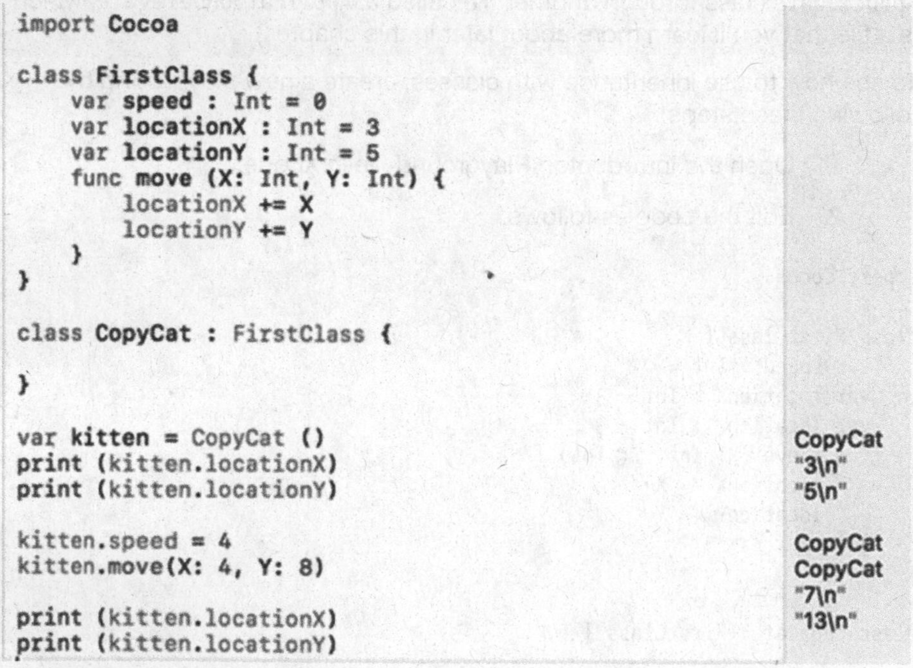

```
import Cocoa

class FirstClass {
    var speed : Int = 0
    var locationX : Int = 3
    var locationY : Int = 5
    func move (X: Int, Y: Int) {
        locationX += X
        locationY += Y
    }
}

class CopyCat : FirstClass {

}

var kitten = CopyCat ()              CopyCat
print (kitten.locationX)             "3\n"
print (kitten.locationY)             "5\n"

kitten.speed = 4                     CopyCat
kitten.move(X: 4, Y: 8)              CopyCat
                                     "7\n"
print (kitten.locationX)             "13\n"
print (kitten.locationY)
```

Figure 14-1. Showing how inheritance works

> **Note**   Some programming languages, such as C++, allow one class to inherit
> from two or more classes, which is known as multiple inheritance. However
> in Swift, a class can only inherit from only one other class, which is known as
> single inheritance.

In the above example, the CopyCat class inherits three properties (speed, locationX, and locationY) and one method (move) from FirstClass. Since the CopyCat class didn't define any properties or methods of its own, the CopyCat class is basically identical to FirstClass.

In actual use, there's no reason for a class to inherit from another class as an exact duplicate. Instead, it's more common for one class (known as the subclass) to inherit from another class (known as the superclass or parent class) and then add additional properties and methods of its own.

In this way, the subclass only needs to include the code for these new properties and methods while still having access to all the properties and methods of the superclass. For example, consider the following class:

```
class CopyDog : CopyCat {
    var name : String = ""
}
```

This class inherits all of the code from the CopyCat class and adds one new property of its own called name that can hold a string. The above class definition that defines a name property and inherits code from the CopyCat class is equivalent to the following:

```
class CopyDog {
    var speed : Int = 0
    var locationX : Int = 3
    var locationY : Int = 5
    func move (X: Int, Y: Int) {
        locationX += X
        locationY += Y
    }
        var name : String = ""
}
```

Remember, the CopyCat class inherited everything from FirstClass, which defined the speed, locationX, and locationY properties along with the move method. In comparison, the CopyDog class that inherits code from the CopyCat class is much shorter and simpler.

Inheritance works like a daisy chain. If class A inherits from class B, but class B inherits everything from class C, then class A inherits everything from both class B and class C. For example, the CopyDog class inherits everything from the CopyCat class. The CopyCat class, in turn, inherits everything from FirstClass. This means the CopyDog class ultimately inherits everything from both the CopyCat class and FirstClass, as shown in Figure 14-2.

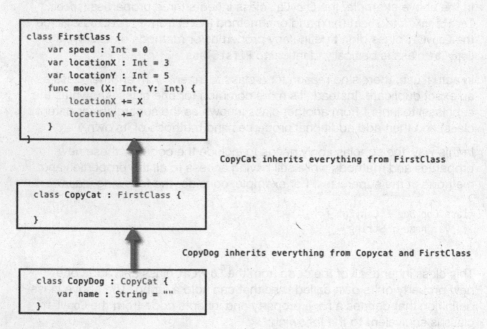

```
class FirstClass {
    var speed : Int = 0
    var locationX : Int = 3
    var locationY : Int = 5
    func move (X: Int, Y: Int) {
        locationX += X
        locationY += Y
    }
}
```

CopyCat inherits everything from FirstClass

```
class CopyCat : FirstClass {

}
```

CopyDog inherits everything from Copycat and FirstClass

```
class CopyDog : CopyCat {
    var name : String = ""
}
```

Figure 14-2. Classes inherit everything from previous classes

This daisy chain effect of inheritance is how the Cocoa framework is designed. At its simplest level, there's a basic class called NSObject. Another class named NSControl inherits everything from NSObject and adds new properties and methods of its own. When you create a text field for your user interface, that text field is based on a class called NSTextField, which is inherits everything from NSControl. If you click a user interface object in the Object Library, Xcode lists which class the user interface object is based on, as shown in Figure 14-3.

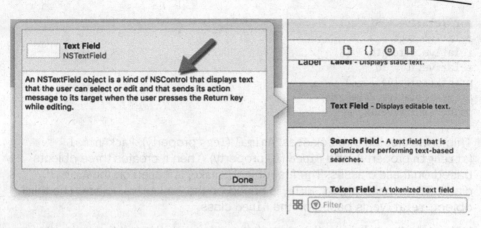

Figure 14-3. Clicking an item in the Object Library can identify the parent class for that user interface object

To see how to use inheritance works between multiple classes, follow these steps:

1. Make sure the IntroductoryPlayground file is loaded in Xcode.

2. Edit the code as follows:

```
import Cocoa
class Animal {
    var legs : Int = 0
}

class PackAnimal : Animal {
    var strength : Int = 100
}

class Biped : PackAnimal {
    var IQ : Int = 75
}

var snake = Animal()
print (snake.legs)

var mule = PackAnimal()
mule.legs = 4
mule.strength = 120
print (mule.legs)
print (mule.strength)
```

```
var relative = Biped()
relative.legs = 2
relative.strength = 55
relative.IQ = 10
print (relative.legs)
print (relative.strength)
print (relative.IQ)
```

This code creates three classes: Animal (legs property), PackAnimal (strength property), and Biped (IQ property). Then it creates three objects based on these classes. The first object, snake, is based on the Animal class. The second object, mule, is based on the PackAnimal class. The third object, relative, is based on the Biped class.

Ultimately, the relative object contains properties from all three classes, the mule object only contains properties from the Animal and PackAnimal class, and the snake object only contains properties from the Animal class, as follows:

Object	Based on these classes	Contains these properties
snake	Animal	legs
mule	PackAnimal, Animal	legs, strength
relative	Biped, PackAnimal, Animal	legs, strength, IQ

The snake, mule, and relative objects contain different properties based on their different classes and the classes that they inherit from, as shown in Figure 14-4.

```
import Cocoa

class Animal {
    var legs : Int = 0
}

class PackAnimal : Animal {
    var strength : Int = 100
}

class Biped : PackAnimal {
    var IQ : Int = 75
}

var snake = Animal()                          Animal
print (snake.legs)                            "0\n"

var mule = PackAnimal()                        PackAnimal
mule.legs = 4                                  PackAnimal
mule.strength = 120                            PackAnimal
print (mule.legs)                              "4\n"
print (mule.strength)                          "120\n"


var relative = Biped()                         Biped
relative.legs = 2                              Biped
relative.strength = 55                         Biped
relative.IQ = 10                               Biped
print (relative.legs)                          "2\n"
print (relative.strength)                      "55\n"
print (relative.IQ)                            "10\n"
```

Figure 14-4. Seeing how inheritance works among properties stored in different classes

Understanding Polymorphism

When one class (subclass) inherits from another class (superclass), it contains all the properties and methods stored in the superclass. Although a subclass inherits all properties and methods from a superclass, those properties and methods aren't displayed inside the subclass. The only code that appears in each class are properties and methods unique to that class.

Properties inherited from another class retain the same name and data type. Methods inherited from another class retain the same method name and code that makes it do something useful.

The problem with inheriting methods is that you may want to modify the code in an inherited method. For example, suppose you had a video game where you have dogs running on the ground and birds flying in the air. You could create a basic class like this:

```
class GameObject {
    var speed : Int = 0
    var locationX : Int = 3
    var locationY : Int = 3
    func move (X: Int, Y: Int) {
        locationX += X + speed
        locationY += Y + speed
    }
}

var dog = GameObject()
```

Now the dog object, created from the GameObject class, has three properties (speed, locationX, and locationY) and one method (move) that changes the locationX and locationY properties.

A dog can only run on the ground, but a bird can move in two-dimensions, so it needs an additional height property. To move a flying object, the move method needs to change the height property. This means the move method needs to be different.

One clumsy way around this problem is to create a different name for the move method such as changing its name from "move" to "fly":

```
class FlyingObject : GameObject {
    var height : Int = 0
        func fly (X: Int, Y: Int) {
        locationX += X + speed
        locationY += Y + speed
        height += (X + Y) / 2
    }
}

var bird = FlyingObject()
```

The problem with this solution is that the bird object, created from the FlyingObject class, now has two methods: the move method inherited from GameObject and the new fly method defined in FlyingObject.

You could simply ignore the move method and use the fly method, but this risks creating errors if you accidentally use the move method to change the position of a bird instead of the correct fly method that moves a bird in two-dimensions instead of one.

That's why polymorphism exists. Polymorphism basically lets you reuse a method name (such as move) but replace it with completely different code to make it work. To identify when you're using polymorphism to reuse a method name but modify its code, you must use the override keyword in front of the method you're changing, such as

```
override func move (X: Int, Y: Int) {
    locationX += X + speed
    locationY += Y + speed
    height += (X + Y) / 2
}
```

When you override a method (using polymorphism), you essentially have two identically named methods, but one version is defined in one class and the second version is defined in another class. The computer never gets confused because you can only run each method by specifying both the object name and the method name. Even though the method names are identical, the object names are not.

To see how polymorphism works, follow these steps:

1. Make sure your IntroductoryPlayground file is loaded into Xcode.

2. Edit the code as follows:

```
import Cocoa

class GameObject {
    var speed : Int = 0
    var locationX : Int = 3
    var locationY : Int = 3
    func move (X: Int, Y: Int) {
        locationX += X + speed
        locationY += Y + speed
    }
}

var dog = GameObject()

class FlyingObject : GameObject {
    var height : Int = 0
    override func move (X: Int, Y: Int) {
        locationX += X + speed
        locationY += Y + speed
        height += (X + Y) / 2
    }
}
```

```
var bird = FlyingObject()

dog.speed = .1
dog.move (X: 4, Y: 7)
bird.speed = 3
bird.move (X: 4, Y: 7)

print (dog.locationX)
print (dog.locationY)
print (dog.speed)

print (bird.locationX)
print (bird.locationY)
print (bird.height)
print (bird.speed)
```

To override a method, the flying Object class must first inherit from another class. In this case, flyingObject inherits from gameObject. Now the flyingObject class can use the override keyword to specify that it's changing the code that makes the move method work. In this case, the only change was adding code to modify the height property, but you could have added completely different code inside the overridden move method.

Notice that when you run the move method for the dog object (dog.move), the move method only changes the values of locationX and locationY, but when you run the move method for the bird object (bird.move), the overridden method runs and also changes the height property, as shown in Figure 14-5.

```
import Cocoa

class GameObject {
    var speed : Int = 0
    var locationX : Int = 3
    var locationY : Int = 3
    func move (X: Int, Y: Int) {
        locationX += X + speed
        locationY += Y + speed
    }
}

var dog = GameObject()                              GameObject

class FlyingObject : GameObject {
    var height : Int = 0
    override func move (X: Int, Y: Int) {
        locationX += X + speed
        locationY += Y + speed
        height += (X + Y) / 2
    }
}

var bird = FlyingObject()                           FlyingObject

dog.speed = 1                                       GameObject
dog.move (X: 4, Y: 7)                               GameObject
bird.speed = 3                                      FlyingObject
bird.move (X: 4, Y: 7)                              FlyingObject

print (dog.locationX)                               "8\n"
print (dog.locationY)                               "11\n"
print (dog.speed)                                   "1\n"

print (bird.locationX)                              "10\n"
print (bird.locationY)                              "13\n"
print (bird.height)                                 "5\n"
print (bird.speed)                                  "3\n"
```

Figure 14-5. Overridden methods can behave differently

When overriding methods, you can only change the code inside the method. You cannot change the parameter list of the method. For example, consider this class:

```
class BasicDesign {
    var location : Int = 0
    func moveMe (X : Int) {
        location += X
    }
}
```

To override the moveMe method, this next class needs to inherit from the basicDesign class and change only the code inside the overridden method. The following would not work:

```
class NewDesign : BasicDesign {
    override moveMe (X: Int, Y: Int) { // Does NOT work

    }
}
```

Notice that the original moveMe method only has one parameter (X : Int) but the moveMe method in the newDesign class has two parameters (X: Int, Y: Int). Despite having the same name, this method has a different parameter list so it won't work. When overriding methods, you can only change the code, not the parameter list.

Overriding Properties

Besides overriding methods, Swift also lets you override properties. When you override properties, you must keep the same property name and data type. What you can change are the getters and setters along with the property observers of a variable.

At the simplest level, a getter simply returns a value of a variable. On a more sophisticated level, a getter calculates a value. Consider the following:

```
class BasicDesign {
    var location: Int {
        get {
            return 4
        }
    }
}
```

This basicDesign class defines a single property called location with a getter that returns the value 4 in the location property. To override this property, you need to retain the variable name and data type (Int), but you can change the getter code, such as

```
class NewDesign : BasicDesign {
    override var location: Int {
        get {
            return 7
        }
    }
}
```

This newDesign class inherits the location property from the basicDesign class. However, it overrides the location property with a new getter that returns a value of 7.

To see how overriding properties work, follow these steps:

1. Make sure your IntroductoryPlayground file is loaded into Xcode.

2. Edit the code as follows:

```
import Cocoa

class BasicDesign {
    var location: Int {
        get {
            return 4
        }
    }
}

class NewDesign : BasicDesign {
    override var location: Int {
        get {
            return 7
        }
    }
}

var ant = BasicDesign()
var fly = NewDesign()
ant.location
fly.location
```

In this example, the ant object is based on the BasicDesign class, which defines the location property with a value of 4. The fly object is based on the NewDesign class, which inherits the location property. However, the NewDesign class overrides the location property's getter code so instead of storing a value of 4 in the location property, it stores a value of 7 instead, as shown in Figure 14-6.

```
import Cocoa

class BasicDesign {
    var location: Int {
        get {
            return 4                                    4
        }
    }
}

class NewDesign : BasicDesign {
    override var location: Int {
        get {
            return 7                                    7
        }
    }
}

var ant = BasicDesign()                            BasicDesign
var fly = NewDesign()                              NewDesign
ant.location                                       4
fly.location                                       7
```

Figure 14-6. Overriding properties with new getter code

Remember, when overriding methods and properties, you can only change

- Code in the method
- Code in the property's getter/setter or property observer

You can never change the

- Method name
- Method parameter list
- Property name
- Property data type

Preventing Polymorphism

In some cases, you may want to prevent a method, property, or even an entire class from being modified through polymorphism. To do this, you just need to insert the final keyword. If you want to prevent an entire class from being inherited, just put the final keyword in front of the class name, like this:

```
final class ClassName {
    var propertyName = initialValue
    func methodName() {

    }
}
```

> **Note** If you place "final" in front of a class name, it automatically prevents that class's properties and methods from being overridden so you don't need to place "final" in front of each property or method name.

If you want to prevent an individual property or method from being overridden, just place the `final` keyword in front of the property or method like this:

```
class ClassName {
        final var propertyName = initialValue
        func methodName() {

        }
}
```

The `final` keyword in the above example prevents the property from being overridden while allowing the method to be overridden. If you want to prevent the method from being overridden while allowing the property to be overridden, you place the `final` keyword in front of the method like this:

```
class ClassName {
        var propertyName = initialValue
        final func methodName() {

        }
}
```

Using Extensions

If there's a class that contains the properties and methods you need, the object-oriented approach is to inherit from that class (create a subclass). The problem with constantly creating subclasses is that it can get awkward to create objects from slightly different class files.

This can be especially true when you want to extend the features of classes that are part of the Cocoa framework. For example, if you're working with String data types, you probably don't want to create a subclass of the String data type and then create objects based on this new subclass. Ideally, you want to continue using String data types but have added features as well.

That's why Swift offers extensions. Extensions essentially let you add code to an existing class without creating a subclass. This way you can still get to use the original class but you also get to add new features to that class without going through inheritance, polymorphism, or subclasses. The structure of an extension looks like this:

```
extension ClassName {

}
```

Extensions can define methods along with properties that contain code such as

- Getters and setters
- Initializers
- Property observers

While extensions add new properties methods to a class without inheritance, extensions cannot override existing methods or properties in a class. Extensions also can't create properties assigned an initial value, such as

```
var temperature : Int = 100    // Cannot be used in an extension
```

To see how to an extension can add properties and methods to a class, create a new playground by following these steps:

1. Make sure your IntroductoryPlayground file is loaded into Xcode.

2. Edit the code as follows:

```
import Cocoa

class EmptyClass {

}

extension EmptyClass {
    var age : Int {
        get {
            return 50
        }
    }
    func retire (testAge : Int) -> String {
        if testAge < 62 {
            return "Keep working"
        } else {
            return "Time to retire"
        }
    }
}
```

```
var aWorker = EmptyClass ()
aWorker.retire(testAge: 65)
aWorker.age
```

This code creates a completely empty class, and then creates an extension that adds an age property and a retire method to the empty class. Finally, it creates an object from that empty class, calls the retire method (defined in the extension) and displays the value stored in the age property, as shown in Figure 14-7.

```
import Cocoa

class EmptyClass {

}

extension EmptyClass {
    var age : Int {
        get {
            return 50                                    50
        }
    }
    func retire (testAge : Int) -> String {
        if testAge < 62 {
            return "Keep working"
        } else {
            return "Time to retire"                      "Time to retire"
        }
    }
}

var aWorker = EmptyClass ()                              EmptyClass
aWorker.retire(testAge: 65)                             "Time to retire"
aWorker.age                                              50
```

Figure 14-7. Using an extension to add a property and method to an empty class

You can see that the class itself does nothing, but with extensions, the class now gets added features that it didn't have before.

Using Protocols

In the beginning of this chapter, you were first introduced to something that appears in the class AppDelegate.swift file that you've been creating to learn the basic principles of each chapter. This class AppDelegate declaration looks like this:

```
class AppDelegate: NSObject, NSApplicationDelegate {
```

This line of code creates a class called AppDelegate, which inherits properties and methods from the NSObject class that's part of the Cocoa framework. However, NSApplicationDelegate is the name of another file used to extend classes without going through inheritance or subclasses.

The NSApplicationDelegate file is a protocol file. The above Swift code creates a class called AppDelegate, inherits properties and methods from the NSObject class, and also inherits code from the NSApplicationDelegate file. (You can see more details about the NSApplicationDelegate protocol by viewing it in the Xcode Documentation window.)

The main difference between a class (such as NSObject) and a protocol (such as NSApplicationDelegate) is that a class defines properties and methods while a protocol only defines properties and method names without any code that actually implements them. A protocol is sometimes called an empty class because it never defines any Swift code to make anything actually work.

A protocol defines a group of property and method names for solving a particular type of problem. Now it's up to the class that adopts or conforms to this protocol to provide the actual Swift code that implements each method or property declaration.

A protocol declaration looks identical to a class or structure declaration. The only difference is that a protocol declaration uses the protocol keyword:

```
protocol ProtocolName {

}
```

Within this protocol declaration you can define properties and methods without implementing any Swift code, like this:

```
protocol ProtocolName {
    var property1 : datatype { get }        // read-only
    var property2 : datatype { get set }    // read-write
    func methodName (parameters) -> datatype
}
```

When a protocol defines a property or method, any class that adopts that protocol must implement that property or method exactly as defined in the protocol. In the above example, property1 is defined with a getter and property2 is defined with a getter and a setter.

This means when a class implements those two properties, it must define a getter only for property1 and both a getter and a setter for property2.

Likewise, the method defined in the protocol must be exact when adopted in the class file. This means if the method is defined in the protocol with two integer parameters, then the implementation of that method must also have the exact same two integer parameters.

Protocols are generally used when working with common user interface items that require specific types of methods to manipulate them, but can't define exactly how to manipulate them because the data may differ from one program to another.

For example, table views are a user interface item that displays a list of data in rows. The table view needs to know how many rows of data to hold and what type of data to display in each row. Since every table view needs to know this information, it makes sense to create standard methods to do this, but since every table view needs to contain different information, it also makes sense to avoid writing Swift code to actually fill a table view with data.

Any program that includes a table view can take advantage of predefined method names stored in a protocol for manipulating data. All you need to do is add Swift code to fill the table view with data.

By using protocols, you can manipulate table views using identical method names from one program to another. Without table view protocols, you'd be forced to make up your own method names for adding and displaying data in a table view. Thus, protocols are typically used in the Cocoa framework to provide a consistent list of methods for performing common tasks.

To see how protocols work, follow these steps:

1. Make sure the IntroductoryPlayground file is loaded into Xcode.

2. Edit the code as follows:

```
import Cocoa

protocol TestMe {
    var cash : Int { get }
    var creditCheck : Int { get set }
    func purchase (price : Int) -> String
}

class WindowShopper : TestMe {
    var tempValue : Int = 0

    var cash : Int = 0
    var creditCheck : Int {
        get {
            return tempValue
        }
```

```
    set (newValue) {
        tempValue = newValue
        cash -= 10
    }
}
func purchase (price : Int) -> String {
    cash -= price
    return "Bought something!"
}
}

var shopper = WindowShopper ()
shopper.cash = 450
shopper.purchase (price: 129)
shopper.cash
```

Notice that the TestMe protocol defines two properties and a method. The cash property is defined only with a getter. The creditCheck property is defined with both a getter and a setter. The purchase method only lists its parameters (price as an integer) and its return value, which is a String. Notice that the protocol doesn't actually implement any of the necessary Swift code.

When the WindowShopper class is created, it adopts or conforms to the TestMe protocol. That means it must provide Swift code to define the getter for the cash property and the getter and setter for the creditCheck property. It will also need to implement the Swift code for the purchase method.

If you fail to write Swift code for all the properties and methods defined in the TestMe protocol, Xcode will give an error saying the WindowShopper class failed to conform to the protocol. When adopting a protocol, make sure you implement all the necessary properties and methods.

Running the above code displays the results shown in Figure 14-8.

```
import Cocoa

protocol TestMe {
    var cash : Int { get }
    var creditCheck : Int { get set }
    func purchase (price : Int) -> String
}

class WindowShopper : TestMe {
    var tempValue : Int = 0

    var cash : Int = 0
    var creditCheck : Int {
        get {
            return tempValue
        }
        set (newValue) {
            tempValue = newValue
            cash -= 10
        }
    }
    func purchase (price : Int) -> String {          "Bought something!"
        cash -= price
        return "Bought something!"
    }
}

var shopper = WindowShopper ()                        WindowShopper
shopper.cash = 450                                    WindowShopper
shopper.purchase (price: 129)                         "Bought something!"
shopper.cash                                          321
```

Figure 14-8. A class conforming to a protocol

Defining Optional Methods and Properties in Protocols

When you create a protocol, every property and method you define must be implemented by any class that adopts that protocol. However, you can also make one or more properties and methods optional so they can be ignored. To define optional properties or methods, you need to identify the protocol with the @objc keyword and identify individual properties or methods with the optional keyword as well, such as

```
@objc protocol ProtocolName {
    var requiredProperty : dataType { get }
    optional var optionalProperty : dataType { get }
    optional func optionalMethod ()
}
```

To adopt or conform to this protocol, a class only needs to implement any property or method that is not identified by the `optional` keyword. To implement required properties or methods, you need to identify them with the @objc keyword, such as

```
class ClassName : ProtocolName {
    @objc var requiredProperty : dataType = initialValue
}
```

However, if you want to implement an optional property or method, you can omit the @objc keyword, like this:

```
class ClassName : ProtocolName {
    @objc var requiredProperty : dataType = initialValue
    var optionalProperty : dataType = initialValue
}
```

To see how to create optional properties and methods in a protocol, follow these steps:

1. Make sure the IntroductoryPlayground file is loaded into Xcode.

2. Edit the code as follows:

```
import Cocoa

@objc protocol Person {
    var name : String { get }
    @objc optional var age : Int { get }
    @objc optional func move (X: Int) -> Int
}

class Politician : Person {
    @objc var name : String = ""
}

var candidate = Politician ()
candidate.name = "John Doe"
```

Notice that the only required item in the person protocol defined above is the property name. That's why the politician class only needs to implement the name property, but it must identify it with the @objc keyword.

Try experimenting with making different properties and methods optional so you can see how they affect how you need to implement them in the class.

Using Inheritance with Protocols

Protocols can even inherit properties and methods from other protocols. This lets one protocol inherit properties and methods from multiple protocols. Now a class must adopt or conform to all the properties and methods defined in all of the protocols.

To see how to inherit properties and methods from multiple protocols, follow these steps:

1. Make sure the IntroductoryPlayground file is loaded into Xcode.

2. Edit the code as follows:

```
import Cocoa

protocol First {
    var name : String { get }
}

protocol Second {
    var ID : Int { get }
}

protocol Third: First, Second {
    var email : String { get }
}

class InheritProtocols : Third {
    var name : String = ""
    var ID : Int = 0
    var email : String = ""
}

var friend = InheritProtocols()
friend.name = "Cindy Smith"
friend.ID = 12
friend.email = cindysmith@isp.com

print (friend.name)
print (friend.ID)
print (friend.email)
```

In this example, the name, ID, and email properties are defined in three different protocols. The third protocol inherits from the first and second protocols.

Now when a class adopts the last protocol, it must implement the properties and methods stored in all the protocols. Even though the name, ID, and email properties were all declared in different protocols, the inheritProtocols class can access them all, as shown in Figure 14-9.

```
import Cocoa

protocol First {
    var name : String { get }
}

protocol Second {
    var ID : Int { get }
}

protocol Third: First, Second {
    var email : String { get }
}

class InheritProtocols : Third {
    var name : String = ""
    var ID : Int = 0
    var email : String = ""
}

var friend = InheritProtocols()          InheritProtocols
friend.name = "Cindy Smith"              InheritProtocols
friend.ID = 12                           InheritProtocols
friend.email = "cindysmith@isp.com"      InheritProtocols

print (friend.name)                      "Cindy Smith\n"
print (friend.ID)                        "12\n"
print (friend.email)                     "cindysmith@isp.com\n"
```

Figure 14-9. Inheriting properties and methods from multiple protocols

Using Delegates

Protocols are closely related to delegation. The main idea behind delegation is for a class to hand off or delegate responsibility to code stored in another class. So rather than create a new subclass to add new features, you can use a delegate that contains additional features.

One common way to use delegates is to allow the view (the user interface) to communicate to the controller. Normally, the controller communicates to the view through IBOutlets that allow the controller to display data on the user interface or retrieve data from the user interface.

However, the view can also communicate back to the controller through protocols. The protocol file defines methods and delegates the responsibility to the controller for implementing those methods. The most common types of methods the controller implements involve method names that include "will," "should," and "did" such as applicationDidFinishLaunching or applicationWillTerminate.

Figure 14-10 shows how the controller communicates to the view through IBOutlets and the view communicates with the controller through protocols.

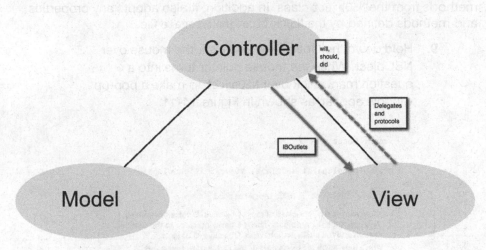

Figure 14-10. Views can communicate to controllers through protocols.

To see how a view uses delegates to communicate with the controller, follow these steps:

1. From within Xcode choose File ➤ New ➤ Project.

2. Click Application under the macOS category.

3. Click Cocoa Application and click the Next button. Xcode now asks for a product name.

4. Click in the Product Name text field and type **DelegateProgram**.

5. Make sure the Language pop-up menu displays Swift and that no check boxes are selected.

6. Click the Next button. Xcode asks where you want to store the project.

7. Choose a folder to store your project and click the Create button.

8. Click the AppDelegate.swift file in the Project Navigator. The contents of the AppDelegate.swift file appear in the middle of the Xcode window. Look for the following line of code:

```
class AppDelegate: NSObject, NSApplicationDelegate {
```

This line defines a class called AppDelegate that inherits properties and methods from the NSObject class. In addition, it also adopts any properties and methods defined by the NSApplicationDelegate file.

9. Hold down the Option key and click the mouse over NSObject. When the mouse pointer turns into a question mark, click over NSObject to make a pop-up window appear, as shown in Figure 14-11.

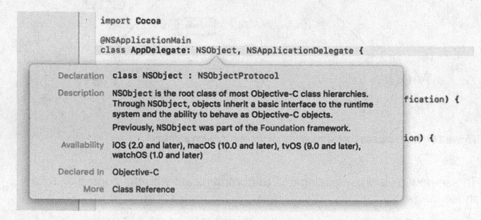

Figure 14-11. Option-clicking on a class name displays information about that class

10. Release the Option key and click the mouse over the Class Reference hyperlink at the bottom of the pop-up window. The Documentation window appears, showing details about the different properties and methods available in the NSObject class, as shown in Figure 14-12. All those properties and methods are also available in your AppDelegate class as well.

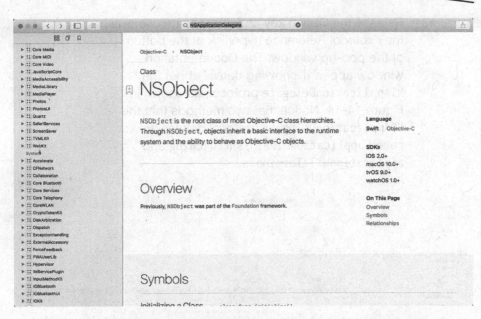

Figure 14-12. The Documentation window displaying information about the NSObject class

11. Click the close button (the red dot) in the upper left corner of the Documentation window to make it go away.

12. Hold down the Option key and click the mouse over NSApplicationDelegate. When the mouse pointer turns into a question mark, click over NSApplicationDelegate to make a pop-up window appear, as shown in Figure 14-13.

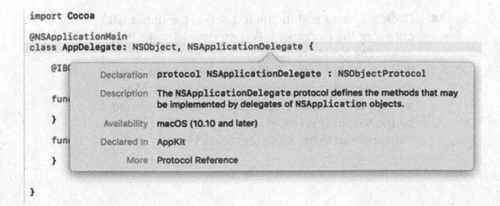

Figure 14-13. Option-clicking displays information about the NSApplication protocol

13. Release the Option key and click the mouse over the Protocol Reference hyperlink at the bottom of the pop-up window. The Documentation window appears, showing details about the NSApplicationDelegate protocol, as shown in Figure 14-14. Notice that two methods that the NSApplicationDelegate protocol defines are called applicationDidFinishLaunching and applicationWillTerminate.

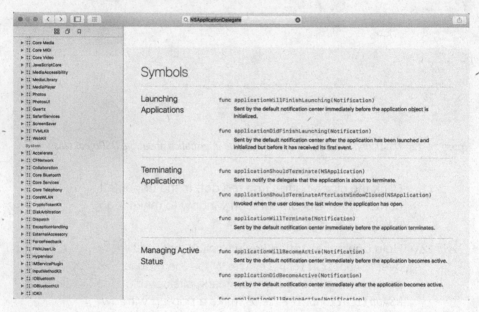

Figure 14-14. Viewing the NSApplicationDelegate protocol in the Documentation window

14. Click the close button (the red dot) in the upper left corner of the Documentation window to make it go away. The Xcode window appears again. Notice that the AppDelegate.swift file contains two empty functions called applicationDidFinishLaunching and applicationWillTerminate. These are defined by the NSApplicationDelegate protocol file but implemented in the AppDelegate.swift file.

15.   Modify both of these functions as follows:

```
func applicationDidFinishLaunching(aNotification: NSNotification) {
    print ("This line should print after the program runs")
}

func applicationWillTerminate(aNotification: NSNotification) {
    print ("This line should print before your program stops")
}
```

16.   Choose Product ➤ Run. Xcode runs your DelegateProgram project and displays an empty user interface.

17.   Choose DelegateProgram ➤ Quit DelegateProgram. The Xcode window appears.

18.   Choose View ➤ Debug Area ➤ Show Debug Area. The debug area appears at the bottom of the Xcode window and displays the text that the two print commands printed. Notice that the print command inside the applicationDidFinishLaunching function ran first, as shown in Figure 14-15.

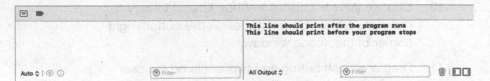

Figure 14-15. The methods defined by the NSApplicationDelegate file tell the program what the user interface is doing

Using Inheritance in a macOS Program

Inheritance lets you create method names that remain the same while the underlying code changes between two classes. In the following sample program, you'll define one class and then inherit properties and methods for a second class. This second class will also override a method and add code to make that overridden method behave slightly differently.

To create the sample program that shows how inheritance works, follow these steps:

1. From within Xcode choose File ➤ New ➤ Project.

2. Click Application under the macOS category.

3. Click Cocoa Application and click the Next button. Xcode now asks for a product name.

4. Click in the Product Name text field and type **InheritProgram**.

5. Make sure the Language pop-up menu displays Swift and that no check boxes are selected.

6. Click the Next button. Xcode asks where you want to store the project.

7. Choose a folder to store your project and click the Create button.

8. Click the `MainMenu.xib` file in the Project Navigator.

9. Click on the Window icon to make the window of the user interface appear.

10. Choose View ➤ Utilities ➤ Show Object Library to make the Object Library appear in the bottom right corner of the Xcode window.

11. Drag one push button and two labels on the user interface and double-click the push buttons and labels to change the text that appears on them so that they look similar to Figure 14-16.

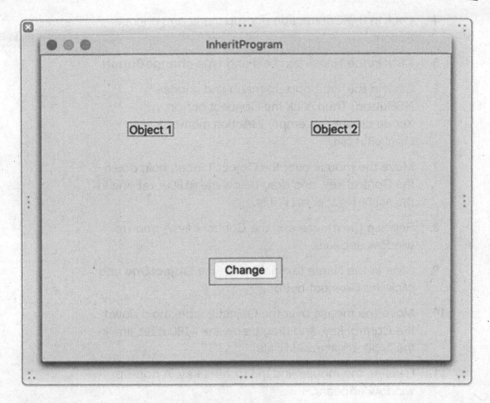

Figure 14-16. The user interface of the InheritProgram

This user interface displays two labels that represent two different objects. Object 1 only contains one property and a method to alter that property. Object 2 inherits from Object 1 and contains one additional property along with overriding the method defined in Object 1.

When you click the Change button, both labels will change their appearance based on the properties and method defined by each object. To connect your user interface to your Swift code, follow these steps:

1. With your user interface still visible in the Xcode window, choose View ➤ Assistant Editor ➤ Show Assistant Editor. The AppDelegate.swift file appears next to the user interface.

2. Move the mouse over the Change button, hold down the Control key, and drag just above the last curly bracket at the bottom of the AppDelegate.swift file.

3. Release the mouse and the Control key. A pop-up window appears.

4. Click in the Connection pop-up menu and choose Action.

5. Click in the Name text field and type **changeButton**.

6. Click in the Type pop-up menu and choose NSButton. Then click the Connect button.
    Xcode creates an empty IBAction method called changeButton.

7. Move the mouse over the Object 1 label, hold down the Control key, and drag below the @IBOutlet line in the AppDelegate.swift file.

8. Release the mouse and the Control key. A pop-up window appears.

9. Click in the Name text field and type **ObjectOne** and click the Connect button.

10. Move the mouse over the Object 2 label, hold down the Control key, and drag below the @IBOutlet line in the AppDelegate.swift file.

11. Release the mouse and the Control key. A pop-up window appears.

12. Click in the Name text field and type **ObjectTwo** and click the Connect button. You should now have the following IBOutlets that represent all the labels on your user interface:

```
@IBOutlet weak var window: NSWindow!
@IBOutlet weak var ObjectOne: NSTextField!
@IBOutlet weak var ObjectTwo: NSTextField!
```

13. Type the following directly underneath the IBOutlet lines of code:

```
class One {
var myColor : NSColor = NSColor.black
func change () {
    myColor = NSColor.red
}
}
```

```
class Two : One {
    var myBackground : NSColor = NSColor.white
    override func change() {
        myColor = NSColor.blue
        myBackground = NSColor.green
    }
}

var ThingOne = One ()
var ThingTwo = Two()
```

14. Modify the IBAction changeButton method as follows:

```
@IBAction func changeButton(_ sender: NSButton) {
    ThingOne.change()
    ThingTwo.change()
    ObjectOne.textColor = ThingOne.myColor
    ObjectTwo.textColor = ThingTwo.myColor
    ObjectTwo.drawsBackground = true
    ObjectTwo.backgroundColor = ThingTwo.myBackground
}
```

This IBAction method runs the change method in both the ThingOne and ThingTwo objects, which are based on the one and two classes, respectively. The two classes inherit from the one class, but override the change method to modify an additional property called myBackground.

After both ThingOne and ThingTwo change their properties, the first label (represented by ObjectOne) assigns its text color to the myColor property from the ThingOne object. The second label (represented by ObjectTwo) changed its myColor and myBackground properties, so it sets those properties to the label.

The complete contents of the AppDelegate.swift file should look like this:

```
import Cocoa

@NSApplicationMain
class AppDelegate: NSObject, NSApplicationDelegate {

    @IBOutlet weak var window: NSWindow!
    @IBOutlet weak var ObjectOne: NSTextField!
    @IBOutlet weak var ObjectTwo: NSTextField!

    class One {
        var myColor : NSColor = NSColor.black
        func change () {
            myColor = NSColor.red
        }
    }
```

```
class Two : One {
    var myBackground : NSColor = NSColor.white
    override func change() {
        myColor = NSColor.blue
        myBackground = NSColor.green
    }
}
var ThingOne = One()
var ThingTwo = Two()

func applicationDidFinishLaunching(_ aNotification: Notification) {
    // Insert code here to initialize your application
}

func applicationWillTerminate(_ aNotification: Notification) {
    // Insert code here to tear down your application
}

@IBAction func changeButton(_ sender: NSButton) {
    ThingOne.change()
    ThingTwo.change()
    ObjectOne.textColor = ThingOne.myColor
    ObjectTwo.textColor = ThingTwo.myColor
    ObjectTwo.drawsBackground = true
    ObjectTwo.backgroundColor = ThingTwo.myBackground

}
}
```

To see how this program works, follow these steps:

1. Choose Product ➤ Run. Xcode runs your InheritProgram project. Notice that both labels look identical.

2. Click the Change button. The Object 1 label only changes its text color because it represented a class that only has one property (myColor). The Object 2 label changes both its text color and its background color because it has two properties (myColor and myBackground), as shown in Figure 14-17. Even though the change method name is identical in both classes, it's been overridden in the second class to modify the myBackground property.

3. Choose InheritProgram ➤ Quit InheritProgram.

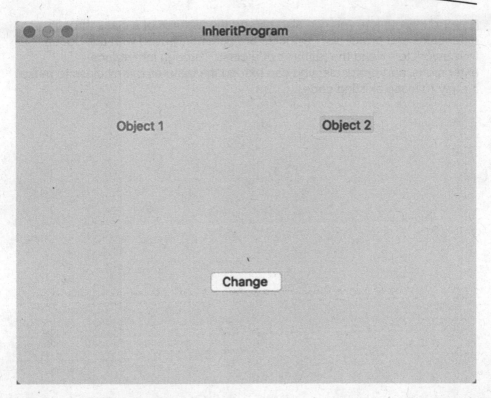

Figure 14-17. Clicking the Change button modifies two different objects with the same method name

Summary

Classes let you organize related code together where data (properties) and functions (methods) that manipulate that data are stored in the same place. The most straightforward way to extend the features of a class is through inheritance where you create a subclass.

Inheritance lets you inherit all the properties and methods of another class. A class can only inherit from one other class, but it's possible for that other class to inherit from another class as well, creating a daisy-chain effect of classes inheriting from other classes. The Cocoa framework is based on this idea of inheritance among daisy chains of classes.

To block inheritance, you can use the final keyword. To identify when you're overriding a property or method, you need to use the override keyword.

Beyond inheritance, you can also extend the features of a class through extensions and protocols. Protocols are commonly used with the Cocoa framework to extend the features of a class. Through inheritance, extensions, and protocols, you can extend the features of any class to make it easy to reuse existing code.

Chapter 15

Creating a User Interface

While it's possible to create programs that never interact with a user at all (such as a program that controls a traffic light), it's far more common to create programs that display a user interface of some kind. Typically, this means showing a window filled with different items such as labels to display text, text fields to allow the user to type something in, and buttons or pull-down menus to give the user control over the program.

Creating an effective user interface depends entirely on the purpose of your program. A business program typically follows standard conventions with pull-down menus and buttons, but a video game may create a custom interface that may not look anything like a standard macOS program. Ultimately, a user interface needs to meet the needs of the user. Given a choice between following standard user interface design conventions or making a user interface easier for the user, focus on the user every time.

To help you better understand user interface design, Apple provides a free document called "The macOS Human Interface Guidelines." This document gives a brief overview of what makes a typical macOS user interface work effectively with special emphasis on taking advantage of the latest features of macOS. By doing this, your macOS program will look modern and up to date. Failure to take advantage of the latest macOS features means your program could look dated even if it's brand new.

In previous chapters, you designed simple user interfaces using Xcode. In this chapter, you'll dig a little deeper into the different parts of Xcode that focus on helping you design user interfaces.

© Wallace Wang 2017
W. Wang, *macOS Programming for Absolute Beginners*,
DOI 10.1007/978-1-4842-2662-9_15

Remember, there is no "perfect" design for a user interface. The "perfect" user interface is one that makes tasks as simple and effortless as possible to the point where the user doesn't even notice interacting with any user interface whatsoever. A user interface acts as the middleman or translator between you and the program. The goal of any user interface is to make users feel as if they're communicating and manipulating a program directly.

Understanding User Interface Files

The Cocoa framework defines classes for creating every possible user interface item from a button (the NSButton class) and a text field (NSTextField) to a slider (NSSlider) or a date picker (NSDatePicker). Theoretically, it's possible to create an entire user interface using nothing but Swift code. However, this can be tedious because you can't see how your user interface looks until you actually run your program. This can be as clumsy as trying to paint a picture by describing exactly where you need to put a paintbrush on a canvas and the specific angle and direction to move your hand.

Rather than force you to write Swift code to define your user interface, Xcode offers a feature called Interface Builder. The idea behind Interface Builder is that you can design your user interface by dragging and dropping items on to a window.

The advantage of dragging and dropping items to create a user interface means you can see how your user interface looks so you can rapidly adjust and modify it. In addition, by separating the design of your user interface from your Swift code, you can now make changes to your user interface without affecting your Swift code and vice versa.

In the old days when programmers had to write code to create a user interface, modifying the user interface code risked affecting the code that made the program worked (and vice versa). So modifying a program went slowly because you had to constantly test to make sure your changes didn't affect another part of your program.

By keeping your user interface isolated from your Swift code, Xcode lets you create reliable programs faster than before. Now you can swap out one user interface and replace it with another one without affecting your code, or you can modify your code without affecting your user interface.

Xcode gives you two choices for how to store your user interface:

- In a .xib file
- In a .storyboard file

A .xib file (which stands for Xcode Interface Builder) typically contains a single window or view of your user interface. A simple program might have one .xib file for its user interface but a more sophisticated program will likely need several .xib files to store different windows.

A .storyboard file consists of one or more views and segues where a view typically represents a window that appears on the screen and a segue defines the transition from one view to the next.

You can actually combine both .xib and .storyboard files in a single project to create your program's user interface. Since .storyboard files are used to create iOS apps, .storyboard files are becoming more common for creating macOS user interfaces as well. (Chapter 16 explains more about storyboards and segues.)

The basic component of a user interface is a view, which displays information on the screen. A view can be an entire window or just a box that can display information, such as a table, a scrolling list of text, or a picture. Whether you're using .xib or .storyboard files, user interfaces always consist of one or more views containing other user interface items, such as buttons and text fields.

Searching the Object Library

To display your program's user interface, you need to click the .xib or .storyboard file in the Project Navigator pane. Once you've selected a user interface file to modify, you can then drag items from the Object Library (in the bottom right corner of the Xcode window) and place it anywhere on your user interface. To view the Object Library, choose View ➤ Utilities ➤ Show Object Library.

There are two ways to search the Object Library. One way is to simply scroll up and down until you find the item you want. Since the Object Library lists every possible user interface item available, scrolling can be clumsy and slow.

A faster method is to use the search field at the bottom of the Object Library pane, as shown in Figure 15-1. Just type part of the name of the user interface item you want to use and the Object Library filters out every item that doesn't match what you typed.

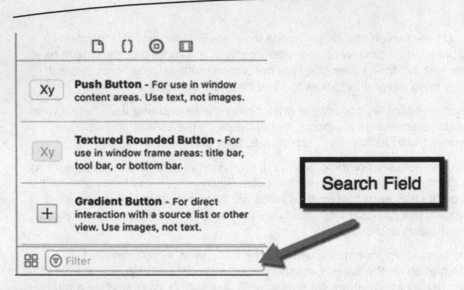

Figure 15-1. *The search field lets you quickly find user interface items in the Object Library*

To learn how to search the Object Library, follow these steps:

1. From within Xcode choose File ➤ New ➤ Project.

2. Click Application under the macOS category.

3. Click Cocoa Application and click the Next button. Xcode now asks for a product name.

4. Click in the Product Name text field and type **UIProgram**.

5. Make sure the Language pop-up menu displays Swift and that no check boxes are selected. Notice at this point you could choose to use storyboards by selecting the "Use Storyboards" check box, as shown in Figure 15-2. Keep the "Use Storyboards" check box clear for now.

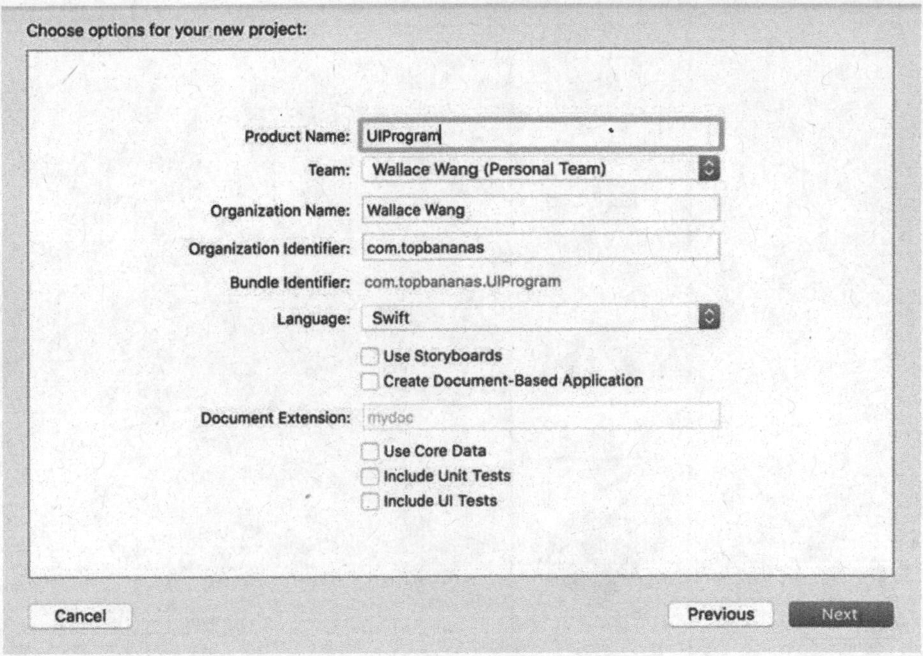

Choose options for your new project:

Product Name:	UIProgram
Team:	Wallace Wang (Personal Team)
Organization Name:	Wallace Wang
Organization Identifier:	com.topbananas
Bundle Identifier:	com.topbananas.UIProgram
Language:	Swift
	☐ Use Storyboards
	☐ Create Document-Based Application
Document Extension:	mydoc
	☐ Use Core Data
	☐ Include Unit Tests
	☐ Include UI Tests

Cancel   Previous   Next

Figure 15-2. When creating a new project, you have the option of using storyboards for your user interface

6. Click the Next button. Xcode asks where you want to store the project.

7. Choose a folder to store your project and click the Create button.

8. Click the `MainMenu.xib` file in the Project Navigator. Your program's user interface appears.

9. Click the Window icon, as shown in Figure 15-3, to display the window of your program's user interface.

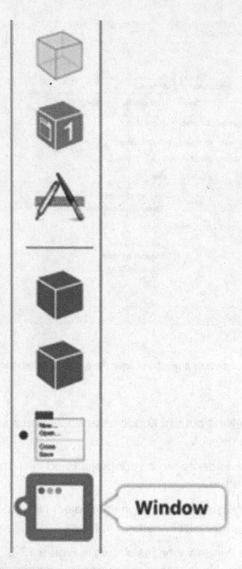

Figure 15-3. *The Window icon represents your user interface window*

10. Click the Window icon, as shown in Figure 15-3, to display the window of your program's user interface

11. Choose View ➤ Utilities ➤ Show Object Library. The Object Library appears in the bottom right corner of the Xcode window.

12. Scroll up and down through the Object Library. Notice the names and variety of different items you can add to your user interface.

13. Click in the search field at the bottom of the Object Library and type **text**. Notice that the Object Library now only shows those items that have "text" in their names or descriptions, as shown in Figure 15-4.

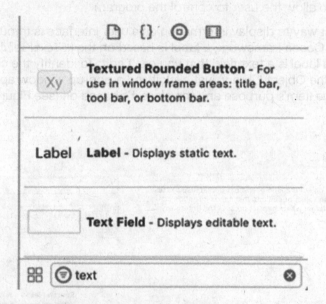

Figure 15-4. *Searching the Object Library for "text"*

14. Click in the search field at the bottom of the Object Library and click the close icon (the X inside the gray circle on the far right of the search field) to clear the search field.

15. Type **button**. Notice that the Object Library now only shows those items that have "button" in their names or descriptions. If you know all or even part of the name or purpose of the item you want, it's far faster to search for it in the Object Library than scrolling through the lengthy list of every user interface item available.

User Interface Items That Display and Accept Text

Although the Object Library contains a huge number of available items you can place on a user interface, most items can be grouped into categories by function. Remember, a user interface has three functions:

- To display information to the user
- To accept data from the user
- To allow the user to control the program

The simplest way to display information on a user interface is through a label. In the Cocoa framework, a label is based on the NSTextField class. Essentially a label is a text field that you can't edit. To identify the class of any item in the Object Library, just click it and a pop-up window appears that describes the item's purpose and the class it's based on (see Figure 15-5).

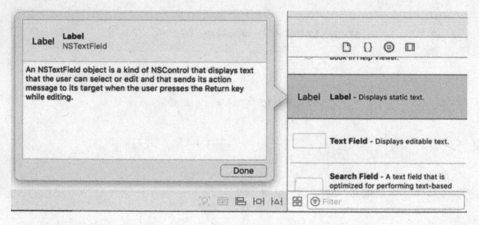

Figure 15-5. Identifying the class of a user interface item in the Object Library

Any user interface item based on the NSTextField can be used to display and accept text, although it's more common to use a label for displaying text and any other type of text field for letting the user type in text. The list of user interface items based on the NSTextField is shown in Figure 15-6:

- **Label**: Displays text but does not allow the user to enter or edit text
- **Text Field**: Lets the user enter and edit text
- **Text Field with Number Formatter**: Lets the user enter and edit formatted numbers easily
- **Wrapping Label**: Displays text on multiple lines

- **Wrapping Text Field**: Lets the user enter and edit text that appears on multiple lines

- **Text Field Cell**: Lets you display text in color in a cell such as in a table

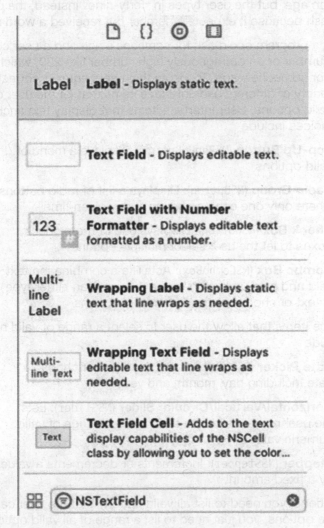

Label **Label** - Displays static text.

Text Field - Displays editable text.

123 **Text Field with Number Formatter** - Displays editable text formatted as a number.

Multi-line Label **Wrapping Label** - Displays static text that line wraps as needed.

Multi-line Text **Wrapping Text Field** - Displays editable text that line wraps as needed.

Text **Text Field Cell** - Adds to the text display capabilities of the NSCell class by allowing you to set the color...

NSTextField

Figure 15-6. User interface items based on the NSTextField class

User Interface Items That Restrict Choices

Letting the user enter data in a text field provides maximum flexibility. However, this flexibility also means that your program has no idea what type of data the user might enter. If a program expects the user to type in a number for an age, but the user types in "forty-nine" instead, the program will likely crash because it expects a number but received a word instead.

Even worse, a program could ask for someone's age and a user could type a negative number or an outrageously high number like 239, which is clearly impossible for someone's age. To insure that users enter in correct data, you can use a variety of different user interface items that let the user choose a range of valid options. User interface items that display text (including numbers) choices include

- **Pop-Up Button** (NSPopUpButton): Displays a menu of valid options

- **Radio Group** (NSButton): Displays a list of radio buttons where only one can be chosen at any given time

- **Check Box** (NSButton): Displays one or more check boxes to let the user select multiple options

- **Combo Box** (NSComboBox): Acts like a combination text field and pop-up button where the user can either type in text or choose from a list of valid options

User interface items that allow the user to select a range of valid numeric options include

- **Date Picker** (NSDatePicker): Lets the user choose a date including day, month, and year

- **Horizontal/Vertical/Circular Slider** (NSSlider): Lets the user move a slider to select a fixed range of valid numeric values

- **Stepper** (NSStepper): Increments or decrements a value by a fixed amount

With text options, you need to list all valid options that the user can choose. With numeric options, you just need to list a range of all valid options, such as letting the user choose a number between 1 and 100.

User Interface Items That Accept Commands

The most common user interface item is one that accepts commands so the user can control a program. The two most common types of user interface items that accept commands are buttons and menus. Each button or menu item represent a single command, so when the user clicks on a button or menu item, that command tells the program to do something.

Both buttons and menu items allow the view to communicate back to the controller using something called target-action, as shown in Figure 15-7. The target is a button or menu item, which triggers an action back in the controller, such as running an IBAction method.

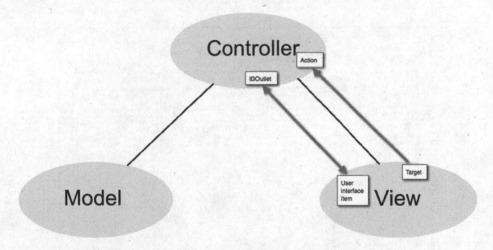

Figure 15-7. Buttons and menu items let a view communicate back to a controller

User interface buttons are based on the NSButton class. Menu items are based on the NSMenuItem class. The Object Library displays a variety of different types of buttons and menu items, but they all work alike where the button or menu item represents a command. To make that command work, you need to connect the button on the user interface to an IBAction method in a Swift file.

User Interface Items That Group Items

One type of user interface item does nothing but group and organize other items on the user interface, such as displaying a box around related buttons or text. These use interface items are more decorative so you likely won't need to connect them to Swift code using IBOutlets or IBAction methods.

Some examples of items that group and organize other user interface items include

- **Table View** (NSTableView): Displays data in rows

- **Collection View** (NSCollectionView): Displays data in rows and columns

- **Box** (NSBox): Displays a box that draws a border around related items

- **Tab View** (NSTabView): Displays a two or more tabs that can change the data that appears inside a box, as shown in Figure 15-8

Figure 15-8. A tab view can group two or more groups of related items in the same box.

- **Windows** (NSWindow): Displays a window that can hold other user interface items

- **Toolbar** (NSToolbar): Displays icons that represent commands

Although the Object Library contains many other items, they typically fall in one of these four categories:

- Items that display or accept text
- Items that let the user choose from a limited range of valid options
- Items that let the user choose a command to control the program
- Items that group or organize other user interface items

Using Constraints in Auto Layout

No matter what type of items you place on a user interface, you need to consider what happens if the user resizes the window. A window that's too big might leave too much empty space on the user interface. A window that's too small might cut off items, as shown in Figure 15-9.

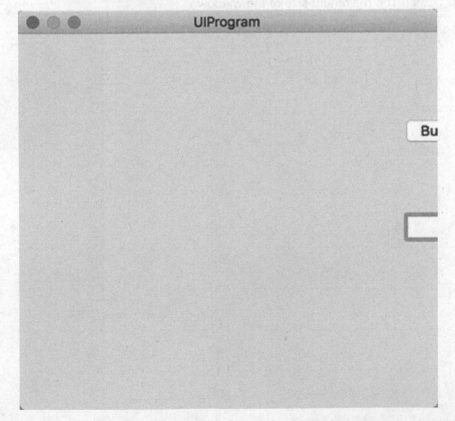

Figure 15-9. A user interface that doesn't adapt when the user resizes a window risks cutting off items

There are two ways to make sure a user interface remains usable when the user resizes a window. First, you can define minimum and maximum sizes for a window to keep a window from shrinking or expanding too much. Second, you can set constraints on individual items that define the distance between neighboring items and the edges of the window.

In most cases, you can use both methods. This way you can define a minimum and maximum size for a window, and define how items on your user interface should adapt to changes in the window size.

Defining Window Sizes

A window displays your program's user interface on the screen. Xcode lets you define the following for a window (as shown in Figure 15-10):

- The initial size of the window
- The minimum size of the window
- The maximum size of the window
- The initial position of the window on the screen

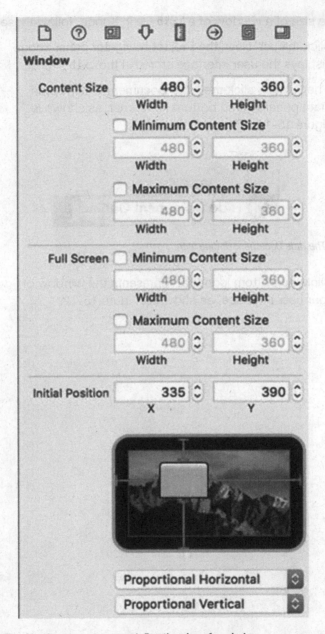

Figure 15-10. The Size Inspector lets you define the size of a window

To define the size of a window of a `.xib` file in Xcode, follow these steps:

1. Click the .xib file in the Project Navigator pane. Xcode displays the user interface stored in the `.xib` file.

2. If necessary, click the Hide Document Outline icon that appears in the bottom left corner, as shown in Figure 15-11.

Figure 15-11. The Hide Document Outline icon

3. Click the bottom icon that represents the window of your user interface, as shown in Figure 15-12.

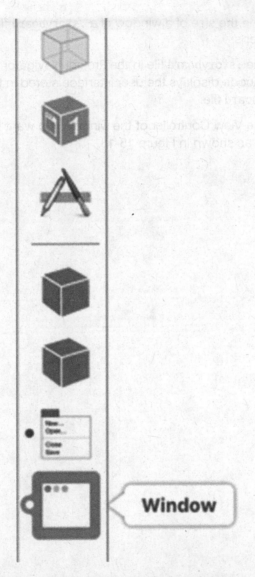

Figure 15-12. The bottom icon represents your user interface window

4.   Choose View ➤ Utilities ➤ Show Size Inspector. The
     Size Inspector pane appears (see Figure 15-10).

Windows stored in `.storyboard` files work slightly differently than `.xib` files.
When you create a macOS project, you have a choice between using `.xib`
files or `.storyboard` files. If you create a project that uses `.storyboard`

files, you can define the size of a window of a .storyboard file in Xcode by following these steps:

1. Click the .storyboard file in the Project Navigator pane. Xcode displays the user interface stored in the .storyboard file.

2. Click the View Controller of the window you want to modify, as shown in Figure 15-13.

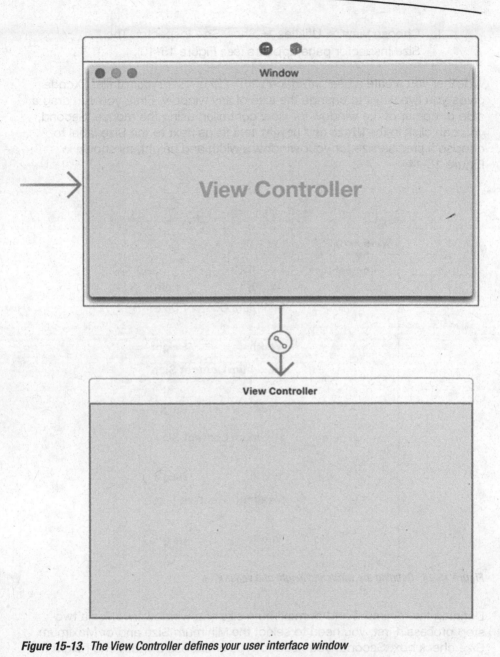

Figure 15-13. The View Controller defines your user interface window

3.   Choose View ➤ Utilities ➤ Show Size Inspector. The
     Size Inspector pane appears (see Figure 15-10).

Whether you create a user interface with .xib or .storyboard files, Xcode
gives you two ways to change the size of any window. First, you can drag a
side or corner of the window (or view controller) using the mouse. Second,
you can click in the Width and Height text fields next to the Size label to
choose a precise size for your window's width and height, as shown in
Figure 15-14.

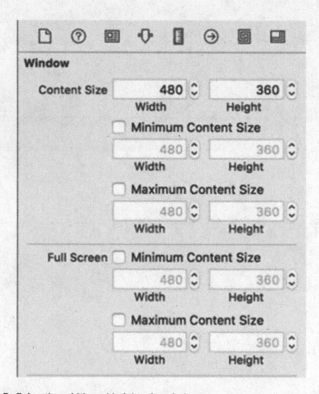

Figure 15-14. Defining the width and height of a window

Defining the minimum and/or maximum size of a window involves a two-
step process. First, you need to select the Minimum Size and/or Maximum
Size check box. Second, you need to type or choose a width and height to
define the minimum or maximum size for your window.

Finally, you can define the initial position of a window when it first appears.
You can do this by either dragging on the window icon on the simulated
screen or by typing in an X and Y value into the Initial Position text fields, as
shown in Figure 15-15.

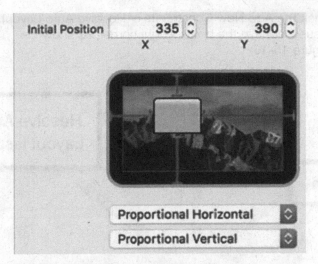

Figure 15-15. Defining the initial position of a window

The two pop-up menus underneath the simulated screen let you define how to determine the initial position of a window:

- **Fixed from Left/Right**: Defines a fixed value between the window edge and the screen edge

- **Proportional Horizontal/Vertical**: Defines a proportional value between the window edge and the screen edge, based on the size of the screen

- **Center Horizontally/Vertically**: Defines the window to appear in the center of the screen

Placing Constraints on User Interface Items

Defining a minimum size for a window can keep the user from shrinking a window so small that it cuts off the items that appear on the user interface. However, what happens if the user expands a window? Then the items in the window should ideally adjust their position to adapt to the expanded window size.

Constraints define the distance between two items, such as between a button and the edge of the window or between two buttons. Xcode gives you three ways to place constraints on a user interface item:

- Control-drag the mouse from a user interface item to another item or the edge of a window

- Choose Editor ➤ Resolve Auto Layout Issues

- Click the Add New Constraints or Resolve Auto Layout Issues icons in the bottom right corner, as shown in Figure 15-16

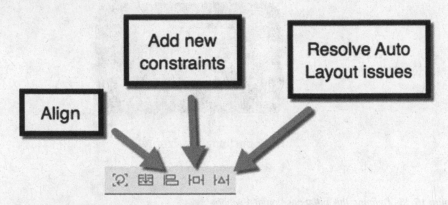

Figure 15-16. The Align, Pin, and Resolve Auto Layout Issues icons

To use the Control-drag method to place a constraint, follow these steps:

1. Move the mouse pointer over the user interface item you want to constrain.

2. Hold down the Control key and drag the mouse towards another user interface item or the edge of the window.

3. Release the Control key and the mouse button when the mouse pointer appears near the other user interface item or window edge. A pop-up window appears, similar to Figure 15-17.

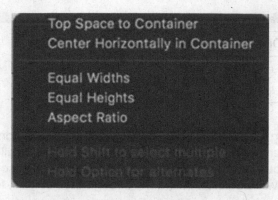

Figure 15-17. Releasing the Control key and the mouse displays a pop-up window

Depending on the direction you Control-drag the mouse, you'll see different options in the pop-up window, as shown in Table 15-1.

Table 15-1. Pop-Up Options

Direction to Window Edge	Constraint Option
Up	Top space to container
Bottom	Bottom space to container
Right	Trailing space to container
Left	Leading space to container

Besides Control-dragging to a window edge, you can also Control-drag from one user interface item over another user interface item. Doing this lets you define the distance between two items on the user interface, such as the distance between two buttons or one button and a text field.

When you Control-drag the mouse over another user interface item, a pop-up window appears. If you're defining the distance between two items that are side by side, the pop-up window will display the Horizontal Spacing option. If you're defining the distance between two items that are stacked one on top of another, the pop-up window will display the Vertical Spacing option, as shown in Table 15-2.

Table 15-2. Spacing Options

Direction to Another Item	Constraint Option
Left/Right	Horizontal spacing
Up/Down	Vertical spacing

The Control-drag method lets you place constraints visually on different user interface items. Another way to define constraints is to click the user interface item you want to constrain, and then click the Pin icon to display a pop-up window. To define constraints through the Pin icon, follow these steps:

1. Click the user interface item that you want to constrain.

2. Click the Add New Constraints icon. A pop-up window appears, showing four constraints to the left, right, up, and down. In Figure 15-18, the distance to the top of the window is 139, the distance to the left of the window is 145, the distance to the right of the window is 239, and the distance to the bottom of the window is 199.

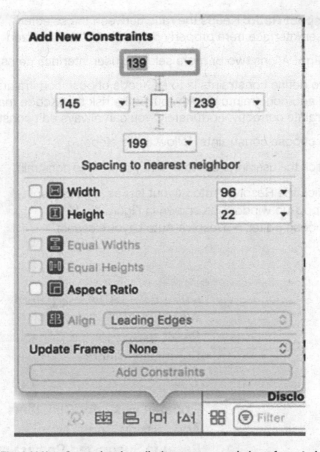

Figure 15-18. The Add New Constraints icon displays a pop-up window of constraints

3. Click a constraint to select it. When you click a constraint, it appears in red. If a constraint appears as a dotted line, this means the constraint has not been selected yet.

4. Click in any of the additional check boxes.

5. Click the Add Constraints button at the bottom of the pop-up window to define one or more constraints.

The Add New Constraints pop-up window lets you define additional types of constraints for your selected user interface item:

- **Width or Height**: Keeps the size of your selected user interface item at a fixed size

- **Equal Widths or Heights**: Keeps two or more selected user interface items at the same fixed size

■ **Aspect Ratio**: Keeps the ratio between the selected user interface item properly proportioned if it's resized

■ **Align**: Aligns two or more selected user interface items

A third way to define constraints is to let Xcode choose constraints for you. This lets you add constraints quickly, but at the risk that Xcode may not define constraints correctly. Fortunately, you can always edit constraints later.

To let Xcode choose constraints, follow these steps:

1. Click the user interface item that you want to constrain.

2. Click the Resolve Auto Layout Issues icon to display a pop-up window, as shown in Figure 15-19 (or choose Editor ➤ Resolve Auto Layout Issues).

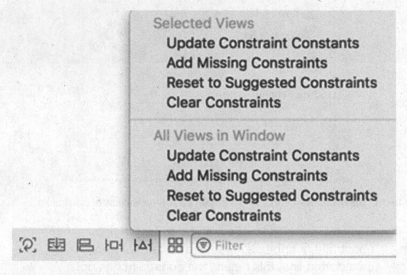

Figure 15-19. The Resolve Auto Layout Issues pop-up window

3. Choose either the "Add Missing Constraints" or "Reset to Suggested Constraints" option.

If you choose the options in the top half of the window, you'll affect only the selected user interface item. If you choose the options in the bottom half of the window, you'll affect all user interface items whether you selected them or not.

Remember, adding constraints can be a trial-and-error process of defining a constraint and seeing how it works before modifying or deleting it altogether. As you add constraints, Xcode displays constraint lines around your user interface item. If Xcode doesn't think you have enough constraints, all constraints on that item will appear as orange. The moment Xcode thinks you have enough constraints on an item, the constraints will appear in blue.

Editing Constraints

Once you've defined one or more constraints, you can always delete or edit existing constraints. To delete a constraint, you have several options:

- Click the constraint and then press the Delete or Backspace key

- Click the user interface item that has the constraint and open the Size Inspector pane, then click the constraint and press the Delete or Backspace key

You can also delete or clear all constraints from a single user interface item or from all items on the currently displayed user interface. To do this, you have two options:

- Choose Editor ➤ Resolve Auto Layout Issues

- Click the Resolve Auto Layout Issues icon in the bottom right corner of the window

With either option, you'll see a menu divided in a top half and a bottom half (see Figure 15-19). Clicking the Clear Constraints option in the top half clears constraints only from any currently selected items. Clicking the Clear Constraints option in the bottom half clears constraints from all items in the currently displayed user interface whether you selected them or not.

Rather than delete a constraint, you can edit it. Editing lets you modify how it behaves. Three values you can modify about a constraint are

- **Constant**: A fixed value that defines the value of the constraint

- **Priority**: A numeric value that determines which constraints must be followed first

- **Modifier**: A numeric value that defines a ratio that affects two values such as an item's height to its width or one item's width to a second item's width

To edit a constraint, follow these steps:

1. Click the user interface item that contains the constraint you want to edit.

2. Choose View ➤ Utilities ➤ Show Size Inspector. The Size Inspector pane lists all defined constraints, as shown in Figure 15-20.

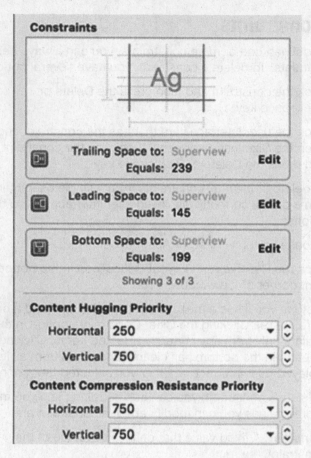

Figure 15-20. Viewing a list of defined constraints in the Size Inspector pane

3. Click the Edit button on the far right of the constraint
    you want to modify. A pop-up window appears, as
    shown in Figure 15-21.

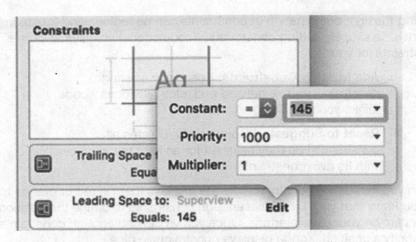

Figure 15-21. A pop-up window lets you modify a constraint

Notice that to the right of the Constant: label, there's a pop-up menu showing an equal sign (=). If you click this pop-up menu, you can select greater than or equal to, less than or equal to, or equal to.

Further to the right of the Constant label is a drop-down field that displays a number. If you click the downward-pointing arrow, you'll be able to choose between three options:

- A numeric value that you can type or edit
- **Use Standard Value**: Lets Xcode decide the best value
- **Use Canvas Value**: Uses the current distance on the screen to define a fixed value

Keep in mind that a fixed value or a canvas value may behave differently on different size monitors. You may need to experiment until you find the right value for your particular user interface.

Priorities are used to resolve conflicts between two or more constraints that may contradict each other, such as one constraint keeping a button pinned to the right edge of a window and a second constraint keeping the same button pinned to the left edge of a window while a third constraint keeps the button a fixed width. By modifying priorities, you can make sure your constraints don't conflict.

Finding the right combination of constraints can be tedious and frustrating at times. To simplify setting constraints, Xcode offers two ways to define constraints for you:

- **Add Missing Constraints**: Keeps any existing constraints you've defined and adds new ones Xcode thinks you're missing

- **Reset to Suggested Constraints**: Deletes all constraints you may have set for an item and replaces it with its own constraints

When you first define constraints, Xcode displays them in red or orange to let you know that you don't have enough constraints to define the position of an item on your user interface. Once you've defined enough constraints to specify a position, Xcode displays constraints in blue.

Defining Constraints in a macOS Program

To fully understand constraints, you need to see how they work in an actual program. Then you can see how your user interface adjusts each time you resize its window. In the following sample program, you'll define relationships constraints for a push button and a text field, and you'll also define an aspect ratio for an image.

Earlier in this chapter you created an macOS project called UIProgram so let's use it to see how constraints work:

1. Make sure your UIProgram project is loaded in Xcode.

2. Click the MainMenu.xib file in the Project Navigator.

3. Click the UIProgram icon to make the window of the user interface appear.

4. Choose View ➤ Utilities ➤ Show Object Library to make the Object Library appear in the bottom right corner of the Xcode window.

5. Drag one push button, one text field, and one text view on the user interface so that it looks similar to Figure 15-22.

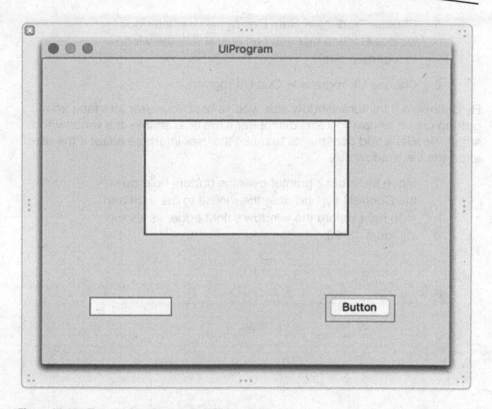

Figure 15-22. The user interface of the UIProgram

While this user interface may look fine right now, it will look awful as soon as the user resizes the window. Choose Product ➤ Run and then resize the window to see how shrinking the window cuts off or hides items on the user interface. Now expand the size of the window and notice all the empty space inside the expanded window. Exit out of your program by choosing UIProgram ➤ Quit UIProgram.

First, let's define the window's minimum size by following these steps:

1. Click the Main.xib file in the Project Navigator.

2. Click the Window icon in the left pane to select the entire window.

3. Choose View ➤ Utilities ➤ Show Size Inspector to display the window constraints (see Figure 15-14).

4. Click to select the top Minimum Size check box to define the current window size as its minimum size.

5.   Choose Product ➤ Run. Resize the user interface window. Notice that you can only shrink the window to a certain size.

6.   Choose UIProgram ➤ Quit UIProgram.

By defining a minimum window size, you've kept your user interface from getting cut off or having items disappear if the user shrinks the window too small. Now let's add constraints to make the user interface adapt if the user expands the window size.

1.   Move the mouse pointer over the button, hold down the Control key, and drag the mouse to the right and stop right before the window's right edge, as shown in Figure 15-23.

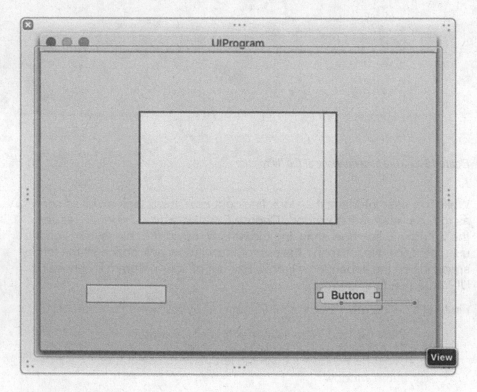

Figure 15-23. Adjusting the size of the user interface window

2.   Release the Control key and the mouse. A pop-up window appears.

3. Choose Trailing Space to Container. Notice that the button appears in red to show that you don't have enough constraints on the button yet.

4. Move the mouse pointer over the button, hold down the Control key, and drag the mouse down and stop right before the window's bottom edge.

5. Release the Control key and the mouse. A pop-up window appears.

6. Choose Bottom Space to Container. Notice that the button now appears in blue to show you have enough constraints.

7. Click the text field to select it.

8. Choose Editor ➤ Resolve Auto Layout Issues ➤ Add Missing Constraints. Xcode adds constraints automatically, as shown in Figure 15-24.

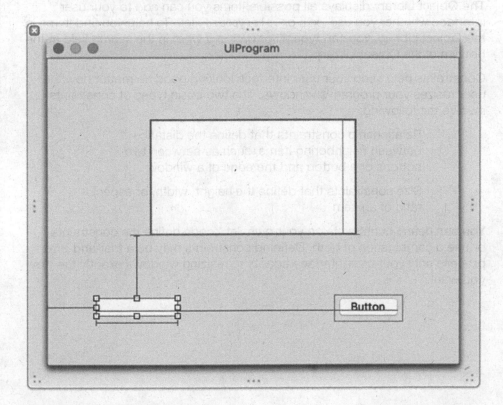

Figure 15-24. Constraints on the text field

9. Choose Product ➤ Run.

10. Resize the window. Notice how the user interface items adjust when you expand the window size. As you can see, constraints keep user interface items in their proper place and size no matter how the user resizes the window. Feel free to experiment with editing your constraints to see how they work.

11. Choose UIProgram ➤ Quit UIProgram.

Summary

Your program's user interface determines how people interact with your program. Every user interface needs to display information, retrieve information from the user, and allow the user to choose commands. Ideally, a user should focus more on using your program and less on figuring out how the user interface works.

The Object Library displays all possible items you can add to your user interface whether you use .xib or .storyboard files. To help you find items in the Object Library, you can type all or part of a word in the search field at the bottom of the Object Library.

Constraints help keep your user interface looking good no matter how the user resizes your program's windows. The two basic types of constraints involve the following:

- Relationship constraints that define the distance between neighboring items, such as between two buttons or a button and the edge of a window

- Size constraints that define the height, width, or aspect ratio of an item

You can define constraints on your own, let Xcode define the constraints, or use a combination of both. Defining constraints may be a trial-and-error process until your user interface adapts to resizing windows exactly the way you want.

Chapter 16

Working with Storyboards

The most common part of every program's user interface is a window that displays items such as buttons and text fields. In Xcode, windows are called views. In all but the simplest programs, a user interface will likely consist of two or more windows or views. This means your program needs to know how to open additional windows and close them again.

The two ways to create and store views are in .xib files and .storyboard files. A .xib file holds one view so if you need to display multiple views, you'll need to create multiple .xib files. A .storyboard file can hold one or more views.

You can create user interfaces with either .xib or .storyboard files, or a combination of both. Originally, you could use either .xib or .storyboard files to create iOS apps, but Xcode 8 now only creates .storyboard files for iOS apps. For creating macOS programs, you can still use either .xib or .storyboard files, but since iOS apps relies primarily on .storyboard files, Apple will likely shift macOS programming to .storyboard files as well. For this reason, you should learn more about using .storyboards for creating user interfaces.

Ultimately, whether you use .xib or .storyboard files is less important than knowing how to design a good user interface that makes performing tasks as easy as possible for the user.

Each time you create a new project, Xcode gives you a choice between using storyboards or not, as shown in Figure 16-1. If you choose not to use storyboards, then Xcode will create and store your user interface in a .xib file. If you choose to use storyboards, then Xcode will store your user interface in a .storyboard file.

© Wallace Wang 2017
W. Wang, *macOS Programming for Absolute Beginners*,
DOI 10.1007/978-1-4842-2662-9_16

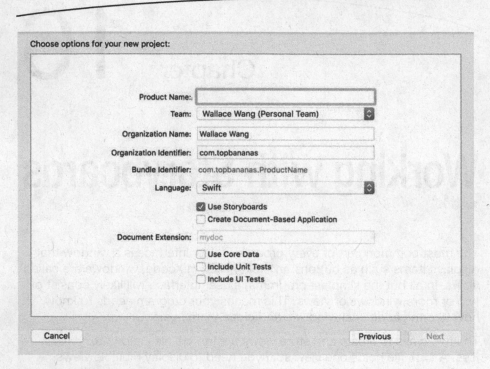

Choose options for your new project:

Product Name::	
Team:	Wallace Wang (Personal Team)
Organization Name:	Wallace Wang
Organization Identifier:	com.topbananas
Bundle Identifier:	com.topbananas.ProductName
Language:	Swift
	☑ Use Storyboards
	☐ Create Document-Based Application
Document Extension:	mydoc
	☐ Use Core Data
	☐ Include Unit Tests
	☐ Include UI Tests

Cancel   Previous   Next

Figure 16-1. When creating a macOS project, Xcode gives you a choice of choosing storyboards or not

To experiment with storyboards, you need to create a project that uses storyboards by following these steps:

1. From within Xcode choose File ➤ New ➤ Project.

2. Click Application under the macOS category.

3. Click Cocoa Application and click the Next button. Xcode now asks for a product name.

4. Click in the Product Name text field and type **StoryProgram**.

5. Make sure the Language pop-up menu displays Swift and that only the "Use Storyboards" check box is selected (see Figure 16-1).

6. Click the Next button. Xcode asks where you want to store the project.

7. Choose a folder to store your project and click the Create button.

8. Click the Main.storyboard file in the Project
    Navigator pane. The .storyboard user interface
    appears, as shown in Figure 16-2.

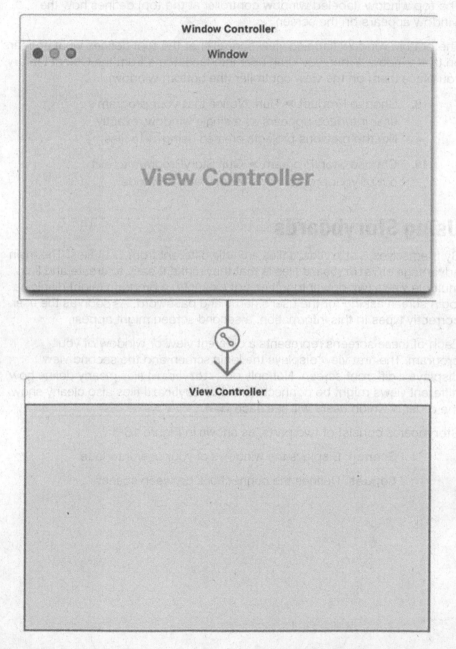

Figure 16-2. A .storyboard file displays a window controller and a view controller.

Unlike .xib files that display a single window for laying out user interface items like buttons, text fields, and labels, .storyboard files display two windows.

The top window (labeled window controller at the top) defines how the window appears on the screen.

The bottom window (labeled view controller at the top) defines what appears on that window. When you drag user interface items from the Object Library, you place them on the view controller (the bottom window).

9.   Choose Product ➤ Run. Notice that your program's user interface appears as a single window, exactly like the previous projects created using .xib files.

10. Choose StoryProgram ➤ Quit StoryProgram to exit out of your program and return back to Xcode.

Using Storyboards

By themselves, .storyboard files are little different from .xib files. The main advantage of .storyboard files is that they make it easy to create and link multiple views (windows) together. For example, a program might display a login screen asking for the user's name and password. As soon as the user correctly types in this information, a second screen might appear.

Each of these screens represents a different view or window of your program. The first view displays the login screen and the second view displays a different screen. Not only do .storyboard files clearly define how different views might be connected, but .storyboard files also clearly show the order in which users will see each view.

Storyboards consist of two parts, as shown in Figure 16-3:

■ **Scenes**: Displays the windows of your user interface

■ **Segues**: Defines the connections between scenes

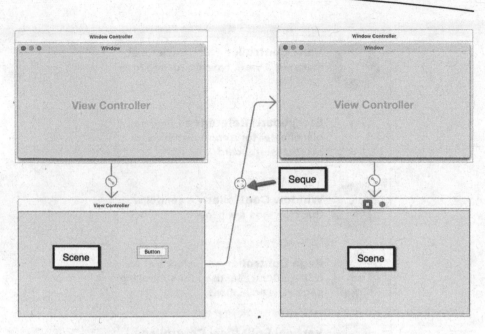

Figure 16-3. *Storyboards organize a user interface into scenes and seques.*

Scenes contain user interface items like buttons and text fields. Segues show the order in which users will view the user interface.

When you first create a new project using storyboards, Xcode includes a window controller that controls a single view where you can place user interface items like buttons or text fields. To add additional views to a storyboard, you must use the Object Library and add additional controllers.

In addition to displaying user interface items, the Object Library also contains controllers for storyboards, as shown in Figure 16-4.

The five types of controllers you can place on a storyboard include

- **View Controller**: Controls a .xib file so you can include it with a storyboard

- **Window Controller**: Controls a single window or view

- **Page Controller**: Defines the animation between views

- **Vertical/Horizontal Split View Controller**: Displays two views side by side or stacked on top of each other

- **Tab View Controller**: Displays a tabbed interface that controls two or more views

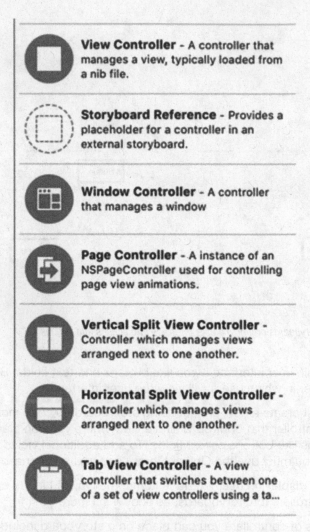

View Controller - A controller that manages a view, typically loaded from a nib file.

Storyboard Reference - Provides a placeholder for a controller in an external storyboard.

Window Controller - A controller that manages a window

Page Controller - A instance of an NSPageController used for controlling page view animations.

Vertical Split View Controller - Controller which manages views arranged next to one another.

Horizontal Split View Controller - Controller which manages views arranged next to one another.

Tab View Controller - A view controller that switches between one of a set of view controllers using a ta...

Figure 16-4. Controllers in the Object Library that you can add to a storyboard

A window controller is nothing more than a window that contains a view. The view displayed inside the window is identified by an arrow pointing from the window controller to the view (see Figure 16-2).

A page controller displays a view that allows multiple pages that can appear or disappear, creating an animated effect. This lets you hide user interface items on the view so they can appear (and disappear) later.

A vertical/horizontal split view controller acts like a window that holds two views either side by side or stacked on top of each other, as shown in Figure 16-5.

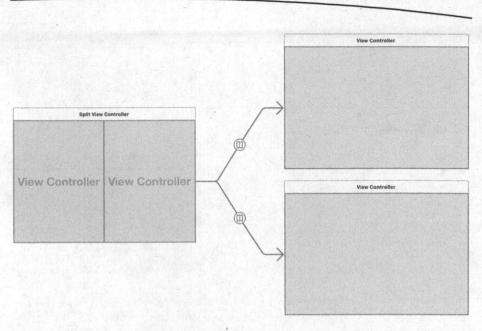

Figure 16-5. A split view controller contains two views.

A tab view controller also consists of a single window that can contain two or more views. The difference is that it can display tabs where each tab represents a different view, as shown in Figure 16-6. You can also add more than two views to a tab view controller.

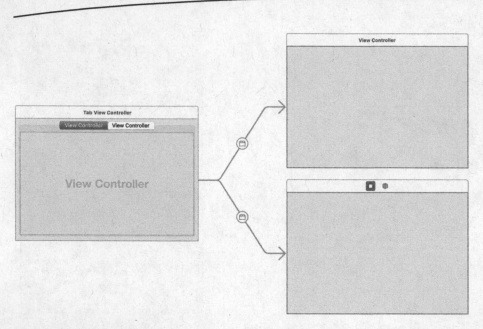

Figure 16-6. *A tab view controller displays two or more views in one window identified by tabs.*

Adding Scenes to a Storyboard

To add scenes to a storyboard, you must add additional controllers. To see how to create a new scene on a storyboard, follow these steps:

1. Make sure your StoryProgram project is loaded into Xcode.

2. Click the `Main.storyboard` file in the Project Navigator pane.

3. Choose View ➤ Utilities ➤ Show Object Library.

4. Drag the blue window controller from the Object Library (see Figure 16-4) and place it next to the existing window controller in your storyboard.

5. Drag the window controller and its accompanying view controller so they appear as shown in Figure 16-7.

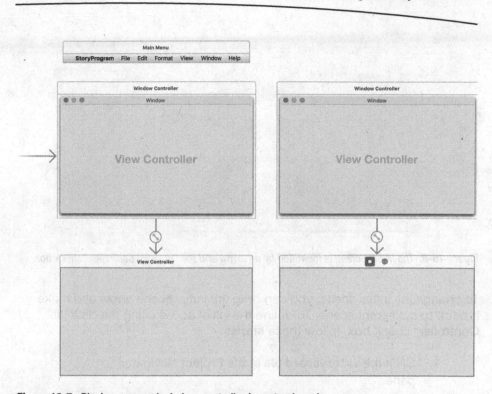

Figure 16-7. *Placing a second window controller in a storyboard*

When you start adding additional scenes to a storyboard, those scenes will never appear on the screen. To make a scene appear, you must either connect that scene to existing scenes using segues, or define that new scene as the initial scene.

Defining the Initial Scene in a Storyboard

In every storyboard, one scene must always be defined as the initial scene, which is the first window or view that appears when your program runs. Xcode identifies the initial scene with an arrow pointing to the right.

Another way to identify the initial scene is to click on the blue icon in the top middle part of the controller and open the Show Attributes Inspector pane. If the "Is Initial Controller" check box is selected, then the currently selected window is the initial scene, as shown in Figure 16-8.

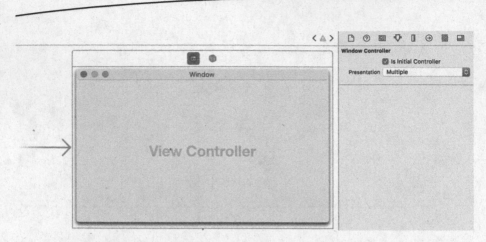

Figure 16-8. The initial screen is identified by an arrow and the "Is Initial Controller" check box.

To change the initial scene, you can drag the initial scene arrow and make it point to a different scene. To define the initial scene using the "Is Initial Controller" check box, follow these steps:

1. Click the .storyboard file in the Project Navigator pane.

2. Click the scene that you want to make the initial scene.

3. Click the blue controller icon at the top of the scene, as shown in Figure 16-9.

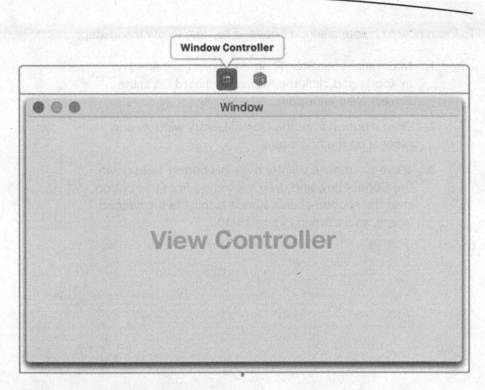

Figure 16-9. Selecting the controller icon of a scene

4. Choose View ➤ Utilities ➤ Show Attributes
    Inspector. The Windows Controller category appears
    in the Attributes Inspector window in the right pane
    (see Figure 16-8).

5. Select the "Is Initial Controller" check box.

Note that there can only be one initial scene at a time. As soon as you check
the "Is Initial Controller" check box for one scene, Xcode automatically clears
that "Is Initial Controller" check box if it's selected for a different scene.

Connecting Scenes with Segues

When a storyboard consists or two or more scenes, only the initial scene will
appear if you run your program. To display other scenes in a storyboard, you
need to create a segue between scenes. A segue creates a link between two
scenes so the user can view one scene after another.

To learn how to create a segue between scenes, follow these steps:

1. Make sure your StoryProgram project is loaded in Xcode and click the Main.storyboard file in the Project Navigator pane.

2. Drag a button from the Object Library window and place it on the first scene.

3. Move the mouse pointer over this button, hold down the Control key, and drag the mouse from this button over the second scene. Xcode highlights the second scene, as shown in Figure 16-10.

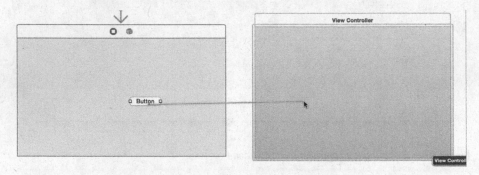

Figure 16-10. Control-dragging the mouse from a button to another scene creates a segue.

4. Release the Control key and the mouse. Xcode displays a pop-up menu, as shown in Figure 16-11.

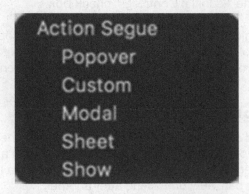

Figure 16-11. A pop-up menu lets you define how to display the scene.

5. Choose Show. Xcode creates a segue between the two scenes.

6. Drag a label on to the second scene and change its text to read "Second scene here".

7. Choose Product ➤ Run. Xcode runs your program and displays the window with the push button on it.

8. Click the button. The second window appears that contains the label "Second scene here", as shown in Figure 16-12.

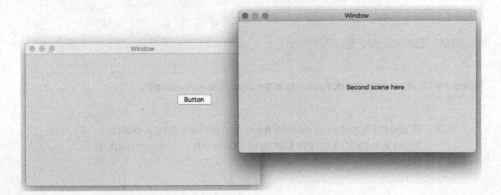

Figure 16-12. A segue opens a second view.

Displaying Scenes from a Segue

Segues serve two purposes. First, a segue connects one scene to another scene. Second, a segue defines how that second scene appears. When creating a segue, you have five options:

■ **Show**: Displays a scene as a separate window that can be moved and resized

■ **Custom**: Lets you create a custom appearance for the scene

■ **Modal**: Displays a scene as a dialog that won't let the user do anything else until dismissing this scene

■ **Popover**: Displays a scene with an arrow pointing to an object, as shown in Figure 16-13.

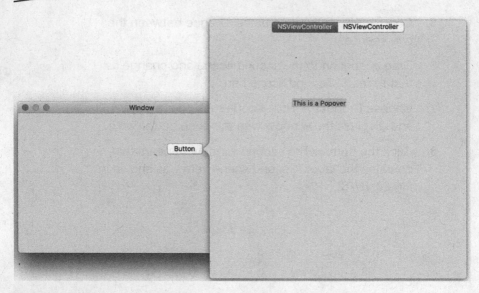

Figure 16-13. A popover appears pointing at the object the user clicked.

- ■ **Sheet**: Displays a scene as a sheet that drops down from a window's title bar and covers it up, as shown in Figure 16-14.

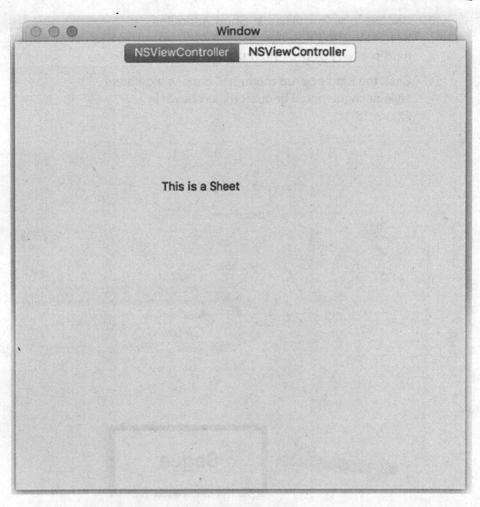

Figure 16-14. A sheet drops down from a window's title bar.

When you first create a segue, you can define how the segue should display the scene. However, you can always change this by following these steps:

1. Make sure your StoryProgram project is loaded in Xcode and click the Main.storyboard file in the Project Navigator pane.

2. Click the segue you want to modify. Xcode highlights your chosen segue.

3. Choose View ➤ Utilities ➤ Show Attributes
    Inspector. The Attributes Inspector pane displays the
    Kind property pop-up menu.

4. Click the Kind pop-up menu and choose a different
    style such as modal or custom, as shown in
    Figure 16-15.

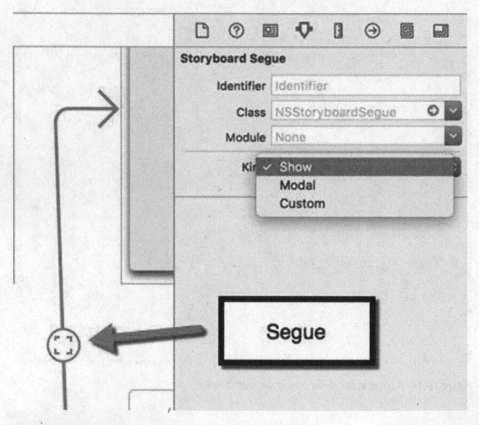

Figure 16-15. You can change how a segue displays a scene.

Adding a Controller File to a Scene

Each time you add a different scene to a storyboard, you're essentially
adding another window of your program's user interface. However, each
scene also needs its own Swift file to control it. This way, if you add buttons
or other user interface items, you can write Swift code to display data on
that scene or handle any commands the user might choose, such as clicking
a button.

First, you must create one Swift file for each additional scene you add to a storyboard. Second, you must link this Swift file to the scene so the scene can use it.

To learn how to create a Swift file to control a scene, follow these steps:

1. Make sure your StoryProgram project is loaded in Xcode and click the Main.storyboard file in the Project Navigator pane.

2. Choose File ➤ New ➤ File. Xcode displays different templates you can use.

3. Choose Source under macOS and click the Cocoa Class icon, as shown in Figure 16-16. Then click the Next button. Another dialog appears, asking for a name and a subclass.

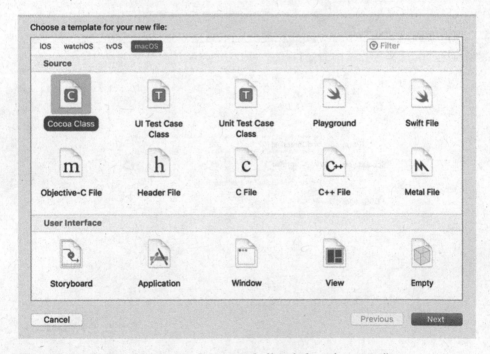

Figure 16-16. Creating a Cocoa class file to store Swift code for a view controller

4. Click in the Name text field and type a descriptive name for your class to control your scene, such as SecondController.

5. Click in the Subclass of: pop-up menu and choose NSViewController. (If you are creating a Swift file for a different type of controller such as a page controller or a tab view controller, choose a different subclass, such as NSPageController or NSTabView.)

6. Clear the "Also create XIB file for user interface" check box.

7. Make sure the Language pop-up menu displays Swift, as shown in Figure 16-17. Click the Next button. Xcode asks where you want to save your new Swift class.

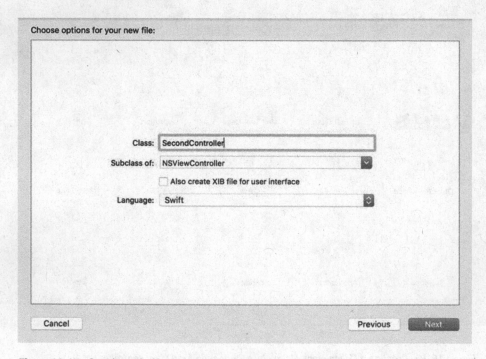

Choose options for your new file:

Class:	SecondController
Subclass of:	NSViewController
	☐ Also create XIB file for user interface
Language:	Swift

Cancel   Previous   Next

Figure 16-17. Creating a Swift class to control a scene in a storyboard

8. Choose a folder and click the Create button. Xcode displays your Swift class in the Project Navigator pane. At this point, the Swift class and the scene aren't connected so you must make the scene's view controller a class of the Swift file you just created.

9. Click the `Main.storyboard` file to display your user interface.

10. Click the blue View Controller icon on the scene that has the label "Second scene here" on it.

11. Choose View ➤ Utilities ➤ Show Identity Inspector.

12. Click in the Class pop-up menu and choose SecondController, the view controller you created earlier, as shown in Figure 16-18.

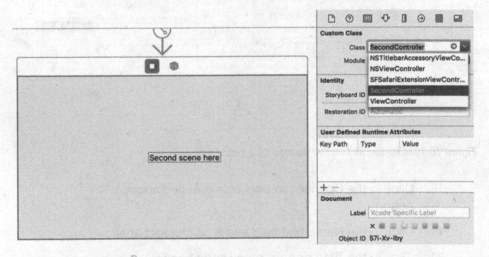

Figure 16-18. Connecting a scene to a Swift view controller file

13. Drag a push button onto this second scene.

14. Choose View ➤ Assistant Editor ➤ Show Assistant Editor. The Assistant Editor displays the `SecondController.swift` file you just created.

15. Move the mouse pointer over the label on this second scene, hold down the Control key, and drag the mouse under the `class SecondController` line. A pop-up window appears.

16.   Type **labelName** in the Name field and click the
       Connect button. The following line should appear in
       your code:

```
@IBOutlet weak var labelName: NSTextField!
```

17.   Move the mouse pointer over the push button on this
       second scene, hold down the Control key, and drag
       the mouse just above the last curly bracket in the
       bottom of the SecondController.swift file, as shown
       in Figure 16-19. A pop-up window appears.

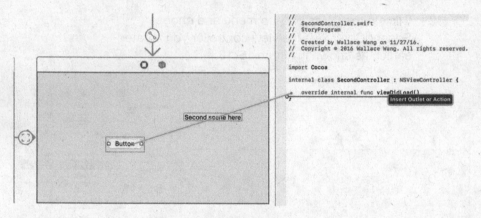

Figure 16-19.   Creating an IBAction method for a button

18.   Click in the Connection pop-up menu and choose
       Action.

19.   Click in the Name text field and type changeLabel.

20.   Click in the Type pop-up menu and choose
       NSButton. Then click the Connect button. Xcode
       displays an empty IBAction method.

21.   Modify the IBAction method as follows:

```
@IBAction func changeLabel(_ sender: NSButton) {
    labelName.stringValue = "Button clicked"
}
```

22.   Choose Product ➤ Run. Your program's initial scene
       appears with the button.

23. Click the button on this first scene. Your second scene appears as another window.

24. Click the button on this second scene. The label on the second scene changes from "Second scene here" to "Button clicked".

25. Choose StoryProgram ➤ Quit StoryProgram.

This exercise showed how to create a Swift file as a Cocoa Class file. Then it showed how to link this Swift file to the second view controller. Once you connect a Swift file to a view controller, you can write Swift code to make any user interface items actually respond to Swift code.

Summary

You can create your user interface and store them in multiple .xib files or a single .storyboard file that contains multiple scenes. Storyboard files are used for creating iOS apps so it's best to use storyboard files for macOS programs as well since storyboard files will likely become the standard way for creating user interfaces.

Storyboards let you define the order in which scenes appear that make up your program's user interface. When you add additional scenes to a storyboard, you need to create Swift files that control those scenes. These Swift files need to be of the NSViewController class and then you must connect your scene to that Swift file.

Designing your program's user interface involves using .xib or .storyboard files, or a combination of both. Storyboards reduce the need to write Swift code, but with both types of files, you still need to write some Swift code to make your user interface completely work.

Chapter **17**

Choosing Commands with Buttons

Every program needs to give the user a way to control the computer. In the old days, that meant knowing how to type the proper commands to make a program work, but with today's graphical user interfaces, the easier way to control a program is to choose from a list of available commands. The simplest way to give a command to a program is through a button.

By displaying multiple buttons on the screen, a user interface offers multiple choices for the user at all times. Instead of memorizing cryptic commands, the user just needs to select a command by pointing at it with the mouse and clicking to choose it.

Xcode provides a variety of different types of buttons you can place on a user interface but they all work the same way. A button represents a single command and clicking that button runs the Swift code stored in an IBAction method.

To use buttons, just place them on a user interface (either a .xib or .storyboard file), modify the label to display the command you want the button to represent, and connect your button to Swift code through an IBAction method.

All buttons are based on the NSButton class defined in the Cocoa framework. While most buttons display text that can contain the command the button represents, some buttons don't display text at all. Despite the differences in appearance, all buttons work the same way and can be

© Wallace Wang 2017
W. Wang, *macOS Programming for Absolute Beginners*,
DOI 10.1007/978-1-4842-2662-9_17

changed into another button type at any time. The different button types available are shown in Figure 17-1:

- Push Button

- Textured Rounded Button

- Gradient Button (does not display text)

- Pop-Up Button

- Checkbox Button

- Radio Button

- Recessed Button

- Inline Button

- Rounded Rectangle Button

- Disclosure Triangle (does not display text)

- Help Button (does not display text)

- Image Button (does not display text)

- Disclosure Button (does not display text)

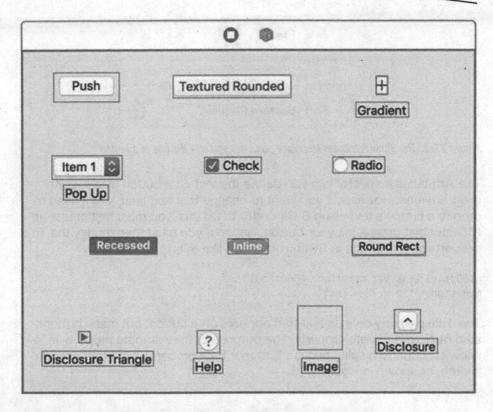

Figure 17-1. The different types of buttons you can place on a user interface

Buttons without text titles take up less space but may appear cryptic because the user has no idea what that button might do. The Image button is often used to display icons that represent commands.

Modifying Text on a Button

For those buttons that display text, Xcode gives you two ways to modify a button's text:

- Double-click directly on the button's text and edit the text.

- Click a button to select it, choose View ➤ Utilities ➤ Show Attributes Inspector, and edit the Title property, as shown in Figure 17-2.

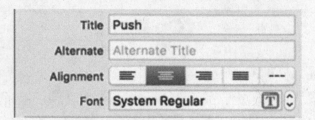

Figure 17-2. The Show Attributes Inspector pane lets you edit the title of a button

The Attributes Inspector lets you define the text on a button when your program runs. However, if you want to change that text later, you'll need to modify a button's text using Swift code. To do this, you must first create an IBOutlet that represents your button. Second, you must then modify the Title property of that button in Swift using code like this:

```
@IBOutlet weak var myButton: NSButton!
myButton.title = "New Text"
```

The Title property defines text that appears on a button, but many buttons also offer an Alternate property. The purpose of the Alternate property is to allow a button to display text if a button's Type property is set to toggle or switch, as shown in Figure 17-3.

Figure 17-3. Changing the Type property of a button

When a button's Alternate Title text is non-empty and the button's Type property is toggle or switch, clicking a Toggle or Switch button alternates between showing the Title text and the Alternate Title text. To see how the Title and Alternate Title properties of a button work, follow these steps:

1. From within Xcode choose File ➤ New ➤ Project.

2. Click Application under the macOS category.

3. Click Cocoa Application and click the Next button. Xcode now asks for a product name.

4. Click in the Product Name text field and type **ButtonProgram**.

5. Make sure the Language pop-up menu displays Swift and that the "Use Storyboards" check box is selected.

6. Click the Next button. Xcode asks where you want to store the project.

7. Choose a folder to store your project and click the Create button.

8. Click the `Main.storyboard` file in the Project Navigator. Your program's user interface appears.

9. Choose View ➤ Utilities ➤ Show Object Library. The Object Library appears in the bottom right corner of the Xcode window.

10. Drag a push button and a text field on to the view controller window and resize both items so they look like Figure 17-4.

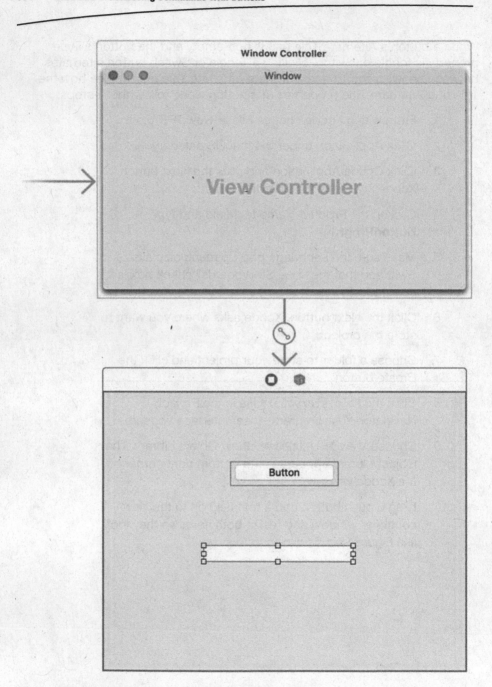

Figure 17-4. The user interface of the ButtonProgram

11. Click the push button and choose View ➤ Utilities ➤ Show Attributes Inspector. The Show Attributes Inspector pane appears in the upper right corner of the Xcode window.

12. Click the Type pop-up menu and choose Toggle.

13. Click in the Title text field, type **Change Me** and press Enter.

14. Click in the Alternate text field and type **Alternate Text**.

15. Choose Product ➤ Run. Your user interface appears.

16. Click the Change Me button. Notice that the text on the button now displays "Alternate Text".

17. Click the same button again. Notice that the text alternates between Change Me and Alternate Text.

18. Choose ButtonProgram ➤ Quit ButtonProgram.

Now let's see how to modify the title of a button by taking text from the text field and storing it in the Title property of the button by following these steps:

1. Click the `Main.storyboard` file in the Project Navigator pane.

2. Click the push button that currently displays the text "Change Me".

3. Choose View ➤ Assistant Editor ➤ Show Assistant Editor. The `ViewController.swift` file appears next to the `Main.storyboard` file.

4. Move the mouse pointer over the push button, hold down the Control key, and drag the mouse underneath the `@IBOutlet` line in the `ViewController.swift` file.

5. Release the Control key and the mouse. A pop-up menu appears.

6. Click in the Name text field and type **myButton**.

7. Move the mouse pointer over the text field, hold down the Control key, and drag the mouse underneath the `@IBOutlet` line in the `AppDelegate.swift` file.

8. Release the Control key and the mouse. A pop-up menu appears.

9. Click in the Name text field and type changeText. You should now have created two IBOutlets that look like this:

    ```
    @IBOutlet weak var myButton: NSButton!
      @IBOutlet weak var changeText: NSTextField!
    ```

10. Move the mouse pointer over the push button, hold down the Control key, and drag the mouse above the last curly bracket in the bottom of the AppDelegate. swift file.

11. Release the Control key and the mouse. A pop-up menu appears.

12. Click in the Connection pop-up menu and choose Action.

13. Click in the Name text field and type changeTitle.

14. Click in the Type pop-up menu and choose NSButton and then click the Connect button. Xcode creates an empty IBAction method.

15. Modify this IBAction method as follows:

    ```
    @IBAction func changeTitle(_ sender: NSButton) {
        myButton.title = changeText.stringValue
    }
    ```

This Swift code retrieves the text in the text field (the IBOutlet changeText) and stores it in the Title property of the button (the IBOutlet myButton).

16. Choose Product ➤ Run. Your user interface appears.

17. Click in the text field and type **Hello there!.**

18. Click the Change Me button. The alternate text appears on the button.

19. Click the button again. The text from the text field now appears.

20. Choose ButtonProgram ➤ Quit ButtonProgram.

Adding Images and Sounds to a Button

Buttons typically display text that lists the command that the button represents, such as OK or Cancel. However, you can also display images on a button. This can be useful for creating toolbar icons that display a descriptive icon that represents a command (such as showing a printer to represent the Print command). Images can appear on a button by themselves or with descriptive text.

Besides displaying images, buttons can also play sounds to give the user audio feedback. While most people click a button using the mouse (or trackpad), some people prefer using keystroke shortcuts, so you can also assign keystrokes to run an IBAction method linked to a particular button.

To add images to a button, you just need to modify the Image and/or the Alternate property directly underneath the Image property in the Attributes Inspector, as shown in Figure 17-5.

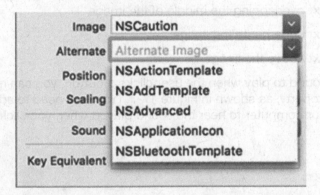

Figure 17-5. The Image and Alternate pop-up menus let you choose from a list of predefined images.

You can also define an image to display on a button using the Image and alternateImage properties of an NSButton. When defining an image to appear on a button, you can also choose the position of that image relative to any text that also appears on that image.

The Position property defines how an image appears with text where text is represented by a horizontal line and the image is represented by a square, as shown in Figure 17-6.

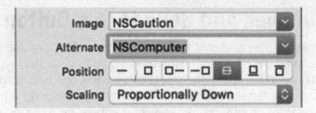

Figure 17-6. The Position property lets you align text and images on a button.

The seven different positions from left to right are

- Text only

- Image only

- Image on the left and text on the right

- Text on the left and image on the right

- Text overlapping the middle of the image

- Text underneath the image

- Text above the image

To define a sound to play when the user clicks a button, you can modify the Sound property, as shown in Figure 17-7. (You may need to adjust the volume of your computer to hear the sound played when you click on a button.)

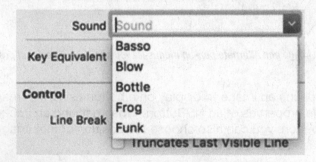

Figure 17-7. The Sound property lets you choose a sound to play.

To learn how to add images and a sound to a button, make sure your ButtonProgram project is loaded in Xcode and then follow these steps:

1. Click in the Main.storyboard file in the Project Navigator pane.

2. Click the push button on your user interface to select it.

3. Choose View ➤ Utilities ➤ Show Attributes Inspector. The Show Attributes Inspector pane appears in the upper right corner of the Xcode window.

4. Click in the Image pop-up menu and choose NSCaution.

5. Click in the Alternate pop-up menu and choose NSComputer (see Figure 17-5).

6. Click in the Position property to choose the icon (third from the left) that displays the image on the left and the text on the right (see Figure 17-6).

7. Click in the Sound pop-up menu and choose a sound such as Frog.

8. Choose Product ➤ Run. Your program appears. Notice that the caution icon appears on the button.

9. Click in the text field and type **Hello there!**

10. Click the button. The text on the button displays the alternate text and plays your chosen sound. Each time you click the button, it alternates between showing the Title and Image properties and the Alternate (Text and Image) properties.

11. Choose ButtonProgram ➤ Quit ButtonProgram.

Connecting Multiple User Interface Items to IBAction Methods

Typically, you link one IBAction method to one user interface item such as a button. However, it's possible to connect multiple items to a single IBAction method. When doing this, the IBAction method needs to know what user interface item called the IBAction method to run.

To identify a particular user interface item, you need to change the Tag property of each item linked to the same IBAction method. The Tag property can hold an integer value so you can use distinct Tag values to identify different user interface items.

Once you've given each user interface item a distinct Tag value, you can create an IBAction method normally using the Control-drag method from one user interface item into your Swift file. Then you use the same Control-drag method to connect the remaining user interface items to that existing IBAction method.

There's no limit to the number of items you can link to the same IBAction method just as long as you use the Tag property to identify which user interface item called the IBAction method.

To see how to connect multiple items to a single IBAction method, follow these steps:

1. From within Xcode choose File ➤ New ➤ Project.

2. Click Application under the macOS category.

3. Click Cocoa Application and click the Next button. Xcode now asks for a product name.

4. Click in the Product Name text field and type **MultipleButtons**.

5. Make sure the Language pop-up menu displays Swift and that the "Use Storyboards" check box is selected.

6. Click the Next button. Xcode asks where you want to store the project.

7. Choose a folder to store your project and click the Create button.

8. Click the Main.storyboard file in the Project Navigator pane.

9. Drag a push button, recessed button, inline button, and label onto the user interface and resize with width of the label, as shown in Figure 17-8.

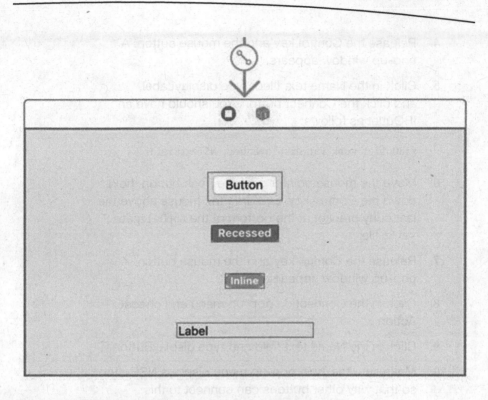

Figure 17-8. The user interface of the MultipleButtons program

At this point, you have three different types of buttons on the window and a label. You'll create a single IBAction method that all three buttons can run. When you click on a button, the label will display the button title to show you which button you just clicked.

First, you need to modify the Tag property of each button. The top button will have a Tag value of 0, the middle button will have a Tag value of 1, and the lowest button will have a Tag value of 2.

Then, you create an IBAction method that identifies the Tag property and displays the button's title in the label. To do this, follow these steps:

1. Click the `Main.storyboard` file in the Project Navigator pane.

2. Choose View ➤ Assistant Editor ➤ Show Assistant Editor. Xcode displays the `ViewController.swift` file next to the user interface.

3. Move the mouse pointer over the Label, hold down the Control key, and drag the mouse under the IBOutlet line in the `AppDelegate.swift` file.

4. Release the Control key and the mouse button. A pop-up window appears.

5. Click in the Name text filed, type displayLabel, and click the Connect button. You should have an IBOutlet as follows:

```
@IBOutlet weak var displayLabel: NSTextField!
```

6. Move the mouse pointer over the push button, hold down the Control key, and drag the mouse above the last curly bracket at the bottom of the AppDelegate. swift file.

7. Release the Control key and the mouse button. A pop-up window appears.

8. Click in the Connection pop-up menu and choose Action.

9. Click in the Name text field and type displayButton.

10. Make sure the Type pop-up menu displays NSButton so that way other buttons can connect to this IBAction method.

11. Click the Connect button. Xcode displays an empty IBAction method.

12. Move the mouse pointer over the Recessed Button, hold down the Control key, and drag the mouse over the func keyword in the IBAction method until Xcode highlights the entire method, as shown in Figure 17-9.

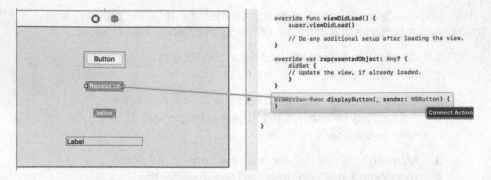

Figure 17-9. Connecting to an existing IBAction method to another user interface item

13. Release the Control key and the mouse button. Xcode connects the IBAction method to the recessed button.

14. Move the mouse pointer over the inline button, hold down the Control key, and drag the mouse over the func keyword in the IBAction method until Xcode highlights the entire IBAction method.

15. Release the Control key and the mouse button. Xcode connects the inline button to the IBAction method.

16. Click the recessed button to select it and choose View ➤ Utilities ➤ Show Attributes Inspector. The Show Attributes Inspector pane appears in the upper right corner of the Xcode window.

17. Scroll down to the View category (it may initially be hidden out of sight), click in the Tag text field and type **1**. (The push button has the default Tag value of 0, the recessed button will have a Tag value of 1, and the inline button will have a Tag value of 2.)

18. Click the inline button to select it.

19. Scroll down to the View category, click in the Tag text field and type **2**.

20. Modify the IBAction method as follows:

```
@IBAction func displayButton(_ sender: NSButton) {
    switch sender.tag {
    case 0:
        displayLabel.stringValue = "Clicked Push Button"
    case 1:
        displayLabel.stringValue = "Clicked Recessed Button"
    case 2:
        displayLabel.stringValue = "Clicked Inline Button"
    default:
        displayLabel.stringValue = "Unknown"
    }
}
```

The sender: NSButton means that the IBAction method can connect to any type of user interface item that's an NSButton type. First, you'll use the Tag property of the sender (NSButton) to determine which button the user clicked using a switch statement. Second, you'll display the proper message in the label depending on which button the user clicked.

21. Choose Product ➤ Run. Your program's user interface appears.

22. Click the three different buttons to see the proper message appear in the label.

23. Choose MultipleButtons ➤ Quit MultipleButtons.

Working with Pop-up Buttons

Buttons can be handy for displaying commands on the screen, but if you need to offer several options, then having each button represent one command can get cumbersome and crowded. One option is to condense multiple options into a single pop-up button. A pop-up button takes less space and can provide a large number of options for the user to select.

When the user chooses an option in the pop-up button, that selected choice gets stored in the pop-up button's `titleOfSelectedItem` property.

To see how pop-up buttons work, follow these steps:

1. From within Xcode choose File ➤ New ➤ Project.

2. Click Application under the macOS category.

3. Click Cocoa Application and click the Next button. Xcode now asks for a product name.

4. Click in the Product Name text field and type **PopupProgram**.

5. Make sure the Language pop-up menu displays Swift and that the "Use Storyboards" check box is selected.

6. Click the Next button. Xcode asks where you want to store the project.

7. Choose a folder to store your project and click the Create button.

8. Click the `Main.storyboard` file in the Project Navigator. Your program's user interface appears.

9. Choose View ➤ Utilities ➤ Show Object Library. The
    Object Library appears in the bottom right corner of
    the Xcode window.

10. Drag a pop-up button and a label on to the user
    interface window and resize the width of the label so
    it looks like Figure 17-10.

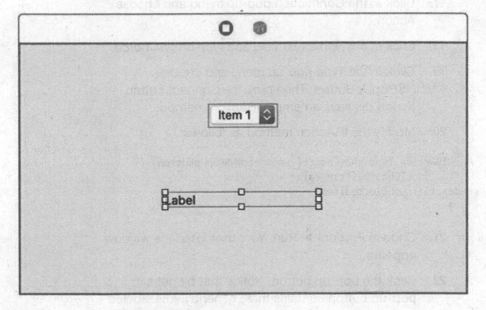

Figure 17-10. The user interface of the PopupProgram

11. Choose View ➤ Assistant Editor ➤ Show Assistant
    Editor. Xcode displays the ViewController.swift file
    next to your user interface.

12. Move the mouse pointer over the label, hold down
    the Control key, and drag underneath the IBOutlet
    line in the ViewController.swift file.

13. Release the Control key and the mouse. A pop-up
    window appears.

14. Click in the Name text field, type **labelChoice**, and
    click the Connect button. Xcode creates an IBOutlet
    as follows:

    ```
    @IBOutlet weak var labelChoice: NSTextField!
    ```

15. Move the mouse pointer over the pop-up button, hold down the Control key, and drag the mouse above the last curly bracket in the bottom of the AppDelegate.swift file.

16. Release the Control key and the mouse. A pop-up window appears.

17. Click in the Connection pop-up menu and choose Action.

18. Click in the Name text field and type **showChoice**.

19. Click in the Type pop-up menu and choose NSPopUpButton. Then click the Connect button. Xcode displays an empty IBAction method.

20. Modify the IBAction method as follows:

```
@IBAction func showChoice(_ sender: NSPopUpButton) {
    labelChoice.stringValue =
sender.titleOfSelectedItem!
    }
```

21. Choose Product ➤ Run. Your user interface window appears.

22. Click the pop-up button. Notice that by default, a pop-up button contains three generic items labeled Item 1, Item 2, and Item 3.

23. Click an option. Notice that your chosen option appears in the label.

24. Choose PopupProgram ➤ Quit PopupProgram.

Modifying Popup Menu Items Visually

A pop-up button contains a default list of three items. However, you can add, edit, or delete items from that list at any time. To edit a pop-up menu list, follow these steps:

1. Double-click the pop-up button on the user interface. The current list of menu items appears, as shown in Figure 17-11.

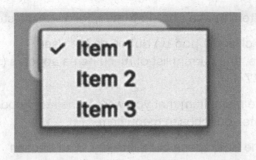

Figure 17-11. Double-clicking a pop-up button displays its list of menu items

2. Double-click the menu item you want to edit.
    Xcode highlights the text of your chosen menu item,
    as shown in Figure 17-12.

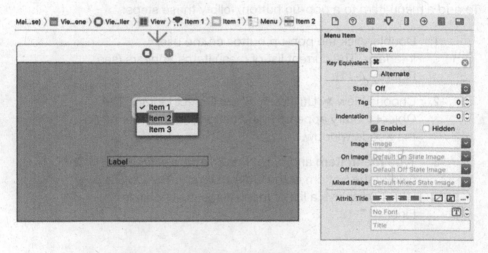

Figure 17-12. Double-clicking a menu item lets you edit the text

Note   You can also choose View ➤ Utilities ➤ Show Attributes Inspector and edit
the text of a menu item by editing the Title property of the selected menu item.

3. Use the arrow keys, Backspace, or Delete key to edit
    the text and type any new text.

4. Press Return. Xcode saves your edited text for the
    menu item.

To delete a menu item from a pop-up button, follow these steps:

1. Double-click the pop-up button on the user interface. The current list of menu items appears (see Figure 17-11).

2. Click the menu item that you want to delete. Xcode highlights your chosen menu item.

3. Press the Backspace or Delete key. Your chosen menu item disappears.

> **Note** If you delete a menu item by mistake, just press Command + Z or choose Edit ➤ Undo to reverse the delete command.

To add a menu item to a pop-up button, follow these steps:

1. Double-click the pop-up button on the user interface. The current list of menu items appears (see Figure 17-11).

2. Choose View ➤ Utilities ➤ Show Object Library. The Object Library appears in the bottom right corner of the Xcode window.

3. Type **menu item** and press Return in the search field at the bottom of the Object Library. The Object Library displays a list of menu items, as shown in Figure 17-13.

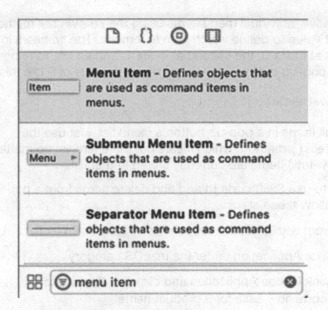

Figure 17-13. The list of menu items in the Object Library

4. Drag the menu item from the Object Library over the list of menu items stored in the pop-up button on the user interface. A horizontal blue line shows where the new menu item will appear in the pop-up button's list.

5. Release the mouse button. Xcode adds a menu item to the pop-up button list.

Adding Pop-up Menu Items with Swift Code

As an alternative to modifying menu items in a pop-up button visually, you can also use Swift code to add, delete, or change a menu item. Pop-up button menu items are based on the NSMenuItem class, but you can find the methods you need to manipulate a list of pop-up button menu items in the NSMenu class.

If you want to add just one new menu item to a pop-up button, you can use the addItemWithTitle method and specify a string, such as

```
myPopUp.addItem(withTitle: "New Item")
```

You can also add a list of new menu items by storing them in an array and using the addItemsWithTitles method, such as

```
myPopUp.addItems(withTitles: ["Cat", "Dog", "Bird", "Fish", "Reptile"])
```

You can remove individual menu items using the `removeItem` method that needs an Int value to define which item to remove. The first item in a pop-up button list is at index 0, the second at index 1, and so on. To remove the first item from a pop-up button list, you use an index value of 0 like this:

```
myPopUp.removeItem(at: 0)
```

To remove all items in a pop-up button's menu list, just use the `removeAllItems()` method, which clears out the entire list no matter how many (or how few) items are currently stored in that list.

To see how to use Swift code to add and delete items from a pop-up button menu list, follow these steps:

1. From within Xcode, choose File ➤ New ➤ Project.

2. Click Application under the macOS category.

3. Click Cocoa Application and click the Next button. Xcode now asks for a product name.

4. Click in the Product Name text field and type **EditPopProgram**.

5. Make sure the Language pop-up menu displays Swift and that the "Use Storyboards" check box is selected.

6. Click the Next button. Xcode asks where you want to store the project.

7. Choose a folder to store your project and click the Create button.

8. Click the `Main.storyboard` file in the Project Navigator. Your program's user interface appears.

9. Choose View ➤ Utilities ➤ Show Object Library. The Object Library appears in the bottom right corner of the Xcode window.

10. Drag a pop-up button, three push buttons, and a text field on to the user interface window and edit the titles on both push buttons so they look like Figure 17-14.

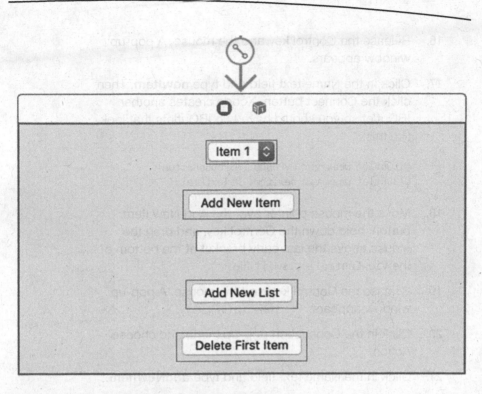

Figure 17-14. The user interface of the EditPopProgram

11. Choose View ➤ Assistant Editor ➤ Show Assistant
     Editor. Xcode displays the ViewController.swift file
     next to your user interface.

12. Move the mouse pointer over the pop-up button,
     hold down the Control key, and drag the mouse
     underneath the IBOutlet line near the top of the
     ViewController.swift file.

13. Release the Control key and the mouse. A pop-up
     window appears.

14. Click in the Name text field and type **myPopUp**.
     Then click the Connect button. Xcode creates an
     IBOutlet.

15. Move the mouse pointer over the text field,
     hold down the Control key, and drag the mouse
     underneath the IBOutlet line near the top of the
     ViewController.swift file.

16. Release the Control key and the mouse. A pop-up window appears.

17. Click in the Name text field and type **newItem**. Then click the Connect button. Xcode creates another IBOutlet so you should have two IBOutlets that look like this:

```
@IBOutlet weak var myPopUp: NSPopUpButton!
@IBOutlet weak var newItem: NSTextField!
```

18. Move the mouse pointer over the Add New Item button, hold down the Control key, and drag the mouse above the last curly bracket at the bottom of the `ViewController.swift` file.

19. Release the Control key and the mouse. A pop-up window appears.

20. Click in the Connection pop-up menu and choose Action.

21. Click in the Name text field and type **addNewItem**.

22. Click in the Type pop-up menu and choose NSButton. Then click the Connect button. Xcode creates an empty IBAction method.

23. Move the mouse pointer over the Delete First Item button, hold down the Control key, and drag the mouse above the last curly bracket at the bottom of the `ViewController.swift` file.

24. Release the Control key and the mouse. A pop-up window appears.

25. Click in the Connection pop-up menu and choose Action.

26. Click in the Name text field and type **deleteFirstItem**.

27. Click in the Type pop-up menu and choose NSButton. Then click the Connect button. Xcode creates an empty IBAction method.

28. Move the mouse pointer over the Add New List button, hold down the Control key, and drag the mouse above the last curly bracket at the bottom of the ViewController.swift file.

29. Release the Control key and the mouse. A pop-up window appears.

30. Click in the Connection pop-up menu and choose Action.

31. Click in the Name text field and type **addList**.

32. Click in the Type pop-up menu and choose NSButton. Then click the Connect button. Xcode creates another empty IBAction method.

33. Modify all three IBAction methods as follows:

```
@IBAction func addNewItem(_ sender: NSButton) {
    myPopUp.addItem(withTitle: newItem.stringValue)
}

@IBAction func addList(_ sender: NSButton) {
    myPopUp.removeAllItems()
    myPopUp.addItems(withTitles: ["Cat", "Dog", "Bird", "Fish", "Reptile"])
}

@IBAction func deleteFirstItem(_ sender: NSButton) {
    myPopUp.removeItem(at: 0)
}
```

The addNewItem IBAction method takes text from the text field and uses the addItem method to add that text as a new menu item in the pop-up button's list. The deleteFirstItem IBAction method uses the removeItem method to delete the first menu item in the pop-up button's list. The addList IBAction method uses the removeAllItems method to clear out the current list in the pop-up button, and then replaces it with a new array of strings.

34. Choose Product ➤ Run. Your user interface appears.

35. Click the pop-up button. Notice that the menu item list displays three items labeled Item 1, Item 2, and Item 3.

36. Click away from the pop-up button so the menu item list no longer appears.

37. Click the Delete First Item button.

38. Click the pop-up button. Notice that the menu item list now displays only two items labeled Item 2 and Item 3.

39. Click in the text field and type **My Item.**

40. Click the Add New Item button.

41. Click the pop-up button. Notice that now the menu item list displays three items labeled Item 2, Item 3, and My Item.

42. Click the Add New List button.

43. Click the pop-up button. Notice that now the menu item list displays the array of strings defined inside the addList IBAction method.

44. Choose EditPopProgram ➤ Quit EditPopProgram.

Summary

Buttons represent commands that users can click in order to choose an option. Xcode offers several different types of buttons you can place on a user interface but they're all based on the same NSButton class defined in the Cocoa frameworks.

Not all buttons display text, but those buttons that do display text use a Title property to hold text. If you want to display an image on a button, you can define an image using the Image property. If you change the Type property of a button to switch or toggle, then you can make a button display text stored in the Title property along with text displayed in the Alternate Text property and/or the Alternate Image property as well.

If you need to offer multiple options to the user, placing more than a handful of buttons on the user interface can get messy and cluttered. A simpler alternative is to use a pop-up button instead that displays a list of options that you can modify visually or through Swift code.

Buttons often connect to a single IBAction method, but you can link multiple to a single IBAction method. When connecting multiple user interface items to an IBAction method, you need to use Swift code to identify the user interface item that called the IBAction method by uniquely identifying each button's Tag property. Buttons represent the most straightforward way to offer users an option to select.

Chapter 18

Making Choices with Radio Buttons, Check Boxes, Date Pickers, and Sliders

Rather than let the user choose a specific command through a button, user interfaces often give choices to pick from. Such choices let the user pick one or more options, such as customizing the way a program works. When a user interface needs to offer multiple choices, the two most common ways to offer options are through radio buttons and check boxes.

Radio buttons get their name from car radios that let you press a button to switch to a different radio station. Since you can only listen to one radio station at a time, radio buttons give you multiple options but limit you to choosing only one button. The moment you select a different button, your previous choice is no longer selected. With radio buttons, you can either select zero buttons or select exactly one button at a time.

Check boxes work slightly differently. Like radio buttons, check boxes offer multiple choices. The main difference is that with a group of check boxes, you can select zero or more check boxes at the same time, so you can choose multiple options at once.

When you need to limit the user to zero or one choices, use radio buttons. When you need to let the user choose zero or more choices, use check boxes. Figure 18-1 shows the Xcode Preferences dialog that uses both radio buttons and a check box to let the user customize how Xcode behaves.

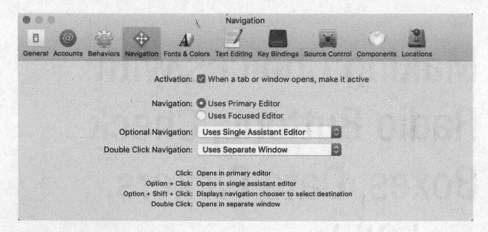

Figure 18-1. The Xcode Preferences dialog uses both radio buttons and check boxes to let the user select options.

While radio buttons and check boxes are commonly used to display choices displayed as text, a date picker displays different types of dates for the user to choose from. Then the date picker stores the user's choice in a special date format (rather than separate text representing months or numbers representing days or years).

By storing dates in a special format, your program can properly display dates according to the user's settings on their computer. For example, in some parts of the world, they display dates like this: mm/dd/yyyy. Yet in other parts of the world they display dates like this: dd/mm/yyyy.

Rather than worry about a particular date format setting on each user's computer, a date picker uses a special date format so this way the computer can properly display the correct format based on the user's current settings.

Date pickers, like radio buttons and check boxes, give users a fixed but limited range of valid options to select. This insures that whatever choice the user makes, the choice will be acceptable to your program.

Check boxes and radio buttons are good for offering users a limited range of choices that are usually text options. For offering users a range of numeric values to select, you can use a slider. Sliders let the user visually select a range of valid options.

Using Check Boxes

You can use a check box by itself or grouped together with other check boxes. A check box is actually based on the NSButton class although it looks and behaves much differently than a typical button. For a check box, the three most important properties are

- **Title**: The text that appears next to a check box that describes an option for the user to choose.

- **State**: Determines if the check box is selected (1) or clear (0).

- **Alternate**: Text that appears when the check box is clear. (The Title text appears when the check box is selected.)

To see how check boxes work, follow these steps:

1. From within Xcode choose File ➤ New ➤ Project.

2. Click Application under the macOS category.

3. Click Cocoa Application and click the Next button. Xcode now asks for a product name.

4. Click in the Product Name text field and type **CheckProgram**.

5. Make sure the Language pop-up menu displays Swift and that the "Use Storyboards" check box is selected.

6. Click the Next button. Xcode asks where you want to store the project.

7. Choose a folder to store your project and click the Create button.

8. Click the MainMenu.xib file in the Project Navigator. Your program's user interface appears.

9. Choose View ➤ Utilities ➤ Show Object Library. The Object Library appears in the bottom right corner of the Xcode window.

10. Drag a push button, three check boxes, and a wrapping text field on to the user interface window. Make sure you resize the wrapping text field and all the check box widths so they look like Figure 18-2.

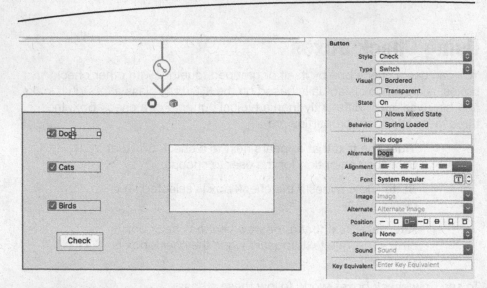

Figure 18-2. The user interface of the CheckProgram

11. Choose View ➤ Utilities ➤ Show Attributes Inspector. The Show Attributes Inspector pane appears in the upper right corner of the Xcode window.

12. Click the top check box and in the Show Attributes Inspector pane, change its title to **No dogs** and its alternate to **Dogs**.

13. Click the middle check box and in the Show Attributes Inspector pane, change its title to **No cats** and its alternate to **Cats**.

14. Click the top check box and in the Show Attributes Inspector pane, change its title to **No birds** and its alternate to **Birds**.

15. Double-click the push button and change its title to **Check**.

16. Choose View ➤ Assistant Editor ➤ Show Assistant Editor. Xcode displays the ViewController.swift file next to the user interface.

17. Move the mouse pointer over the Dogs check box, hold down the Control key, and drag the mouse under the IBOutlet line in the ViewController.swift file.

18. Release the Control key and the mouse. A pop-up window appears.

19. Click in the Name text field, type **dogBox**, and click the Connect button.

20. Move the mouse pointer over the Cats check box, hold down the Control key, and drag the mouse under the IBOutlet line in the ViewController.swift file.

21. Release the Control key and the mouse. A pop-up window appears.

22. Click in the Name text field, type **catBox**, and click the Connect button.

23. Move the mouse pointer over the Birds check box, hold down the Control key, and drag the mouse under the IBOutlet line in the ViewController.swift file.

24. Release the Control key and the mouse. A pop-up window appears.

25. Click in the Name text field, type **birdBox**, and click the Connect button.

26. Move the mouse pointer over the wrapping text field, hold down the Control key, and drag the mouse under the IBOutlet line in the ViewController.swift file.

27. Release the Control key and the mouse. A pop-up window appears.

28. Click in the Name text field, type **messageBox**, and click the Connect button. You should now have four new IBOutlets that look like this:

```
@IBOutlet weak var dogBox: NSButton!
@IBOutlet weak var catBox: NSButton!
@IBOutlet weak var birdBox: NSButton!
@IBOutlet weak var messageBox: NSTextField!
```

29. Move the mouse pointer over the check push button, hold down the Control key, and drag the mouse over the last curly bracket in the bottom of the ViewController.swift file.

30. Release the Control key and the mouse. A pop-up window appears.

31. Click in the Connection pop-up menu and choose Action.

32. Click in the Name text field and type **checkBoxes**.

33. Click in the Type pop-up menu and choose NSButton.

34. Click the Connect button. Xcode creates an empty IBAction method.

35. Modify this checkboxes IBAction method as follows:

```
@IBAction func checkBoxes(_ sender: NSButton) {
    let nextLine = "\r\n"
    var message : String = ""
    if dogBox.state == 1 {
        message = "Dog check box selected" + nextLine
    } else {
        message = "Dog check box NOT selected" + nextLine
    }

    if catBox.state == 1 {
        message = message + "Cat check box selected" + nextLine
    } else {
        message = message + "Cat check box NOT selected" + nextLine
    }

    if birdBox.state == 1 {
        message = message + "Bird check box selected" + nextLine
    } else {
        message = message + "Bird check box NOT selected" + nextLine
    }

    messageBox.stringValue = message
}
```

This code creates a constant (nextLine) that represents a carriage return (\r) and a new line (\n) character. It declares a message variable that can hold String data types and initially contains "", which is an empty string. The multiple if-else statements check the State property of each check box to determine if it's selected (state = 1) or clear (state = 0). Then it displays the results in the wrapping text field, which is represented by an IBOutlet variable called messageBox.

36.   Choose Product ➤ Run. Your user interface appears.

37.   Click the different check boxes. Notice that each time you select or clear a check box, the title or alternate text appears.

38.   Click the Check push button. The wrapping text field identifies which check boxes you selected and which ones are clear.

39.   Choose CheckProgram ➤ Quit CheckProgram.

Using Radio Buttons

Unlike check boxes that allow the user to select multiple options, radio buttons display multiple options but only let the user select one at a time. The moment the user selects another radio button, the currently selected radio button gets cleared.

To identify which radio button a user selected, you need to change the Tag property of each radio button individually. Then you can retrieve the selected radio button by using the selectedTag() method.

To see how to use radio buttons, follow these steps:

1.   From within Xcode choose File ➤ New ➤ Project.

2.   Click Application under the macOS category.

3.   Click Cocoa Application and click the Next button. Xcode now asks for a product name.

4.   Click in the Product Name text field and type **RadioProgram**.

5.   Make sure the Language pop-up menu displays Swift and that the "Use Storyboards" check box is selected.

6.   Click the Next button. Xcode asks where you want to store the project.

7.   Choose a folder to store your project and click the Create button.

8. Click the Main.storyboard file in the Project
    Navigator. Your program's user interface appears.

9. Click the RadioProgram icon to display the window
    of your program's user interface.

10. Choose View ➤ Utilities ➤ Show Object Library. The
    Object Library appears in the bottom right corner of
    the Xcode window.

11. Drag a push button and four radio buttons on to the
    user interface window so it looks like Figure 18-3.

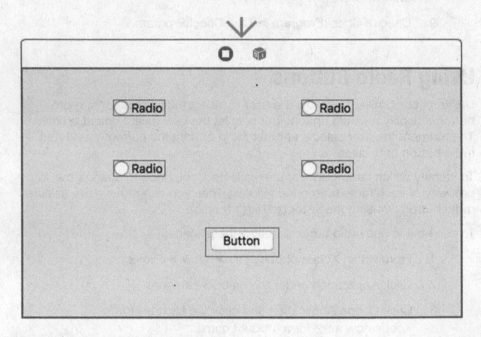

Figure 18-3. The user interface of the RadioProgram

12. Click the top radio button in the upper left corner
    and make sure its Tag property in the View category
    of the Attributes Inspector pane is set to 0.

13. Click the top radio button in the upper right column
    and make sure its Tag property is set to 1.

14. Click the bottom radio button in the lower left
    column and make sure its Tag property is set to 2.

15. Click the bottom radio button in the lower right column and make sure its Tag property in the Show Attributes Inspector pane is set to 3.

16. Choose View ➤ Assistant Editor ➤ Show Assistant Editor. The ViewController.swift file appears next to your user interface.

17. Move the mouse pointer over the radio button in the upper left corner, hold down the Control key, and drag underneath the IBOutlet line.

18. Release the Control key and the mouse. A pop-up window appears.

19. Click in the Name text field and type **radioZero**. An IBOutlet appears as follows:

```
@IBOutlet weak var radioZero: NSButton!
```

20. Choose View ➤ Utilities ➤ Show Attributes Inspector.

21. Scroll down the Attributes Inspector pane and make sure the Tab property is 0.

22. Move the mouse pointer over the radio button in the upper right corner, hold down the Control key, and drag underneath the IBOutlet line.

23. Release the Control key and the mouse. A pop-up window appears.

24. Click in the Name text field and type **radioOne**.

25. Choose View ➤ Utilities ➤ Show Attributes Inspector.

26. Scroll down the Attributes Inspector pane and change the Tab property to **1**.

27. Move the mouse pointer over the radio button in the lower left corner, hold down the Control key, and drag underneath the IBOutlet line.

28. Release the Control key and the mouse. A pop-up window appears.

29. Click in the Name text field and type **radioTwo**.

30. Choose View ➤ Utilities ➤ Show Attributes Inspector.

31. Scroll down the Attributes Inspector pane and change the Tab property to **2**.

32. Move the mouse pointer over the radio button in the lower right corner, hold down the Control key, and drag underneath the IBOutlet line.

33. Release the Control key and the mouse. A pop-up window appears.

34. Click in the Name text field and type **radioThree**. You should have four IBOutlets as follows:

```
@IBOutlet weak var radioZero: NSButton!
@IBOutlet weak var radioOne: NSButton!
@IBOutlet weak var radioTwo: NSButton!
@IBOutlet weak var radioThree: NSButton!
```

35. Choose View ➤ Utilities ➤ Show Attributes Inspector.

36. Scroll down the Attributes Inspector pane and change the Tab property to **3**.

37. Type the following underneath the four IBOutlets:

```
var radioButtonSelected : String?
```

38. Move the mouse pointer over the push button, hold down the Control key, and drag the mouse over the last curly bracket at the bottom of the ViewController.swift file.

39. Release the Control key and the mouse. A pop-up window appears.

40. Click in the Connect pop-up menu and choose Action.

41. Click in the Name text field and type **displayButton**.

42. Click in the Type pop-up menu and choose NSButton.

43. Click the Connect button. Xcode creates an empty
     IBAction method.

44. Modify the IBAction method as follows:

```
@IBAction func displayButton(_ sender: NSButton) {
    let myAlert = NSAlert()
    if radioButtonSelected != nil {
        myAlert.messageText = "You clicked the radio button in the " +
        radioButtonSelected!
    } else {
        myAlert.messageText = "No radio button selected"
    }
    myAlert.runModal()
}
```

45. Move the mouse pointer over the upper left radio
     button, hold down the Control key, and drag the
     mouse over the last curly bracket at the bottom of
     the ViewController.swift file.

46. Release the Control key and the mouse. A pop-up
     window appears.

47. Click in the Connect pop-up menu and choose
     Action.

48. Click in the Name text field and type
     whichRadioButton.

49. Click in the Type pop-up menu and choose
     NSButton.

50. Click the Connect button. Xcode creates an empty
     IBAction method.

51. Modify the IBAction method as follows:

```
@IBAction func whichRadioButton(_ sender: NSButton) {
    switch sender.tag {
        case 0 : radioOne.state = 0
                 radioTwo.state = 0
                 radioThree.state = 0
                 radioButtonSelected = "Upper left"
        case 1 : radioZero.state = 0
                 radioTwo.state = 0
                 radioThree.state = 0
                 radioButtonSelected = "Upper right"
```

```
        case 2 : radioZero.state = 0
                 radioOne.state = 0
                 radioThree.state = 0
                 radioButtonSelected = "Lower left"
        case 3 : radioZero.state = 0
                 radioOne.state = 0
                 radioTwo.state = 0
                 radioButtonSelected = "Lower right"
      default: radioButtonSelected = "No radio button selected"
    }
}
```

52. Move the mouse pointer over the upper right radio button, hold down the Control key, and drag the mouse over the func keyword in the whichRadioButton IBAction function in the ViewController.swift file until the entire function appears highlighted.

53. Release the mouse and the Control key.

54. Move the mouse pointer over the lower left radio button, hold down the Control key, and drag the mouse over the func keyword in the whichRadioButton IBAction function in the ViewController.swift file until the entire function appears highlighted.

55. Release the mouse and the Control key.

56. Move the mouse pointer over the lower right radio button, hold down the Control key, and drag the mouse over the func keyword in the whichRadioButton IBAction function in the ViewController.swift file until the entire function appears highlighted.

57. Release the mouse and the Control key. All four radio buttons should now be connected to the whichRadioButton IBAction function.

58. Choose Product ➤ Run. Your user interface appears.

59. Click a radio button and then click the push button. An alert dialog appears, displaying the radio button you selected.

60.   Click the OK button to make the alert dialog go away.

61.   Choose RadioProgram ➤ Quit RadioProgram.

The purpose of the `radioButtonSelected` variable is to hold a string that identifies which radio button the user chose. Initially, no radio button is selected so the `radioButtonSelected` variable is an optional variable.

The `displayButton` IBAction function creates an alert dialog and checks if there's a value in the `radioButtonSelected` variable. If so, then it displays that value. If not, then it displays "No radio button selected".

The `whichRadioButton` IBAction function identifies which radio button the user clicked by the radio button's Tag property. In addition, clicking any radio button deselects all the other radio buttons so this way only one radio button can be selected at a time.

Notice that you connected all four radio buttons to the IBAction `whichRadioButton` function. That means the `whichRadioButton` function runs any time you click any of the four radio buttons.

Using a Date Picker

A date picker makes it easy for users to choose a date and/or time in a proper format. The three types of date picker appearances are shown in Figure 18-4:

■   **Textual**: Displays a date in a text field that requires the user to type in a proper date

■   **Textual with Stepper**: Displays a date in a text field that the user can change by clicking on a stepper to modify the currently selected part of the date

■   **Graphical**: Displays a calendar so the user can click on a date

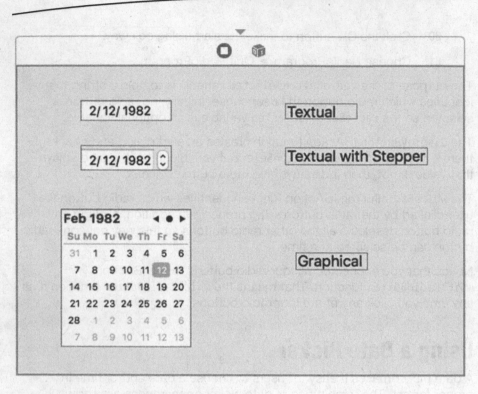

Figure 18-4. The three variations of a date picker

Some of the properties to modify in a date picker are shown in Figure 18-5:

- **Style**: Determines the date picker's appearance

- **Selects**: Determines whether the user can select a single date or a range of dates

- **Elements**: Determines what date and time elements to display such as month, day, year, hour, minute, and second

- **Minimum Date**: Defines the earliest date possible

- **Maximum Date**: Defines the latest date possible

- **Date**: Defines the currently displayed date and/or time

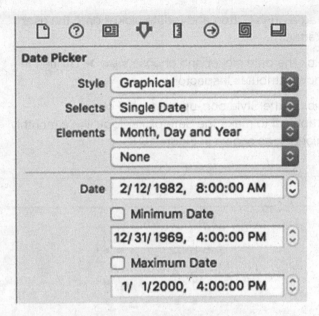

Figure 18-5. The date picker properties in the Show Attributes Inspector pane

To retrieve the user's chosen date from a date picker, you need to access the dateValue property, which represents an NSDate type.

To learn how to use a date picker, follow these steps:

1. From within Xcode choose File ➤ New ➤ Project.

2. Click Application under the macOS category.

3. Click Cocoa Application and click the Next button. Xcode now asks for a product name.

4. Click in the Product Name text field and type **DateProgram**.

5. Make sure the Language pop-up menu displays Swift and that all check boxes are clear and not selected.

6. Click the Next button. Xcode asks where you want to store the project.

7. Choose a folder to store your project and click the Create button.

8. Click the Main.storyboard file in the Project Navigator pane.

9. Drag a push button and a date picker onto the user interface.

10. Click the date picker and choose View ➤ Utilities ➤ Show Attributes Inspector.

11. Click in the Style pop-up menu and choose Graphical to make the date picker look like a monthly calendar, as shown in Figure 18-6.

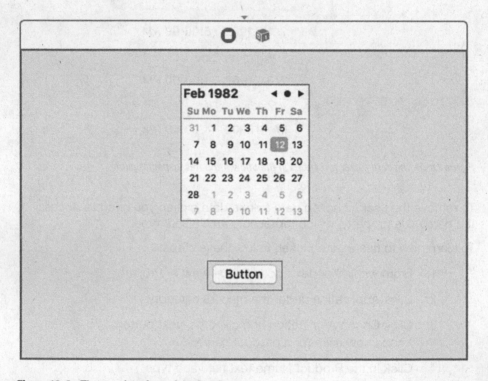

Figure 18-6. The user interface of the DateProgram

12. Choose View ➤ Assistant Editor ➤ Show Assistant Editor. Xcode displays the `ViewController.swift` file next to the user interface.

13. Move the mouse pointer over the date picker, hold down the Control key, and drag the mouse under the IBOutlet line in the `ViewController.swift` file.

14. Release the Control key and the mouse button. A pop-up window appears.

15. Click in the Name text field, type **chooseDate**, and click the Connect button. Xcode creates an IBOutlet like this:

```
@IBOutlet weak var chooseDate: NSDatePicker!
```

16. Move the mouse pointer over the push button, hold down the Control key, and drag the mouse over the last curly bracket in the bottom of the ViewController.swift file.

17. Release the Control key and the mouse. A pop-up window appears.

18. Click in the Connect pop-up menu and choose Action.

19. Click in the Name text field and type **showDate**.

20. Click in the Type pop-up menu and choose NSButton. Then click the Connect button. Xcode creates an IBAction method.

21. Modify this IBAction method as follows:

```
@IBAction func showDate(_ sender: NSButton) {
    let myAlert = NSAlert()
    myAlert.messageText = "You chose this date = \(chooseDate.
    dateValue)"
    myAlert.runModal()

}
```

22. Choose Product ➤ Run. Your user interface appears.

23. Choose a date on the date picker and click the push button. An alert dialog appears, displaying the date you chose.

24. Click the OK button to make this alert dialog go away.

25. Choose DateProgram ➤ Quit DateProgram.

Using Sliders

A slider can appear vertically or horizontally. Sliders visually represent a range of values that the user can select by dragging the slider back and forth (or up and down). One end represents the minimum value (left or bottom) while the other end represents the maximum value (right or top). To help users understand the different values a slider represents, you can also choose to display tick marks, as shown in Figure 18-7.

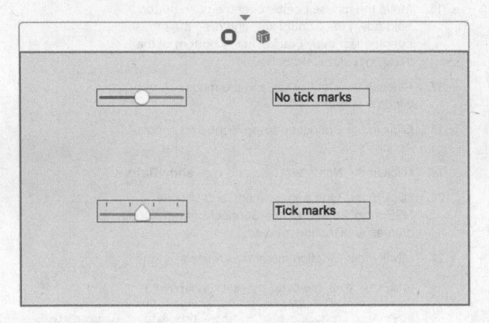

Figure 18-7. The appearance of a slider with and without tick marks

Some of the more important properties to define on a slider include

- **Tick Marks**: Defines the position of tick marks and how many tick marks to display

- **Minimum**: Defines the smallest value possible

- **Maximum**: Defines the largest value possible

- **Current**: Identifies the initial value of the slider when it first appears on the user interface

You can use the integerValue property to retrieve the current value of the slider and display this value in another user interface item such as a text field. To see how to do this, follow these steps:

1. From within Xcode choose File ➤ New ➤ Project.

2. Click Application under the macOS category.

3. Click Cocoa Application and click the Next button. Xcode now asks for a product name.

4. Click in the Product Name text field and type **SliderProgram**.

5. Make sure the Language popup menu displays Swift and that the "Use Storyboards" check box is selected.

6. Click the Next button. Xcode asks where you want to store the project.

7. Choose a folder to store your project and click the Create button.

8. Click the Main.storyboard file in the Project Navigator pane.

9. Click the SliderProgram icon to make the window of the user interface appear.

10. Drag a horizontal slider and a text field on to the user interface so it looks like Figure 18-8.

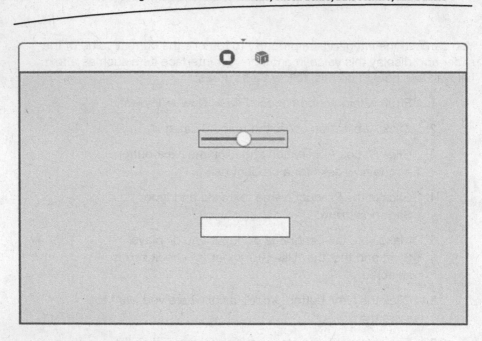

Figure 18-8. The user interface of the SliderProgram

11.   Choose View ➤ Assistant Editor ➤ Show Assistant
       Editor. Xcode shows the `ViewController.swift` file
       next to the user interface.

12.   Move the mouse pointer over the horizontal slider,
       hold down the Control key, and drag the mouse
       under the IBOutlet line in the `ViewController.swift`
       file.

13.   Release the Control key and the mouse. A pop-up
       window appears.

14.   Click in the Name text field, type **mySlider**, and click
       the Connect button.

15.   Move the mouse pointer over the text field, hold
       down the Control key, and drag the mouse under the
       IBOutlet line in the `ViewController.swift` file.

16.   Release the Control key and the mouse. A pop-up
       window appears.

17.   Click in the Name text field, type **sliderValue**, and
       click the Connect button. You should now have these
       two IBOutlets:

```
@IBOutlet weak var mySlider: NSSlider!
@IBOutlet weak var sliderValue: NSTextField!
```

18. Move the mouse pointer over the horizontal slider, hold down the Control key, and drag the mouse just above the last curly bracket at the bottom of the `AppDelegate.swift` file.

19. Release the Control key and the mouse. A pop-up window appears.

20. Click in the Connection pop-up menu and choose Action.

21. Click in the Name text field and type **getValue**.

22. Click in the Type pop-up menu and choose NSSlider. Then click the Connect button. Xcode creates an empty IBAction method.

23. Modify this IBAction method as follows:

```
@IBAction func getValue(_ sender: NSSlider) {
    sliderValue.integerValue = mySlider.integerValue
}
```

24. Choose Product ➤ Run. Your user interface appears.

25. Drag the slider left and right. Notice that each time you drag the slider and release the mouse button, the slider's current value appears in the text box.

26. Choose SliderProgram ➤ Quit SliderProgram.

Summary

Check boxes, radio buttons, and date pickers let you provide the user with a range of valid options to select. This insures that the user can't give a program invalid data by mistake (or deliberately).

Check boxes allow the user to choose zero or more options. A group of radio buttons only allow the user to choose one option. A date picker allows the user to choose a correctly formatted date.

To identify which check boxes a user selected, examine the State property of each check box. If the State value is 1, the check box is selected. If the State value is 0, the check box is clear.

It's possible to display alternate text on a check box and radio button. This way, text appears when the check box or radio button is selected and different text appears when the check box or radio button is clear.

To identify which radio button a user may have selected, you need to use the Tag property. Each radio button needs a unique Tag value, which can be an integer. By identifying the Tag value, you can identify the radio button that the user selected.

The date picker makes it easy for the user to choose a date and/or a time. The date picker stores the selected date/time in a special NSDate format that you can access through the dateValue property of the date picker.

Sliders let users choose from a range of valid numeric values. By using check boxes, radio buttons, date pickers, and sliders, a program insures that users can only choose from a range of valid options.

Chapter 19

Using Text with Labels, Text Fields, and Combo Boxes

When a program needs to offer a limited range of valid options to the user, that's when you want to use check boxes, radio buttons, date pickers, or sliders. However, sometimes a program needs to allow the user to type in data that can never be predicted ahead of time, such as a person's name. When a program needs to allow the user to type in data, that's when you need to use a text field or a combo box.

A text field lets the user type in numbers, unusual characters, or ordinary letters. This means a program may need to verify that the user typed in valid data.

Sometimes a program can offer the user the option of choosing from a limited selection of valid options or typing in data instead. For example, a program might ask the user to choose a country. Then the program can offer a limited range of likely options or give the user the freedom to type something else.

This ability to either choose from a limited range of options or type something in is the main advantage of a combo box. The combo box gets its name because it combines the features of a pop-up button (displaying a list of valid options) with the freedom to type anything in (like a text field).

© Wallace Wang 2017
W. Wang, *macOS Programming for Absolute Beginners*,
DOI 10.1007/978-1-4842-2662-9_19

While text fields and combo boxes are used to accept data from the user, labels are used to display information to the user. When you just need to display information such as displaying instructions or identifying the purpose of a text field (such as telling a user to type a name or address), you'll want to use a label. Labels, text fields, and combo boxes work together to accept and display text on a user interface.

Using Text Fields

Since a user can type anything into a text field, a text field stores data as a string, which you can retrieve using the `stringValue` property. However, since users can type in integer or decimal numbers, a text field is versatile enough to recognize such numbers.

If the user types in an integer, you can retrieve that value by accessing the `intValue` property. If the user types in a decimal number, you can retrieve that value by accessing either the `floatValue` or `doubleValue` properties.

No matter what the user types into a text field, you can retrieve the proper value. Since text fields can accept strings or numbers, your program can retrieve the proper value by accessing one of the following properties:

- `intValue`: Retrieves an integer value. If the user types a string, this property stores 0. If the user types a decimal number such as 10.9, it stores only the integer value such as 10.

- `floatValue` or `doubleValue`: Retrieves a floating point or double value. If the user types a string, this property stores 0.0. If the user types an integer such as 4, the `floatValue` and `doubleValue` properties store it as a decimal such as 4.0.

- `stringValue`: Retrieves a string value. If the user types a number, it stores that number as a string (such as "4.305").

> **Note**   When the user types text into a text field, that typed text gets stored in all four properties: `intValue`, `floatValue`, `doubleValue`, and `stringValue`.

Beyond the standard text field, Xcode offers several text field variations for handling different types of text entry:

- **Text Field with Number Formatter**: Defines the type of numbers that can be typed in

- **Secure Text Field**: Masks typed text

- **Search Field**: Stores a list of previously entered text

- **Token Field**: Allows the user to enter tokens of content in addition to typing ordinary text

Using a Number Formatter

A number formatter lets you define valid numeric values the user can type into the text box such as a minimum or maximum value, or a specific way to enter data, such as with a % sign or by typing "four" instead of 4.

Xcode gives you two ways to create a text field with a number formatter. First, you can drag and drop the text field with number formatter from the Object Library and place it on your user interface. Second, you can drag and drop the number formatter from the Object Library and place it on an existing text field on your user interface.

To quickest way to find these items is to type "Number Formatter" in the search text field at the bottom of the Object Library, as shown in Figure 19-1.

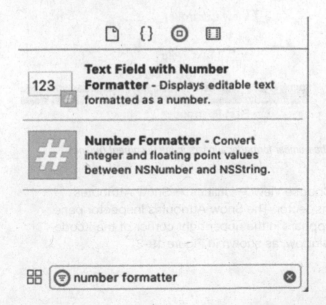

Figure 19-1. The text field with number formatter and number formatter in the Object Library

Whether you create a new text field with the text field with number formatter item or apply a number formatter to an existing text field, you'll need to define the number formatter settings. To do this, you need to follow several steps:

1. Click the Show Document Outline icon to display the Document Outline.

2. Click the disclosure triangle to the left of the text field that uses the number formatter.

3. Click the disclosure triangle that appears to the left of the text field cell underneath the text field.

4. Click the number formatter, as shown in Figure 19-2.

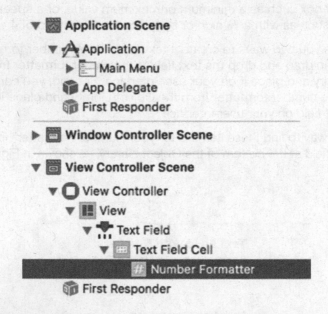

Figure 19-2. The number formatter appears in the Document Outline

5. Choose View ➤ Utilities ➤ Show Attributes Inspector. The Show Attributes Inspector pane appears in the upper right corner of the Xcode window, as shown in Figure 19-3.

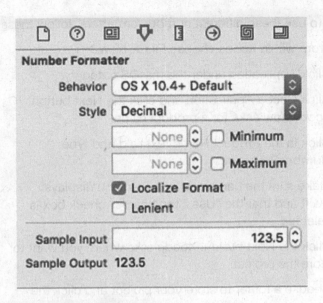

Figure 19-3. The Show Attributes Inspector pane

The Minimum and Maximum check boxes let you define a minimum and/or maximum value that the text field will accept. If you define a minimum value of 10 and the user types in a number less than 10, the text field won't accept the number.

The Localize Format check box tells Xcode to use the user's local settings to determine the appearance of a decimal point and currency symbol. In some parts of the world, they use a period for a decimal point, while in others they use a comma.

Likewise for currency, Europeans use the Euro symbol, Americans use the dollar symbol, and British users use the British pound symbol. Selecting the Localize check box insures that your text field number formatter works no matter where in the world the program is used.

The Style pop-up menu lets you define different ways to format numbers. When you choose a style, the Unformatted and Formatted text fields under the Sample category displays how your numbers may look.

For example, in Figure 19-3, choosing the None style means that if the user types in 1,234.75 into a text field with a number formatter and presses Return, the text field formats that number as simply 1235.

However, if the style is Currency, Percent, Scientific, or Spell Out, that means the user can enter a number as defined by the Formatted example, and the text field will store the number as shown in the Unformatted example.

To see how to use these different number formatters, follow these steps:

1. From within Xcode choose File ➤ New ➤ Project.

2. Click Application under the macOS category.

3. Click Cocoa Application and click the Next button. Xcode now asks for a product name.

4. Click in the Product Name text field and type **NumberProgram**.

5. Make sure the Language pop-up menu displays Swift and that the "Use Storyboards" check box is selected.

6. Click the Next button. Xcode asks where you want to store the project.

7. Choose a folder to store your project and click the Create button.

8. Click the Main.storyboard file in the Project Navigator. Your program's user interface appears.

9. Choose View ➤ Utilities ➤ Show Object Library. The Object Library appears in the bottom right corner of the Xcode window.

10. Drag a pop-up button, a push button, and a text field with number formatter (it looks like a normal text field) on to the user interface window so it looks like Figure 19-4.

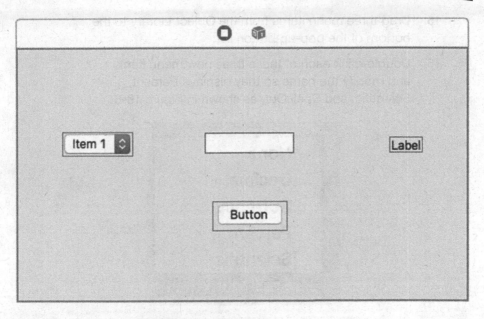

Figure 19-4. The user interface of the NumberProgram

11. Double-click the pop-up button. Xcode displays a list of three choices labeled Item 1, Item 2, and Item 3, as shown in Figure 19-5.

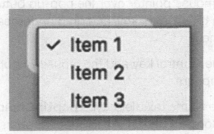

Figure 19-5. Modifying a pop-up button

12. Double-click Item 1, and when Xcode highlights it, type **None**.

13. Double-click Item 2, and when Xcode highlights it, type **Decimal**.

14. Double-click Item 3, and when Xcode highlights it, type **Currency**.

15. Drag three menu items from the Object Library to the bottom of the pop-up button list.

16. Double-click each of these three new menu items and modify the name so they displays Percent, Scientific, and Spell Out, as shown in Figure 19-6.

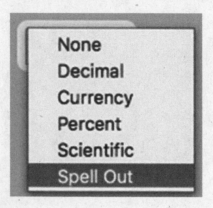

Figure 19-6. The modified pop-up button menu

17. Choose View ➤ Assistant Editor ➤ Show Assistant Editor. The `ViewController.swift` file appears next to your user interface.

18. Move the mouse pointer over the pop-up button, hold down the Control key, and drag underneath the IBOutlet line.

19. Release the Control key and the mouse. A pop-up window appears.

20. Click in the Name text field, type **popUpChoice**, and click the Connect button. An IBOutlet appears.

21. Move the mouse pointer over the text field, hold down the Control key, and drag the mouse under the IBOutlet line.

22. Release the Control key and the mouse. A pop-up window appears.

23. Click in the Name text field, type **textBox**, and click the Connect button.

24. Move the mouse pointer over the label, hold down the Control key, and drag the mouse under the IBOutlet line.

25. Release the Control key and the mouse. A pop-up window appears.

26. Click in the Name text field, type **labelResult**, and click the Connect button.

27. Click the Show Document Outline icon to reveal the Document Outline.

28. Move the mouse pointer over Number Formatter, hold down the Control key, and drag the mouse under the IBOutlet line.

29. Release the Control key and the mouse. A pop-up window appears.

30. Click in the Name text field, type **numberFormat**, and click the Connect button. You should have four IBOutlet lines as follows:

```
@IBOutlet weak var popUpChoice: NSPopUpButton!
@IBOutlet weak var textBox: NSTextField!
@IBOutlet weak var labelResult: NSTextField!
@IBOutlet weak var numberFormat: NumberFormatter!
```

31. Click the Hide Document Outline icon to hide the document outline.

32. Move the mouse pointer over the push button, hold down the Control key, and drag the mouse above the last curly bracket in the bottom of the ViewController.swift file.

33. Release the Control key and the mouse button. A pop-up window appears.

34. Click in the Connect pop-up menu and choose Action.

35. Click in the Name text field and type **showResults**.

36. Click in the Type pop-up menu, choose NSButton, and click the Connect button. Xcode creates an empty IBAction method.

37.   Modify the IBAction method as follows:

```
@IBAction func showResults(_ sender: NSButton) {
    if popUpChoice.titleOfSelectedItem! == "None" {
        numberFormat.numberStyle = NumberFormatter.Style.none
    } else if popUpChoice.titleOfSelectedItem! == "Decimal" {
        numberFormat.numberStyle = NumberFormatter.Style.decimal
    } else if popUpChoice.titleOfSelectedItem! == "Currency" {
        numberFormat.numberStyle = NumberFormatter.Style.currency
    } else if popUpChoice.titleOfSelectedItem! == "Percent" {
        numberFormat.numberStyle = NumberFormatter.Style.percent
    } else if popUpChoice.titleOfSelectedItem! == "Scientific" {
        numberFormat.numberStyle = NumberFormatter.Style.scientific
    } else if popUpChoice.titleOfSelectedItem! == "Spell Out" {
        numberFormat.numberStyle = NumberFormatter.Style.spellOut
    }
    labelResult.stringValue = String(stringInterpolationSegment:
    textBox.doubleValue)
}
```

38.   Choose Product ➤ Run. Your user interface appears.

39.   Click the pop-up button, choose Decimal, type **2.3**
into the text field, and then click the push button.
The label displays 2.3 in the text field's number
formatter.

40.   Click the pop-up button, choose Currency, type
$4.56 into the text field, and then click the push
button. The label displays 4.56.

41.   Click the pop-up button, choose Percent, type **25%**
into the text field, and then click the push button.
The label displays 0.25.

42.   Click the pop-up button, choose Scientific, type
1.2E3 into the text field, and then click the push
button. The label displays 1200.0.

43.   Click the pop-up button, choose Spell Out, type
forty-five into the text field, and then click the push
button. The label displays 45.0.

44.   Choose NumberProgram ➤ Quit NumberProgram.

The above Swift code in the IBAction method uses the `titleOfSelectedItem`
property to determine which option the user chose. Then it uses multiple
if-else if statements to change the number style property of the number
formatter.

The pop-up button lets you choose different number formatting styles so you can see how they work when you type a formatted number into the text field. By choosing different formatting styles, you can see how the text field lets you type in differently formatted numbers such as 25% (which gets converted into 0.25) or 1.2E3 (which gets converted into 1200.0).

Using a Secure Text Field, a Search Field, and a Token Field

A secure text field simply hides text behind bullets when the user types. This can be handy for masking actual text such as passwords, credit card numbers, or other sensitive information from view. Beyond masking anything typed in, a secure text field works exactly like a regular text field where you can retrieve the value typed using the intValue, floatValue, doubleValue, or stringValue properties.

A search text field looks like a typical search field you might find in a browser that displays a magnifying glass icon and close icon that can delete the text in the search field with one click. Each time the user types something in the search field and presses Return, the search field stores the text as a list stored in the recentSearches property.

By accessing this recentSearches property, you can view a list of everything the user previously typed in that search field.

A token field lets you type text and then it encloses that text inside a token. Despite the appearance of tokens, you can still retrieve the text of a token field by accessing the stringValue property.

To see how to use a secure text field, a search field and a token field, follow these steps:

1. From within Xcode choose File ➤ New ➤ Project.

2. Click Application under the macOS category.

3. Click Cocoa Application and click the Next button. Xcode now asks for a product name.

4. Click in the Product Name text field and type **TextProgram**.

5. Make sure the Language pop-up menu displays Swift and that the "Use Storyboards" check box is selected.

6. Click the Next button. Xcode asks where you want to store the project.

7. Choose a folder to store your project and click the Create button.

8. Click the `Main.storyboard` file in the Project Navigator pane.

9. Click the TextProgram icon to make the window of the user interface appear.

10. Drag three push buttons, a search field (on top), a token field (in the middle), a secure text field (at the bottom), and three labels resized to expand their width on to the user interface, as shown in Figure 19-7.

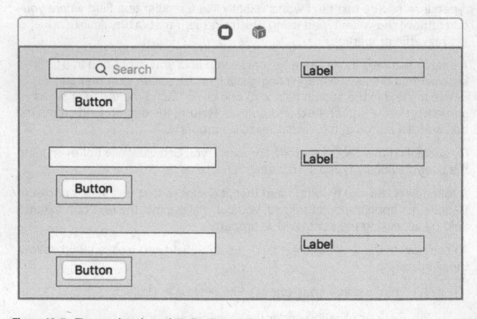

Figure 19-7. The user interface of the TextProgram

11. Choose View ➤ Assistant Editor ➤ Show Assistant Editor. Xcode displays the `ViewController.swift` file next to the user interface.

12. Move the mouse pointer over the search field, hold down the Control key, and drag the mouse under the IBOutlet line in the `ViewController.swift` file.

13. Release the Control key and the mouse button.
    A pop-up window appears.

14. Click in the Name text field, type **searchBox**, and
    click the Connect button.

15. Move the mouse pointer over the label to the right of
    the search field, hold down the Control key, and drag
    the mouse under the IBOutlet line.

16. Release the Control key and the mouse button.
    A pop-up window appears.

17. Click in the Name text field, type **historyBox**, and
    click the Connect button. You should have two
    IBOutlets like this:

    ```
    @IBOutlet weak var searchBox: NSSearchField!
    @IBOutlet weak var historyBox: NSTextField!
    ```

18. Move the mouse pointer over the Token field, hold
    down the Control key, and drag the mouse under the
    IBOutlet line in the ViewController.swift file.

19. Release the Control key and the mouse button.
    A pop-up window appears.

20. Click in the Name text field, type **tokenBox**, and
    click the Connect button.

21. Move the mouse pointer over the label to the right of
    the search field, hold down the Control key, and drag
    the mouse under the IBOutlet line.

22. Release the Control key and the mouse button.
    A pop-up window appears.

23. Click in the Name text field, type **tokenResult**, and
    click the Connect button. You should have two more
    IBOutlets like this:

    ```
    @IBOutlet weak var tokenBox: NSTokenField!
    @IBOutlet weak var tokenResult: NSTextField!
    ```

24. Move the mouse pointer over the secure text field, hold
    down the Control key, and drag the mouse under the
    IBOutlet line in the ViewController.swift file.

25. Release the Control key and the mouse button.
    A pop-up window appears.

26. Click in the Name text field, type **secureBox**, and
    click the Connect button.

27. Move the mouse pointer over the label to the right of
    the search field, hold down the Control key, and drag
    the mouse under the IBOutlet line.

28. Release the Control key and the mouse button.
    A pop-up window appears.

29. Click in the Name text field, type **secureResults**,
    and click the Connect button. You should have two
    more IBOutlets like this:

    ```
    @IBOutlet weak var secureBox: NSSecureTextField!
    @IBOutlet weak var secureResults: NSTextField!
    ```

30. Move the mouse pointer over the push button under
    the search field, hold down the Control key, and drag
    the mouse over the last curly bracket in the bottom
    of the ViewController.swift file.

31. Release the Control key and the mouse. A pop-up
    window appears.

32. Click in the Connect pop-up menu and choose
    Action.

33. Click in the Name text field and type **showHistory**.

34. Click in the Type pop-up menu and choose
    NSButton. Then click the Connect button. Xcode
    creates an IBAction method.

35. Move the mouse pointer over the push button under
    the token field, hold down the Control key, and drag
    the mouse over the last curly bracket in the bottom
    of the ViewController.swift file.

36. Release the Control key and the mouse. A pop-up
    window appears.

37. Click in the Connect pop-up menu and choose
    Action.

38. Click in the Name text field and type **showToken**.

39. Click in the Type pop-up menu and choose NSButton. Then click the Connect button. Xcode creates an IBAction method.

40. Move the mouse pointer over the push button under the secure text field, hold down the Control key, and drag the mouse over the last curly bracket in the bottom of the ViewController.swift file.

41. Release the Control key and the mouse. A pop-up window appears.

42. Click in the Connect pop-up menu and choose Action.

43. Click in the Name text field and type **showSecret**.

44. Click in the Type pop-up menu and choose NSButton. Then click the Connect button. Xcode creates an IBAction method.

45. Modify these IBAction methods as follows:

```
@IBAction func showHistory(_ sender: NSButton) {
    historyBox.stringValue = String(string
    InterpolationSegment: searchBox.recentSearches)
}

@IBAction func showToken(_ sender: NSButton) {
    tokenResult.stringValue = tokenBox.stringValue
}

@IBAction func showSecret(_ sender: NSButton) {
    secureResults.stringValue = secureBox.stringValue
}
}
```

46. Choose Product ➤ Run. Your user interface appears.

47. Click in the search field, type **Yahoo**, and press Return.

48. Click the close icon (the X in the gray circle) to clear the search field, type **Google**, and press Return.

49. Click the push button underneath the search field. Notice that the label to the right displays the two search results.

50.   Click in the Token field, type **Yahoo**, and press
      Return. Notice that the token field displays your
      typed text as a token.

51.   Click in the Token field and next to the Yahoo token,
      type **Google** and press Return.

52.   Click the push button underneath the Token field.
      Notice that the label to the right displays your two
      text tokens.

53.   Click in the secure text field and type **password**.
      Notice that the secure text field masks the text.

54.   Click the push button underneath the secure text
      field. Notice the label to the right displays the text
      from the secure text field, as shown in Figure 19-8.

55.   Choose TextProgram ➤ Quit TextProgram.

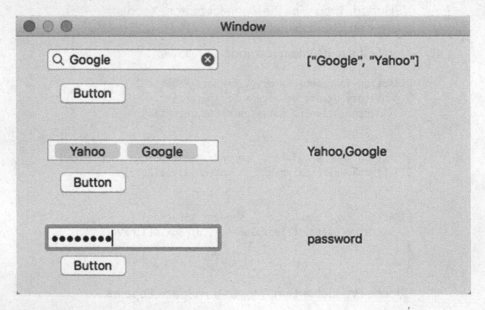

Figure 19-8. The results of the TextProgram

Although search fields, token fields, and secure text fields look differently,
they behave exactly like a text field when you need to access the values
stored inside them.

Using Combo Boxes

A text field lets the user type in anything while a pop-up button displays a fixed range of options. When you want to display a fixed range of options and let the user type in text, that's when you can use a combo box.

A combo box is based on the NSComboBox class, which is based on the NSTextField class that defines all text fields. As a result, you can retrieve values from a combo box using the intValue, floatValue, doubleValue, or stringValue properties.

When using a combo box, you have two ways to fill its pop-up list of options. First, you can create an internal list using the Show Attributes Inspector pane. Second, you can use an external data source so the combo box retrieves data from a database file or over the Internet.

Creating an Internal List

An internal list is best when you know ahead of time exactly how many and which items you want to store in a combo box, such as a list of countries or product names. To create an internal list, follow these steps:

1. Place a combo box on your program's user interface.

2. Click to select that combo box.

3. Choose View ➤ Utilities ➤ Show Attributes Inspector. The Items list appears, as shown in Figure 19-9.

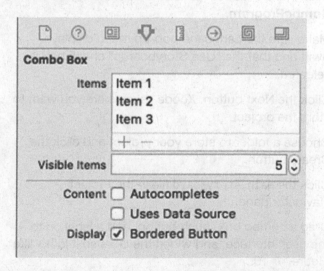

Figure 19-9. The Items list lets you define items to appear in a combo box

To edit an existing item in the list, click that item to select it and press Return. Now you can edit the text.

To remove an existing item, click that item to select it and click the minus sign icon.

To add a new item, click the plus sign icon. Then click the newly added item, press Return, and edit the text.

The Visible Items text field defines how many items the combo box menu displays.

The Autocompletes check box lets the combo box displays items in its list that match what the user started to type in. So if the user types one letter, autocomplete displays a list of all items in the combo box list that begins with the same letter the user typed.

The Uses Data Source check box determines if the combo box uses its internal Items list to display menu items, or retrieves data from another source. If the Uses Data Source check box is selected, then you'll need to write Swift code to fill a combo box with data.

To see how to fill a combo box using an internal list, follow these steps:

1. From within Xcode choose File ➤ New ➤ Project.

2. Click Application under the macOS category.

3. Click Cocoa Application and click the Next button. Xcode now asks for a product name.

4. Click in the Product Name text field and type **ComboProgram**.

5. Make sure the Language pop-up menu displays Swift and that the "Use Storyboards" check box is selected.

6. Click the Next button. Xcode asks where you want to store the project.

7. Choose a folder to store your project and click the Create button.

8. Click the `Main.storyboard` file in the Project Navigator pane.

9. Drag a combo box, push button, and a label on to the user interface, and widen the label so it looks like Figure 19-10.

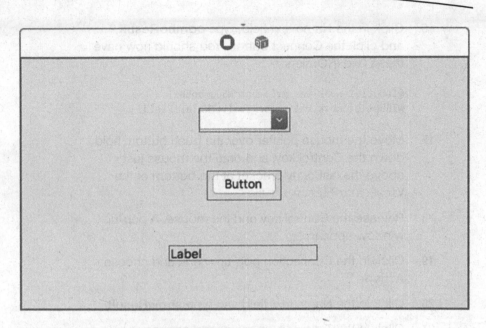

Figure 19-10. *The user interface of the ComboProgram*

10. Choose View ➤ Assistant Editor ➤ Show Assistant Editor. Xcode shows the ViewController.swift file next to the user interface.

11. Move the mouse pointer over the combo box, hold down the Control key, and drag the mouse under the IBOutlet line in the ViewController.swift file.

12. Release the Control key and the mouse. A pop-up window appears.

13. Click in the Name text field, type **myCombo**, and click the Connect button.

14. Move the mouse pointer over the label, hold down the Control key, and drag the mouse under the IBOutlet line in the ViewController.swift file.

15. Release the Control key and the mouse. A pop-up window appears.

16. Click in the Name text field, type **comboResult**, and click the Connect button. You should now have these two IBOutlets:

    ```
    @IBOutlet weak var myCombo: NSComboBox!
    @IBOutlet weak var comboResult: NSTextField!
    ```

17. Move the mouse pointer over the push button, hold down the Control key, and drag the mouse just above the last curly bracket at the bottom of the ViewController.swift file.

18. Release the Control key and the mouse. A pop-up window appears.

19. Click in the Connection pop-up menu and choose Action.

20. Click in the Name text field and type **showResult**.

21. Click in the Type pop-up menu and choose NSButton. Then click the Connect button. Xcode creates an empty IBAction method.

22. Modify this IBAction method as follows:

    ```
    @IBAction func showResult(sender: NSButton) {
        comboResult.stringValue = myCombo.stringValue
    }
    ```

23. Choose Product ➤ Run. Your user interface appears.

24. Click in the combo box and type Hello.

25. Click the push button. The word Hello appears in the label.

26. Click the downward-pointing arrow on the right edge of the combo box to display its list of items. Since you didn't modify the default list, the combo box list contains three items labeled Item 1, Item 2, and Item 3.

27. Click Item 3 and then click the push button. The label underneath displays Item 3.

28. Choose ComboProgram ➤ Quit ComboProgram.

This example used the default item list for the combo box. Experiment by adding or modifying this combo box item list and select the Autocompletes check box to see how these options modify the combo box.

Using a Data Source

A data source is best when a combo box needs to display data that may change over time, such as displaying a list of information from a database. To use a data source, you need to write Swift code. First, you need to adopt the NSComboBoxDataSource protocol in the ViewController.swift file like this:

```
class ViewController: NSViewController, NSComboBoxDataSource {
```

Next, you need to write two functions. One function needs to count the number of items to display in the combo box. The second function needs to retrieve data to insert in the combo box's list of items.

Finally, you need to specify a data source (the file that contains the data you want to display in the combo box) and make sure the combo box's Uses Data Source check box is selected in the Show Attributes Inspector pane or set the usesDataSource property to true using Swift code.

To see how a data source works to fill a combo box with a list of items, follow these steps:

1. Make sure the ComboProgram project is loaded in Xcode.

2. Click the ViewController.swift file in the Project Navigator pane.

3. Modify the class name in the AppDelegate.swift file to include the NSComboBoxDataSource protocol as follows:

   ```
   class ViewController: NSViewController, NSComboBoxDataSource {
   ```

4. Underneath the IBOutlet lines, add the following line to create an array of strings that will fill the combo box's item list:

   ```
   let myArray = ["Sandwich", "Chips", "Soda", "Salad"]
   ```

5. Modify the `viewDidLoad` function as follows:

```
override func viewDidLoad() {
    super.viewDidLoad()

    // Do any additional setup after loading the view.
    self.myCombo.usesDataSource = true
    self.myCombo.dataSource = self
}
```

This Swift code defines the data source for the combo box (identified by the `myCombo` IBOutlet) as self, which means the same class is also the data source. It makes sure the `usesDataSource` property is true to use a data source.

6. Above the IBAction method, add the following two function implementations:

7. Above the last curly bracket in the `ViewController.swift` file, add the following:

```
func numberOfItems (in comboBox: NSComboBox) -> Int {
    return myArray.count
}

func comboBox(_ comboBox: NSComboBox, objectValueForItemAt
index: Int) -> Any? {
    return myArray[index]
}
```

The `numberOfItems` function counts all the items in the myArray array and returns that integer. The comboBox function places each array item in the combo box's item list.

8. Choose Product ➤ Run.

9. Click the downward-pointing arrow of the combo box. Notice that its item list contains the items defined in myArray ("Sandwich", "Chips", "Soda", and "Salad").

10. Click Sandwich in the combo box to select it and then click the push button. Notice that the label underneath displays Sandwich.

11. Choose ComboProgram ➤ Quit ComboProgram.

This simple program shows how to retrieve a list of items from another data source (in this case an array called myArray) to fill an item list for a combo box. The complete code for the ViewController.swift file should look like this:

```swift
import Cocoa

class ViewController: NSViewController, NSComboBoxDataSource {

    @IBOutlet weak var myCombo: NSComboBox!
    @IBOutlet weak var comboResult: NSTextField!

    let myArray = ["Sandwich", "Chips", "Soda", "Salad"]

    override func viewDidLoad() {
        super.viewDidLoad()

        // Do any additional setup after loading the view.
        self.myCombo.usesDataSource = true
        self.myCombo.dataSource = self
    }

    override var representedObject: Any? {
        didSet {
        // Update the view, if already loaded.
        }
    }

    @IBAction func showResult(_ sender: NSButton) {
        comboResult.stringValue = myCombo.stringValue
    }

    func numberOfItems(in comboBox: NSComboBox) -> Int {
        return myArray.count
    }

    func comboBox(_ comboBox: NSComboBox, objectValueForItemAt index: Int)
-> Any? {
        return myArray[index]
    }

}
```

Summary

Text fields allow the user to type anything such as numbers or strings, so a text field offers multiple properties (`intValue`, `floatValue`, `doubleValue`, and `stringValue`) to store typed information in the proper data type. To restrict numeric information the user may type, you can use a number formatter to define minimum and/or maximum values along with defining different ways the user can enter numeric data, such as with a percentage sign or a currency sign.

Besides ordinary text fields, Xcode offers several variations of text fields for specialized purposes. Labels are designed for simply displaying text without allowing the user to edit the displayed text. A secure text field masks typed-in data to keep it safe from prying eyes. A token field displays typed-in data as groups or tokens while a search field offers a property to remember previously typed-in data.

Combo boxes combine the features of a text field with a pop-up button. A combo box can display a list of valid options that the user can click, or the user can type in data. You can define a combo box's list of options in the Show Attributes Inspector pane, or you can retrieve data from another source such as from an array.

The main purpose of text fields and combo boxes is to allow the user to type in any type of data. When the user types in data, you may need to write Swift code to verify that the entered data is valid for your program.

Chapter 20

Designing a User Interface with Constraints

A user interface lets people control a program, give a program data, and receive data back again. Since people can only interact with a program through its user interface, it's crucial that the user interface is uncluttered and easy to understand.

When designing a program's user interface, experiment with different designs. What may seem intuitive and simple for you to use may seem completely foreign and confusing to a novice.

To help you create and experiment with different user interface designs, Xcode makes it easy for you to drag and arrange items on a user interface such as buttons, text fields, and check boxes. Once you've found the best possible user interface design, the next challenge is making sure that user interface always looks right.

With macOS programs, the user interface appears in a window that the user can resize. This means the user might stretch a window wider (or skinnier), taller (or shorter), or do both at the same time, so your user interface must adapt to the different window sizes. Even the best user interface will be worthless if the program window shrinks and cuts off or hides part of the user interface from view, as shown in Figure 20-1.

© Wallace Wang 2017
W. Wang, *macOS Programming for Absolute Beginners*,
DOI 10.1007/978-1-4842-2662-9_20

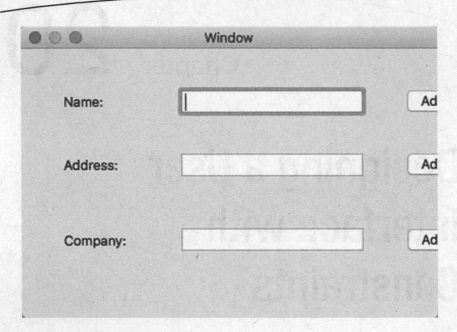

Figure 20-1. Resizing a window may cut off or hide a program's user interface

To make sure resizing a window won't distort a user interface, you need to use constraints. Constraints can define one or more of the following:

- The maximum and minimum size a user interface item can expand or shrink

- The position of a user interface item in relation to the borders of the window

- The distance between two user interface items

By applying constraints to all parts of your user interface, you can insure that your user interface will always look good no matter how the user may resize the window.

Constraining a Window Size

By default, every window of your program can be resized by the user. This means the user can shrink or expand a window. When the user shrinks a window, the window risks cutting off or hiding part of the user interface. When the user expands a window, the window will contain mostly empty space.

To constrain the maximum and minimum size of a window, follow these steps:

1. Click the .xib or .storyboard file that contains your program's user interface. With storyboards, make sure you click the window controller (not the view controller).

2. Choose View ➤ Utilities ➤ Show Size Inspector. The Size Inspector pane appears, as shown in Figure 20-2.

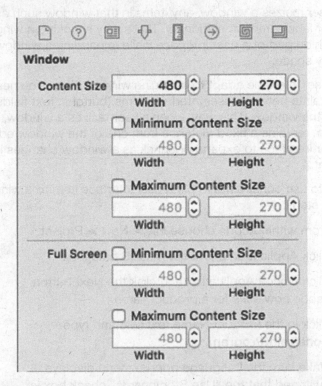

Figure 20-2. The Size Inspector lets you define a maximum and minimum window size

3. Click the Minimum Content Size check box under the Content Size category and type a value in the Width and Height text fields. The values you define here will be the minimum size of the window.

4. Click the Maximum Content Size check box under the Content Size category and type a value in the Width and Height text fields. The values you define here will be the maximum size of the window.

By defining a minimum size, you can insure that shrinking the window won't cut off or hide part of the user interface. By defining a maximum size, you can insure that expanding the size of a window won't create a large empty space.

Constraining User Interface Items to Window Edges

When the user resizes a window, any items in that window such as buttons, text fields, or labels, remain stationary. That's why shrinking a window can cover up or hide part of a user interface while expanding a window can create empty space.

To make a user interface adapt to changing window sizes, you need to place constraints between user interface items (buttons, text fields, etc.) to the sides of the window. This way, when a user resizes a window, the user interface item remains a fixed distance from one of the window edges. This allows a user interface to expand or shrink as a window changes its width and/or height.

To see how to use constraints to pin a user interface item to a window edge, follow these steps:

1. From within Xcode choose File ➤ New ➤ Project.

2. Click Application under the macOS category.

3. Click Cocoa Application and click the Next button. Xcode now asks for a product name.

4. Click in the Product Name text field and type **ConstraintProgram**.

5. Make sure the Language pop-up menu displays Swift and that the "Use Storyboards" check box is selected.

6. Click the Next button. Xcode asks where you want to store the project.

7. Choose a folder to store your project and click the Create button.

8. Click the Main.storyboard file in the Project Navigator. Your program's user interface appears.

9. Choose View ➤ Utilities ➤ Show Object Library.

10. Place a push button anywhere on the scene. (Make sure you place it on the view controller and not on the window controller.)

11. Choose Product ➤ Run. The user interface appears.

12. Move the mouse pointer over the bottom right corner of the program window and drag the mouse to the right and down. Notice that although the window changes size, the push button remains in place.

13. Choose ConstraintProgram ➤ Quit ConstraintProgram. Xcode appears again.

    The push button remained in place when you resized the window because the button had no constraints. By placing a constraint on the button to the right window edge, you can make the button move as the right window edge moves as well.

14. Click the Main.storyboard file in the Project Navigator and then click the push button to select it.

15. Move the mouse pointer over the push button, hold down the Control key, and drag the mouse to the right towards the right edge of the window. Xcode displays a blue line, as shown in Figure 20-3.

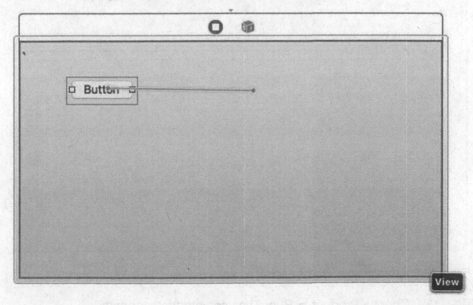

Figure 20-3. Control-dragging the mouse creates a constraint

16. Release the Control key and left mouse button in-between the push button and the right edge of the window. A pop-up menu appears, as shown in Figure 20-4.

Figure 20-4. *A pop-up menu for choosing constraints*

17. Choose the "Trailing Space to Container" option. Xcode draws a constraint from the push button to the right edge of the window, as shown in Figure 20-5.

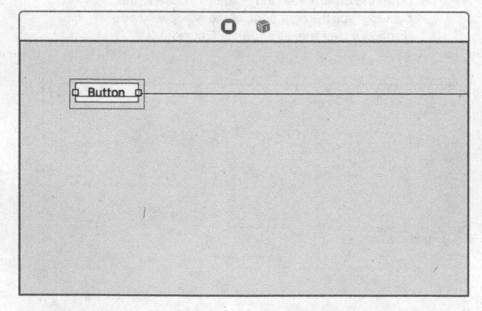

Figure 20-5. *A constraint appears as a line*

18. Choose Product ➤ Run. The user interface appears.

19. Move the mouse pointer over the bottom right corner of the program window and drag the mouse to the right and down. Notice that because the push button has a constraint that links it to the right window edge, each time the window changes size, the push button moves to remain a fixed distance from the right edge of the window.

20. Choose ConstraintProgram ➤ Quit ConstraintProgram. Xcode appears again.

When you place one constraint on the push button, Xcode displays a red border around the push button. This red border lets you know that you don't have enough constraints on the user interface item.

In this case, the constraint defines how the push button reacts when the right edge of the window moves. However, the push button lacks constraints that define how the push button reacts when the window shrinks or expands in height.

Ideally, you should place enough constraints on every user interface item so they define all possible variations if the window changes width or height. To fix this problem for the push button, you need to add another constraint that defines the push button's vertical position to the top or bottom of the window.

1. Click the push button to select it.

2. Hold down the Control key and drag the mouse down towards the bottom of the window.

3. Release the Control key and left mouse button in-between the push button and the bottom edge of the window. A pop-up menu appears, as shown in Figure 20-6.

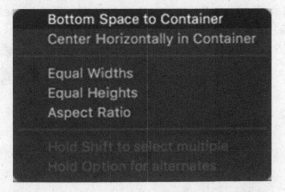

Figure 20-6. Another pop-up menu for applying constraints to the push button

4. Choose the "Bottom Space to Container" option. Xcode draws a constraint from the push button to the bottom of the window. Notice that Xcode no longer highlights the border around the push button in red because you have enough constraints.

5. Choose Product ➤ Run. The user interface appears.

6. Move the mouse pointer over the bottom right corner of the program window and drag the mouse to the right and down. Notice that because the push button has a constraint that links it to the right and bottom window edges, each time the window changes size, the push button moves to remain a fixed distance from the right and bottom edge of the window.

7. Choose ConstraintProgram ➤ Quit ConstraintProgram.

    With each user interface item, you can define a constraint to the top, left, right, or bottom of the window:

- **Trailing Space to Container**: Constrains an item to the right edge of a window.

- **Leading Space to Container**: Constrains an item to the left edge of a window.

- **Top Space to Container**: Constrains an item to the top edge of a window.

- **Bottom Space to Container**: Constrains an item to the bottom edge of a window.

Once you've placed one or more constraints on a user interface item, you can see more details about those constraints in the Size Inspector pane, as shown in Figure 20-7.

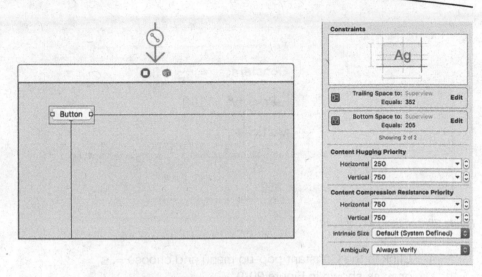

Figure 20-7. The Size Inspector pane lists details of each constraint

Editing a Constraint

Once you create a constraint, you can modify it later. Some ways to modify a constraint include

- **Changing the length of a constraint**: The constraint length can be equal to, less than or equal, or greater than or equal a fixed value.

- **Changing the priority of a constraint**: The priority defines which constraints are most important.

- **Changing the multiplier of the constraint**: (The default is 1, which represents 100% or 1:1.) Multipliers alter the way the constraints resize user interface items.

To modify a constraint, follow these steps:

1. Click the user interface item that has the constraints you want to modify.

2. Choose View ➤ Utilities ➤ Show Size Inspector. The Size Inspector pane appears and displays the constraints on that item (see Figure 20-7).

3. Click the Edit button that appears to the right of the constraint you want to modify. A pop-up window appears, as shown in Figure 20-8.

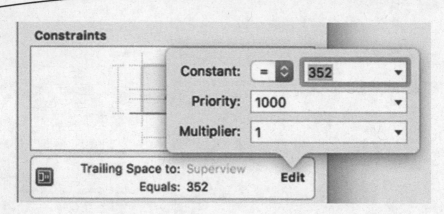

Figure 20-8. Editing a constraint

4. Click in the Constant pop-up menu and choose =, ≤, or ≥, as shown in Figure 20-9.

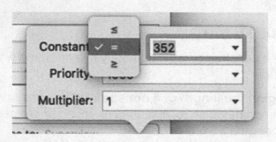

Figure 20-9. Editing a constraint

5. Click in the text field to the right of the Constant: label and type a value or choose standard value (Xcode uses recommended values) or canvas value (Xcode uses the distance of items on the user interface to define a numeric value). In most cases, standard value is the safest option that will work on different types of screens.

6. Click in the Priority text field and type a value. The higher the value, the higher the priority of the constraint. Priorities determine which constraint to follow if two or more constraints conflict.

7. Click in the Multiplier text field and type a value such as 0.5 or 2. The Multiplier value defines how a user interface item may stretch or shrink.

To see how multiple constraints can affect the appearance of user interface items, follow these steps:

1. Make sure your ConstraintProgram is loaded in Xcode.

2. Click the `Main.storyboard` file in the Navigator pane. Your program's user interface appears.

3. Click the push button. There should be a constraint connecting the button to the right edge of the window and a second constraint connecting the button to the bottom of the window.

4. Move the mouse pointer over the push button, hold down the Control key, and drag the mouse towards the left edge of the window.

5. Release the Control key and the left mouse button. A pop-up menu appears, as shown in Figure 20-10.

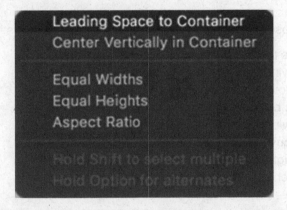

Figure 20-10. Defining a new constraint for the left window edge

6. Choose Leading Space to Container. Xcode draws a constraint from the push button to the left window edge. At this point, you should have three constraints to the left, right, and bottom edges of the window, as shown in Figure 20-11.

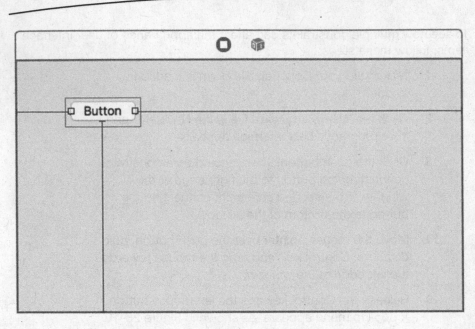

Figure 20-11. Three constraints on a push button

7.   Choose Product ➤ Run. The user interface appears.

8.   Move the mouse pointer over the right edge of the window and drag the mouse to resize the window. Notice that the left constraint keeps the push button's left edge a fixed distance from the left window edge while the right constraint keeps the push button's right edge a fixed distance from the right window edge, which forces the button to stretch, as shown in Figure 20-12.

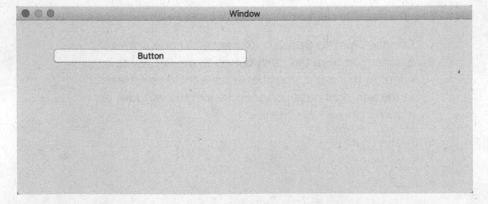

Figure 20-12. Multiple constraints can alter the appearance of items when a window resizes

9. Choose ConstraintProgram ➤ Quit
    ConstraintProgram.

Because you created two constraints for the left and right sides of the push
button, the push button expands when the window resizes. That's because
both the left and right constraints define a fixed distance between the push
button and the left and right edges of the window.

One way to keep the push button from expanding is to modify its left and
right constraints. Instead of a fixed value, the right constraint can define a
greater than or equal to value. To see how this works, follow these steps:

1. Make sure the ConstraintProgram is loaded in
    Xcode.

2. Click the `Main.storyboard` file in the Project
    Navigator pane.

3. Click the push button.

4. Choose View ➤ Utilities ➤ Show Size Inspector.
    The Size Inspector pane appears, displaying the
    constraints on the push button (see Figure 20-7).

5. Click the Edit button that appears to the right of the
    Trailing Space constraint (the right constraint).
    A pop-up window appears (see Figure 20-8).

6. Click in the Constant pop-up menu and choose ≥, as
    shown in Figure 20-13.

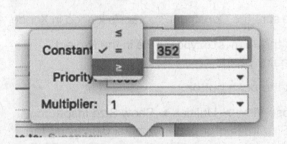

Figure 20-13. Changing a constraint from = to ≥

7. Choose Product ➤ Run. Your user interface appears.

8. Move the mouse pointer over the right edge of the window and drag the mouse to resize the window. Notice that the left constraint keeps the push button's left edge a fixed distance from the left window edge but the push button no longer expands when you widen the window. That's because the right constraint defines that the distance of the push button to the right edge of the window must be equal or greater than a fixed value.

9. Choose ConstraintProgram ➤ Quit ConstraintProgram.

Creating Size Constraints

The previous example showed how to keep a push button from expanding in size by modifying a constraint from = to ≥. However, another way to keep user interface items a fixed size is to apply size constraints. A size constraint can define one of the following:

- Height
- Width
- Aspect Ratio

The aspect ratio keeps the ratio between the height and width a fixed value so widening the item also makes it taller (and vice versa). To define a size constraint, you simply Control-drag within the boundaries of a user interface item. To see how to define a size constraint, follow these steps:

1. Make sure the ConstraintProgram is loaded in Xcode.

2. Click the Main.storyboard file in the Project Navigator pane.

3. Click the push button.

4. Choose View ➤ Utilities ➤ Show Size Inspector. The Size Inspector pane appears, displaying the constraints on the push button (see Figure 20-7).

5. Move the mouse pointer over the push button.

6. Hold down the Control key and drag the mouse to the left or right but stay within the boundaries of the push button.

7. Release the Control key and the left mouse button. A pop-up menu appears, as shown in Figure 20-14.

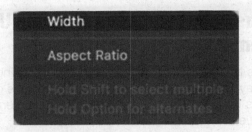

Figure 20-14. Creating a size constraint

8. Choose Width. Notice that Xcode displays a width
    constraint under the push button, as shown in
    Figure 20-15. This width constraint keeps the push
    button a fixed size.

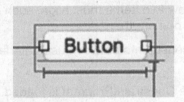

Figure 20-15. A width constraint appears under the item

9. Click the Edit button that appears to the right of the
    Width constraint. A pop-up window appears.

10. Click the Constant pop-up menu and change
    the = to a ≤.

11. Click in the Constant text field and whatever value is
    there (such as 70), enter double that value (such as
    140). This defines the width constraint to make the
    push button width equal or less than a specific value.

12. Choose Product ➤ Run. Your user interface appears.
    Notice that you can only resize the window width to
    a limited size. When you widen the window, the push
    button expands in width up to a certain size. Then
    the constraint keeps the window from resizing any
    wider.

13. Choose ConstraintProgram ➤ Quit
    ConstraintProgram.

Creating Constraints Between Multiple User Interface Items

Constraining items to the edge of a window and constraining the size of an item are two ways to use constraints. A third way to use constraints is to define distances between two separate user interface items such as a button and a text field.

By defining constraints between user interface items, you can insure that your entire user interface looks good no matter how the user may resize the program windows. In addition, creating constraints between user interface items keeps you from exhaustively defining constraints to the window edges for every user interface item.

To create constraints between user interface items, Control-drag the mouse from one user interface item to another. You can define a fixed distance between two items or how two items must align, such as keeping their tops or bottoms aligned with one another.

To learn how to create constraints between user interface items, follow these steps:

1. Make sure the ConstraintProgram is loaded in Xcode.

2. Click the Main.storyboard file in the Project Navigator pane.

3. Click the push button. There should be three constraints between the push button and the right, left, and bottom window edges. In addition, there should be a size constraint underneath the push button.

4. Place a text field to the right of the push button.

5. Move the mouse pointer over the text field, hold down the Control key, and drag the mouse until the mouse pointer appears over the push button, as shown in Figure 20-16.

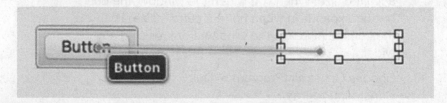

Figure 20-16. Defining a constraint between user interface items

6. Release the Control key and the left mouse button. A pop-up menu appears, as shown in Figure 20-17.

Figure 20-17. Choosing a constraint between user interface items

7. Choose the Horizontal Spacing option. Xcode displays a constraint between the push button and the text field. Notice that Xcode displays a red border around the text field because there aren't enough constraints to define the text field's position in the window. You could manually add more constraints but you can also let Xcode add the constraints automatically. The only drawback is that Xcode doesn't always guess the correct constraints you need.

8. Make sure the text field is still selected and then choose Editor ➤ Resolve Auto Layout Issues ➤ Add Missing Constraints in the top half of the submenu, as shown in Figure 20-18. (If you choose Add Missing Constraints in the bottom half of the submenu, Xcode will add constraints to all items currently on the user interface.) Xcode adds additional constraints and removes the red border around the text field.

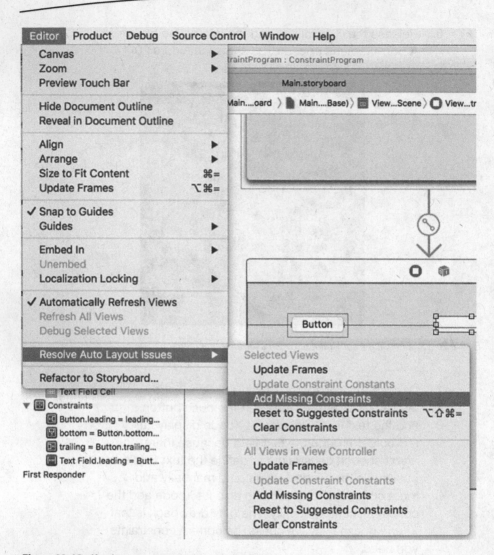

Figure 20-18. Xcode can automatically add constraints

9. Choose Product ➤ Run. Your user interface appears.
    Notice that when you resize the window, the text
    field always moves to maintain a fixed distance from
    the push button.

10. Choose ConstraintProgram ➤ Quit
    ConstraintProgram.

> **Note**   If you choose Editor ➤ Resolve Auto Layout Issues ➤ Reset to
> Suggested Constraints, Xcode will automatically add all necessary constraints
> to the currently selected user interface item (if you choose Reset to Suggested
> Constraints in the top half of the submenu) or to all user interface items (if you
> choose Reset to Suggested Constraints in the bottom half of the submenu).

Deleting Constraints

Defining constraints can often be a process of trial and error until you get the
results you want. If you define a constraint that doesn't work the way you
want, you can always delete that constraint. To delete a single constraint,
you have two choices:

- Click the constraint on the user interface and then press
  the Backspace key.
- Click the constraint in the Size Inspector pane and then
  press the Backspace key.

If you want to remove all constraints from a single user interface item such
as a button or text field, follow these steps:

1. Click the user interface item that contains the
   constraints you want to delete.

2. Choose Editor ➤ Resolve Auto Layout Issues ➤
   Clear Constraints (in the top half of the submenu).

If you want to remove all constraints from a user interface, follow these
steps:

1. Click the user interface item that contains the
   constraints you want to delete.

2. Choose Editor ➤ Resolve Auto Layout Issues
   ➤ Clear Constraints (in the bottom half of the
   submenu).

Summary

Constraints insure that your user interface will always look good no matter how the user may resize the program windows. You can define three types of constraints:

- From a user interface item to a window edge

- A size constraint that defines the height and/or width of a user interface item

- Between two user interface items

When working with multiple constraints, you can assign a fixed value or a greater than or less than comparison value. You can also assign priorities to constraints so that if two or more constraints conflict, the constraint with the higher priority gets used first.

Xcode can automatically add constraints but they may not always work right, so be prepared to experiment with different constraints until you get your user interface to behave the way you want it to.

Chapter **21**

Using Alerts and Panels

In every program, you can design the unique features of your program while letting the Cocoa framework worry about making your program look and behave like a standard macOS program. To create the common features of nearly every macOS program, you can use alerts and panels.

An alert typically pops up on the screen to inform the user, such as asking the user to verify the deletion of a file or to alert the user of a problem. A panel displays common user interface items such as a print panel that macOS programs typically display to give you options for printing, or an open panel for selecting a file.

By using alerts and panels, you can add common macOS user interface elements without having to create your own user interface or without needing to write Swift code. Alerts and panels are part of the Cocoa framework that your macOS programs can use to create a standard macOS user interface.

Using Alerts

An alert is based on the NSAlert class in the Cocoa framework. At the simplest level, you can create an alert with two lines of Swift code:

```
let myAlert = NSAlert()
myAlert.runModal()
```

The first line declares an object called myAlert that is based on the NSAlert class. Then the second line uses the runModal() method to display the alert. When an alert appears, it's considered modal, which means the alert won't let the user do anything until the user dismisses the alert.

© Wallace Wang 2017
W. Wang, *macOS Programming for Absolute Beginners*,
DOI 10.1007/978-1-4842-2662-9_21

The above two lines of code create a generic alert that displays an OK button, a generic graphic image, and a generic text message, as shown in Figure 21-1.

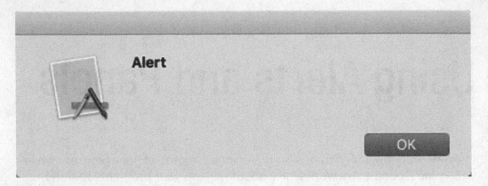

Figure 21-1. Creating a generic alert

To customize an alert, you can modify the following properties:

- messageText: Displays the main alert message in bold. In Figure 21-1, **Alert** is the messageText.

- informativeText: Displays non-bold text directly underneath the messageText. In Figure 21-1, there is no informativeText.

- icon: Displays an icon. By default, the icon is the program's icon.

- alertStyle: Displays a critical icon when set to NSAlertStyle.critical. Otherwise, it displays the default alert icon.

- showsSuppressionButton: Displays a check box with the default text of "Do not show this message again" unless the suppressionButton?.title property is defined.

- suppressionButton?.title: Replaces the default text ("Do not show this message again") with custom text for the check box.

To see how to customize an alert, follow these steps:

1. From within Xcode choose File ➤ New ➤ Project.

2. Click Application under the macOS category.

3. Click Cocoa Application and click the Next button. Xcode now asks for a product name.

4. Click in the Product Name text field and type
    AlertProgram.

5. Make sure the Language pop-up menu displays
    Swift and that the "Use Storyboards" check box is
    selected.

6. Click the Next button. Xcode asks where you want to
    store the project.

7. Choose a folder to store your project and click the
    Create button.

8. Click the Main.storyboard file in the Project
    Navigator. Your program's user interface appears.

9. Choose View ➤ Utilities ➤ Show Object Library. The
    Object Library appears in the bottom right corner of
    the Xcode window.

10. Drag a Push Button on to the user interface window.

11. Choose View ➤ Assistant Editor ➤ Show Assistant
    Editor. The ViewController.swift file appears next
    to your user interface.

12. Move the mouse pointer over the push button,
    hold down the Control key, and drag the mouse
    above the last curly bracket in the bottom of the
    ViewController.swift file.

13. Release the Control key and the mouse button.
    A pop-up window appears.

14. Click in the Connect pop-up menu and choose
    Action.

15. Click in the Name text field and type **showAlert**.

16. Click in the Type pop-up menu, choose NSButton,
    and click the Connect button. Xcode creates an
    empty IBAction method.

17.   Modify the IBAction method as follows:

```
@IBAction func showAlert(_ sender: NSButton) {
    let myAlert = NSAlert()
    myAlert.messageText = "Warning!"
    myAlert.informativeText = "Zombies approaching"
    myAlert.alertStyle = NSAlertStyle.critical
    myAlert.showsSuppressionButton = true
    myAlert.suppressionButton?.title = "Stop scaring me"
    myAlert.runModal()
}
```

18.   Choose Product ➤ Run. Your user interface appears.

19.   Click the push button. An alert appears, as shown in
Figure 21-2.

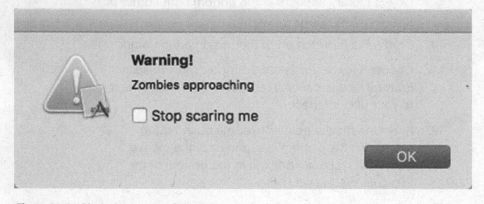

Figure 21-2. Displaying a customized alert

20.   Click the OK button on the alert to make it go away.

21.   Choose AlertProgram ➤ Quit AlertProgram.

Getting Feedback from an Alert

An alert typically displays a single OK button so the user can dismiss the
alert. However, an alert can get feedback from the user in one of two ways:

■   Selecting the suppression check box

■   Clicking a button other than the OK button

To determine if the user selected the suppression check box or not, you
need to access the suppressionButton!.state property. If the check box is

selected, the suppressionButton!.state property is 1. If the check box is clear, the suppressionButton!.state property is 0.

The second way to get feedback from an alert is by displaying two or more buttons on an alert. To add more buttons to an alert, you need to use the addButton method. Then, to determine which button the user selected, you need to use the NSAlertFirstButtonReturn, NSAlertSecondButtonReturn, or NSAlertThirdButtonReturn constants.

If you have four or more buttons on an alert, you can check for the fourth button by using NSAlertThirdButtonReturn + 1, a fifth button by using NSAlertThirdButtonReturn + 2, and so on for each additional button beyond the third one.

To see how to identify what options the user chose in an alert, follow these steps:

1. Make sure your AlertProgram project is loaded in Xcode.

2. Click the ViewController.swift file in the Project Navigator pane.

3. Modify the IBAction showAlert method as follows:

```
@IBAction func showAlert(_ sender: NSButton) {
    let myAlert = NSAlert()
    myAlert.messageText = "Warning!"
    myAlert.informativeText = "Zombies approaching"
    myAlert.alertStyle = NSAlertStyle.critical
    myAlert.showsSuppressionButton = true
    myAlert.suppressionButton?.title = "Stop scaring me"

    myAlert.addButton(withTitle: "Ignore it")
    myAlert.addButton(withTitle: "Run")
    myAlert.addButton(withTitle: "Panic")
    myAlert.addButton(withTitle: "Do nothing")

    let choice = myAlert.runModal()

    switch choice {
    case NSAlertFirstButtonReturn:
        print ("User clicked Ignore it")
    case NSAlertSecondButtonReturn:
        print ("User clicked Run")
    case NSAlertThirdButtonReturn:
        print ("User clicked Panic")
    case NSAlertThirdButtonReturn + 1:
        print ("User clicked Do nothing")
```

```
                default: break
                }

                if myAlert.suppressionButton!.state == 1 {
                    print ("Checked")
                } else {
                    print ("Not checked")
                }

        }
```

The addButton methods create buttons on the alert where the first addButton method creates a default button and the other addButton methods create additional buttons. To capture the button that the user clicked, the above code creates a constant called "choice".

Then it uses a switch statement to identify which button the user clicked. Notice that the fourth button is identified by adding 1 to the NSAlertThirdButtonReturn constant.

The suppressionButton!.state property checks if the user selected the check box that appears on the alert. If its value is 1, then the user selected the check box. Otherwise, if its value is 0, the check box is clear.

4.   Choose Product ➤ Run. Your user interface appears.

5.   Click the button. The alert appears, as shown in Figure 21-3.

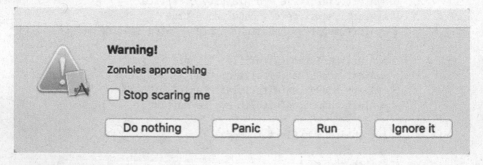

Figure 21-3. The alert created by Swift code

6.   Click in the "Stop scaring me" check box to select it.

7.   Click one of the buttons, such as Panic or Run. No matter which button you click, the alert goes away.

8. Choose AlertProgram ➤ Quit AlertProgram. Xcode appears again and displays text in the Debug Area such as "User clicked Panic" and "Checked."

Displaying Alerts as Sheets

Alerts typically appear as a modal dialog that creates another window that you can move separately from the main program window. Another way to display an alert is as a sheet that appears to scroll down from the title bar of the currently active window.

To make an alert appear as a sheet, you need to use the beginSheetModalForWindow method, like this:

```
alertObject.beginSheetModal (for: window, completionHandler: closure)
```

The first parameter defines the window where you want the sheet to appear. In the AlertProgram project, the IBOutlet representing the user interface window is called window. The second parameter is the completion handler label, which identifies the name of a special function called a closure.

A closure represents a shorthand way of writing a function. Instead of writing a function the traditional way, like

```
func functionName(parameters) -> Type {
    // Insert code here
    return value
}
```

you can write a closure like this:

```
    let closureName = { (parameters) -> Type in
    // Insert code here
}
```

To see how to turn an alert into a sheet and use closures, follow these steps:

1. Make sure your AlertProgram project is loaded in Xcode.

2. Click the ViewController.swift file in the Project Navigator pane.

3. Modify the IBAction showAlert method as follows:

```
@IBAction func showAlert(_ sender: NSButton) {
```

```
let myAlert = NSAlert()
myAlert.messageText = "Warning!"
myAlert.informativeText = "Zombies approaching"
myAlert.alertStyle = NSAlertStyle.critical
myAlert.showsSuppressionButton = true
myAlert.suppressionButton?.title = "Stop scaring me"

myAlert.addButton(withTitle: "Ignore it")
myAlert.addButton(withTitle: "Run")
myAlert.addButton(withTitle: "Panic")
myAlert.addButton(withTitle: "Do nothing")

let myCode = { (choice:NSModalResponse) -> Void in
    switch choice {
    case NSAlertFirstButtonReturn:
        print ("User clicked Ignore it")
    case NSAlertSecondButtonReturn:
        print ("User clicked Run")
    case NSAlertThirdButtonReturn:
        print ("User clicked Panic")
    case NSAlertThirdButtonReturn + 1:
        print ("User clicked Do nothing")
    default: break
    }

    if myAlert.suppressionButton!.state == 1 {
        print ("Checked")
    } else {
        print ("Not checked")
    }
}
myAlert.beginSheetModal(for: NSApp.keyWindow!, completionHandler:
myCode)
}
```

4. Choose Product ➤ Run. The user interface appears.

5. Click the button. Notice that now the alert drops
    down as a sheet, as shown in Figure 21-4.

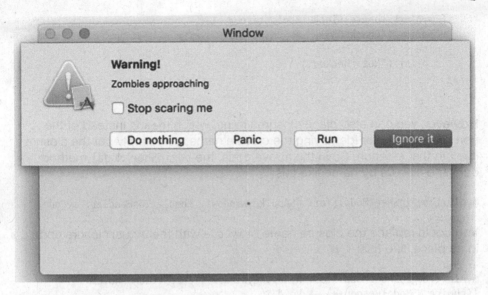

Figure 21-4. The alert as a sheet

6. Click in the "Stop scaring me" check box to select it.

7. Click one of the buttons, such as Panic or Run. No matter which button you click, the alert goes away.

8. Choose AlertProgram ➤ Quit AlertProgram. Xcode appears again and displays text in the Debug Area such as "User clicked Run" and "Checked."

In the above Swift code, the closure is defined as follows:

```
let myCode = { (choice:NSModalResponse) -> Void in
switch choice {
case NSAlertFirstButtonReturn:
    print ("User clicked Ignore it")
case NSAlertSecondButtonReturn:
    print ("User clicked Run")
case NSAlertThirdButtonReturn:
    print ("User clicked Panic")
case NSAlertThirdButtonReturn + 1:
    print ("User clicked Do nothing")
default: break
}
```

```
    if myAlert.suppressionButton!.state == 1 {
        print ("Checked")
    } else {
        print ("Not checked")
    }
}
```

However, you can also place closures inline, which means instead of the completion handler identifying the closure name, you simply put the closure itself in that location. So in the above code, the beginSheetModal method calls the closure by name like this:

```
myAlert.beginSheetModal(for: NSApp.keyWindow!, completionHandler: myCode)
```

You could replace the closure name of myCode with the actual closure code in its place, like this:

```
myAlert.beginSheetModal(for: NSApp.keyWindow!, completionHandler:
{(choice:NSModalResponse) -> Void in
    switch choice {
    case NSAlertFirstButtonReturn:
    print ("User clicked Ignore it")
    case NSAlertSecondButtonReturn:
    print ("User clicked Run")
    case NSAlertThirdButtonReturn:
    print ("User clicked Panic")
    case NSAlertThirdButtonReturn + 1:
    print ("User clicked Do nothing")
    default: break
    }

    if myAlert.suppressionButton!.state == 1 {
    print ("Checked")
    } else {
    print ("Not checked")
    }
})
```

Putting closures inline directly within a method shortens the amount of code you need to write, but at the possible expense of making the overall code harder to understand. Separating the closure by name and then calling it by name makes it easier to reuse that closure elsewhere in your program if necessary, but also makes your code clearer at the expense of forcing you to write more code.

Choose whatever method you like best but, as in all aspects of programming, stick to one style to make it easy for other programmers to understand your code later if you're not around to explain how it works.

Using Panels

Panels represent common user interface elements that macOS programs need, such as displaying an Open panel to let users select a file to open and a Save panel to let users choose a folder to store a file. The Open panel is based on the NSOpenPanel class while the Save panel is based on the NSSavePanel class.

Creating an Open Panel

An Open panel let the user select a file to open. The Open panel needs to return a file name if the user selected a file. Some properties that the Open panel uses include

- canChooseFiles: Lets the user select a file

- canChooseDirectories: Lets the user select a folder or directory

- allowsMultipleSelection: Lets the user select more than one item

- urls: Holds the name of the chosen item. If the allowsMultipleSelection property is set to true, then the urls property holds an array of items. Otherwise, it holds a single item.

To see how to use an Open panel, follow these steps:

1. From within Xcode choose File ➤ New ➤ Project.

2. Click Application under the macOS category.

3. Click Cocoa Application and click the Next button. Xcode now asks for a product name.

4. Click in the Product Name text field and type **PanelProgram**.

5. Make sure the Language pop-up menu displays Swift and that the "Use Storyboards" check box is selected.

6. Click the Next button. Xcode asks where you want to store the project.

7. Choose a folder to store your project and click the Create button.

8. Click the `Main.storyboard` file in the Project Navigator. Your program's user interface appears.

9. Choose View ➤ Utilities ➤ Show Object Library. The Object Library appears in the bottom right corner of the Xcode window.

10. Drag a push button on to the user interface window and double-click it to change its title to **Open**.

11. Choose View ➤ Assistant Editor ➤ Show Assistant Editor. The `ViewController.swift` file appears next to your user interface.

12. Move the mouse pointer over the push button, hold down the Control key, and drag the mouse above the last curly bracket in the bottom of the `ViewController.swift` file.

13. Release the Control key and the mouse button. A pop-up window appears.

14. Click in the Connect pop-up menu and choose Action.

15. Click in the Name text field and type **openPanel**.

16. Click in the Type pop-up menu, choose NSButton, and click the Connect button. Xcode creates an empty IBAction method.

17. Modify the IBAction method as follows:

```
@IBAction func openPanel(_ sender: NSButton) {
    let myOpen = NSOpenPanel()
    myOpen.canChooseFiles = true
    myOpen.canChooseDirectories = true
    myOpen.allowsMultipleSelection = true

    myOpen.begin { (result) -> Void in
        if result == NSFileHandlingPanelOKButton {
            print (myOpen.urls)
        }
    }

}
```

18. Choose Product ➤ Run. The user interface appears.

19. Click the button. An Open panel appears, as shown in Figure 21-5.

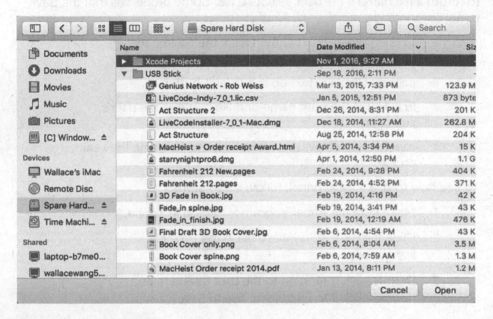

Figure 21-5. The Open panel

20. Hold down the Command key and click two different items, such as two different files or a file and a folder.

21. Click the Open button.

22. Choose PanelProgram ➤ Quit PanelProgram. Xcode appears again. In the Debug area, you should see a list of the files/folders you can chose.

Note   The Open panel only selects a file/folder but you still need to write Swift code to actually open any file the user selects.

Creating a Save Panel

A Save panel looks similar to an Open panel, but its purpose is to let the user select a folder and define a file name to save. The Save panel needs to return a file name if the user selects a file. Some properties that the Save panel uses include

- `title`: Displays text at the top of the Save panel. If undefined, it defaults to displaying "Save".

- `prompt`: Displays text on the default button.

- `url`: Holds the path name and file name of the user's selection.

- `nameFieldStringValue`: Holds just the file name the user chose.

To see how to use a Save panel, follow these steps:

1. Make sure the PanelProgram is loaded in Xcode.

2. Click the `Main.storyboard` file in the Project Navigator pane.

3. Drag a push button on to the user interface and double-click it to change its title to Save.

4. Choose View ➤ Assistant Editor ➤ Show Assistant Editor. Xcode shows the `ViewController.swift` file next to the user interface.

5. Move the mouse pointer over the Save button, hold down the Control key, and drag the mouse under the IBOutlet line in the `ViewController.swift` file.

6. Release the Control key and the mouse. A pop-up window appears.

7. Click in the Connection pop-up menu and choose Action.

8. Click in the Name text field, type **savePanel**, and click the Connect button.

9. Click in the Type pop-up menu and choose NSButton. Then click the Connect button. Xcode creates an empty IBAction method.

10.   Modify this IBAction method as follows:

```
@IBAction func savePanel(_ sender: NSButton) {
    let mySave = NSSavePanel()
    mySave.title = "Save a File Here"
    mySave.prompt = "Save Me"

    mySave.begin { (result) -> Void in
        if result == NSFileHandlingPanelOKButton {
            print (mySave.url!)
            print (mySave.nameFieldStringValue)
        }
    }

}
```

11.   Choose Product ➤ Run. Your user interface appears.

12.   Click the Save button. A Save panel appears, as
       shown in Figure 21-6. Notice that the title property
       creates the text that appears at the top of the Save
       panel while the prompt property creates the text that
       appears on the default button in the bottom right
       corner of the Save panel.

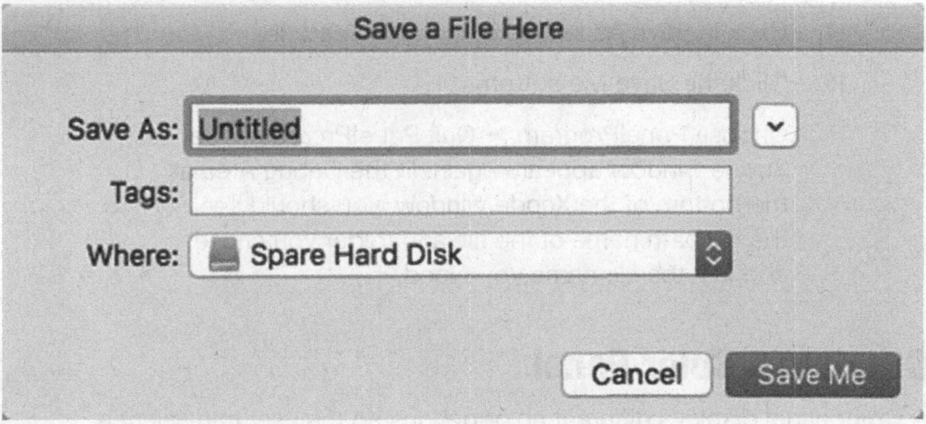

Figure 21-6. The condensed Save panel

13.   Click the Expand button that appears to the far right
       of the Save As text field. The Save panel expands, as
       shown in Figure 21-7.

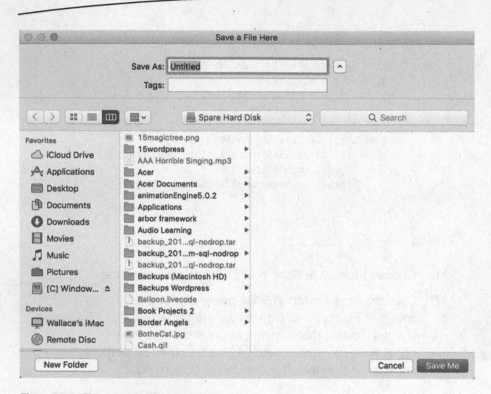

Figure 21-7. The expanded Save panel

14. Click in Save As text field and type **TestFile**.

15. Click the Save Me button.

16. Choose PanelProgram ➤ Quit PanelProgram. The Xcode window appears again. In the Debug Area at the bottom of the Xcode window, you should see the full path name of the file and folder you chose, and just the file name you typed.

Creating a Color Panel

A Color panel displays different color options so the user can select a different color. The Color panel needs to return a color that the user selects. Some properties that the Color panel uses include

- `activate`: Displays the color panel

- `action`: Defines the function to run when the Color panel is opened

- `color`: Stores the color value that the user chose as part of the `NSColor` class

To learn how to use a Color panel, follow these steps:

1. From within Xcode choose File ➤ New ➤ Project.

2. Click Application under the macOS category.

3. Click Cocoa Application and click the Next button. Xcode now asks for a product name.

4. Click in the Product Name text field and type **ColorPanelProgram**.

5. Make sure the Language pop-up menu displays Swift and that the "Use Storyboards" check box is selected.

6. Click the Next button. Xcode asks where you want to store the project.

7. Choose a folder to store your project and click the Create button.

8. Click the `Main.storyboard` file in the Project Navigator. Your program's user interface appears.

9. Choose View ➤ Utilities ➤ Show Object Library. The Object Library appears in the bottom right corner of the Xcode window.

10. Drag a push button on to the user interface window and double-click it to change its title to **Color**.

11. Drag a label on to the user interface window and double-click it to change its displayed text to **You chose this color**, as shown in Figure 21-8.

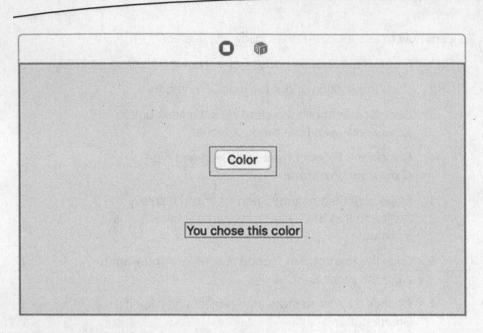

Figure 21-8. The user interface for the ColorPanelProgram

12. Choose View ➤ Assistant Editor ➤ Show Assistant Editor. The `ViewController.swift` file appears next to your user interface.

13. Move the mouse pointer over the label, hold down the Control key, and drag the mouse underneath the last `class ViewController` line in the `ViewController.swift` file.

14. Release the Control key and the mouse button. A pop-up window appears.

15. Click in the Name text field, type **myLabel**, and click the Connect button. Xcode creates an IBOutlet as follows:

```
@IBOutlet weak var myLabel: NSTextField!
```

16. Underneath this IBOutlet type the following code:

```
let colorPanel = NSColorWell()
```

17. Move the mouse pointer over the push button, hold down the Control key, and drag the mouse above the last curly bracket in the bottom of the ViewController.swift file.

18. Release the Control key and the mouse button. A pop-up window appears.

19. Click in the Connect pop-up menu and choose Action.

20. Click in the Name text field and type **chooseColor**.

21. Click in the Type pop-up menu, choose NSButton, and click the Connect button. Xcode creates an empty IBAction method.

22. Modify the IBAction method as follows:

```
@IBAction func chooseColor(_ sender: NSButton) {
    colorPanel.activate(true)
    colorPanel.action = #selector(changeColor(_:))
    }
```

The activate command displays the color panel and the #selector command runs the changeColor function, which you'll need to create.

23. Above this IBAction method, type the following function:

```
override func changeColor(_ sender: Any?) {
    myLabel.textColor = colorPanel.color
    }
```

This changeColor function simply takes whatever color the user chose in the color panel and assigns it to the text of the label.

24. Choose Product ➤ Run. The user interface appears.

25. Click the Color button on your program's user interface. A Color panel appears, as shown in Figure 21-9.

Figure 21-9. The Color panel

26.   Click a color. Notice that each time you click a color, the color of the text in the label changes.

27.   Choose ColorPanelProgram ➤ Quit ColorPanelProgram.

Summary

When designing a standard macOS user interface, you don't have to create everything yourself. By taking advantage of the Cocoa framework, you can create alerts and panels that look and behave like other macOS programs with little extra coding on your own part.

Alerts let you display brief messages to the user, such as warnings. You can customize an alert with text and graphics, and place two or more buttons on the alert. If you place two or more buttons on an alert, you need to write Swift code to identify which button the user clicked.

An alert typically appears as a separate window, but you can also make it appear as a sheet that drops down from a window's title.

Panels display commonly used user interface items such as an Open panel to select a file to open and a Save panel to select a folder and a file name in which to save data. The Open and Save panels are part of the Cocoa framework, but you need to write additional Swift code to make the Open and Save panels actually open or save a file to a hard disk.

The Color panel lets the user select a different color. To retrieve the color the user chose, use the color property of the NSColorWell class.

Alerts and panels let you create standard macOS user interface elements with little additional coding. By using these features of the Cocoa framework, you can create standard macOS programs that work reliably and behave like users expect a macOS program to look and behave.

Chapter 22

Creating Pull-Down Menus

Pull-down menus represent the standard way to interact with a macOS program. While your program may display buttons to represent commands, too many buttons can clutter the screen. To avoid trying to cram multiple buttons on the screen, you can group related commands in multiple pull-down menus. By default, Xcode creates every macOS project with the following pull-down menu titles:

- **File**: Displays commands for opening, saving, creating, and printing

- **Edit**: Displays commands for copying, cutting, pasting, undoing, and redoing commands

- **Format**: Displays commands for modifying text or graphics such as changing fonts

- **View**: Displays commands for changing the way data appears in the window such as zooming in and out or displaying other user interface items such as toolbars

- **Window**: Displays commands for manipulating document windows such as switching between multiple open windows

- **Help**: Displays commands for getting help using a program

© Wallace Wang 2017
W. Wang, *macOS Programming for Absolute Beginners*,
DOI 10.1007/978-1-4842-2662-9_22

Although Xcode can create pull-down menu titles for you, you'll still need to write Swift code to make them actually work. Besides using the standard pull-down menu titles, you can add your own or delete the existing ones. To organize commands within a pull-down menu, you can use horizontal lines to group similar commands together or store them in submenus. For the user's convenience, you can also assign keystroke shortcuts to commands.

Pull-down menus represent a standard way for users to control a program. By creating pull-down menus for your own programs, you can create a familiar user interface so others can learn and use your program quickly with little or no additional training.

Editing Pull-Down Menus

Each time you create a Cocoa Application project, Xcode creates a default pull-down menu that contains common menu titles and commands. Without writing a single line of Swift code, many of these commands already work. For example, the Quit command under the application menu (the name of your program, such as MenuProgram) knows how to quit your program and the Zoom and Minimize commands under the Window menu title know how to zoom and minimize the user interface window.

In most cases, you'll need to customize these pull-down menus by editing existing commands, adding new commands, and deleting existing commands. To modify a program's pull-down menus, you have two options:

- Edit the pull-down menus directly
- Open the Document Outline and edit the menus

To edit pull-down menus directly, click the .xib or .storyboard file in the Project Navigator pane and then click directly on your program's pull-down menus, as shown in Figure 22-1.

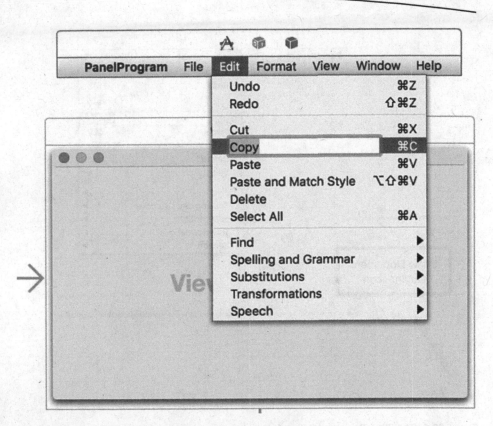

Figure 22-1. *You can click directly on a program's pull-down menus to select individual items*

A second way to edit pull-down menus is to open the Document Outline by clicking the Show Document Outline icon, as shown in Figure 22-2.

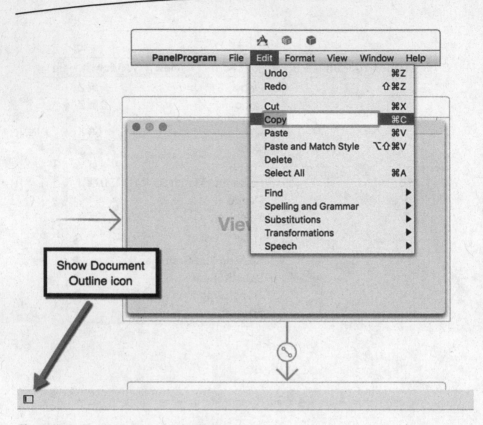

Figure 22-2. *The Show Document Outline icon*

With the Document Outline open, you can click the disclosure triangles to view the different pull-down menus and their commands, as shown in Figure 22-3.

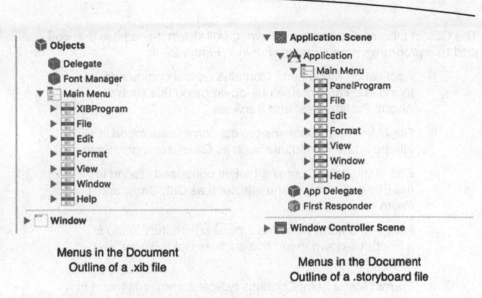

Menus in the Document
Outline of a .xib file

Menus in the Document
Outline of a .storyboard file

Figure 22-3. Viewing menus in the Document Outline pane

To delete a menu item, click it to select it (either by clicking directly on the pull-down menu item or on the menu item in the Document Outline pane) and press the Backspace or Delete key. This lets you delete individual menu items or entire menu titles, such as the File or Edit pull-down menu title.

> **Note** If you delete a menu item or entire pull-down menu title by mistake, just choose Edit ➤ Undo or press Command + Z to recover it right away.

To add items to a program's pull-down menus, you have two choices:

- Add a new menu item to an existing pull-down menu title, such as File or Edit

- Add a new pull-down menu title that lists its own commands

Adding New Pull-Down Menu Titles to the Menu Bar

You can add menu items and pull-down menu titles either directly on the pull-down menu, or inside the Document Outline.

The Object Library displays the following pull-down menu titles that you can add to a program's menu bar, as shown in Figure 22-4:

- Application Menu Item: Contains typical commands found in an application pull-down menu title such as About, Preferences, and Services

- File Menu Item: Contains typical commands found in a File pull-down menu title such as Open, New, and Save

- Edit Menu Item: Contains typical commands found in the Edit pull-down menu title such as Cut, Copy, and Paste

- Font Menu Item: Contains typical commands found in a Font pull-down menu title such as Bold, Bigger, and Copy Style

- Format Menu Item: Contains typical commands found in a Format pull-down menu title such as Font and Text

- Text Menu Item: Contains typical commands found in a Text pull-down menu title such as Center, Writing Direction, and Show Ruler

- Find Menu Item: Contains typical commands found in a Find pull-down menu title such as Find, Find and Replace, and Find Next

- Window Menu Item: Contains typical commands found in a Window pull-down menu title such as Minimize, Bring to Front, and Zoom

- Help Menu Item: Contains typical commands found in a Help pull-down menu title such as Application Help

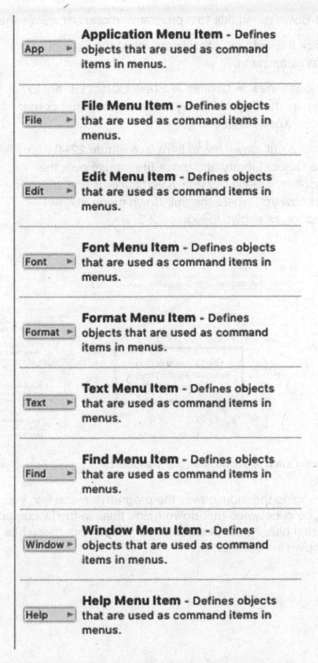

Application Menu Item - Defines objects that are used as command items in menus.

File Menu Item - Defines objects that are used as command items in menus.

Edit Menu Item - Defines objects that are used as command items in menus.

Font Menu Item - Defines objects that are used as command items in menus.

Format Menu Item - Defines objects that are used as command items in menus.

Text Menu Item - Defines objects that are used as command items in menus.

Find Menu Item - Defines objects that are used as command items in menus.

Window Menu Item - Defines objects that are used as command items in menus.

Help Menu Item - Defines objects that are used as command items in menus.

Figure 22-4. The pull-down menu titles you can add to a program's menu bar

To add a pull-down menu title to a program's menu bar, follow these steps:

1. Click the .xib or .storyboard file in the Project Navigator pane.

2. Choose View ➤ Utilities ➤ Show Object Library to display the Object Library in the bottom right corner of the Xcode window.

3. Drag a pull-down menu item (see Figure 22-4) from the Object Library and move the mouse over the program's menu bar until a vertical blue line appears to show you where the pull-down menu title will appear, as shown in Figure 22-5.

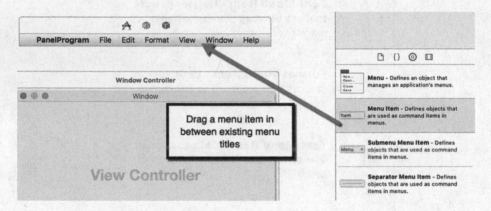

Figure 22-5. Adding a new pull-down menu title to a menu bar

Instead of dragging the mouse over the program's menu bar, you can also drag the mouse in between pull-down menu titles in the Document Outline until a horizontal blue line appears to show where your menu title will appear, as shown in Figure 22-6.

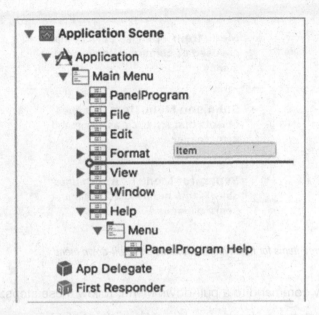

Figure 22-6. Adding a new pull-down menu title to a menu bar using the Document Outline

4.   Release the mouse. Your new pull-down menu title
appears on the menu bar.

To rearrange the pull-down menu titles, move the mouse pointer over the
menu title you wish to move (either on the menu bar or in the Document
Outline), and drag the mouse to move the menu title to a new location.

Adding New Commands to a Pull-Down Menu

You can always delete, rearrange, and add commands on any pull-down
menu. To delete a command, simply select it and press the Backspace or
Delete key. To rearrange a command, drag and drop it to a new location.

To add a new command to a pull-down menu, you need to use the following
three items from the Object Library, as shown in Figure 22-7:

■   Menu Item: Represents a single command

■   Submenu Menu Item: Represents a submenu of
additional commands

■   Separate Menu Item: Displays a horizontal line to
separate commands on a pull-down menu

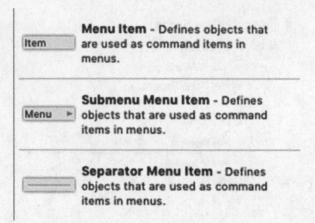

Figure 22-7. *Three items for modifying commands on a pull-down menu*

To add a new command to a pull-down menu, follow these steps:

1. Click the `.xib` or `.storyboard` file in the Project Navigator pane.

2. Choose View ➤ Utilities ➤ Show Object Library to display the Object Library in the bottom right corner of the Xcode window.

3. Click the pull-down menu where you want to add a new command. You can either click directly on the pull-down menu title on the menu bar or click a disclosure triangle to open a pull-down menu title in the Document Outline, as shown in Figure 22-8.

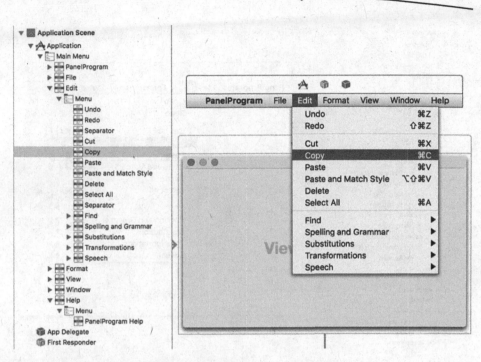

Figure 22-8. *You can add a new command directly on a pull-down menu or through the Document Outline*

4. Drag a menu item (see Figure 22-7) from the Object Library and move the mouse in the pull-down menu list until a horizontal blue line appears to show you where the command will appear, as shown in Figure 22-9.

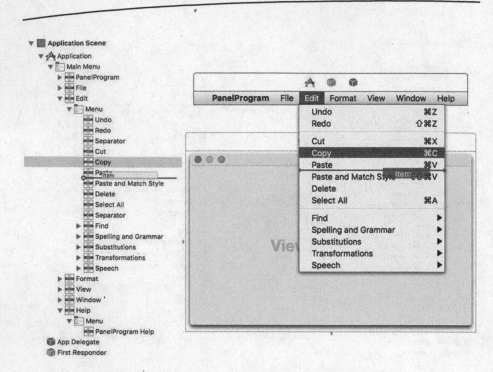

Figure 22-9. Dragging and dropping a new command in a pull-down menu list

5.   Release the mouse. Xcode adds your new menu
      item to the pull-down menu. If you added a submenu
      menu item, you can now edit the commands stored
      on its submenu.

Editing Commands

Once you've modified the pull-down menu titles that appear on a menu bar
and modified the commands that appear on each pull-down menu, you may
want to further edit each individual command using the Inspector pane. The
Inspector pane can be useful to modify the following properties:

- Title: Displays the text of the menu command

- Key Equivalent: Defines a keystroke shortcut for a
  command

To edit a command (or a pull-down menu title), follow these steps:

1. Click the `.xib` or `.storyboard` file in the Project Navigator pane.

2. Click the pull-down menu command (or pull-down menu title) that you want to edit either in the Document Outline or directly on the pull-down menu itself.

3. Choose View ➤ Utilities ➤ Show Attributes Inspector. The Show Attributes Inspector pane appears, as shown in Figure 22-10.

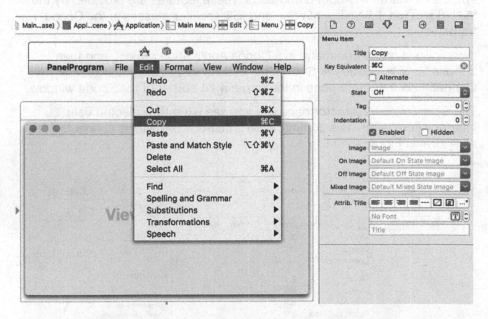

Figure 22-10. Dragging and dropping a new command in a pull-down menu list

4. Click in the Title text field in the Inspector pane to edit the text of the command.

5. Click in the Key Equivalent text field and press (not type) the keystroke shortcut you want to assign to your command. Make sure this keystroke shortcut isn't used by another command (such as Command+X for the Cut command). Xcode displays your keystroke shortcut to the right of the command on the pull-down menu.

Connecting Menu Commands to Swift Code

Once you've modified your pull-down menu titles and filled them with the proper commands, you'll eventually need to make these commands actually do something. This means linking your menu commands to IBAction methods, much like connecting buttons or other user interface items to a file containing Swift code. You can Control-drag from either the menu command on the pull-down menu itself or from the menu command displayed in the Document Outline.

When you create a Cocoa Application project, you'll find that many menu commands already work, such as the File ➤ Print, Window ➤ Minimize, and application name ➤ About commands. These features are provided by the NSApplication, NSWindow, NSView, and NSResponder classes in the Cocoa framework.

If you click a menu command in a Cocoa Application project, and then choose View ➤ Utilities ➤ Show Connections Inspector, you'll see the Connections Inspector pane in the upper right corner of the Xcode window.

The Connections Inspector pane lets you see what the selected user interface item (such as a command on a pull-down menu) is connected to, as shown in Figure 22-11.

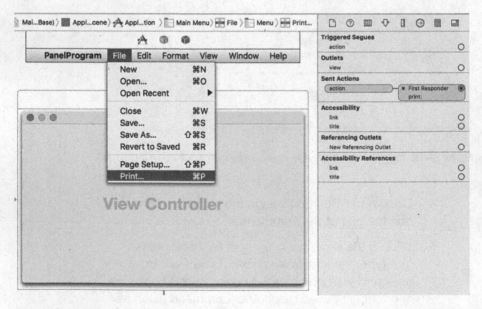

Figure 22-11. The Connections Inspector pane shows what IBAction method a user interface is connected to

In Figure 22-11, the Print menu command on the File menu is connected to the print IBAction method, but this IBAction method isn't stored in a specific file. Instead, it's connected to something called First Responder, which is defined by the NSResponder class.

A user interface consists of several objects based on NSApplication, NSWindow, and NSView so First Responder simply points to the first object that should respond to the user clicking a user interface item (such as the Print command on the File menu). If this first object doesn't have a print IBAction method, then it searches for this IBAction method in the next object.

So if you have a text field on a window and click the Print command on the File menu, the Print command will look for the print IBAction method in the text field (based on NSTextfield, which is based on NSView) first. If it fails to find the print IBAction method in the NSTextfield class, it will look next in the window (based on NSWindow) or the application itself (based on NSApplication).

If you click the First Responder icon and then choose View ➤ Utilities ➤ Show Connections Inspector, you can see the Connections Inspector pane for the First Responder, which identifies all the IBAction methods connected to the default pull-down menus of a typical Cocoa Application project, as shown in Figure 22-12.

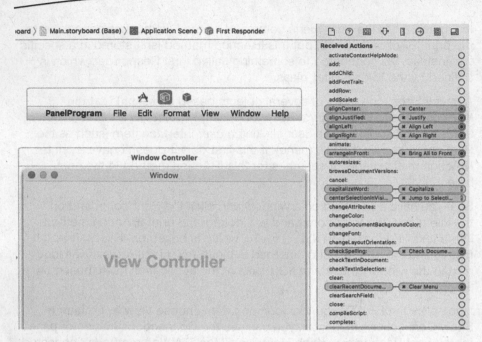

Figure 22-12. *The First Responder Connections Inspector pane lists all the IBAction methods connected to the default pull-down menus of a Cocoa Application project*

> **Note** Another way to view the Connections Inspector is to right-click the First Responder icon, as shown in Figure 22-13.

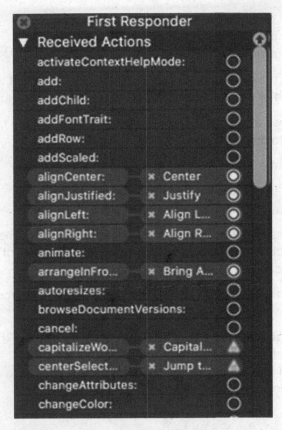

Figure 22-13. Right-clicking the First Responder icon lists all the IBAction methods connected to the default pull-down menus of a Cocoa Application project

Although the Cocoa Application template creates standard pull-down menus and commands, you'll still need to write Swift code to make many of these commands actually work. For example, the Save command doesn't know what to save or how to save it and the New command doesn't know what type of document to create.

To see how menu commands work with IBAction methods like other user interface items with .xib files, follow these steps:

1. From within Xcode choose File ➤ New ➤ Project.

2. Click Application under the macOS category.

3. Click Cocoa Application and click the Next button.
    Xcode now asks for a product name.

4. Click in the Product Name text field and type
    MenuProgram.

5. Make sure the Language pop-up menu displays Swift and that no check boxes are selected. This project will use `.xib` files for its user interface.

6. Click the Next button. Xcode asks where you want to store the project.

7. Choose a folder to store your project and click the Create button.

8. Click the `MainMenu.xib` file in the Project Navigator.

9. Click the Window icon in the Document Outline to display the program's user interface.

10. Choose View ➤ Utilities ➤ Show Object Library. The Object Library appears in the bottom right corner of the Xcode window.

11. Drag a text field on to the user interface window. You may want to widen the width of the text field.

12. Drag a menu item from the Object Library to the bottom of the File menu. You can either drag the menu item on to the File pull-down menu or in the Document Outline, as shown in Figure 22-14.

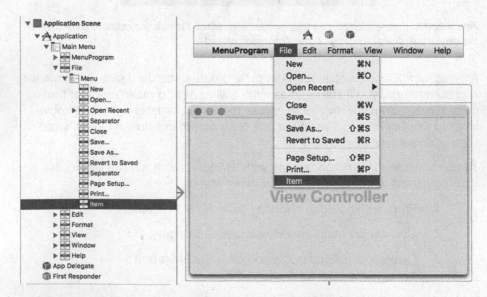

Figure 22-14. Drag a menu item to the bottom of the File pull-down menu

13. Choose View ➤ Assistant Editor ➤ Show Assistant Editor. The `AppDelegate.swift` file appears next to your user interface.

14. Move the mouse pointer over the text field, hold down the Control key, and drag the mouse under the IBOutlet line in the `AppDelegate.swift` file.

15. Release the Control key and the mouse button. A pop-up window appears.

16. Click in the Name text field, type **textResult**, and click the Connect button so your IBOutlet looks like this:

```
@IBOutlet weak var textResult: NSTextField!
```

17. Move the mouse pointer over the menu item you just added to the bottom of the File pull-down menu (either on the pull-down menu or in the Document Outline), hold down the Control key, and drag the mouse above the last curly bracket in the bottom of the `ViewController.swift` file.

18. Release the Control key and the mouse button. A pop-up window appears.

19. Click in the Connection pop-up menu and choose Action.

20. Click in the Name text field and type **myMenu**.

21. Click in the Type pop-up menu, choose NSMenuItem, and click the Connect button. Xcode creates an empty IBAction method.

22. Modify the IBAction method as follows:

```
@IBAction func myMenu(_ sender: NSMenuItem) {
    textResult.stringValue = "Clicked on = " + sender.title
}
```

23. Click the Save command in the File pull-down menu of your program (not on Xcode's File menu).

24. Choose View ➤ Utilities ➤ Show Connections
    Inspector. The Connections Inspector pane
    shows that the Save command is connected to
    the saveDocument IBAction method in the First
    Responder, as shown in Figure 22-15.

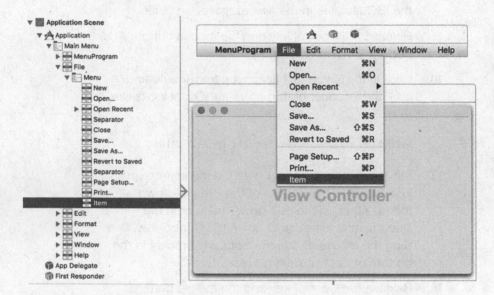

Figure 22-15. The Connections Inspector for the Save command in the File pull-down menu

25. Click the close icon (the X) that appears to the
    left of First Responder. This cuts the connection
    between the Save command and the saveDocument
    IBAction method.

26. Move the mouse pointer over the Save command on
    the File pull-down menu, hold down the Control key,
    and drag the mouse over the myMenu func keyword
    in the IBAction method you created in step 22. Make
    sure Xcode highlights the entire IBAction method and
    displays Connect Action, as shown in Figure 22-16.

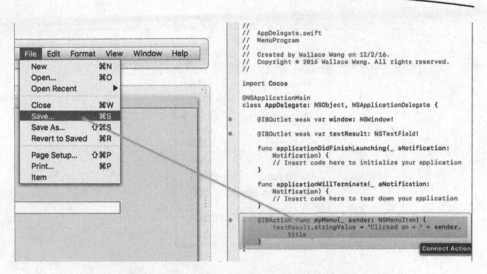

```
//
//  AppDelegate.swift
//  MenuProgram
//
//  Created by Wallace Wang on 12/2/16.
//  Copyright © 2016 Wallace Wang. All rights reserved.
//

import Cocoa

@NSApplicationMain
class AppDelegate: NSObject, NSApplicationDelegate {

    @IBOutlet weak var window: NSWindow!

    @IBOutlet weak var textResult: NSTextField!

    func applicationDidFinishLaunching(_ aNotification:
        Notification) {
        // Insert code here to initialize your application
    }

    func applicationWillTerminate(_ aNotification:
        Notification) {
        // Insert code here to tear down your application
    }

    @IBAction func myMenu(_ sender: NSMenuItem) {
        textResult.stringValue = "Clicked on = " + sender.
            title
    }
}
```

Figure 22-16. Connecting the Save command to an existing IBAction method

27. Release the Control key and the mouse button.
      Xcode connects the Save command to the myMenu
      IBAction method.

28. Choose Product ➤ Run. The user interface appears.

29. Click the File menu title. Notice that your menu item
      (labeled Item) appears at the bottom of the File
      pull-down menu.

30. Click the Save command. The text field displays
      "Clicked on = Save…"

31. Click the File menu title and click Item, which is
      the menu item you added. The text field displays
      "Clicked on = Item".

32. Choose MenuProgram ➤ Quit MenuProgram.

The MenuProgram project shows how to connect a menu command to a
text field so the text field displays the name of the menu command that the
user clicked. However, when working with storyboards, connecting menu
commands works a little differently.

The main difference is that in a storyboard, the pull-down menus are stored
in a separate scene from the actual user interface, as shown in Figure 22-17.

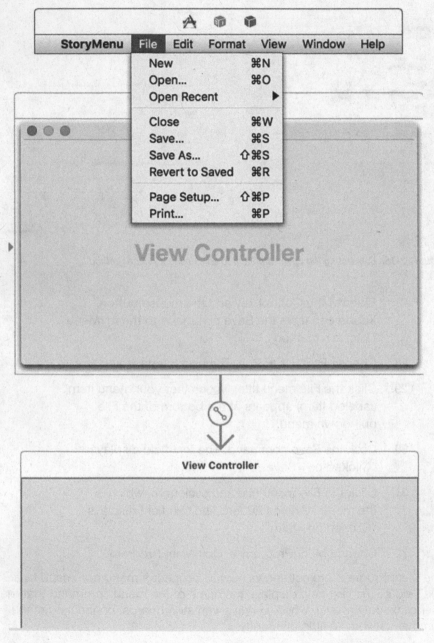

Figure 22-17. Pull-down menus appear in a separate scene from the user interface in a storyboard

This means when you Control-drag on a pull-down menu command, Xcode stores your Swift code in the AppDelegate.swift file, but if you Control-drag on a user interface item such as a text field, Xcode stores your Swift code in the ViewController.swift file.

Essentially this means if you create an IBOutlet for a text field, it's stored in the ViewController.swift file while your IBAction methods for your pull-down menu commands are stored in the AppDelegate.swift file, which means the IBOutlet doesn't know the IBAction methods exist (and vice versa).

The way around this problem is to connect your pull-down menu commands to the First Responder icon. This means that your program will first look for an IBAction method in its AppDelegate.swift file, but then will also look for the same IBAction method in other files as well.

So the trick is to create an empty IBAction method in the AppDelegate. swift file and an identical IBAction method in the ViewController.swift file, except you'll fill this second IBAction method with Swift code to make it retrieve the title of the selected menu command.

To see how menu commands work with storyboards, follow these steps:

1. From within Xcode choose File ➤ New ➤ Project.

2. Click Application under the macOS category.

3. Click Cocoa Application and click the Next button.
    Xcode now asks for a product name.

4. Click in the Product Name text field and type
    StoryMenu.

5. Make sure the Language pop-up menu displays
    Swift and that only the "Use storyboards" check box
    is selected.

6. Click the Next button. Xcode asks where you want to
    store the project.

7. Choose a folder to store your project and click the
    Create button.

8. Click the Main.storyboard file in the Project
    Navigator. Your program's user interface appears.

9. Choose View ➤ Utilities ➤ Show Object Library and
    drag a text field on to the user interface (identified by
    view controller in its title bar). You may want to widen
    the text field width.

10. Choose View ➤ Assistant Editor ➤ Show Assistant Editor. Xcode shows the `ViewController.swift` file next to your user interface.

11. Move the mouse pointer over the text field, hold down the Control key, and drag the mouse under the `class ViewController` line.

12. Release the Control key and the mouse. A pop-up window appears.

13. Click in the Name text field, type **textResult**, and then click the Connect button. Xcode creates the following IBOutlet:

    ```
    @IBOutlet weak var textResult: NSTextField!
    ```

14. Click the File pull-down menu in your program (not the Xcode File menu) to display its entire list. The Assistant Editor should now display the `AppDelegate.swift` file.

15. Drag a menu item from the Object Library to the bottom of the File pull-down menu underneath the Print command.

16. Move the mouse pointer over the new menu item you just added to the bottom of the File pull-down menu, hold down the Control key, and drag the mouse above the last curly bracket at the bottom of the `AppDelegate.swift` file. A pop-up window appears.

17. Click in the Connection pop-up menu and choose Action.

18. Click in the Name text field and type **myMenu**.

19. Click in the Type pop-up menu, choose NSMenuItem, and click the Connect button. Xcode creates an empty IBAction method.

20. Select this empty IBAction method and choose Edit ➤ Copy.

21. Move the mouse pointer over the new Menu Item
     you just added at the bottom of the File menu, hold
     down the Control key, and drag the mouse over the
     First Responder icon, as shown in Figure 22-18.

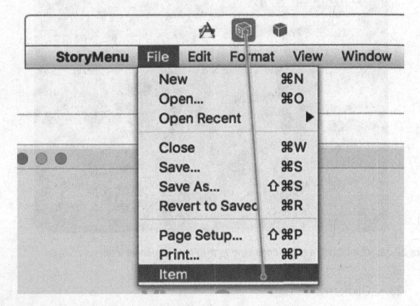

Figure 22-18. Connecting a menu command to the First Responder icon

22. Release the Control key and the mouse. A pop-up
     menu appears, as shown in Figure 22-19.

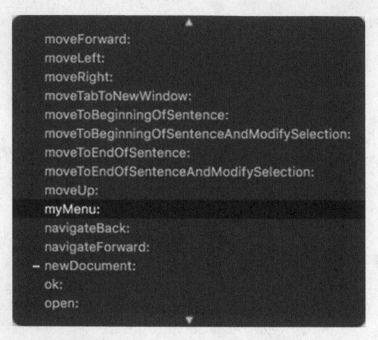

Figure 22-19. Connecting a menu command to the First Responder icon

23. Click myMenu.

24. Move the mouse pointer over the Save command
     in the File pull-down menu in your program (not
     Xcode's File menu).

25. Control-drag from the Save command over the First
     Responder icon.

26. Release the Control key and the mouse. A pop-up
     menu appears (see Figure 22-19).

27. Click myMenu.

28. Choose View ➤ Standard Editor ➤ View Standard
     Editor to display just one file in the Xcode window.

29. Click the ViewController.swift file in the Project
     Navigator pane.

30. Move the cursor above the last curly bracket in
     the ViewController.swift file and choose Edit ➤
     Paste. Xcode pastes your IBAction method from
     step 20.

31. Modify this IBAction method as follows:

```
@IBAction func myMenu(_ sender: NSMenuItem) {
    textResult.stringValue = "Clicked on = " + sender.title
}
```

32. Choose Product ➤ Run. Your user interface appears.

33. Choose File ➤ Save on your StoryMenu menu bar. Notice that the text field displays "Clicked on=Save...".

34. Choose File ➤ Item on your StoryMenu menu bar. Notice that the text field now displays "Clicked on=Item".

35. Choose StoryMenu ➤ Quit StoryMenu.

Summary

When you create a Cocoa Application project, Xcode automatically creates pull-down menus for your program. You can add, delete, or rearrange menu titles on the menu bar or menu commands on the pull-down menus. For the user's convenience, you can even assign keystroke shortcuts to menu commands.

To edit a pull-down menu, you can either edit it directly on the pull-down menu or open the Document Outline. You can Control-drag from either the pull-down menu commands or the Document Outline to connect menu commands to IBAction methods.

When working with .storyboard files, you typically connect menu commands to the First Responder icon. Then you can implement the IBAction method in the correct Swift file to make that menu command work. When working with .xib files, you can directly connect menu commands to IBAction methods.

When Xcode creates pull-down menus for your Cocoa Application, many of those menu commands already know how to work, such as Window ➤ Zoom and File ➤ Close. However, most of the menu commands won't do anything at all until you write Swift code of your own to make them work properly in your particular program.

Menu commands on pull-down menus give you one more way to connect commands to IBAction methods. Since most macOS programs rely on pull-down menus, focus first on organizing your program commands into pull-down menus, then write the Swift code to make each menu command actually work.

Chapter **23**

Programming the Touch Bar

The latest input device for Macintosh computers is the Touch Bar, which appears above the keyboard where the row of function keys used to appear. The Touch Bar displays contextual shortcuts depending on what you're doing at the time. For example, if you're typing, the Touch Bar might display suggested words that you can tap so you don't have to type the entire word out. If you're editing a video, the Touch Bar lets you scroll back and forth through the video.

Because the Touch Bar offers a new way to interact with a Macintosh, all macOS programs will need to know how to display information on the Touch Bar. The main key to programming for the Touch Bar is to realize that not every Macintosh has a Touch Bar. This means you cannot display any crucial information or commands on the Touch Bar that can't also be viewed on the screen at the same time.

A second key feature of the Touch Bar is to display shortcuts to commands the user will most likely need at that particular time. If you're editing text, the Touch Bar should display text formatting shortcuts such as Bold, Italic, and Underline commands. If you're editing graphics, the Touch Bar should change and display graphics editing shortcuts such as a button to choose different colors or change the size of a drawing tool.

© Wallace Wang 2017
W. Wang, *macOS Programming for Absolute Beginners*,
DOI 10.1007/978-1-4842-2662-9_23

The key to the Touch Bar is making it adapt to the user. When adding Touch Bar shortcuts to your own macOS program, you need to

- Add a Touch Bar to a window in your program's user interface

- Add buttons on your Touch Bar

- Create a Swift file to control the window that contains the Touch Bar

- Connect Touch Bar buttons to IBAction methods in your Swift file to make them do something

> **Note** Even if your Macintosh does not come with a Touch Bar, you can use the Touch Bar simulator. To use the Touch Bar simulator, you must have Xcode 8.1 and higher and macOS Sierra 10.12.1 or higher.

Adding a Touch Bar

The Touch Bar is just another item in the Object Library that you can drag on to your window. If you open the Object Library and type **touch** in the search field, you can easily find the Touch Bar and all of the items you can add to it, such as a button or a label (see Figure 23-1).

Figure 23-1. The Object Library contains everything you can add to a Touch Bar

The first step to adding a Touch Bar to your program is to drag the Touch Bar item over the window controller (not the view controller), as shown in Figure 23-2.

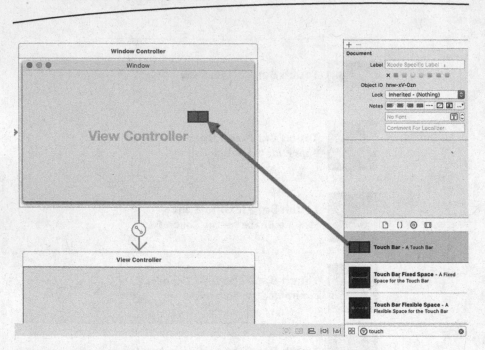

Figure 23-2. Dragging the Touch Bar from the Object Library to a window controller

As soon as you place the Touch Bar over the window controller, it appears underneath, as shown in Figure 23-3. Now you need to create a Swift class file to contain the Swift code to make the Touch Bar work.

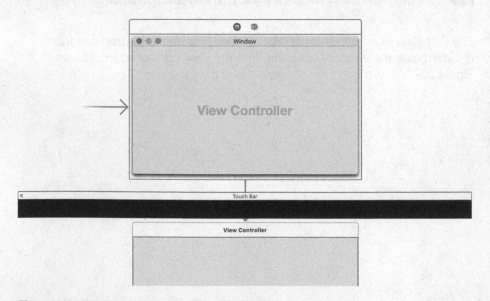

Figure 23-3. The Touch Bar as part of the user interface

Creating a Swift Class File

At this point, the Touch Bar is connected to the window of your user interface, but you can't write any Swift code to make it work because there is no class file yet defined for the window controller.

To create a Swift class file, you need to follow these steps:

1. Choose File ➤ New ➤ File. A template window appears, as shown in Figure 23-4.

Figure 23-4. Choosing a Swift Cocoa Class file

2. Click Cocoa Class under the Source group in the macOS category.

3. Click the Next button. A dialog appears asking for a class name and subclass, as shown in Figure 23-5.

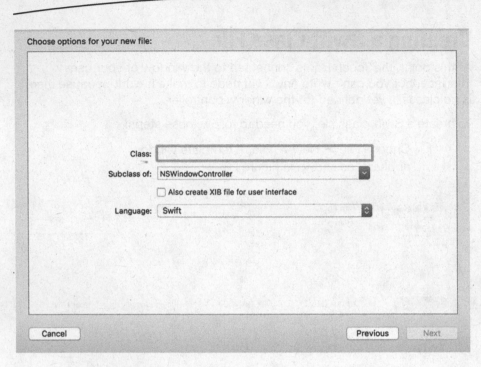

Choose options for your new file:

Class: [   ]

Subclass of: NSWindowController

☐ Also create XIB file for user interface

Language: Swift

Cancel   Previous   Next

Figure 23-5. Defining a class

4. Click in the Class text field and type a name for your class, such as **TouchClass**.

5. Make sure the "Subclass of" field displays NSWindowController.

6. Clear the "Also create XIB file for user interface" check box.

7. Make sure the Language pop-up menu displays Swift.

8. Click the Next button. A Save dialog appears.

9. Click the Create button. The Xcode window appears again.

Once you've created a class file, you need to connect it to the window controller. To connect a class file to the window controller, follow these steps:

1. Click the .storyboard file that contains the window controller and touch bar.

2. Click the blue Window Controller icon in the top, middle of the window.

3. Choose View ➤ Utilities ➤ Show Identity Inspector.

4. Click the downward-pointing arrow to the right of the Class field. You'll see a menu of valid class files you can choose, as shown in Figure 23-6.

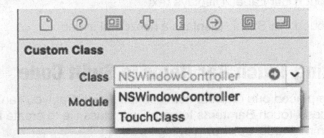

Figure 23-6. Choosing a class file for the window controller

5. Click the class name you created (such as TouchClass).

At this point, your Swift class file is connected to the window controller and the Touch Bar. Now you can add items to the Touch Bar and create IBOutlets and IBAction methods for the Touch Bar in the class file you just chose.

Adding Items to the Touch Bar

The Object Library contains all of the items you can add to the Touch Bar. You can only place Touch Bar items on the Touch Bar, not ordinary buttons or labels. To place an item on the Touch Bar, just drag and drop any Touch Bar item from the Object Library on to the Touch Bar, as shown in Figure 23-7.

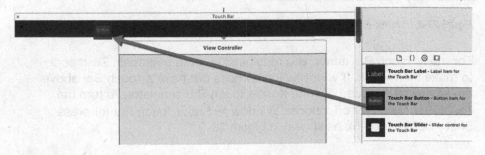

Figure 23-7. Dragging an item from the Object Library to the Touch Bar

Some commonly used items to use on the Touch Bar include

- Touch Bar Button: Displays a single button

- Touch Bar Fixed/Flexible Space: Creates space between multiple Touch Bar items

- Touch Bar Label: Displays text

- Touch Bar Slider: Displays a horizontal slider

Connecting Touch Bar Items to Swift Code

Once you've placed one or more items on the Touch Bar, you can Control-drag from these Touch Bar items to your Swift class file to create IBOutlets and IBAction methods, as shown in Figure 23-8.

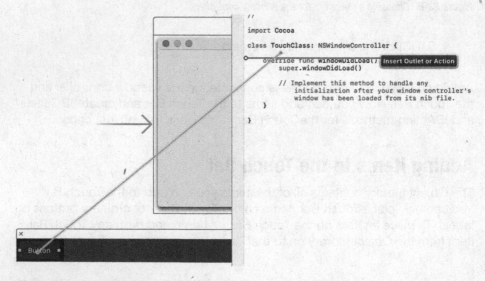

Figure 23-8. Control-dragging from the Touch Bar to a Swift class file

For many Touch Bar items, you may need to write additional Swift code to make them work. If your Macintosh does not have a Touch Bar above the keyboard, you can use the Xcode Touch Bar simulator. To turn the Touch Bar simulator on, choose Window ➤ Show Touch Bar (or press Shift + Command + 5), as shown in Figure 23-9.

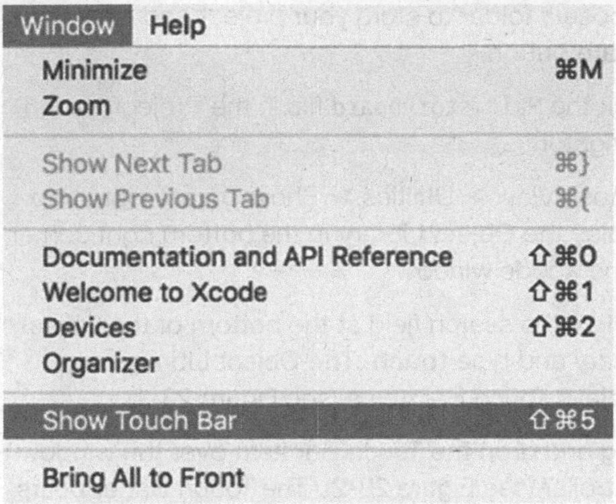

Window	Help	
Minimize		⌘M
Zoom		
Show Next Tab		⌘}
Show Previous Tab		⌘{
Documentation and API Reference		⇧⌘0
Welcome to Xcode		⇧⌘1
Devices		⇧⌘2
Organizer		
Show Touch Bar		⇧⌘5
Bring All to Front		

Figure 23-9. The Show Touch Bar command appears on Xcode's Window menu

If your Macintosh does not have a Touch Bar, you need to run your program, switch to Xcode, choose Window ➤ Show Touch Bar, and then switch back to your running program to see your program's simulated Touch Bar on the screen.

Creating a Touch Bar Program

To create a sample Touch Bar program and see how the Touch Bar simulator works, follow these steps:

1. From within Xcode choose File ➤ New ➤ Project.

2. Click Application under the macOS category.

3. Click Cocoa Application and click the Next button. Xcode now asks for a product name.

4. Click in the Product Name text field and type **TouchProgram**.

5. Make sure the Language pop-up menu displays Swift and that the "Use Storyboards" check box is selected.

6. Click the Next button. Xcode asks where you want to store the project.

7. Choose a folder to store your project and click the Create button.

8. Click the `Main.storyboard` file in the Project Navigator.

9. Choose View ➤ Utilities ➤ Show Object Library to display the Object Library in the bottom right corner of the Xcode window.

10. Click in the search field at the bottom of the Object Library and type **touch**. The Object Library only displays Touch Bar items (see Figure 23-1).

11. Drag and drop the Touch Bar item over the window controller (see Figure 23-2). The Touch Bar appears underneath the window controller.

12. Drag a Touch Bar button, Touch Bar color picker, and Touch Bar slider on to the Touch Bar, as shown in Figure 23-10.

Figure 23-10. The Touch Bar with a button, color picker, and slider

13. Choose File ➤ New ➤ File. A template dialog appears (see Figure 23-4).

14. Click Cocoa Class in the Source group under the macOS category and click the Next button. A dialog appears asking for a class name and subclass (see Figure 23-5).

15. Click in the Class text field and type **TouchClass**.

16. Clear the "Also create XIB file for user interface" check box.

17. Make sure the "Subclass of" field contains NSWindowController and the Language pop-up menu displays Swift.

18. Click the Next button. A Save dialog appears.

19. Click the Create button. The Xcode window appears again.

20. Click the Main.storyboard file in the Navigator pane.

21. Click the blue Window Controller icon in the top,
middle of the window, as shown in Figure 23-11.

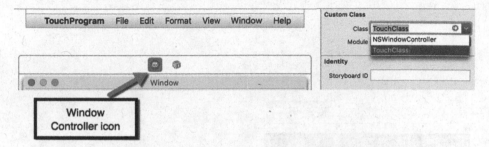

Figure 23-11. Clicking the blue Window Controller icon selects that window controller

22. Choose View ➤ Utilities ➤ Show Identity Inspector.

23. Click the downward-pointing arrow to the right of the
Class field. See the menu of valid class files you can
choose (see Figure 23-6).

24. Choose TouchClass.

25. Choose View ➤ Assistant Editor ➤ Show Assistant
Editor. The Touch Bar appears in the left half and the
TouchClass.swift file appears in the right half of the
middle pane of Xcode.

26. Move the mouse pointer over the Touch Bar button.

27. Hold down the Control key and drag the mouse from
the Touch Bar button to under the class TouchClass
line, as shown in Figure 23-12.

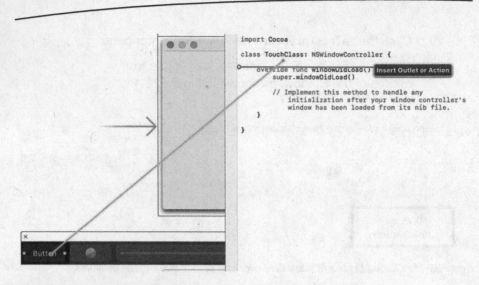

Figure 23-12. Control-dragging from the Touch Bar to the Swift class file

28.   Release the Control key and the left mouse button.
      A pop-up window appears.

29.   Click in the Name text field and type **touchButton**
      and then click the Connect button. This creates an
      IBOutlet to the Touch Bar button:

      ```
      @IBOutlet weak var touchButton: NSButton!
      ```

30.   Move the mouse pointer over the Touch Bar color
      picker icon.

31.   Hold down the Control key and drag the mouse from
      the Touch Bar button to under the class TouchClass
      line.

32.   Click in the Name text field and type **colorIcon**
      and then click the Connect button. This creates an
      IBOutlet to the Touch Bar color picker:

      ```
      @IBOutlet weak var colorIcon: NSColorPickerTouchBarItem!
      ```

33.   Add the following line above the class TouchClass line:

      ```
      @available(OSX 10.12.1, *)
      class TouchClass: NSWindowController {
      ```

This line of Swift code means your program can only run on Macintosh computers that have macOS 10.12.1 or greater installed.

34. Move the mouse pointer over the Touch Bar color picker slider.

35. Hold down the Control key and drag the mouse from the Touch Bar button to under the `class TouchClass` line.

36. Click in the Name text field and type **touchSlider** and then click the Connect button. This creates an IBOutlet to the Touch Bar color picker:

```
@IBOutlet weak var touchSlider: NSSliderAccessory!
```

37. Add the following line above the `class TouchClass` line as shown below:

```
@available(OSX 10.12.2, *)
```

At this point, you've created a Touch Bar and added items to it. You've also created IBOutlets that represent each Touch Bar item. Now the final step is to write Swift code to make each of these Touch Bar items work.

To write Swift code for your Touch Bar items, follow these steps:

1. Move the mouse pointer over the Touch Bar button.

2. Hold down the Control key and drag the mouse from the Touch Bar button to above the last curly bracket in the `TouchClass.swift` file.

3. Release the Control key and the left mouse button. A pop-up window appears.

4. Click in the Connection pop-up menu and choose Action.

5. Click in the Name text field and type **buttonClicked**.

6. Click in the Type pop-up menu and choose NSButton. Then click the Connect button to create an IBAction method.

7. Move the mouse pointer over the Touch Bar color picker icon.

8. Hold down the Control key and drag the mouse from the Touch Bar button to above the last curly bracket in the `TouchClass.swift` file.

9. Release the Control key and the left mouse button. A pop-up window appears.

10. Click in the Connection pop-up menu and choose Action.

11. Click in the Name text field and type **colorPicked**.

12. Click in the Type pop-up menu and choose NSColorPickertouchBarItem, as shown in Figure 23-13.

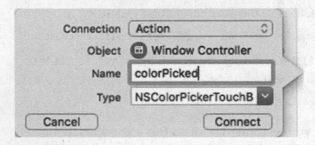

Figure 23-13. Creating an IBAction method for the color picker icon

13. Click the Connect button to create an IBAction method.

14. Click the Show Document Outline icon to display all the parts of your user interface. The Document Outline makes it easy to select the right Touch Bar item. The Touch Bar slider consists of a slider and a horizontal slider. If you click the slider on the Touch Bar directly, you may accidentally select the horizontal slider instead of the slider.

15. Move the mouse pointer over the Slider icon.

16. Hold down the Control key and drag the mouse from the touch bar button to above the last curly bracket in the TouchClass.swift file, as shown in Figure 23-14.

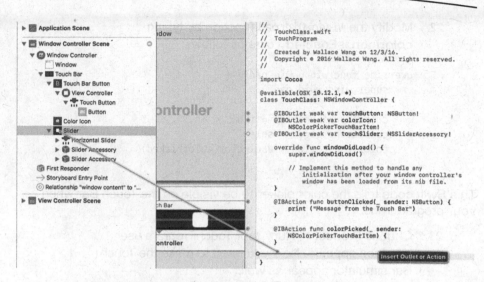

Figure 23-14. Dragging from the Document Outline

17. Release the Control key and the left mouse button. A pop-up window appears.

18. Click in the Connection pop-up menu and choose Action.

19. Click in the Name text field and type **sliderChanged**.

20. Click in the Type pop-up menu and choose NSSliderTouchBarItem. Then click the Connect button.

21. Modify the three IBAction methods as follows:

```
@IBAction func buttonClicked(_ sender: NSButton) {
    print ("Message from the Touch Bar")
    }

@IBAction func colorPicked(_ sender: NSColorPickerTouchBarItem) {
    print ("\(colorIcon.color.cgColor)")
}

@IBAction func sliderChanged(_ sender: NSSliderTouchBarItem) {
    print ("Slider value = \(sender.slider.intValue)")
}
```

22.   Modify the `windowDidLoad` function by typing **colorIcon.isEnabled=true** as follows:

```
override func windowDidLoad() {
    super.windowDidLoad()

    colorIcon.isEnabled = true
    colorIcon.target = self
    colorIcon.action = #selector(colorPicked)
    }
```

This Swift code tells the color picker to be visible on the Touch Bar when your program runs.

23.   Choose Product ➤ Run. Your TouchProgram user interface appears. Now you need to make the Touch Bar simulator appear as well.

24.   Click the Xcode icon on the Dock to switch back to Xcode.

25.   Choose Window ➤ Show Touch Bar (or press Shift + Command + 5). The Touch Bar simulator appears.

26.   Click the Touch Program icon on the Dock to switch back to your TouchProgram. Notice that the Touch Bar simulator now appears and displays the button, color picker, and slider that you added (see Figure 23-15).

Figure 23-15. Displaying the Touch Bar simulator

27.   Click the button on the left of the Touch Bar. The text "Message from the Touch Bar" appears in the debug area at the bottom of the Xcode window.

28.   Drag the slider back and forth. The debug area displays "Slider value = ", followed by a numeric value.

29.   Click the color picker icon in-between the button and the slider on the Touch Bar. The Touch Bar now displays a range of colors, as shown in Figure 23-16.

Figure 23-16. The color picker displays colors to select on the Touch Bar

30. Click any color. Notice that the debug area displays
the name of the color you chose (see Figure 23-17).

```
Message from the Touch Bar
Slider value = 39
Slider value = 71
<CGColor 0x6080000a0ae0> [<CGColorSpace 0x6080000217c0>
(kCGColorSpaceICCBased; kCGColorSpaceModelRGB; Generic RGB
Profile)] ( 1 1 0 1 )
```

All Output ⟳   🔻 Filter   🗑 | ▢▢

Figure 23-17. The debug area of Xcode displays messages from the Touch Bar

31. Click the X in the circle on the left of the Touch Bar
to display the button, color picker, and slider on the
Touch Bar once more.

32. Choose TouchProgram ➤ Quit TouchProgram.

Summary

Until all Macintosh computers come with a Touch Bar, the Touch Bar will
be an optional way for users to interact with a macOS program. Eventually,
every Macintosh will come with a Touch Bar but until then, you'll need to
add the following line of code to make sure Touch Bar programs don't run
on any Macintosh unless it's running macOS 10.12.2 or higher:

```
@available(OSX 10.12.2, *)
```

To create a Touch Bar, you just need to drag a Touch Bar item from the
Object Library on to your window controller (not the view controller). Then
you need to create a Swift class file to hold the IBOutlets and IBAction
methods from any items you place on the Touch Bar, such as buttons,
sliders, or labels. Once you've created a Swift class file, you must define that
class file to work with your window controller by using the Identity Inspector.

To make the Touch Bar simulator appear on a Macintosh without a Touch Bar, you must run your program, switch back to Xcode, and then choose Window > Show Touch Bar. Then you need to switch back to your running program to see the Touch Bar actually working.

The Touch Bar will become a standard input device of the Macintosh so expect to see Apple add new items you can add to the Touch Bar. As more people get comfortable using the Touch Bar, you can be certain every macOS program will need to add Touch Bar support.

Chapter 24

Protocol-Oriented Programming

When Apple introduced Swift during its Worldwide Developer's conference in 2014, it was promoted as an easier, safer, and faster programming language for iOS, macOS, tvOS, and watchOS development than Objective-C. While both Swift and Objective-C allow object-oriented programming, Swift goes one step further and offers protocol-oriented programming as well.

One of the biggest problems with pure object-oriented programming languages is that extending the capabilities of a class means creating additional subclasses. Then you have to create objects based on those new subclasses. This can be a clumsy solution since you now have to keep track of one or more subclasses where each subclass has a different name and may only offer only minor differences between them.

Even worse, Swift (unlike some object-oriented programming languages) only allows single inheritance. This means a class can only inherit from exactly one other class. If you'd really like to inherit properties and methods from two different classes, you can't.

To get around this problem of inheritance and multiple subclasses, Swift offers protocols. Protocols work much like object-oriented programming but with some additional advantages:

- Protocols can extend features of classes, structs, and enums. Inheritance can only extend features of classes.

- A single class, struct, or enum can be extended by one or more protocols. Inheritance can only extend a single class.

© Wallace Wang 2017
W. Wang, *macOS Programming for Absolute Beginners*,
DOI 10.1007/978-1-4842-2662-9_24

This means that protocols are more flexible and versatile than classes, while giving you the advantages of object-oriented programming without its disadvantages. Instead of using classes (object-oriented programming), you can use protocols (protocol-oriented programming), or mix both object-oriented programming and protocol-oriented programming to get the best of both worlds.

Understanding Protocols

Like a class, a protocol can define properties (variables) and methods (functions). The main difference is that unlike a class, a protocol can't set an initial value for a property and can't implement a method. A protocol simply defines a property and its data type. When defining a property in a protocol, you need to define the following three items:

- The property name, which can be any arbitrary, descriptive name

- The data type of the property such as Int, Double, String, etc.

- Whether a property is gettable { get } or gettable and settable { get set }

> **Note**   A gettable/settable { get set } property cannot be assigned to a constant stored property (defined with the let keyword) or a read-only computed property. A gettable { get } property has no such limitations.

Consider the following protocol:

```
protocol Cat {
    var name: String { get set }
    var age: Int { get }
}
```

Now you can create a structure based on this protocol, such as

```
struct pet : Cat {
    var name : String
    //let name : String -- Invalid since "let" defines a constant stored
    property
    //var name : String { return "Fred" } -- Invalid since this is a read-
    only computed property
    let age : Int
}
```

The above code defines a structure called pet that adopts the Cat protocol. This means it needs to declare the name property as a string and the age property as an integer.

Notice that because the age property is defined as gettable { get } by the Cat protocol, you can implement that property as a constant with the let keyword. You could also compute the age property by returning a value like this:

```
struct pet : Cat {
    var name : String
    var age : Int { return 4 }
}
```

To see how to use protocols and structures with different types of properties, follow these steps:

1. From within Xcode choose File > New > Playground. Xcode now asks for a playground name.

2. Click in the Name text field and type **ProtocolPlayground**.

3. Make sure the Platform pop-up menu displays macOS.

4. Click the Next button. Xcode asks where you want to store the playground.

5. Choose a folder to store your project and click the Create button.

6. Edit the playground code as follows:

```
import Cocoa

protocol Cat {
    var name: String { get set }
    var age: Int { get }
}

// Using a computed property
struct pet : Cat {
    var name : String
    var age : Int { return 4 }
}

var animal = pet(name: "Taffy")
print (animal.name)
print (animal.age)
```

```
// Using a constant stored property with "let"
struct feral : Cat {
    var name : String
    let age : Int
}

var pest = feral (name: "Stinky", age: 2)
print (pest.name)
print (pest.age)
```

Notice the differences when you declare a variable based on a structure. With computed properties for age, you don't need to create an initial value when declaring the variable, such as

```
// Using a computed property { return 4 }
struct pet : Cat {
    var name : String
    var age : Int { return 4 }
}
var animal = pet(name: "Taffy")
```

However, if you don't have computed properties, then you must specifically initialize it when creating a variable, such as

```
// Using a constant stored property with "let"
struct feral : Cat {
    var name : String
    let age : Int
}
var pest = feral (name: "Stinky", age: 2)
```

Figure 24-1 shows how you can define two structures based on the same protocol.

```
import Cocoa

protocol Cat {
    var name: String { get set }
    var age: Int { get }
}

// Using a computed property
struct pet : Cat {
    var name : String
    var age : Int { return 4 }                          4
}

var animal = pet(name: "Taffy")                         pet
print (animal.name)                                     "Taffy\n"
print (animal.age)                                      "4\n"


// Using a constant stored property with "let"
struct feral : Cat {
    var name : String
    let age : Int
}

var pest = feral (name: "Stinky", age: 2)               feral
print (pest.name)                                       "Stinky\n"
print (pest.age)                                        "2\n"
```

Figure 24-1. Two different structures can adopt the same protocol

Using Methods in Protocols

When a protocol defines a method, it only defines the method name, any parameters, and any data type it returns, but it does not include any Swift code that actually implements that method, such as

```
protocol Cat {
    var name: String { get set }
    var age: Int { get }
    func meow (sound: String)
}
```

If a class, struct, or enum adopts this Cat protocol, it must not only define a name and age property, but it must also implement the protocol method with Swift code such as

```
struct pet : Cat {
    var name : String
    var age : Int
```

```
    func meow (sound : String) {
    print (sound)
    }
}
```

Even though a class, structure, or enum might adopt the exact same
protocol, the actual implementation of a method can be wildly different. In
the above example, the pet structure defines the meow function with a single
print statement. In the example below, the feral structure defines the meow
function with two print statements:

```
struct feral : Cat {
    var name : String
    var age : Int
    func meow (sound : String) {
        print ("Hear me roar")
        print (sound.uppercased())
    }
}
```

To see how to define methods in protocols and implement them in different
structures, follow these steps:

1. Make sure the ProtocolPlayground file is loaded in
    Xcode.

2. Edit the playground code as follows:

    ```
    import Cocoa

    protocol Cat {
        var name: String { get set }
        var age: Int { get }
        func meow (sound : String)
    }

    // One way to implement the meow method
    struct pet : Cat {
        var name : String
        var age : Int
        func meow (sound : String) {
            print (sound)
        }
    }

    var animal = pet(name: "Taffy", age: 16)
    print (animal.name)
    print (animal.age)
    animal.meow(sound: "Feed me")
    ```

```
        // A second way to implement the same meow method
        struct feral : Cat {
            var name : String
            var age : Int
            func meow (sound : String) {
                print ("Hear me roar")
                print (sound.uppercased())
            }
        }

        var pest = feral(name: "Stinky", age: 2)
        print (pest.name)
        print(pest.age)
        pest.meow(sound: "Growl")
```

Figure 24-2 shows how the two different implementations of the same protocol method work.

```
import Cocoa

protocol Cat {
    var name: String { get set }
    var age: Int { get }
    func meow (sound : String)
}

// One way to implement the meow method
struct pet : Cat {
    var name : String
    var age : Int
    func meow (sound : String) {
        print (sound)                           "Feed me\n"
    }
}

var animal = pet(name: "Taffy", age: 16)        pet
print (animal.name)                             "Taffy\n"
print (animal.age)                              "16\n"
animal.meow(sound: "Feed me")                   pet

// A second way to implement the same meow method
struct feral : Cat {
    var name : String
    var age : Int
    func meow (sound : String) {
        print ("Hear me roar")                  "Hear me roar\n"
        print (sound.uppercased())              "GROWL\n"
    }
}

var pest = feral(name: "Stinky", age: 2)        feral
print (pest.name)                               "Stinky\n"
print(pest.age)                                 "2\n"
pest.meow(sound: "Growl")                       feral
```

Figure 24-2. Method implementations can be different despite adopting the same protocol

Adopting Multiple Protocols

One huge advantage protocols have over object-oriented programming is that a single class, structure, or enum can adopt two or more protocols. To do this, you just need to specify the name of each protocol to adopt, like so:

```
struct structureName : protocolName1, protocolName2, protocolNameN {
```

By letting you adopt multiple protocols, Swift makes coding more flexible since you can pick and choose the protocols you want to use. To see how adopting multiple protocols works, follow these steps:

1. Make sure the ProtocolPlayground file is loaded in Xcode.

2. Edit the playground code as follows:

```
import Cocoa

protocol Cat {
    var name: String { get }
    var age: Int { get }
}

protocol CatSounds {
    func meow (sound : String)
}

struct pet : Cat, CatSounds {
    var name : String
    var age : Int
    func meow (sound : String) {
        print (sound)
    }
}
var animal = pet(name: "Fluffy", age: 6)
print (animal.name)
print (animal.age)
animal.meow(sound : "Wake up!")
```

Figure 24-3 shows how this code works by having a structure adopt two protocols. Notice that this code works exactly the same as if the name and age properties were defined in the same protocol as the meow method. By separating different properties and methods in two or more protocols, you don't have to implement properties and/or methods you don't need.

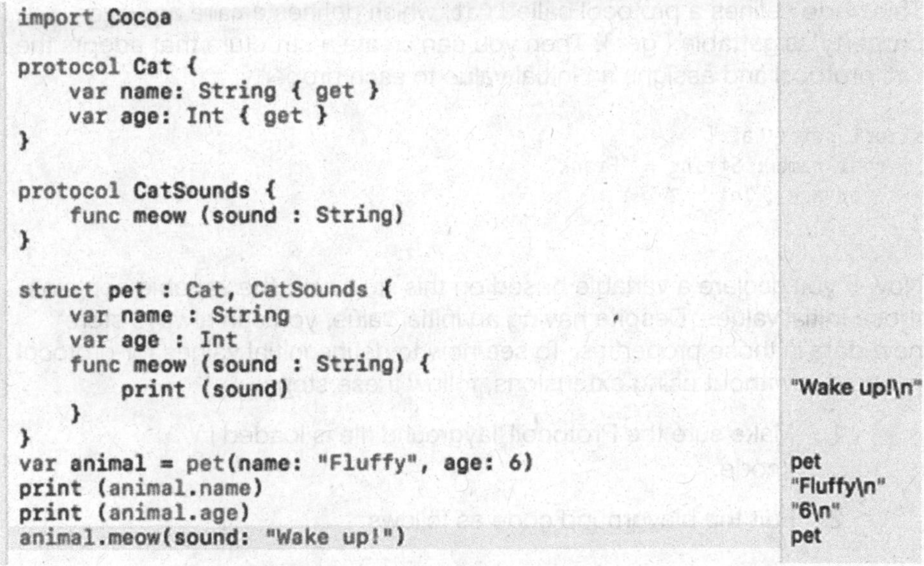

```
import Cocoa

protocol Cat {
    var name: String { get }
    var age: Int { get }
}

protocol CatSounds {
    func meow (sound : String)
}

struct pet : Cat, CatSounds {
    var name : String
    var age : Int
    func meow (sound : String) {
        print (sound)                              "Wake up!\n"
    }
}
var animal = pet(name: "Fluffy", age: 6)           pet
print (animal.name)                                "Fluffy\n"
print (animal.age)                                 "6\n"
animal.meow(sound: "Wake up!")                     pet
```

Figure 24-3. A structure can adopt two or more protocols

Since you can adopt multiple protocols, it's generally best to keep each protocol as short and simple as possible. This makes it easier to use only the protocols you need without being forced to implement additional properties and/or methods you may not need or want.

Protocol Extensions

In the world of object-oriented programming, you can extend a class through inheritance, which inherits every property and method that class may have inherited from other classes. In the world of protocol-oriented programming, you can extend a protocol through protocol extensions.

One purpose for protocol extensions is to define default values for properties. You could define default values by simply assigning values to one or more properties, such as

```
protocol Cat {
    var name: String { get }
    var age: Int { get }
}
```

This code defines a protocol called Cat, which defines a name and age property as gettable { get }. Then you can create a structure that adopts the Cat protocol and assigns an initial value to each property:

```
struct pet : Cat {
    var name : String = "Frank"
    var age : Int = 2
}
```

Now if you declare a variable based on this structure, the variable contains those initial values. Despite having an initial value, you can always store new data in those properties. To see how to define initial values for protocol properties without using extensions, follow these steps:

1. Make sure the ProtocolPlayground file is loaded in Xcode.

2. Edit the playground code as follows:

   ```
   import Cocoa

   protocol Cat {
       var name: String { get }
       var age: Int { get }
   }

   struct pet : Cat {
       var name : String = "Frank"
       var age : Int = 2
   }

   var animal = pet()
   print (animal.name)
   print (animal.age)

   animal.name = "Joey"
   animal.age = 13
   print (animal.name)
   print (animal.age)
   ```

When you first create the animal variable based on the pet structure, the initial name property value is "Frank" and the initial age property value is 2. At any time, you can store a new value in both properties, as shown in Figure 24-4.

```
import Cocoa

protocol Cat {
    var name: String { get }
    var age: Int { get }
}

struct pet : Cat {
    var name : String = "Frank"
    var age : Int = 2
}

var animal = pet()                          pet
print (animal.name)                         "Frank\n"
print (animal.age)                          "2\n"

animal.name = "Joey"                        pet
animal.age = 13                             pet
print (animal.name)                         "Joey\n"
print (animal.age)                          "13\n"
```

Figure 24-4. You can assign initial values to gettable properties defined by a protocol

If you want to set (and keep) an initial value for a property, that's when you can use protocol extensions. Protocol extensions can only work for gettable { get } properties. A protocol extension just uses the extension keyword followed by the name of the protocol you want to extend, such as

```
extension Cat {
    // Set one or more default values for gettable properties here
}
```

Inside the extension you can compute a default value for one or more gettable properties by using the return keyword, such as

```
extension Cat {
    var name : String { return "Frank" }
}
```

Not only does the protocol extension define the name property to hold the string "Frank" but it also eliminates the need to define the name property within a class, structure, or enum, such as

```
extension Cat {
    var name : String { return "Frank" }
}

struct pet : Cat {
    var age : Int = 2
}
```

The above protocol extension and structure is essentially equivalent to this:

```
struct pet : Cat {
    var name : String = "Frank"
    var age : Int = 2
}
```

The main difference is that when the name property is declared inside the structure, you can assign new strings to the name property later. When the name property is declared and set to a value inside a protocol extension, you cannot assign a new string to the name property later. To see how protocol extensions define a default value, follow these steps:

1. Make sure the ProtocolPlayground file is loaded in Xcode.

2. Edit the playground code as follows:

```
import Cocoa


protocol Cat {
    var name: String { get }
    var age: Int { get }
}

extension Cat {
    var name : String { return "Frank" }
}

struct pet : Cat {
    //var name : String = "Frank"
    var age : Int = 2
}

var animal = pet()
print (animal.name)
print (animal.age)

//animal.name = "Joey"
animal.age = 13
print (animal.name)
print (animal.age)
```

In the above code, the two commented lines show you what the protocol extension eliminates. Once you define the name property inside the protocol extension, you no longer need to declare that name property inside the pet structure. You also can't assign a new string (such as "Joey") to the name property after it's been assigned a default value in the protocol extension. Figure 24-5 shows the results of the above code.

```
import Cocoa

protocol Cat {
    var name: String { get }
    var age: Int { get }
}

extension Cat {
    var name : String { return "Frank" }              (2 times)
}

struct pet : Cat {
    //var name : String = "Frank"
    var age : Int = 2
}

var animal = pet()                                    pet
print (animal.name)                                   "Frank\n"
print (animal.age)                                    "2\n"

//animal.name = "Joey"
animal.age = 13                                       pet
print (animal.name)                                   "Frank\n"
print (animal.age)                                    "13\n"
```

Figure 24-5. Defining a default value with a protocol extension

One problem with defining a default value in a protocol extension is that anything that adopts that protocol is forced to also adopt that protocol's extension. This means everything based on that protocol and extension will have the same default value that can't be changed.

If you want the flexibility of defining default values, but only for certain classes, structures, or enums, you can create a protocol extension that only applies to any class, structure, or enum that also adopts a second protocol:

```
extension protocol2Extend where Self: protocol2Use {
    // Set one or more default values for gettable properties here
}
```

The above Swift code extends a protocol defined by protocol2Extend. However, the where Self: keywords identify a second protocol defined by protocol2Use.

So if a class, structure, or enum adopts the protocol defined by protocol2Extend, then the extension only sets a default value if the class, structure, or enum also adopts the second protocol defined by protocol2Use.

Suppose you created the following protocol extension:

```
extension Cat where Self: CatType {
    var name : String { return "Frank" }
}
```

This would define a default value of "Frank" to the name property to any class, structure, or enum that adopts the Cat protocol and the CatType protocol. If a class, structure, or enum only adopts the Cat protocol, its name property won't be assigned a default value of "Frank".

To see how this version of a protocol extension only works when a class, structure, or enum adopts a specific protocol, follow these steps:

1. Make sure the ProtocolPlayground file is loaded in Xcode.

2. Edit the playground code as follows:

```
import Cocoa

protocol Cat {
    var name: String { get }
    var age: Int { get }
}

protocol CatType {
    var species: String { get }
}

extension Cat where Self: CatType {
    var name : String { return "Frank" }
}

struct pet : Cat {
    var name : String = "Max"
    var age : Int = 2
}

var animal = pet()
print (animal.name)
print (animal.age)

animal.name = "Joey"
animal.age = 13
print (animal.name)
print (animal.age)

// New structure that adopts two protocols
```

```
struct wild : Cat, CatType {
    var age : Int = 2
    var species : String = "Lion"
}

var beast = wild()
print (beast.name)
print (beast.age)
print (beast.species)
```

Notice that pet structure adopts the Cat protocol but since it doesn't adopt the CatType protocol as well, you can assign an initial value of "Max" to its name property and you can later assign "Joey" to that same name property.

However, the wild structure adopts both the Cat and CatType protocols, so it also adopts the protocol extension, which assigns "Frank" as a default value to the wild structure's name property, as shown in Figure 24-6.

```
import Cocoa

protocol Cat {
    var name: String { get }
    var age: Int { get }
}

protocol CatType {
    var species: String { get }
}

extension Cat where Self: CatType {
    var name : String { return "Frank" }          "Frank"
}

struct pet : Cat {
    var name : String = "Max"
    var age : Int = 2
}

var animal = pet()                                 pet
print (animal.name)                                "Max\n"
print (animal.age)                                 "2\n"

animal.name = "Joey"                               pet
animal.age = 13                                    pet
print (animal.name)                                "Joey\n"
print (animal.age)                                 "13\n"


// New structure that adopts two protocols
struct wild : Cat, CatType {
    var age : Int = 2
    var species : String = "Lion"
}

var beast = wild()                                 wild
print (beast.name)                                 "Frank\n"
print (beast.age)                                  "2\n"
print (beast.species)                              "Lion\n"
```

Figure 24-6. Protocol extensions can selectively assign default values to a structure that adopts a specific protocol

Using Protocol Extensions to Extend Common Data Types

Perhaps the most interesting use for protocol extensions is to add properties to common data types such as String, Int, and Double. A protocol extension for extending data types looks like this:

```
extension dataType {
    // New property {
    // return computed value
    }
}
```

When you extend a common data type with a protocol, you must create a variable that represents the data type followed by a period and the property name. So if you created an extension for the Int data type like

```
extension Int {
    var name : String {
    return text
    }
}
```

you could store a string value like

```
var status = 25.name    // represents a String
```

To see how to use protocol extensions to extend common data types, follow these steps:

1. Make sure the ProtocolPlayground file is loaded in Xcode.

2. Edit the playground code as follows:

   ```
   import Cocoa

   func checkMe (myAge : Int) -> String {
       if myAge >= 21 {
           return "Legal"
       } else {
           return "Underage"
       }
   }

   var text : String
   var myAge : Int
   ```

```
myAge = 32
text = checkMe (myAge : myAge)

extension Int {
    var name : String {
        return text
    }
}

var status = myAge.name
print (myAge)
print (status)

myAge = 16
text = checkMe (myAge : myAge)
status = myAge.name
print (myAge)
print (status)
```

Figure 24-7 shows the result of running this code. As you can see, when the myAge variable is greater than 21, its name property stores a string, which gets stored in the status variable. Depending on the value of the myAge variable, the name property stores either the string "Legal" or the string "Underage."

```
import Cocoa

func checkMe (myAge : Int) -> String {
    if myAge >= 21 {
        return "Legal"                              "Legal"
    } else {
        return "Underage"                           "Underage"
    }
}

var text : String
var myAge : Int

myAge = 32                                          32
text = checkMe (myAge: myAge)                       "Legal"

extension Int {
    var name : String {
        return text                                 (2 times)
    }
}

var status = myAge.name                             "Legal"
print (myAge)                                       "32\n"
print (status)                                      "Legal\n"

myAge = 16                                          16
text = checkMe (myAge: myAge)                       "Underage"
status = myAge.name                                 "Underage"
print (myAge)                                       "16\n"
print (status)                                      "Underage\n"
```

Figure 24-7. Protocol extensions can extend common data types

Summary

Protocols offer an alternate way to extend existing code. Just like a class, a protocol can define properties and methods. The main difference is that a protocol only defines a method's name and parameters, but does not actually include Swift code that implements that method.

Another difference is that when a protocol defines properties, it must also define whether that property is gettable { get } or gettable and settable { get set }.

Protocols work much like inheritance. While inheritance only allows classes to inherit from exactly one other class, protocols can extend classes, structures, and enums using one or more protocols.

Protocol extensions let you define default values for properties. When combined with common data types like Int, String, and Double, protocol extensions allow a data type to store additional information.

Just remember that you can mix object-oriented programming with protocol-oriented programming so you don't have to choose between one or the other. Both objects and protocols can be useful depending on what you need to accomplish in your particular program. Make sure you understand how to define protocols, use them, and extend them because protocols will be a common feature of Swift programs.

Chapter 25

Defensive Programming

Programmers tend to be optimistic, because when they write code, they assume that it will work correctly. However, it's often better to be more pessimistic when it comes to programming. Instead of assuming your code will work the first time, it's safer to assume your code won't work at all. This forces you to be extra careful when writing Swift code to make sure it does exactly what you want and doesn't do anything unexpected.

No program is error-free. Rather than waste time hunting down problems, it's far better to anticipate them and do your best to prevent them from creeping into your code in the first place. While it's not possible to write error-free code 100% of the time, the more defensive you are in writing code, the less likely you'll need to spend time hunting down errors that keep your code from working properly.

In general, assume nothing. Assumptions will surprise you every time, and rarely for the better. By anticipating problems ahead of time, you can plan for them so they won't wreck your program and force you to spend countless hours trying to fix a problem that you assumed should never have existed at all.

Test with Extreme Values

The simplest way to test your code is to start with extreme values to see how your program handles data way out of range from the expected. When working with numbers, programs often assume that the user will give it valid data within a fixed range, but what happens if the user types a letter or a symbol such as a smiley face instead of a number? What if the user types an integer instead of a decimal number (or vice versa)? What if the user types an extreme number like 42 billion or -0.00000005580?

© Wallace Wang 2017
W. Wang, *macOS Programming for Absolute Beginners*,
DOI 10.1007/978-1-4842-2662-9_25

When working with strings, do the same type of test. How does your program react when it expects a string but receives a number instead? What happens if it receives a huge string consisting of 3,000 characters? What happens if it receives foreign language symbols with accent marks or unusual letters?

By testing your program with extreme values, you can see if your program responds gracefully or simply crashes. Ultimately, the goal is to avoid crashes and respond gracefully. This might mean asking the user for valid data over and over again, or at least warning the user when the program receives invalid data. Reliable programs need to guard against anything that threatens to keep it from working properly.

Working with Optional Variables

One of Swift's most powerful features is the optional variable. An optional variable can contain a value or nothing at all (identified with a nil value). However, you must use optional variables with care because if you try using them when they contain a nil value, your program could crash.

When working with optional variables, you need to worry about the following:

- Whether the optional variable holds a nil value or not

- Unwrapping an optional variable to retrieve its actual value

Normally you can access the value stored inside an optional by using the exclamation mark, which is called unwrapping an optional. The big problem with unwrapping an optional is if you assume its value is not nil. Suppose you had the following:

```
var test : String?

print (test)
print (test!)
```

Since the `test` optional variable hasn't been assigned a value, its default value is nil. The first `print` command simply prints nil. However, the second `print` command tries to unwrap the optional, but since its value is nil, this causes an error, as shown in Figure 25-1.

```
import Cocoa                                                          nil

var test : String?

print (test)                                                        "nil\n"
print(test!)                                                         ● error
      ● error: Execution was interrupted, reason: EXC_BAD_INSTRUCTION (code=EXC_I386_I...
```

Figure 25-1. Unwrapping an optional that has a nil value causes an error

When working with optionals, always test to see if they're nil before you try using them. One way to test for a nil value is to simply test if the optional is equal to nil, like so:

```
import Cocoa

var test : String?

if test == nil {
    print ("Nil value")
} else {
    print (test!)
}
```

In this example, the if-else statement first checks if the test optional is equal to nil. If so, then it prints "Nil value." If not, then it can safely unwrap the optional using the exclamation mark.

Another way to check for a nil value is to assign a constant to an optional, which is known as optional binding. Instead of using the optional variable, you assign or bind its value to a constant, such as

```
if let constant = optionalVariable {
    // Optional is not nil
} else {
    // Optional is a nil value
}
```

If you need to test several optional variables, you can list them on a single line like this:

```
if let constant = optionalVariable, constant2 = optionalVariable2 {
    // No optionals are nil
} else {
    // One or more optionals are nil
}
```

If the constant holds a value, then the if-else statement can use the constant value. If the constant does not hold a value (contains nil), then the if-else statement does something else to avoid using a nil value. By using a constant to store the value of an optional variable, you avoid unwrapping an optional variable using the exclamation mark.

Let's see how to use optional binding:

1. From within Xcode choose File ➤ New ➤ Playground. Xcode now asks for a playground name.

2. Click in the Name text field and type **DefensePlayground**.

3. Make sure the Platform pop-up menu displays macOS.

4. Click the Next button. Xcode asks where you want to store the playground.

5. Choose a folder to store your project and click the Create button.

6. Edit the playground code as follows:

```
import Cocoa

var test : String?
var final : String?

if let checkMe = test, let checkMe2 = final {
    print (checkMe)
} else {
    print ("Nil value in one or both optionals")
}

test = "Hello"
if let checkMe = test, let checkMe2 = final {
    print (checkMe)
} else {
    print ("Nil value in one or both optionals")
}

final = "Bye"
if let checkMe = test, let checkMe2 = final {
    print (checkMe + " & " + checkMe2)
} else {
    print ("Nil value in one or both optionals")
}
```

The above code assigns two different optional variable values to two different constants. Only if both constants contain a non-nil value will the first part of the if-else statement run. If one or both constants contain a nil value, then the else part of the if-else statement runs, as shown in Figure 25-2. Also notice that none of the code unwraps any optional variable using the exclamation mark.

```
import Cocoa

var test : String?                                          nil
var final : String?                                         nil

if let checkMe = test, let checkMe2 = final {
    print (checkMe)
} else {
    print ("Nil value in one or both optionals")            "Nil value in one or both optionals\n"
}

test = "Hello"                                              "Hello"
if let checkMe = test, let checkMe2 = final {
    print (checkMe)
} else {
    print ("Nil value in one or both optionals")            "Nil value in one or both optionals\n"
}

final = "Bye"                                               "Bye"
if let checkMe = test, let checkMe2 = final {
    print (checkMe + " & " + checkMe2)                      "Hello & Bye\n"
} else {
    print ("Nil value in one or both optionals")
}
```

Figure 25-2. Using optional binding to assign an optional variable value to a constant

Working with Optional Chaining

When dealing with optionals, you typically declare an optional variable with a question mark, such as Int?, String?, Float?, and Double?. Besides using common data types, you can declare any type as an optional variable, including classes.

To declare an ordinary data type as an optional variable, you just add a question mark to the data type name, like this:

```
var myNumber : String?
```

Normally, properties in a class hold a common data type like String, Int, or Double. However, a class property can also hold another class. If you can declare a class as a type, you can also declare a class as an optional variable too, like this:

```
class Dreamer {
    var candidate: Politician?
}
```

```
class Politician {
    var name = ""
}
```

Now if you create an object based on the Dreamer class, you'll wind up with a candidate property that holds an optional variable:

```
let person = Dreamer()
```

The person object is based on the Dreamer class, which means it also holds a property called candidate. However, the candidate property is also an optional variable object based on the Politician class. At this point, the candidate property has an initial value of nil.

To see how an object can have another object as an optional variable, follow these steps:

1. Make sure the **DefensePlayground** is loaded into Xcode.

2. Edit the playground code as follows:

    ```
    import Cocoa

    class Dreamer {
        var candidate: Politician?
    }

    class Politician {
        var name : String = ""
    }

    let person = Dreamer()

    if let check = person.candidate?.name {
        print ("Name = \(check)")
    }
    else {
        print ("Nil value here")
    }
    ```

This code fails to create an object from the Politician class, so the candidate property is nil. Because you declared the candidate property as an optional variable, you can use what's called optional chaining to access its name property in the if-else statement, as shown in Figure 25-3.

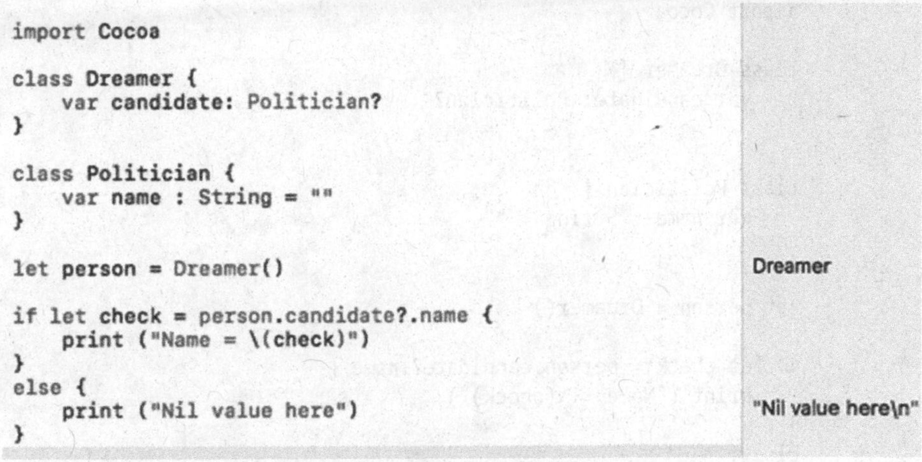

```
import Cocoa

class Dreamer {
    var candidate: Politician?
}

class Politician {
    var name : String = ""
}

let person = Dreamer()                          Dreamer

if let check = person.candidate?.name {
    print ("Name = \(check)")
}
else {
    print ("Nil value here")
}                                               "Nil value here\n"
```

Figure 25-3. Optional chaining can access an optional variable property of a class

To store a value in the candidate property, you need to create another object, like this:

```
person.candidate = Politician()
```

Then you need to store data in the Politician class's name property. To do this, you need to unwrap the optional variable (the Politician class) to access its name property like this:

```
person.candidate!.name = "Sally"
```

Remember, unwrapping optionals with the exclamation mark should only be done when you're absolutely sure the optional variable contains a value. In this case, you're assigning a value ("Sally") to the optional variable so it's safe to unwrap the optional variable.

Let's see how to modify your previous code to store a value in an optional variable property:

1. Make sure the DefensePlayground is loaded into Xcode.

2. Edit the playground code as follows:

```
import Cocoa

class Dreamer {
    var candidate: Politician?
}

class Politician {
    var name : String = ""
}

let person = Dreamer()

if let check = person.candidate?.name {
    print ("Name = \(check)")
}
else {
    print ("Nil value here")
}

person.candidate = Politician ()
person.candidate!.name = "Sally"

if let check = person.candidate?.name {
    print ("Name = \(check)")
}
else {
    print ("Nil value here")
}
```

Notice that the candidate optional variable (Politician) is undefined or nil until you specifically store a value in it. As soon as you store a string ("Sally") into the name property, it no longer holds a nil value, as shown in Figure 25-4.

```
import Cocoa

class Dreamer {
    var candidate: Politician?
}

class Politician {
    var name : String = ""
}

let person = Dreamer()                              Dreamer

if let check = person.candidate?.name {
    print ("Name = \(check)")
}
else {
    print ("Nil value here")                        "Nil value here\n"
}

person.candidate = Politician ()                    Dreamer
person.candidate!.name = "Sally"                    Politician

if let check = person.candidate?.name {
    print ("Name = \(check)")                       "Name = Sally\n"
}
else {
    print ("Nil value here")
}
```

Figure 25-4. You need to unwrap an optional variable to store a value in it

The key when working with optional variables is to make sure you use the question mark and exclamation mark symbols correctly. Fortunately, if you omit either symbol, Xcode can often prompt you to choose the right symbol, as shown in Figure 25-5.

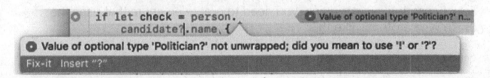

Figure 25-5. Xcode's editor can prompt you when to use the ? or ! symbols when working with optional variables

The question mark symbol is used to create optional variables or safely access optional variables. The exclamation mark symbol is used to unwrap optional variables, so make sure those unwrapped optional variables hold a non-nil value.

In general, any time you see a question mark used with optional variables, your code is likely safe when dealing with nil values. However, any time you see an exclamation mark with optional variables, make sure the optional variable holds a value because if it holds a nil value, your code may be unsafe and could crash.

Error Handling

Since you can't expect to write bug-free code every time, Swift offers a feature called error handling. The idea behind error handling is to identify and catch likely errors so your program handles them gracefully rather than letting the program crash or act unpredictably. To handle errors, you need to go through several steps:

- Define descriptive errors that you want to identify
- Identify one or more functions to detect an error and identify the type of error that occurred
- Handle the error

Defining Errors with Enumerations

In the old days, programs often displayed cryptic error messages filled with hexadecimal numbers and odd symbols. Those types of error messages are generally useless for identifying the problem that may have occurred. That's why the first step in handling errors is to create a list of descriptive error types.

The names you give different errors is completely arbitrary, but you should give meaningful names to different types of error messages. To create a list of descriptive error types, you need to create an enum that uses the ErrorType protocol, like this:

```
enum enumName : Error {
    case descriptiveError1
    case descriptiveError2
    case descriptiveError3
}
```

Replace enumName with a descriptive name that identifies the type of error you want to identify. Then type a descriptive error name as one word (without spaces) using the case keyword. Your list of possible errors can range from one to as many errors as you wish to describe, so you're not limited to a fixed number. If you want to create an enum that lists three error types, you can use code like this:

```
enum ageError : Error {
    case negativeAge // Negative numbers
    case unrealAge   // Numbers > 140
    case underAge    // Under 21
}
```

Creating a Function to Identify Errors

Once you've created a list of descriptive error types, you now need to create one or more functions where you think the error might occur. Normally, you would define a function like this:

```
func functionName {
        // Code goes here
}
```

To make a function identify errors, you need to insert the throws keyword like this:

```
func functionName throws {
        // Code goes here
}
```

The throws keyword means that the function "throws" the error for some other part of your code to handle. Inside a function with the throws keyword you need to use one or more guard statements.

A guard statement identifies what's allowed and works similar to an if-else statement. If the guard statement's Boolean condition is true, then nothing happens. However, if the guard statement is false, then the guard statement can use the throws keyword to identify a specific type of error, like this:

```
guard Booleancondition else {
    throws enumName.descriptiveError
}
```

If you want to allow only values greater than 21, you can create a guard statement like this:

```
guard myAge > 21 else {
    throws ageError.underAge
}
```

This guard statement will do nothing if the Boolean condition (myAge>21) is true. Otherwise, it will throw the ageError.underAge error where "ageError" is the name of the enum that lists different errors to identify and "underAge" is one of the possible errors likely to occur.

The guard statement always defines acceptable behavior (myAge > 21) or else it identifies an error with the throws keyword. A function (identified with the throws keyword) can have one or more guard statements.

Handling the Error

When you've identified one or more functions with the throws keyword where it uses one or more guard statements to identify possible errors, you finally need a way to handle those errors. In Swift you do that using a do-try-catch statement like this:

```
do {
    try callFunctionThatThrows
} catch enumName.descriptiveError {
    // Code to handle the error
}
```

The do-try-catch statement tries to run a function that can identify errors using the throws keyword. If the function doesn't identify any errors with one or more guard statements, then the do-try-catch statement works exactly like a normal function call.

However, if the function identifies an error, the do-try-catch statement is where you need to write code to handle that error. How you handle this error can be as simple as printing a message to let you know of a problem or as complicated as running an entirely new set of code just to deal with the problem.

The point is that if you anticipate possible errors and write code to handle those errors, your program will be less likely to crash. If your program does crash, simply find out why (which may not be easy), create a new descriptive error name to identify it, and then create a new catch statement to deal with that error.

Let's see how error handling works:

1.   Make sure the **DefensePlayground** is loaded into Xcode.

2.   Edit the playground code as follows:

```
import Cocoa

enum ageError : Error {
    case negativeAge // Negative numbers
    case unrealAge   // Numbers > 140
    case underAge    // Under 21
}

func checkAge(myAge : Int) throws {
    print (myAge)

    guard myAge > 0 else {
        throws ageError.negativeAge
    }

    guard myAge <= 140 else {
        throws ageError.unrealAge
    }

    guard myAge > 21 else {
        throws ageError.underAge
    }

}

var oldAge = -9

do {
    try checkAge (myAge: oldAge)
} catch ageError.negativeAge {
    print ("An age can't be a negative number")
} catch ageError.unrealAge {
    print ("An age can't be greater than 140")
} catch ageError.underAge {
    print ("Sorry, you have to be 21 or older")
}

print (oldAge)
```

Notice how a negative number gets identified and handled with a simple message, as shown in Figure 25-6.

```
import Cocoa

enum ageError : Error {
    case negativeAge // Negative numbers
    case unrealAge   // Numbers > 140
    case underAge    // Under 21
}

func checkAge(myAge : Int) throws {
    print (myAge)                                    "-9\n"

    guard myAge > 0 else {
        throw ageError.negativeAge
    }

    guard myAge <= 140 else {
        throw ageError.unrealAge
    }

    guard myAge > 21 else {
        throw ageError.underAge
    }

}

var oldAge = -9                                      -9

do {
    try checkAge (myAge: oldAge)
} catch ageError.negativeAge {
    print ("An age can't be a negative number")     "An age can't be a negative number\n"
} catch ageError.unrealAge {
    print ("An age can't be greater than 140")
} catch ageError.underAge {
    print ("Sorry, you have to be 21 or older")
}

print (oldAge)                                       "-9\n"
```

Figure 25-6. *Error handling involves an enum, a function with guard statements, and a do-try-catch statement*

Change the value of the oldAge variable to 250 to see how the do-try-catch statement catches that number as higher than 140, which makes it unrealistic. Change the value of the oldAge variable to 15 to see how the do-try-catch statement identifies an age under 21.

To use error handling in your programs, you must first identify possible problems, and then you need to decide how to handle these problems. Error handling can only identify errors you already know about, but it can make your programs less fragile when confronted with common types of problems your program may face.

Summary

No matter how talented, skilled, or educated you may be as a programmer, you will make mistakes occasionally. Sometimes these mistakes will be simple errors you can easily correct but sometimes you'll make mistakes that cause a variety of subtle problems that will challenge and frustrate you to find and fix. That's just the nature of programming.

However, any problems you accidentally create are also problems you can learn to discover and fix. Once you learn how one mistake works, you'll likely remember how to fix those types of mistakes in the future if you or someone else makes them again. This frees you up to make new mistakes you'll likely never have experience facing again.

The best way to reduce errors in your program is to examine your code carefully and assume nothing will go right. Then look for every possible way to make sure it can't go wrong. The more you code with a defensive mindset, the more likely you'll prevent problems before they occur.

Programming is more of an art than a science, so learn the best ways that work for you to reduce introducing errors in your programs. When experimenting with new code, it's usually safer to test it out in a Swift playground or in a simple program separate from your real program.

This way you can isolate and test your code safely. When it works, then you can copy and paste it into your program.

Errors are a way of life in the world of programming. Ideally you want to spend more time writing code and less time debugging it.

Chapter 26

Simplifying User Interface Design

Designing a user interface can be challenging. Not only do you need to design a user interface that's easy to use, but you also need to design an adaptive user interface that can respond to any changes the user might make to a window's size. If the user shrinks a window, your user interface must shrink accordingly without cutting any items off. If the user enlarges a window, your user interface must expand accordingly to maintain a consistent appearance.

To help create adaptive user interfaces, Xcode provides constraints that fix the edges of various user interface items to a window's edge or the edge of other user interface items. In this chapter, you'll learn more about constraints and storyboards to help make user interface design easier than ever before.

Using Stack View

If your user interface contains a handful of items such as a text field, a button, and a label, it's fairly straightforward to place constraints on these items so they stay in the correct place. However, if your user interface contains multiple items, then it can get messy to place so many constraints on each item. Change one constraint and your entire user interface can fail to adapt properly, which often means wasting time trying to get your multiple constraints working. Figure 26-1 shows how messy multiple constraints can look on a crowded user interface.

© Wallace Wang 2017
W. Wang, *macOS Programming for Absolute Beginners*,
DOI 10.1007/978-1-4842-2662-9_26

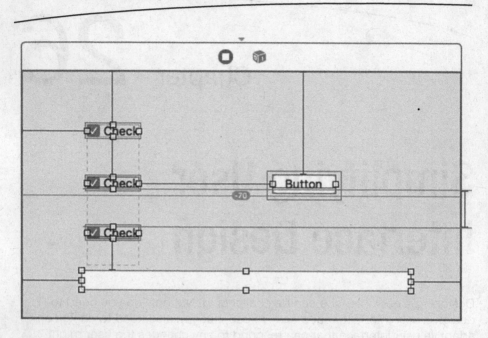

Figure 26-1. Multiple constraints make it hard to correctly lay out a user interface

To solve this problem, Xcode offers a feature called stack view. The idea behind the stack view is that groups of user interface items often need to stay together. Rather than set constraints for each item individually, you group them together in a stack view, then set constraints for that single stack view.

To learn how to create and use a stack view, follow these steps:

1. From within Xcode choose File ➤ New ➤ Project.

2. Click Application under the macOS category.

3. Click Cocoa Application and click the Next button. Xcode now asks for a product name.

4. Click in the Product Name text field and type **StackViewProgram**.

5. Make sure the Language pop-up menu displays Swift and that the "Use Storyboards" check box is selected.

6. Click the Next button. Xcode asks where you want to store the project.

7. Choose a folder to store your project and click the Create button.

8. Click the Main.storyboard file in the Project Navigator. Your program's user interface appears.

9. Choose View ➤ Utilities ➤ Show Object Library. The Object Library appears in the bottom right corner of the Xcode window.

10. Drag three check boxes on to the user interface window so they appear stacked on top of each other. Notice that unless you precisely align each check box, they won't appear organized.

11. Drag the mouse to select all three check boxes, as shown in Figure 26-2. (Another way to select multiple items is to hold down the Shift key and click each item you want to select.)

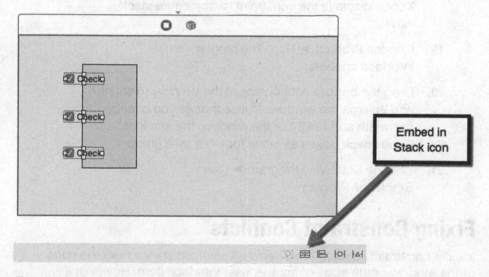

Figure 26-2. Dragging is a fast way to select multiple items

12. Choose Editor ➤ Embed In ➤ Stack View (or click the Embed in Stack icon on the bottom right corner of the middle Xcode pane). Xcode groups your selected items inside a single stack view.

13.   Move the mouse pointer over the stack view of three check boxes, hold down the Control key, and drag the mouse towards the right edge of the window.

14.   Release the Control key and the mouse button. A pop-up window appears.

15.   Choose the "Trailing Space to Container" option. Xcode displays the constraint for the entire stack view.

16.   Move the mouse pointer over the stack view of the three check boxes, hold down the Control key, and drag the mouse towards the bottom edge of the window.

17.   Release the Control key and the mouse button. A pop-up window appears.

18.   Choose the "Bottom Space to Container" option. Xcode displays the constraint for the entire stack view.

19.   Choose Product ➤ Run. The program's user interface appears.

20.   Drag the bottom right corner of the window to shrink and enlarge the window. Notice that as you change the width and height of the window, the stack of three check boxes all move together as a group.

21.   Choose StackViewProgram ➤ Quit StackViewProgram.

Fixing Constraint Conflicts

Ideally, constraints should keep items a specific distance from the edge of the window or the edge of another user interface item. However, if you shrink or expand a window, it's possible for constraints to create unexpected problems.

Let's see how setting two constraints on a user interface item can create a problem:

1. Make sure the StackViewProgram project is loaded in Xcode.

2. Click the `Main.storyboard` file in the Project Navigator pane.

3. Choose Edit ➤ Select All (or press Command+A). Xcode selects your stack view that's currently on the user interface window.

4. Press the Delete key on your keyboard, or choose Edit ➤ Delete to delete all user interface items from the window.

5. Choose View ➤ Utilities ➤ Show Object Library.

6. Drag a single text field in the middle of the user interface window. (Don't worry about the exact positioning.)

7. Move the mouse pointer over the text field, hold down the Control key, and drag the mouse to the right edge of the window.

8. Release the Control key and the mouse. A pop-up window appears.

9. Choose the "Trailing Space to Container" option. Xcode creates a constraint from the right edge of the text field to the right edge of the window.

10. Move the mouse pointer over the text field, hold down the Control key, and drag the mouse to the left edge of the window.

11. Release the Control key and the mouse. A pop-up window appears.

12. Choose the "Leading Space to Container" option. Xcode creates a constraint from the left edge of the text field to the left edge of the window.

13. Choose Product ➤ Run. The user interface window appears.

14.   Move the mouse pointer over the right edge of the window and expand the window width by dragging the mouse to the right. Notice that the text field expands to the right.

15.   Move the mouse pointer over the right edge of the window and shrink the window width by dragging the mouse to the left. Notice that the text field shrinks. If you keep shrinking the window width, the text field eventually disappears altogether.

16.   Choose StackViewProgram ➤ Quit StackViewProgram.

Right now, you have two constraints that keep the text field a fixed distance from the two window edges, but they do nothing to keep the text field from disappearing if the window shrinks too much. One way to fix this is to create a compression constraint.

A compression constraint keeps a user interface item from shrinking or expanding too much. To create a compression constraint, you hold down the Control key and drag the mouse within the boundaries of that user interface element.

1.   Make sure the StackViewProgram project is loaded in Xcode.

2.   Click the Main.storyboard file in the Project Navigator pane.

3.   Move the mouse pointer over the text field.

4.   Hold down the Control key and drag the mouse to the left or right, keeping the mouse pointer within the boundary of the text field.

5.   Release the Control key and the mouse. A pop-up menu appears, as shown in Figure 26-3.

Figure 26-3. Defining a compression constraint

6. Choose Width. Xcode displays a compression constraint underneath the text field, as shown in Figure 26-4.

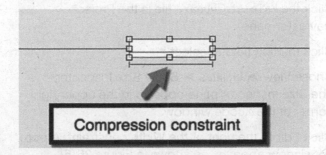

Figure 26-4. A compression constraint appears underneath a user interface item

7. Choose Product ➤ Run. The user interface window appears.

8. Move the mouse pointer over the right edge of the window and try dragging the window to expand or shrink its width. Notice that you can't do this because of the compression constraint.

9. Choose StackViewProgram ➤ Quit StackViewProgram.

The compression constraint tells Xcode to keep the text field a fixed width and the left and right constraints tell Xcode to keep the text field a fixed distance from the left and right edges of the window. To satisfy all of these constraints, the window can no longer be resized in width.

What if you want to keep the text field width no smaller than its current width, but allow the window to resize? One solution is to use constraint priorities.

Priorities define which constraints must be satisfied first. Each time you create a constraint, Xcode gives it a priority of 1000, which is the highest priority possible. If you give a constraint a lower priority, then that constraint will allow constraints with higher priorities to take precedence. Let's see how changing priorities on constraints works:

1. Make sure the StackViewProgram project is loaded in Xcode.

2. Click the Main.storyboard file in the Project Navigator pane.

3. Click the text field to select it.

4. Chose View ➤ Utilities ➤ Show Size Inspector. The Size Inspector pane appears in the upper right corner of the Xcode window.

5. Click Edit to the right of the Width constraint. A pop-up window appears, as shown in Figure 26-5.

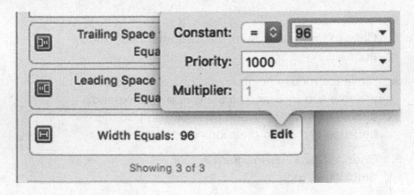

Figure 26-5. Editing a constraint

6. Click the downward-pointing arrow to the right of the Priority text field. A pop-up menu appears, as shown in Figure 26-6.

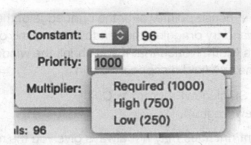

Figure 26-6. *Changing the priority of a constraint*

7. Choose Low (250). Notice that Xcode now displays
    the width constraint as a dotted line to visually show
    you that its priority is lower than the constraints with
    a solid line, as shown in Figure 26-7.

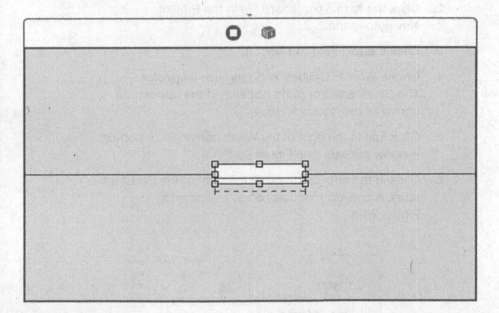

Figure 26-7. *A constraint with a lower priority appears as a dotted line*

8. Choose Product ➤ Run. The user interface window
    appears.

9.   Move the mouse pointer over the right edge of the window and try dragging the window to expand or shrink its width. Notice that if you shrink the window width, the text field disappears again.

10. Choose StackViewProgram ➤ Quit StackViewProgram.

Changing constraint priorities may not always give you the result you want so you may need to change how the constraint works. Most constraints define a fixed value that the constraint must satisfy. For more flexibility, you can also change this equal constraint to a greater than or equal constraint or a less than or equal constraint.

1.   Make sure the StackViewProgram project is loaded in Xcode.

2.   Click the Main.storyboard file in the Project Navigator pane.

3.   Click the text field to select it.

4.   Chose View ➤ Utilities ➤ Show Size Inspector. The Size Inspector pane appears in the upper right corner of the Xcode window.

5.   Click Edit to the right of the Width constraint. A pop-up window appears (see Figure 26-5).

6.   Click in the pop-up menu to the right of the Constant label. A pop-up menu appears, as shown in Figure 26-8.

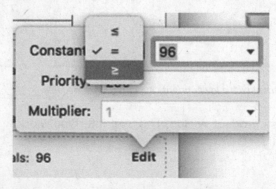

Figure 26-8. Changing an equal sign to a greater-than-or-equal-to sign or a less-than-or-equal-to sign

7. Choose the ≥ (greater-than-or-equal-to sign).

8. Click the downward-pointing arrow to the right of the Priority text field so a menu appears and choose High (750).

9. Choose Product ➤ Run. Notice that if you shrink the width of the window, the compression constraint will only shrink the text field a limited distance before stopping the text field from disappearing altogether. If you expand the width of the window, the text field expands.

10. Choose StackViewProgram ➤ Quit StackViewProgram.

When your user interface doesn't adapt correctly, try one or more of the following options:

- Add or delete constraints

- Change constraint priorities

- Change constraints from equaling a fixed value to greater than or equal or less than or equal relationships

Each user interface problem with adapting to window resizing can be different, so solving that problem could be as simple as modifying one constraint or as complicated as modifying multiple constraints. If groups of user interface items move together, group them in a stack view for simplicity.

Often times you may need to experiment with modifying different constraints to see how they work in various combinations. Just be aware of your options for modifying constraints and you'll eventually find the best solution for your particular user interface.

Working with Storyboard References

The two ways to design user interfaces involve .xib files and .storyboard files. Storyboard files represent scenes (windows) connected by segues. For a simple program that consists of a handful of windows, a storyboard may be fine, but if your program's user interface consists of many windows, then a storyboard can get clumsy and cluttered with multiple segues linking scenes.

The more scenes your user interface needs, the more complicated your storyboard can be to understand, as shown in Figure 26-9.

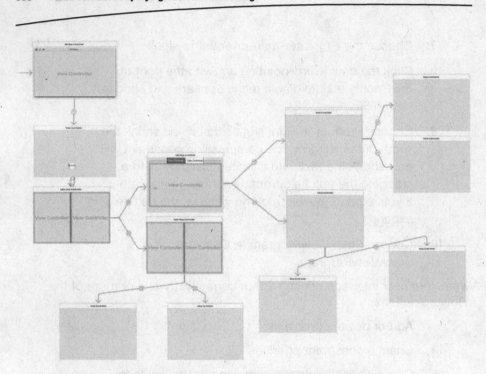

Figure 26-9. Large storyboards can look cluttered and hard to understand

To avoid storing your entire user interface in a single, cluttered storyboard, Xcode lets you divide a storyboard into parts using storyboard references. A storyboard reference lets you store scenes and segues in a separate storyboard file.

A storyboard reference lets you replace one or more scenes and segues with a storyboard reference box, as shown in Figure 26-10. You can have multiple storyboard reference boxes where each one represents a separate storyboard file.

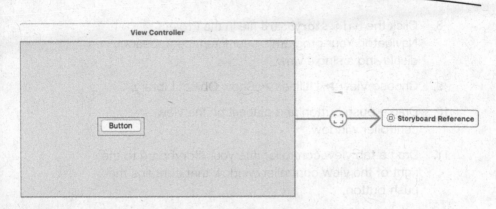

Figure 26-10. Storyboard references represent multiple scenes and segues stored in another storyboard file

You can create a storyboard reference in two ways:

- Select the storyboard scenes you want to separate from a storyboard file and choose Editor ➤ Refactor to Storyboard.

- Drag a storyboard reference from the Object Library and connect it to an existing scene in a storyboard.

To see how to use storyboard references, follow these steps:

1. From within Xcode choose File ➤ New ➤ Project.

2. Click Application under the macOS category.

3. Click Cocoa Application and click the Next button. Xcode now asks for a product name.

4. Click in the Product Name text field and type **StoryReference**.

5. Make sure the Language pop-up menu displays Swift and that "Use Storyboards" check box is selected.

6. Click the Next button. Xcode asks where you want to store the project.

7. Choose a folder to store your project and click the Create button.

8. Click the `Main.storyboard` file in the Project Navigator. Your program's user interface appears, displaying a single view.

9. Choose View ➤ Utilities ➤ Show Object Library.

10. Drag a push button and place it on the view controller window.

11. Drag a tab view controller into your storyboard to the right of the view controller window that contains the push button.

12. Move the mouse pointer over the push button, hold down the Control key, and drag the mouse over the tab view controller, as shown in Figure 26-11.

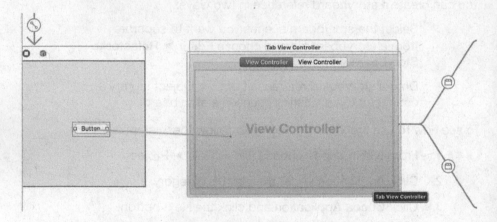

Figure 26-11. Control-dragging creates a segue between view controllers

13. Release the Control key and the mouse. A pop-up window appears.

14. Choose show. Xcode draws a segue between the two view controllers.

15. Click the tab view controller to select it.

16. Choose Editor ➤ Refactor to Storyboard. A sheet drops down to ask the name you want to give your storyboard, as shown in Figure 26-12.

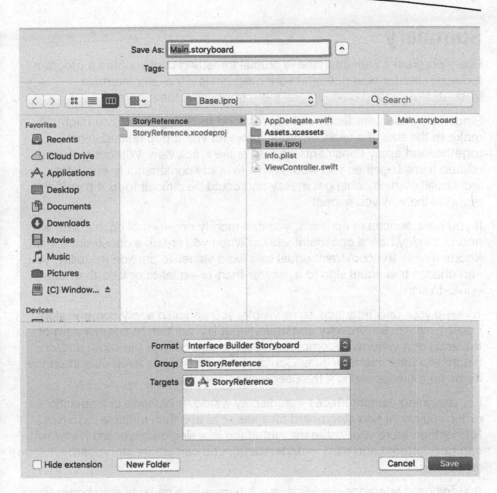

Figure 26-12. Creating a storyboard reference

17. Click in the Save As text field and type **Tab.storyboard**.

18. Click the Save button. Xcode saves the tab view controller in a `Tab.storyboard` file and displays a storyboard reference box in the `Main.storyboard` file.

19. Click the `Tab.storyboard` file in the Project Navigator pane. Xcode shows the tab view controller.

Summary

Every program's user interface is crucial for letting users control a program. It doesn't matter how powerful your program is if the user interface frustrates users and discourages them from using the program.

Since every user interface needs to respond to changes the user might make to the size of a window, stack views let you group related items together and apply constraints on that entire stack view. Without grouping related items together, you would have to apply constraints to each item individually, which could get messy and could be difficult to fix if they don't respond the way you expect.

If you have constraint conflicts, you can modify priorities of each constraint and/or modify how a constraint works. When you create a constraint initially, Xcode makes the constraint equal to a fixed value. To provide flexibility, you can change this equal sign to a greater-than-or-equal-to or less-than-or-equal-to sign.

To keep your user interface items visible, you can also apply compression constraints. Unlike ordinary constraints that link an item to another item or the edge of a window, a compression constraint defines the width and/or height of a user interface item. Compression constraints keep user interface items from disappearing if the user resizes a window.

For designing user interfaces that display windows or views in a specific order, you might find storyboard files easier to use than multiple `.xib` files. Rather than store your entire user interface in a single storyboard file (which can get cluttered and hard to understand), you can create storyboard references.

A storyboard reference divides a user interface into multiple storyboard files. By separating a user interface into multiple storyboard files, you can design and understand the structure of your user interface much easier.

Chapter 27

Debugging Your Programs

In the professional world of software development, you'll actually spend more time modifying existing programs than you ever will creating new ones. However, whether writing new programs or editing existing ones, it doesn't matter how much experience or education you might have because even the best programmers can make mistakes. In fact, you can expect that you will make mistakes no matter how careful you may be. Once you accept this inevitable fact of programming, you can learn how to find and fix your mistakes.

In the world of computers, mistakes are commonly called "bugs," a name based on an incident with an early computer that used physical switches to work. One day the computer failed, and when technicians opened the computer, they found that a moth had been crushed within a switch, preventing the switch from closing. From that point on, programming errors have been called bugs, and fixing computer problems has been known as debugging.

Three common types of computer bugs are

- **Syntax Errors**: Occur when you misspell something such as a keyword, variable name, function name, or class name, or you use a symbol incorrectly

- **Logic Errors**: Occur when you use commands correctly, but the logic of your code doesn't do what you intended

- **Runtime Errors**: Occur when a program encounters unexpected situations such as the user entering invalid data or when another program somehow interferes with your program unexpectedly

© Wallace Wang 2017
W. Wang, *macOS Programming for Absolute Beginners*,
DOI 10.1007/978-1-4842-2662-9_27

Syntax errors are the easiest to find and fix because they're merely misspellings of variable names that you created or misspellings of Swift commands that Xcode can help you identify. If you type a Swift keyword such as var or let, Xcode displays that keyword in pink (or whatever color you specify for displaying keywords in the Xcode editor).

Now if you type a Swift keyword and it doesn't appear in its usual identifying color, then you know you probably typed it wrong somehow. By coloring your code, Xcode's editor helps you visually identify common misspellings or typos.

Besides using color, the Xcode editor provides a second way to help you avoid mistakes when you need to type the name of a method or class defined in the Cocoa framework. As soon as Xcode recognizes that you might be typing something from the Cocoa framework, it displays a pop-up menu of possible options. Now instead of typing the entire command yourself, you can simply click your choice in the pop-up menu and press the Tab key one or more times to let Xcode type your chosen command correctly, as shown in Figure 27-1.

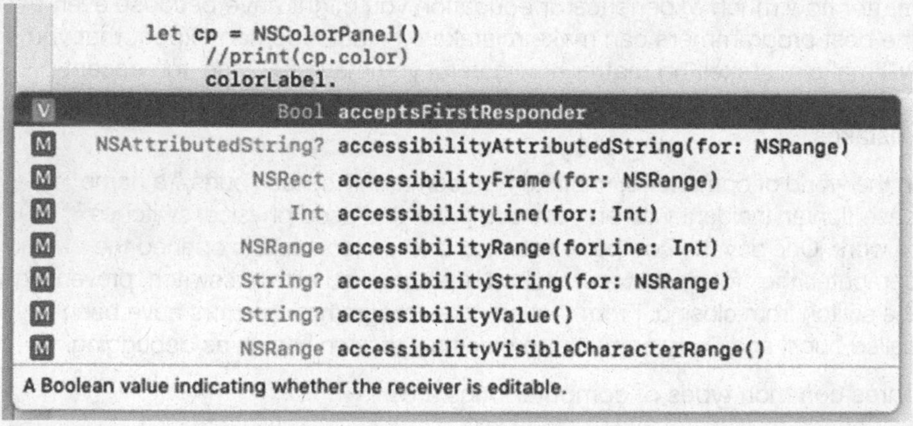

```
let cp = NSColorPanel()
    //print(cp.color)
    colorLabel.
V              Bool  acceptsFirstResponder
M  NSAttributedString?  accessibilityAttributedString(for: NSRange)
M              NSRect  accessibilityFrame(for: NSRange)
M                 Int  accessibilityLine(for: Int)
M             NSRange  accessibilityRange(forLine: Int)
M             String?  accessibilityString(for: NSRange)
M             String?  accessibilityValue()
M             NSRange  accessibilityVisibleCharacterRange()
A Boolean value indicating whether the receiver is editable.
```

Figure 27-1. Xcode displays a menu of possible commands that you might want to use

Syntax errors often keep your program from running at all. When a syntax error keeps your program from running, Xcode can usually identify the line (or the nearby area) of your program where the misspelled commands appears so you can fix it, as shown in Figure 27-2.

```
let cp = NSColorPanel()
    //print(cp.color)
    colorLabel.backgroundColor = NSColor.blue
```
Ⓧ Use of unresolved identifier 'colorabel'
Fix-it Did you mean 'colorLabel'?

Ⓧ Use of unresolved identifier 'colorabel'

Figure 27-2. Syntax errors often keep a program from running, which allows Xcode to identify the syntax error

> **Note** Swift treats uppercase and lowercase letters as completely different characters. One common mistake is to type a lowercase letter instead of an uppercase letter (or vice versa).

Logic errors are much harder to find and detect than syntax errors. Xcode can identify syntax errors because it recognizes the difference between a properly spelled Swift keyword (such as var) and a misspelled Swift keyword (such as varr).

However, logic errors occur when you use Swift code correctly, but it doesn't do what you intended it to do. Since your code is actually valid, Xcode has no way of knowing that it's not working the way you intended. As a result, logic errors can be difficult to debug because you think you wrote your code correctly but you (obviously) did not.

How do you find a mistake in code that you thought you wrote correctly? Finding your mistake can often involve starting from the beginning of your program and exhaustively searching each line all the way until the end. (Of course, there are faster ways than searching your entire program line by line, which you'll learn about later in this chapter.)

Finally, the hardest errors to find and debug are runtime errors. Syntax errors usually keep your program from running so if your program actually runs, you can assume that you have eliminated most, if not all, syntax errors in your code.

Logic errors can be tougher to find, but they're predictable. For example, if your program asks the user for a password but fails to give the user access even though the user types a correct password, you know you have a logic error. Each time you run your program, you can reliably predict when the logic error will occur.

Runtime errors are more insidious because they don't always occur predictably. For example, your program may run perfectly well on your computer, but the moment you run the same program on an identical computer, the program may fail. That's because conditions between two different computers will never be exactly the same.

As a result, the same program can run fine on one computer but fail on the exact same type of computer somewhere else. The problem is that unexpected, outside circumstances can affect your program's behavior. For example, your program may run just fine until the user presses a number key on the numeric keypad instead of the number key at the top of the alphanumeric keys.

Even though the user may be typing the exact same number (such as 5), the program may treat the 5 key above the R and T keys as a completely different key than the 5 key on the numeric keypad. As subtle as that may be, it could be enough to cause a program to fail or crash.

Because runtime errors can't always be duplicated, they can be frustrating to find and even harder to fix since you can't always examine every possible condition your program might face when running on other computers. Some programs have been known to work perfectly, except if the user accidentally presses two keys at the same time. Other programs work just fine until the user happens to save a file at the exact moment that another program tries to receive e-mail over the Internet.

Usually you can eliminate most syntax errors, and find and fix most logic errors. However, it may not be possible to find and completely eliminate all runtime errors in a program. The best way to avoid spending time hunting for bugs is to strive to write good code and test it carefully to make sure it's as error-free as possible.

Simple Debugging Techniques

When your program isn't working, you often have no idea what could be wrong. While you could tediously examine your code from beginning to end, it's often faster to simply guess where the mistake might be.

Once you have a rough idea what part of your program might be causing the problem, you have two choices. First, you can delete the suspicious code and run your program again. If the problem magically goes away, then you'll know that the code you deleted was likely the culprit.

However, if your program still doesn't work, you have to retype your deleted code back into your program. A simpler solution might be to cut and paste the code out of Xcode and store it in a text editor such as the TextEdit program that comes with every Macintosh, but this can be tedious.

That's why a second solution is to just temporarily hide code that you suspect might be causing a problem. Then, if the problem persists, you can simply unhide that code and make it visible again. To do this in Xcode, you just need to turn your code into comments.

Remember, comments are text that Xcode completely ignores. You can create comments in three ways:

- Add the // symbols at the beginning of each line that you want to convert into a comment. This method lets you convert a single line into a comment.

- Add the /* symbols at the beginning of code and add the */ symbols at the end of code you want to convert into a comment. This method lets you convert one or more lines into a comment.

- Select the lines of code you want to turn into a comment and choose Editor ➤ Structure ➤ Comment Selection (or press Command + /). This method lets you convert one or more lines into a comment by placing the // symbols at the beginning of each line of code you selected.

> **Note**   Xcode color codes comments in green (or whatever color you defined to identify comments). After creating a comment, make sure Xcode color codes it properly to insure you have created a comment. If Xcode fails to recognize your comments, it will treat your text as a valid Swift command, which will likely keep your program from running properly.

By turning code into comments, you essentially hide that code from Xcode. Now if you want to turn that comment back into code again, you just remove the // or /* and */ symbols that define your commented-out code.

If you commented out code by choosing Editor ➤ Structure ➤ Comment Selection (or pressing Command + /), just choose Editor ➤ Structure ➤ Uncomment Selection (or press Command + / again) to convert that commented code back to working code once more.

Besides turning your code into comments to temporarily hide it, a second simple debugging technique is to use the print command. The idea is to put the print command in your code to print out the values of a variable.

By doing this, you can see what values one or more variables may contain. Putting multiple print commands throughout your program gives you a chance to make sure your program is running correctly.

To see how using the print command along with commenting out code can work to help you debug a program, follow these steps

1. From within Xcode choose File ➤ New ➤ Project.

2. Click Application under the macOS category.

3. Click Cocoa Application and click the Next button. Xcode now asks for a product name.

4. Click in the Product Name text field and type **DebugProgram**.

5. Make sure the Language pop-up menu displays Swift and that the "Use Storyboards" check box is selected.

6. Click the Next button. Xcode asks where you want to store the project.

7. Choose a folder to store your project and click the Create button.

8. Click the AppDelegate.swift file in the Project Navigator. The contents of the AppDelegate.swift file appear.

9. Edit the applicationDidFinishLaunching method as follows:

```swift
func applicationDidFinishLaunching(_ aNotification: Notification) {
    var myMessage = "Temperature in Celsius:"
    let temp = 100.0
    print (myMessage + "\(temp)")
    myMessage = "Temperature in Fahrenheit:"
    print (myMessage + "\(C2F(tempC: temp))")
}
```

10. Directly above this function, add the following code:

```swift
func C2F (tempC : Double) -> Double {
    var tempF : Double
    tempF = tempC + 32 * 9/5
    return tempF
}
```

11. Choose Product ➤ Run. Your program's user interface appears (which is blank).

12.   Choose DebugProgram ➤ Quit DebugProgram.
      Xcode appears. If you look in the bottom of the
      Xcode window in the Debug Area, you can see
      what your two print commands printed, which is
      "Temperature in Celsius: 100.0" and "Temperature in
      Fahrenheit: 157.6", as shown in Figure 27-3.

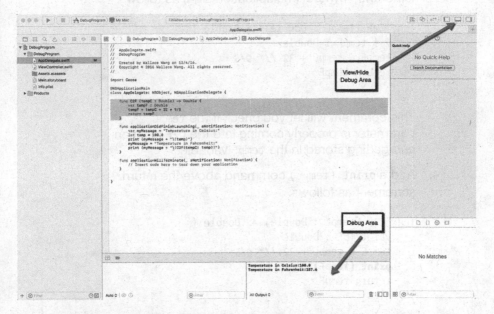

Figure 27-3. The print command displays text in the debug area of the Xcode window

To view or hide the debug area, you have three options:

- Click the View/Hide Debug Area icon in the upper right
  corner of the Xcode window.

- Choose View ➤ Debug Area ➤ Show/Hide Debug Area.

- Press Shift+Command+Y.

By peeking in the debug area, you can see what the print commands
have displayed. If you know anything about temperatures in Fahrenheit and
Celsius, you know that the boiling point in Celsius is 100 degrees and the
boiling point in Fahrenheit is 212 degrees. Yet your temperature conversion
program calculates that 100 degrees Celsius is equal to 157.6 degrees
in Fahrenheit, which means the Fahrenheit temperature should be closer
to 212 than 157.6. Obviously something is wrong, so let's use the print
command and comments to help debug the problem.

1. Make sure the DebugProgram project is loaded in Xcode.

2. Click the AppDelegate.swift file in the Project Navigator pane.

3. Edit the C2F function by typing the // symbols to the left of the * symbol (multiplication sign) as follows:

```
func C2F (tempC : Double) -> Double {
    var tempF : Double
    tempF = tempC + 32 //* 9/5
    return tempF
}
```

This comment will let you check if the tempC parameter is properly coming into the C2F function and getting stored in the tempF variable.

4. Add a print (tempC) command above the return statement as follows:

```
func C2F (tempC : Double) -> Double {
    var tempF : Double
    tempF = tempC + 32 //* 9/5
    print (tempF)
    return tempF
}
```

5. Choose Product ➤ Run. The blank user interface of your program appears.

6. Choose DebugProgram ➤ Quit DebugProgram. Xcode appears again, displaying the result in the Debug Area, which prints

Temperature in Celsius: 100.0

132.0

Temperature in Fahrenheit: 132.0

By commenting out the calculation part of the code and using the print (tempF) command, you can see that the C2F function is storing 100.0 correctly in the tempC variable and adding 32 to this value before storing it in the tempF variable. Because you commented out the calculation part of the code, you can assume that the error must be in your commented-out portion of the code.

Although the formula might look correct, the error occurs because of the way Swift (and most programming languages) calculate formulas. First, they start from left to right. Second, they calculate certain operations such as multiplication before addition.

The error occurs because your conversion formula first multiples 32 by 9 (288), and then divides the result (288) by 5 to get 57.6. Finally, it adds 57.6 to 100.0 to get the incorrect result of 157.6. What it should really be doing is multiplying 9/5 by the temperature in Celsius and then adding 32 to the result.

7. Modify the C2F function as follows:

```
func C2F (tempC : Double) -> Double {
    var tempF : Double
    tempF = tempC * (9/5) + 32
    print (tempF)
    return tempF
}
```

8. Choose Product ➤ Run. Your program's blank user interface appears.

9. Choose DebugProgram ➤ Quit DebugProgram. Xcode appears again.

10. Look in the Debug Area and you'll see that the program now correctly converts 100 degrees Celsius to 212 degrees Fahrenheit.

For simple debugging, turning code temporarily into comments and using the print command can work, but it's fairly clumsy to keep adding and removing comment symbols and print commands. A much better solution is to use breakpoints and variable watching, which essentially duplicates using comments and print commands.

Using the Xcode Debugger

While comments and the print command can help you isolate problems in your code, they can be clumsy to use. The print command can be especially tedious since you have to type it into your code and then remember to remove it later when you're ready to ship your program.

Although leaving one or more print commands buried in your program won't likely hurt your program's performance, it is poor programming practice to leave code in your program that no longer serves any purpose.

As an alternative to typing the print command throughout your program, Xcode offers a more convenient alternative using the Xcode debugger. The debugger gives you two ways to hunt out and identify bugs in your program:

■ Breakpoints

■ Variable watching

Using Breakpoints

Breakpoints let you identify a specific line in your code where you want your program to stop. Once your program stops, you can step through your code line by line. As you do so, you can also peek at the contents of one or more variables to check if the variables are holding the right values.

For example, if your program converts Celsius to Fahrenheit, but somehow converts 100 degrees Celsius into -41259 degrees Fahrenheit, you know your code isn't working right. By inserting breakpoints in your code and examining the values of your variables at each breakpoint, you can identify where your code calculates its values. The moment you spot the line where it miscalculates a value, you know the exact area of your program that you need to fix.

You can set a breakpoint by doing one of the following:

■ Clicking to the left of the code where you want to set the breakpoint

■ Moving the cursor to a line where you want to set the breakpoint and pressing Command + \

■ Choosing Debug ➤ Breakpoints ➤ Add Breakpoint at Current Line

Stepping Through Code

Once a breakpoint has stopped your program from running, you can step through your code line by line using the step command. Xcode offers a variety of different step commands but the three most common are

■ step over

■ step into

■ step out

The step over command examines the next line of code, treating function or method calls as a single line of code.

The step into command works exactly like the step over command until it highlights a function or method call. Then it jumps to the first line of code in that function or method.

The step out command is used to prematurely exit out of a function or method that you entered using the step into command. The step out command returns to the line of code where a function or method was called.

All three step commands are used after a program temporarily stops at a breakpoint. By using a step command, you can examine your code line by line and see how values stored in different variables may change.

Such variable watching lets you examine the contents of one or more variables to verify if it's holding the correct data. The moment you spot a variable holding incorrect data, you can zero in on the line of code that's creating that error.

The best part about breakpoints is that you can easily add and remove them since they don't modify your code at all, unlike comments and multiple print commands. Xcode can remove all breakpoints for you automatically so you don't have to hunt through your code to remove them one by one.

To see how to use breakpoints, step commands, and variable watching, follow these steps:

1. Make sure the DebugProgram project is loaded in Xcode.

2. Click the AppDelegate.swift file in the Project Navigator pane.

3. Modify the C2F function as follows:

```
func C2F (tempC : Double) -> Double {
    var tempF : Double
    tempF = tempC + 32 * 9/5
    return tempF
}
```

4. Move the cursor anywhere inside the following line inside the applicationDidFinishLaunching function:

```
var myMessage = "Temperature in Celsius:"
```

5. Choose Debug ➤ Breakpoints ➤ Add Breakpoint at Current Line. Xcode displays a breakpoint as a blue arrow, as shown in Figure 27-4.

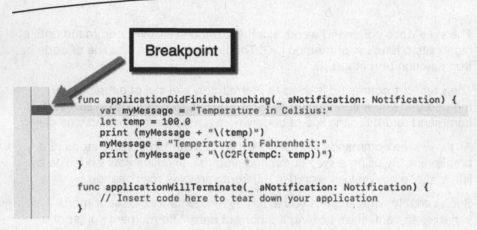

```
func applicationDidFinishLaunching(_ aNotification: Notification) {
    var myMessage = "Temperature in Celsius:"
    let temp = 100.0
    print (myMessage + "\(temp)")
    myMessage = "Temperature in Fahrenheit:"
    print (myMessage + "\(C2F(tempC: temp))")
}

func applicationWillTerminate(_ aNotification: Notification) {
    // Insert code here to tear down your application
}
```

Figure 27-4. A breakpoint appears to the left of your Swift code

6. Choose Product ➤ Run. Notice that Xcode highlights the line where your breakpoint appears, as shown in Figure 27-5. Notice that initially the value of the myMessage variable is not defined.

```
import Cocoa

@NSApplicationMain
class AppDelegate: NSObject, NSApplicationDelegate {

    func C2F (tempC : Double) -> Double {
        var tempF : Double
        tempF = tempC + 32 * 9/5
        print (tempF)
        return tempF
    }

    func applicationDidFinishLaunching(_ aNotification: Notification) {
        var myMessage = "Temperature in Celsius:"          Thread 1: breakpoint 1.1
        let temp = 100.0
        print (myMessage + "\(temp)")
        myMessage = "Temperature in Fahrenheit:"
        print (myMessage + "\(C2F(tempC: temp))")
    }

    func applicationWillTerminate(_ aNotification: Notification) {
        // Insert code here to tear down your application
    }

}
```

Figure 27-5. A breakpoint halts program execution so you can examine its current state

7. Choose Debug ➤ Step Over (or press F6). Xcode highlights the next line under your breakpoint. The information in the left-hand side of the debug area displays the current values that your program is using, as shown in Figure 27-6. Notice that after the breakpoint code runs, the value of the myMessage variable is now defined as the string "Temperature in Celsius:".

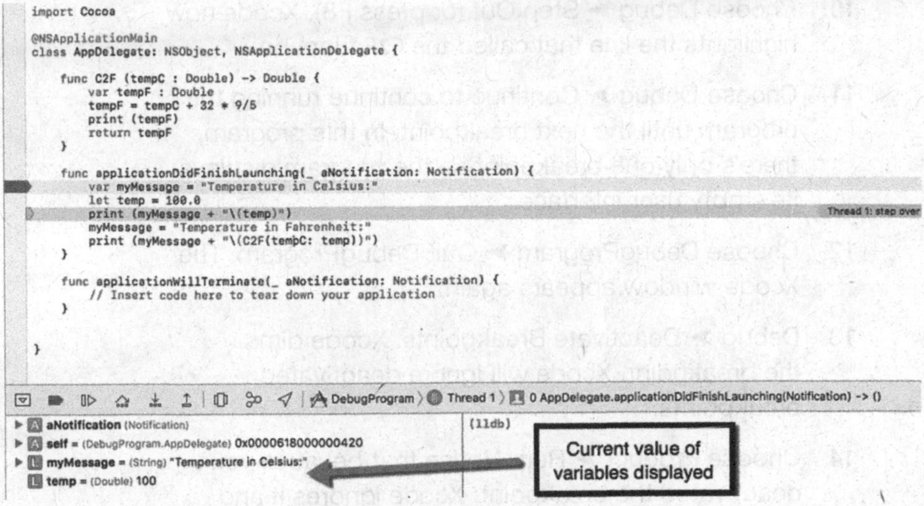
import Cocoa
@NSApplicationMain
class AppDelegate: NSObject, NSApplicationDelegate {
func C2F (tempC : Double) -> Double {
var tempF : Double
tempF = tempC + 32 * 9/5
print (tempF)
return tempF
}
func applicationDidFinishLaunching(_ aNotification: Notification) {
var myMessage = "Temperature in Celsius:"
let temp = 100.0
print (myMessage + "\(temp)")
Thread 1: step over
myMessage = "Temperature in Fahrenheit:"
print (myMessage + "\(C2F(tempC: temp))")
}
func applicationWillTerminate(_ aNotification: Notification) {
// Insert code here to tear down your application
}
}
DebugProgram
Thread 1
0 AppDelegate.applicationDidFinishLaunching(Notification) -> ()
aNotification (Notification)
self = (DebugProgram.AppDelegate) 0x0000618000000420
myMessage = (String) "Temperature in Celsius:"
temp = (Double) 100
(lldb)
Current value of variables displayed

Figure 27-6. By watching how variables change, you can see how each line of code affects each variable

8. Choose Debug ➤ Step Over (or press F6) several more times until Xcode highlights the following line:

```
print (myMessage + "\(C2F(temp))")
```

9. Choose Debug ➤ Step Into (or press F7). Xcode now highlights the first line of code in the `C2F` function, as shown in Figure 27-7.

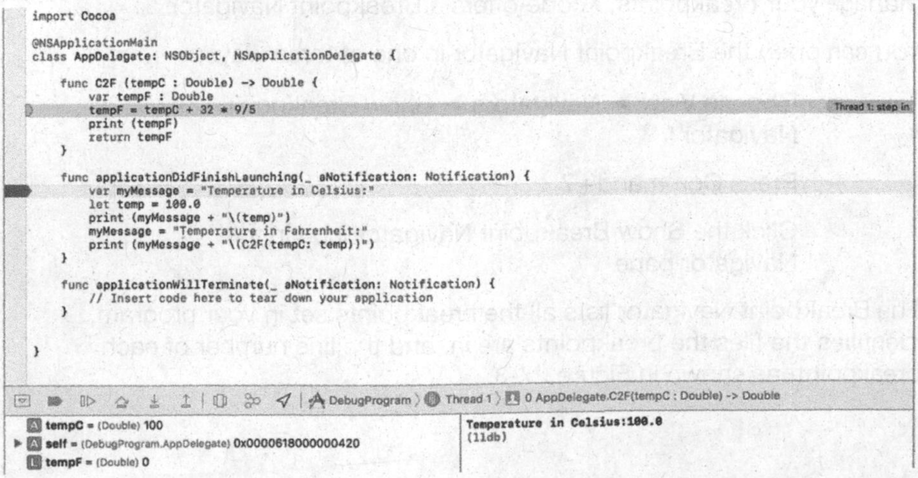
import Cocoa
@NSApplicationMain
class AppDelegate: NSObject, NSApplicationDelegate {
func C2F (tempC : Double) -> Double {
var tempF : Double
tempF = tempC + 32 * 9/5
Thread 1: step in
print (tempF)
return tempF
}
func applicationDidFinishLaunching(_ aNotification: Notification) {
var myMessage = "Temperature in Celsius:"
let temp = 100.0
print (myMessage + "\(temp)")
myMessage = "Temperature in Fahrenheit:"
print (myMessage + "\(C2F(tempC: temp))")
}
func applicationWillTerminate(_ aNotification: Notification) {
// Insert code here to tear down your application
}
}
DebugProgram
Thread 1
0 AppDelegate.C2F(tempC : Double) -> Double
tempC = (Double) 100
self = (DebugProgram.AppDelegate) 0x0000618000000420
tempF = (Double) 0
Temperature in Celsius:100.0
(lldb)

Figure 27-7. The step into command lets you step through the code stored in a function or method

10. Choose Debug ➤ Step Out (or press F8). Xcode now highlights the line that called the C2F function.

11. Choose Debug ➤ Continue to continue running the program until the next breakpoint. In this program, there's only one breakpoint so the program displays its empty user interface.

12. Choose DebugProgram ➤ Quit DebugProgram. The Xcode window appears again.

13. Debug ➤ Deactivate Breakpoints. Xcode dims the breakpoint. Xcode will ignore deactivated breakpoints.

14. Choose Product ➤ Run. Notice that because you deactivated the breakpoint, Xcode ignores it and runs your program by displaying its empty user interface.

15. Choose DebugProgram ➤ Quit DebugProgram. The Xcode window appears again.

Managing Breakpoints

There's no limit to the number of breakpoints you can put in a program so feel free to place as many as you need to help you track down an error. Of course, if you place breakpoints in a program, you may lose track of how many breakpoints you've set and where they might be set. To help you manage your breakpoints, Xcode offers a Breakpoint Navigator.

You can open the Breakpoint Navigator in one of three ways:

- Choose View ➤ Navigators ➤ Show Breakpoint Navigator

- Press Command+7

- Click the Show Breakpoint Navigator icon in the Navigator pane

The Breakpoint Navigator lists all the breakpoints set in your program, identifies the files the breakpoints are in, and the line number of each breakpoint, as shown in Figure 27-8.

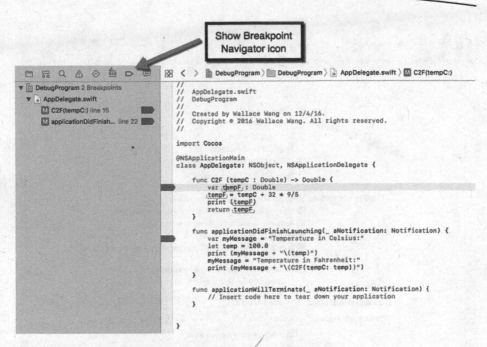

Figure 27-8. The Breakpoint Navigator identifies all your breakpoints

Since the Breakpoint Navigator identifies breakpoints by line number, you might want to display line numbers in the Xcode editor (see Figure 27-8). To turn on line numbers, follow these steps:

1. Choose Xcode ➤ Preferences. The Xcode Preferences window appears.

2. Click the Text Editing icon. The text editing options appear.

3. Select the "Line numbers" check box, as shown in Figure 27-9.

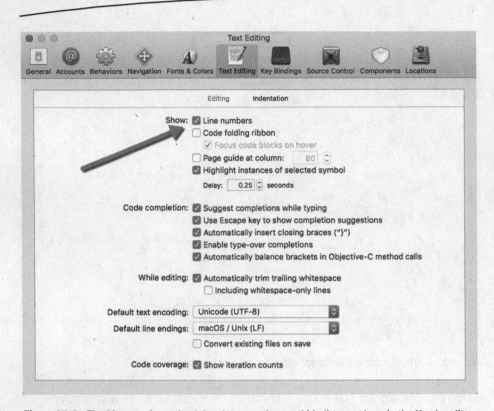

Figure 27-9. The Line numbers check box lets you show or hide line numbers in the Xcode editor

4. Click the close button (the red button) in the upper left corner of the Xcode Preferences window. Xcode now displays line numbers in the left margin of the editor.

To learn how to use the Breakpoint Navigator, follow these steps:

1. Make sure the DebugProgram project is loaded in Xcode.

2. Turn on line numbers in Xcode.

3. Click the AppDelegate.swift file in the Project Navigator pane.

4. Place three breakpoints anywhere in your code using whatever method you like best, such as clicking in the left margin of the Xcode editor, pressing Command+\, or choosing Debug ➤ Breakpoints ➤ Add Breakpoint at Current Line. (The exact location doesn't matter.)

5. Click the Main.storyboard file in the Project Navigator pane. Xcode displays the user interface of your program.

6. Choose View ➤ Navigators ➤ Show Breakpoint Navigator. The Breakpoint Navigator displays your three breakpoints.

7. Click any breakpoint. Xcode displays the file containing your chosen breakpoint.

8. Right-click any breakpoint in the Breakpoint Navigator pane. A pop-up menu appears, as shown in Figure 27-10.

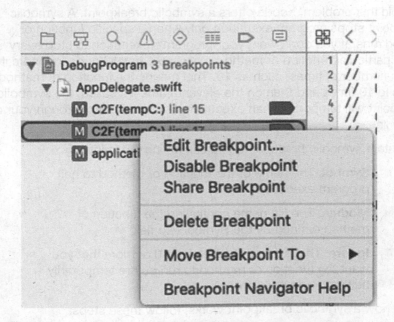

Figure 27-10. A pop-up menu lets you modify breakpoints

9.   Choose Disable Breakpoint. Notice that this lets you deactivate or disable breakpoints individually instead of deactivating all of them at once through the Debug ➤ Deactivate Breakpoints command.

10.   Right-click any breakpoint in the Breakpoint Navigator pane and choose Delete Breakpoint. (Another way to delete a breakpoint is to drag the breakpoint away from your code and release the left mouse button.)

11.   Delete all your breakpoints until no more breakpoints are left.

Using Symbolic Breakpoints

When you create a breakpoint, you must place it on the line where you want your program's execution to temporarily stop. However, this often means guessing where the problem might be and then using the various step commands to examine your code line by line.

To avoid this problem, Xcode offers a symbolic breakpoint. A symbolic breakpoint stops program execution only when a specific function or method runs. If you don't want your program's execution to stop every time a particular function or method runs, you can tell Xcode to ignore it a certain number of times, such as 10. That means the function or method will run up to 10 times and then on the eleventh time it's called, the symbolic breakpoint will temporarily halt execution so you can step through your code line by line.

To create a symbolic breakpoint, you can define the following:

■   **Symbol**: The name of the function or method to halt program execution

■   **Module**: The file name containing the function or method defined by the Symbol text field

■   **Ignore**: The number of times from 0 or more that you want the function or method to run before temporarily halting program execution

To see how a symbolic breakpoint works, follow these steps:

1.   Make sure the DebugProgram project is loaded in Xcode.

2. Choose Debug ➤ Breakpoints ➤ Create Symbolic
    Breakpoint. A Symbolic Breakpoint pop-up window
    appears, as shown in Figure 27-11.

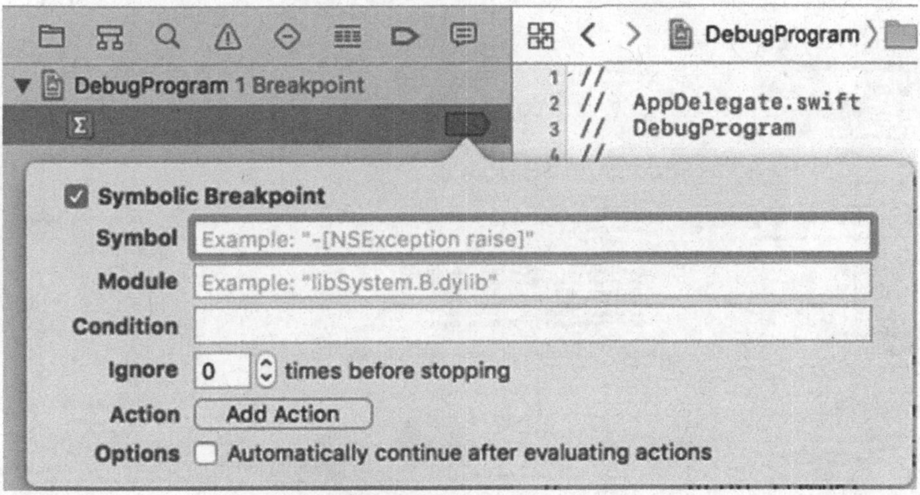

Figure 27-11. The Symbolic Breakpoint pop-up window lets you define a breakpoint

3. Click in the Symbol text field and type **C2F**, which
    is the name of the function or method you want to
    examine.

4. (Optional) If the function or method name you
    specified in the Symbol text field is used in other
    files, click in the Module text field and type a
    file name. This file name will limit the symbolic
    breakpoint only to that function or method in that
    particular file. Since the C2F function is only used
    once, you can leave the Module text field empty.

5. (Optional) Click in the Ignore text field and type
    a number to specify how many times to ignore
    a function or method being called before halting
    program execution. In this case, leave 0 in the Ignore
    text field.

6. Click anywhere away from the Symbolic Breakpoint
    pop-up window to make it disappear.

7. Choose Product ➤ Run. The C2F Symbolic breakpoint causes the program to temporarily halt execution on the first line of code in the C2F function that calculates a result, as shown in Figure 27-12.

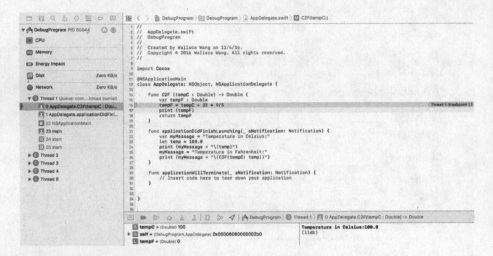

Figure 27-12. The symbolic breakpoint halts program execution in the C2F function defined by the Symbol text field

8. Choose Product ➤ Stop to make your program stop running.

9. Choose View ➤ Navigators ➤ Show Breakpoint Navigator. The Breakpoint Navigator pane appears.

10. Right-click the C2F breakpoint in the Breakpoint Navigator pane and when a pop-up menu appears, choose Delete Breakpoint. There should be no breakpoints displayed in the Breakpoint Navigator pane.

Note   Another way to set a breakpoint without specifying a specific line of code is to create an Exception breakpoint. Normally if your program crashes, Xcode displays a bunch of cryptic error messages and you have no idea what caused the error. If you set an Exception breakpoint, Xcode can identify the line of code that created the crash so you can fix it.

Using Conditional Breakpoints

Breakpoints normally stop program execution at a specific line every time. However, you may want to stop program execution on a particular line only if a certain condition holds true, such as if a variable exceeds a certain value, which can signal when something has gone wrong.

To see how a conditional breakpoint works, follow these steps:

1. Make sure the DebugProgram project is loaded in Xcode.

2. Click the `AppDelegate.swift` file in the Project Navigator pane.

3. Place a breakpoint on the following line by clicking in the left margin or moving the cursor in the line and pressing Command+\ or choosing Debug ➤ Breakpoints ➤ Add Breakpoint at Current Line:

   ```
   print (myMessage + "\(C2F(temp))")
   ```

4. Choose View ➤ Navigators ➤ Show Breakpoint Navigator. The Breakpoint Navigator pane appears, showing the breakpoint you just created.

5. Right-click the breakpoint in the Breakpoint Navigator pane and choose Edit Breakpoint. A pop-up window appears, as shown in Figure 27-13.

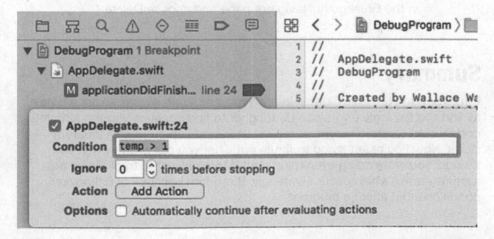

Figure 27-13. The symbolic breakpoint halts program execution in the C2F function defined by the Symbol text field

6.   Click in the Condition text field and type **temp ➤ 1** and press Return.

7.   Choose Product ➤ Run. Xcode highlights your breakpoint to temporarily stop program execution, which means that the condition (temp ➤ 1) must be true.

8.   Choose Product ➤ Stop to halt and exit out of your program and return back to Xcode.

9.   Choose View ➤ Navigators ➤ Show Breakpoint Navigator, right-click the breakpoint you created, and choose Edit Breakpoint. The pop-up window appears.

10. Click in the Condition text field and edit the text so it reads (**temp ➤ 500**). Press Return.

11. Choose Product ➤ Run. Notice that this time your breakpoint does not stop program execution because its condition (temp ➤ 500) is not true. Because the breakpoint didn't stop your program, your program's blank user interface appears.

12. Choose DebugProgram ➤ Quit DebugProgram.

13. Drag the breakpoint away from the left margin and release the left mouse button to delete the breakpoint. (You can also right-click the breakpoint in the Breakpoint Navigator pane and choose Delete Breakpoint.)

Summary

Errors or bugs are unavoidable in any program. While syntax errors are easy to find and fix, logic errors can be tougher to find because you thought your code would create one type of result but it winds up creating a different result. Now you're left trying to figure out what you did wrong when you thought you were doing everything right. More difficult to track down are runtime errors, which occur seemingly at random because of unknown conditions that affect a program

To help you track down and eliminate most bugs, you can use the print command along with comments, but for more robust debugging, you should use Xcode's built-in debugger. With the debugger you can set breakpoints in your code and watch how values get stored in one or more variables.

A conditional breakpoint only stops program execution when a certain condition occurs. A symbolic breakpoint only stops program execution when a specific function or method gets called. Once a breakpoint stops a program, you can continue examining your code line by line using various step commands. The step into command lets you view code stored inside a function or method while the step out command lets you prematurely exit out of a function or method and jump back to the function or method call.

By using breakpoints and step commands, you can exhaustively examine how your program works, line by line, to eliminate as many errors as possible. The fewer errors your program contains, the happier your users will be.

Chapter 28

Planning a Program Before and After Coding

Before you invest days, weeks, months, or years working on a program, make sure the world even wants your program in the first place. If you're writing a program for yourself, then you can ignore what the rest of the world thinks. However, if you plan on selling your programs to others, make sure your program has a future before you even begin.

Here's one way to determine if there's a market for your program. Look for competition. Most people think it's better to target a market with no competition, but if there's no competition, this could be a big clue that there's also no market.

However, if you look for a market loaded with lots of competitors, this means there's a thriving market for that type of program. Just do a quick search for lottery picking software or astrology programs and you'll find plenty of competition. The more competition, the more active the market.

If only one or two big companies dominate a particular market, chances are good that the opportunity in that market has already passed. For example, despite the availability of macOS and Linux, Windows is still the dominant operating system for PCs. Similarly, iOS and Android dominate the mobile computer market so you'll probably waste your time trying to write a rival operating system to compete against Windows, Android, or iOS.

Likewise, there are only a handful of major word processors, spreadsheets, and presentation programs on the market today, which means trying to write another general word processor, spreadsheet, or presentation program will likely be an exercise in futility.

© Wallace Wang 2017
W. Wang, *macOS Programming for Absolute Beginners*,
DOI 10.1007/978-1-4842-2662-9_28

Lots of competition means an active market. Little or no competition means that the market has probably already settled on a leader and your program likely will never be able to overthrow that leader. Trying to convince people to buy your word processor instead of using Microsoft Word or Pages will likely be a waste of time.

So look for niche markets. For example, the word processor market may already be dominated by Microsoft Word, but specialized word processors are still in demand. Although Microsoft Word can be used to write screenplays and novels, it's not optimized for that purpose. That's why other companies can successfully sell screenplay-writing word processors or novel-writing word processors that help you organize your ideas.

Such specialized niches are too small for big companies to worry about, which means you'll never have to compete directly against any of these big companies. Besides targeting niche markets that big companies ignore, a second approach is to find out what the big companies are lacking in their software, and then write a program that solves that missing need.

For example, Microsoft Office offers a password protection feature to lock files. However, Microsoft's encryption feature is weak and easily broken. As a result, there's a market for software that can encrypt files much better than Microsoft Office while offering a similar user interface as Microsoft Office.

Most importantly, write a program because you're interested in that particular field, not because you think it will make you a lot of money. There may be money selling real estate management software or software for controlling drones, but unless you're interested in those fields, you likely won't have the passion or long-term interest to spend the long hours needed to develop and market a program for those users.

As a general rule, avoid competing directly against a big company. Even Apple couldn't compete against Microsoft Windows for the PC operating system market and a free offering like Linux hasn't succeeded much against Windows either.

Instead of directly competing against a big company, look for niche markets that are too small for big companies to tackle, or look for ways to supplement a big company's existing programs. Above all, look for a problem in a field that you're passionately committed to solving and this will give you the motivation to create the best program possible.

Identifying the Purpose of Your Program

When programmers first get an idea, their natural tendency is to rush to the computer and start writing code. However, this is like living in Los Angeles, getting an idea to visit New York, and hopping in your car to drive there.

You may get there eventually, but without a plan, you'll likely waste time by not planning which roads to take or what to bring with to make your trip more enjoyable.

Just as you should take your time and plan ahead before rushing off to visit another city, so should you also take your time and plan ahead when developing a new program. If you start writing Swift code in a flurry of inspiration, you'll likely run out of energy and ideas long before you finish your program. This will likely create a half-completed, poorly designed program that will need to be heavily modified to make it work or, worse, may need to be dumped completely.

Writing code is actually the most straightforward part of creating any program. The hardest part of programming can be deciding what you hope to get out of a program when it's finished.

For example, if you're learning and experimenting with Swift, you might want to create programs just to learn a specific feature such as how to retrieve data from a stock market website or how to create animation for a game. In this case, your goal is just to create short, disposable programs that let you understand how to use specific programming features.

If you're planning to create programs for other people to use, then you need to do some additional planning. First of all, why do you want to create a program for other people? Perhaps you want to create a custom program for a particular person. Maybe you want to create a program that offers features that current programs lack. Whatever the reason, every program must ultimately satisfy the user.

If you're creating a program for your own use, then you're the user. However, if you're creating programs for other people, then the user can be a specific person and computer (such as one dentist in your neighborhood dental office), or a general group of users (any dentist in who needs to manage a dental office). Whoever the user might be, identify the single most important task your program must solve for that user. Then make sure your program accomplishes that one crucial task correctly.

> **Note**   Between 2000 and 2005, the FBI spent $170 million creating a program called Virtual Case File. The government eventually abandoned the entire project because of constantly changing specifications for what the program was supposed to do and how it was supposed to work. If you don't know what a program is supposed to do, you won't know how it's supposed to achieve that result.

Before writing any program, identify the following:

- Who is the user of the program?

- What is the program supposed to do for the user?

- How will the program achieve that result for the user?

The user of your program completely determines the design of your program's user interface. Compare the cockpit of a 777 jet airliner to the dashboard of a typical car. To the average person, a 777 cockpit may look intimidating, but to an experienced pilot, everything is within arm's reach and is easy to understand. If your program caters to specialists, your user interface can rely on the user's knowledge to work. If your program caters to the general public, your user interface may need to guide the user more often.

Every program must create a useful result for the user. Word processors organize text into neatly formatted pages, spreadsheets automatically and accurately calculate mathematical formulas, and even games provide entertainment. Imagine your program giving the user superpowers that the user can't achieve any other way. What superpower will your program give to the user?

Once you know what your program should do for the user, the final step is to determine how it will achieve that result. Programs typically accept input from the user, manipulate that input somehow, and provide a new result. As a programmer, you need to determine how to achieve that new result step by step. Then you need to translate these steps into a programming language like Swift.

Ultimately, programming is a creative talent that requires clear, specific goals and methodical persistence to succeed.

Designing the Structure of a Program

Once you know what your program needs to do and how it can do it, the next step is to design how your program will actually work. There's no single "best" way to write a program since you can write the same program a million different ways. However, you need to design a program that not only works, but is also easy to understand and modify in the future.

Every program can always be improved. Sometimes that improvement means optimizing the program so it runs faster or uses less memory. Other times improvement means adding new features to the program. In either case, every program will likely go through several modifications during its lifetime, so it's crucial that you design your program from the start so it's easy to understand and modify.

In the world of object-oriented programming, the common way to design a program is to separate a large program into multiple objects that represent logical features. For example, if you are designing a program to control a car, you can divide the program into the following objects:

- Engine object
- Steering object
- Stereo object
- Transmission object

Now, if you need to improve the program's steering ability, you can just replace the steering object with a new steering object without the risk that your changes will affect the rest of the program.

How you divide a program into objects is completely arbitrary. You could just as well design the same car program into the following objects:

- Front object
- Back object
- Inside object
- Undercarriage object

If you design your program well from the start, you'll make it easy for yourself or other programmers to modify it easily in the future.

Designing the User Interface of a Program

Besides the structure of your program's design, the other crucial element of your program is the user interface. With Xcode, you can design the structure of your program (its various objects) in complete isolation from the user interface (and vice versa). This gives you the freedom to easily design and modify the structure of your program or the user interface without affecting the other part of your program.

The user interface defines how your user sees your program. A poor user interface makes a program hard to use. A good user interface makes a program easy to use. Even if the underlying structure of a program is poor, a good user interface can make that program appear responsive, elegant, and well-designed.

So what is a good user interface? Ideally a user interface dissolves in the background to the point where the user isn't even aware that it exists. When you pinch two fingers on the screen of an iPhone or iPad, you can make an image appear larger or smaller.

From the user's point of view, the user interface doesn't even exist because the user gets the sensation of directly manipulating an image. In reality, the user interface translates the user's fingertip positions into magnifying an image's appearance. The user interface is still there, but the user doesn't need to read a thick training manual and follow multiple steps to manipulate it. A good user interface essentially melts into the background.

Here's how a clumsy user interface would accomplish the exact same task. First, the user would have to tap a button on the screen to display a menu. Second, the user would have to choose a Zoom command from that menu. Third, the user would have to type in a number that represents the magnification percentage, such as 50% or 125%. Fourth, the user would have to tap an OK button to finally complete the task and change the magnification of an image.

Which user interface would you rather use?

As a general rule, the more steps needed to accomplish a task, the harder the user interface is to use because if the user omits one step or does one step out of order, the entire task fails. Often programmers try to fix poor user interface designs by simply adding more ways to accomplish the same task through keystroke shortcuts or toolbar icons. Unfortunately, if you have a poor user interface, adding more ways to accomplish the same task won't necessarily make your user interface easier to use.

If you have a poor user-interface, it may be easier to redesign the whole interface rather than try to fix a faulty design.

Design a User Interface with Paper and Pencil

As a general rule, your first idea for a user interface will rarely be the final design. That's because what you think will work won't work, and what you may not even consider could be vitally important to your users. So rather than design your user interface and be forced to change it later, it's far faster and simpler to design your user interface with paper and pencil instead.

Once you have a rough design on paper, show it to your eventual users to get their feedback. Even though looking at static images of crudely drawn user interfaces might seem pointless, it can give you feedback on the general design of your user interface. When evaluating a preliminary user interface, ask your users the following questions:

- What's missing? Are there commands or features that need to be displayed but aren't?

- What's not needed? Are there commands or features that are currently displayed but aren't necessary?

- What could be easier? How can the user interface be rearranged or organized to make it simpler?

- What's confusing? Is there anything that users don't understand? Help menus and descriptive tool tips can never substitute for clean user interface designs.

- What's intuitive? What will users expect to do with your user interface? Does your user interface support or frustrate user's expectations?

Designing user interfaces on paper is quick, fast, and easy. Since you don't have much time invested in any particular user interface design, it's much easier to throw away bad designs rather than try to defend and justify keeping them.

In addition, paper designs make it easy for you or others to scribble on them to redesign them. Because paper user interface designs are so fast and simple for anyone to make, feel free to experiment. The more user interface designs you can create, the more likely you'll stumble across one that will work.

Study existing programs and see what you like best and what you like least. Then put both features (the ones you like and the ones you dislike) into different user interface designs. The design you may think is best may be the ones others like the least, and the design you like the least may be the one others find is the best.

Design a User Interface with Software

Once you've experimented with different user interface designs and found one or more that seem promising, it's time to move beyond paper and pencil and create a user interface prototype that people can actually see on a computer screen.

What may look nice on paper may not work on a computer screen. More importantly, a computer screen can create a simple form of interaction. When the user clicks on a button, a new screen can appear just like the real user interface would work. This interactivity is something you can only poorly mimic with paper and pencil designs.

A fast way to create an interactive user interface prototype is to use presentation software such as PowerPoint or Keynote. Presentation software lets you create slides where each slide can represent a window of your user interface. You can place buttons and graphics to create rough user interface designs, and then create links between those buttons and slides to create a limited form of interactivity.

An interactive user interface prototype lets you test how users expect the user interface to respond. For example, users might expect to see a certain window after clicking a command. If your interactive prototype shows users a different window, then you'll know what you need to fix.

Like paper and pencil designs, the goal of a user interface prototype is to find out what works and what doesn't work while spending as little time designing your prototype. The less time you spend designing your prototype, the more time you can spend coming up with alternate ideas and testing them.

In addition to creating user interface prototypes using presentation software, you can also buy special mockup software that contains common user interface elements such as buttons, windows, and check boxes that you can quickly drag and drop to create a simulated user interface, as shown in Figure 28-1.

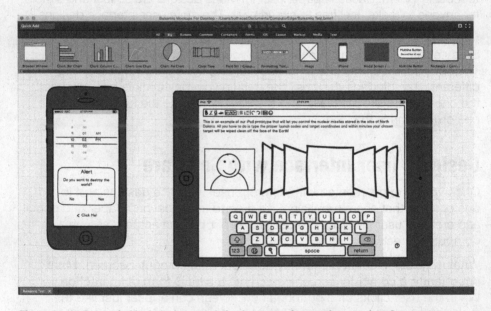

Figure 28-1. Balsamiq Mockups is a specialized program for creating user interface prototypes

A software version of your user interface prototype provides interactivity. When you're satisfied with your user interface design as a prototype, the final step is to convert your prototype into an actual Xcode user interface.

Remember, Xcode lets you create your Swift code completely separate from your user interface. This means you can create user interfaces in Xcode without writing a single line of code. When you're happy with the appearance and design of your user interface, you can connect its various items (buttons, menus, etc.) to IBOutlets and IBAction methods to link your user interface to your Swift code.

Marketing Your Software

Once you create a program, you'll need to test it to make sure it works. Such early testers (known as alpha and beta testers) can help spot bugs in your program so you can fix them right away. When your program is as bug-free as possible, that's the time to release your software on the market.

Here's the biggest mistake most people make: they write a program, put up a website advertising the program or their company, and wait for the orders to roll in. In the macOS world, Apple offers a special Mac App Store that gives every Macintosh user potential access to your software.

However, it's never enough to advertise your software on a website or the Mac App Store and wait for people to buy it. To maximize sales, you must also promote your software.

To many people, marketing means spending money advertising. While you could do that, it's always best to spend as little as possible. It's easy to spend money on advertising and marketing, but unless your advertising and marketing expenses are less than the sales that the advertising and marketing generates, you risk going bankrupt slowly. Where most people go wrong is that they spend money on advertising and marketing, but they have no idea if all that advertising and marketing is generating enough sales to justify the expense.

This is why you should focus on free ways to advertise and market your software so you can find out what people like about your software, what types of people are more likely to buy your software, and the best ways to reach your potential users, all without going broke to do it.

For example, suppose you sell software that makes video look aged as if it had been filmed decades ago on film, complete with scratches, faded images, and sound effects of film threading through a movie projector. You might initially target people who want to turn their videos into older movies for fun, but you may find that your actual market is Hollywood studios that need to create visual effects to simulate older films.

Your initial market may not care about your software but an entirely different market just might. If you spent money advertising to your initial market, you would have wasted money targeting people who didn't really want your program after all. Only later might you find the real market for your software and it could come from an unexpected niche that you never thought about before.

So don't substitute spending money for doing market research. It's easy to spend more money. It's harder to take the time to determine how effective your marketing and advertising really is and whether you're even targeting the most lucrative market for your software in the first place.

Beyond spending a minimal amount of money promoting your software through a website, here are some other ways to promote your software for little or no cost:

- Start a blog.
- Give away free software.
- Post videos of your software on video sharing sites like YouTube.
- Create and give away free information stored in PDF files offering tips for people who are potential customers of your software.
- Find the social networks where your potential customers gather and participate in discussions to answer their questions.

Blogging About Your Software

A website is like putting a billboard in the middle of the desert and hoping people will magically find it. While search engines can help people find your website, it's far better to include a blog on your website as well.

A blog serves several purposes. First, by constantly blogging at least once a week, you generate new content for your website. New content tells search engines that your site is active and thus search engines will rank it as more relevant than a site that hasn't been updated in months or even years. So blogs increase your search engine rank, increasing the chance that potential customers can find your product.

Second, a blog puts a human face behind your software. By discussing the challenges you faced creating the software and responding to questions from people about your software, you demonstrate that there's someone who cares and is willing to respond to questions about that software. Given a choice between buying from a faceless corporation or someone who seems like a real person, this subtle difference can increase the likelihood that potential customers will buy your software.

Third, each blog post acts like another miniature ad for your software. Most people create a website describing their software and hope it will convince people to buy their product. A blog lets you focus on different aspects of your software. One blog post might talk about a special feature that you're particularly proud to highlight. A second blog post might tell a story of a happy customer who used your software to solve a problem. A third blog post might explain why you designed your program the way you did.

Since each blog post is slightly different, you avoid repetition. Yet since each blog post continually promotes your software, you're constantly advertising your software from different points of view. This increases the chance that one of your blog posts will convince someone to buy your software.

Blogging simply costs time, yet provides higher search engine rankings while promoting your software over and over again. Think of blogs as a free way to advertise on the Internet.

Giving Away Free Software

There's a reason companies give away free samples of everything from food to toothpaste. They know once you try a product and like it, you'll be far more likely to buy it. If you never try a product, it's much harder for a company to convince you to buy it.

Giving away free software works the same way. Some companies give away free "lite" versions of their software, which are fully functional. This lets customers try and use your software at no cost. A certain percentage of people will eventually want more advanced features, and those people will translate into paying customers.

The more people you get using your free software, the more people you'll get paying for the advanced version.

For example, assume 1% of all people trying your free software decide to buy your advanced version. If you can get your free software in the hands of 100 people, that translates into one sale. However, if you can get your free software in the hands of 10,000 people, that translates into 100 sales.

Since distributing free software doesn't cost you anything to duplicate or distribute, your advertising and marketing costs are essentially zero.

Besides offering a free "lite" version of your program, you could also offer free software related to your main program. For example, suppose you sell a word processor targeted for scientists that writes complex mathematical and chemical formulas. Rather than give away a free "lite" version of your program, you could give away free software that your target audience (engineers and scientists) might like, such as an interactive periodic table of elements or a simple equation solving program.

Such free software simply gives potential customers something for free. Now if they like your free software, they'll be far more likely to trust your commercial software. If your free software is well-designed and useful, potential customers will believe your commercial software must also be just as well-designed and useful. Free software lets potential customers sample your products without risk.

Posting Videos About Your Software

Blogging about your software can be great for people who like reading. Unfortunately, in today's busy world, many people don't have time to read. Another approach is to make short videos demonstrating how your software works so people can see what problems your software solves and how it does it.

In general, nobody wants to buy or use your software. What they really want are the solutions your software offers, and that's what you need to emphasize in your videos. Don't explain the menu system or the organization of your user interface. Focus on solving a single problem and emphasize something unique about your software.

For example, suppose your software is designed to help real estate agents. Your potential customers will either want to save time or make money, so show how your software can help real estate agents do both. Show a feature that simplifies an existing, time-consuming process. Show another feature that increases the number of potential buyers of a property with little additional work. Always focus on how your software benefits the user.

Keep your videos short and to the point. More people will watch a video demonstrating a single feature that runs under a minute. Far fewer people will watch a 30 minute video demonstrating multiple features. With many video sharing sites, like YouTube, you can even link multiple videos together so when one video ends, a second one begins. Now each video acts like another advertisement for your product, and by linking each video to another one, each new video increases the chance that someone will find and watch at least one of them.

Give Away Free Information

People tend to buy more from people they trust, so one way to get people to trust you is to give out free, useful information. For example, if your software helps edit photographs, write up a list of tips for capturing better pictures. Now share that list of tips as a PDF file and give it away for free, with a link back to your website promoting your software.

Free, useful information acts as a subtle advertisement. Traditional ads blatantly promote a product, which can immediately turn off even your best potential customers. Free information subtly promotes a product. Since the free information is useful to your potential customer, they'll be more willing to look at it and even share it with others. If they want more information, they can visit your website.

One visually appealing way to provide free information is through a combination of text and graphics known as infographics. An infographic presents information in a colorful manner so it's easy to read and understand without wading through large amounts of text. As Figure 28-2 shows, even IBM creates and distributes free infographics to promote their services and products.

Figure 28-2. IBM provides an infographics as a PDF file to promote how their services helped American Greetings

By providing free, useful information, you establish yourself as an authority. If you can provide free, useful information as PDF files and blog posts on your website, you'll give people additional reasons to keep coming back to your website/blog over and over again. The more times people visit, the more likely they'll eventually buy your software or tell others about your website/blog.

Free, useful information establishes you as trustworthy, which lowers the barrier to buying your software. The more people trust you, the more likely they'll believe your product will do what you claim it does.

Join Social Networks

Giving away free, useful information in your blog or as PDF files can help establish you as an authority in your field. However, a blog requires that someone visits your site and a PDF file requires someone download that file. Another way to share useful information for free is to stay in constant contact with popular social networks.

Find out which social networks your potential customers visit and join those networks. As people post questions, jump in and answer them with useful advice. The purpose is to answer people's questions and establish yourself as trustworthy. Then make sure each post you make includes a link back to your website or blog.

Visiting social networks lets you reach potential customers far faster than hoping they'll visit your blog or find your PDF file. Just make sure you provide useful information instead of thinly disguised advertising copy that will simply annoy others. The more people learn to trust you on a social network, the more likely they'll also visit your website/blog.

With all of these techniques, the goal isn't to get someone to buy your product right away (although that's always nice). The real goal is to draw them one step closer towards learning more about you and your product. The more people know about your product, the more likely they'll buy from you.

Advertising and marketing are basically numbers games. Keep helping others for free in ways that don't take up much time or money, and you'll eventually find that others will find you and buy your software. The more you help others, the more others will trust and buy from you.

The old way of marketing and advertising involves trying to force people to listen to ads and buy against their will (which is why so many people dislike marketing and advertising). The far more effective way of marketing and advertising is to give potential customers something of value before you ask them to buy from you.

Summary

Most programmers focus on increasing their technical knowledge of programming. While knowing as much as possible about Swift's features and the Cocoa framework can always be helpful, technical knowledge alone is rarely enough.

Programming involves more than just writing code. Before you even start writing Swift code, you need to make sure there's a market for your program. Rather than trying to compete against big companies, look for niche markets that big companies are ignoring, or look for ways your program can supplement programs offered by a big company. Big companies have far more resources that they can use to crush any direct competitors, so by targeting a niche market or a way to supplement their own products, you can avoid directly competing with a much bigger company.

Before you start writing Swift code, create prototypes of your software's user interface. Although user interface design may not sound as appealing to programmers as digging into the intricacies of writing code, it's a vital part of any software project. The user interface determines how people view your program. A well-designed user interface can make your program easier to use. A poorly designed user interface can make a program seem harder to use, despite any technical features it may offer.

Test your user interface designs as quickly and cheaply as possible using paper and pencil. When you need to create an interactive version of your user interface, create simple mockups using presentation software like Keynote or PowerPoint, or consider buying special mockup construction software.

When you have a final user interface design, create it in Xcode. Just remember that as your program continues to evolve, you'll likely still need to make changes to your user interface.

Finally, when your program is complete, your work still isn't done. You'll still need to advertise and market your software. Rather than spend money buying ads, it's far less expensive and often more effective to pursue free options instead.

Start a blog, give away free information, and provide something of value to others. The more you give to others, the more likely others will be attracted to your product and buy from you.

As you can see, coding is just one stage of creating and marketing software. Technical knowledge can create software, but you still need additional skills before and after coding to properly design your program and successfully sell it afterwards.

Index

Get the eBook for only $4.99!

Why limit yourself?

Now you can take the weightless companion with you wherever you go and access your content on your PC, phone, tablet, or reader.

Since you've purchased this print book, we are happy to offer you the eBook for just $4.99.

Convenient and fully searchable, the PDF version enables you to easily find and copy code—or perform examples by quickly toggling between instructions and applications.

To learn more, go to http://www.apress.com/us/shop/companion or contact support@apress.com.

Printed in the United States
By Bookmasters